The General Textile Strike of 1934

The General Textile Strike of 1934

FROM MAINE TO ALABAMA

John A. Salmond

University of Missouri Press
Columbia and London

Library of Congress Cataloging-in-Publication Data

Salmond, John A.
  The general textile strike of 1934 : from Maine to Alabama / John A. Salmond.
    p.   cm.
  Includes bibliographical references and index.
  ISBN 0-8262-1395-2 (alk. paper)
  1. Textile Workers' Strike, Southern States, 1934.   2. Textile workers—United States.
3. Textile industry—United States.   I. Title.
HD5325.T42 1934 S35 2002
331.892'877'097329043–dc21   2002024567

⊗™ This paper meets the requirements of the
American National Standard for Permanence of Paper
for Printed Library Materials, Z39.48, 1984.

Designer: Stephanie Foley
Typesetter: Bookcomp, Inc.
Printer and binder: Thomson-Shore, Inc.
Typefaces: Galliard and Spring Light

Portions of "The Fellowship of Southern Churchmen and International Change
in the South" and " 'The Burlington Dynamite Plot': The Textile Strike and Its
Aftermath in Burlington, North Carolina," previously appeared in the
North Carolina Historical Review and are reprinted here with permission.

To Fiona Innes Salmond
December 11, 1999

Contents

Preface

IN JANUARY 1933, THE UNITED TEXTILE WORKERS OF America had, in the words of its historian Robin R. Brooks, reached the "nadir of its fortunes." Its membership probably no more than 15,000, and those largely concentrated in the dying New England cotton mills, its southern forays of 1929 and 1930 both disastrous failures, constantly assailed from the left by the Communist-led National Textile Workers Union, the likelihood of its becoming a serious force in American labor seemed remote. Yet barely eighteen months later, with a dues-paying membership of around 300,000, with newly established or revived branches concerned with woolen and worsted workers, with silk and jacquard weavers, with dyers and finishers, even with rayon workers, with locals in 208 cities, towns, and mill villages, it was about to embark on what was at the time "the greatest single industrial conflict in the history of American Labor." The general textile strike of 1934, in Brooks's view, invited comparison with the 1926 general strike in Great Britain. Time may well have diminished its significance, yet it remains true that the 1934 textile strike was an important event in American labor history, one which shaped the future of labor relations in the industry and the lives of those who participated in it. The event has not received from historians the attention it deserves, thus the main purpose of this book is to tell the strike story.[1]

Those historians who have discussed the 1934 strike, Janet Irons in her excellent dissertation and subsequent monograph, Jacquelyn Hall and her colleagues in *Like a Family,* James Hodges, and filmmaker George Stoney in *The Uprising of 1934,* have, because of the nature of their larger works, concentrated on its southern aspect. Indeed, it has often been presented as a southern rather than a national outbreak. Similarly, these historians have concentrated on cotton mill workers as the main, indeed the only, actors in the drama. Almost everything written about the strike has been from the perspective of the South and its cotton mill people, and Stoney's moving film, too, focuses solely on the region.

There are of course plenty of reasons to emphasize both the South and cotton in telling the strike's story. It was the militancy of cotton textile workers, their anger that the National Industrial Recovery Act and its provisions, which had promised so much in 1933, had in fact led to a worsening of their lives, that had forced a reluctant UTW leadership to support a strike vote. Moreover, no industry leader was more intransigent, less willing to concede anything to labor, more devious in evading or ignoring NRA's section 7(a) giving workers the right to join unions and bargain collectively than the chair of the Cotton Code Authority and head of the Cotton Textile Institute, George Sloan. Nevertheless, the strike of 1934 was a nationwide affair, involving hundreds of thousands of silk, woolen, and rayon workers, all represented by the UTW and most living outside the South, in New England, in Pennsylvania, in New Jersey. Peter Van Horn and Arthur Besse, heads of the Silk and Woolen Code Authorities, respectively, lost little to Sloan in their determination to evade as many of the NRA labor provisions as they could. Finally, though the great transfer of the cotton industry from New England to the South was almost complete, there were still little pockets left in Maine, Massachusetts, Rhode Island, and even in Connecticut, and they need to be brought into the story. This book's purpose is to do just that, to study the strike from a national perspective, an industrywide perspective, not just from that of its most important region.

This strike narrative is much more concerned with the events of September 1934 than with what happened afterward. Historians like James Hodges, Robert Zieger, and now Janet Irons have already plowed that patch and with much more skill and learning than I could hope to achieve. Moreover, it tries to tell the strike's story from two perspectives, that of the nation as a whole, using primarily national sources, including national newspapers, to do so, and that of the various localities and regions that, together, made the decision to support the strike call, often for quite different reasons. Here, I have tried to use local sources as far as possible. Inevitably, there is some repetition, the same story told from two perspectives, the same voices heard at two levels, descriptions of the same struggles, the same funerals. I hope readers will understand my purpose and bear with me.

For this reason, I have divided the book into four distinct sections or parts. The first part, comprising the first three chapters, examines the reasons for the strike, and the strike itself, from an overall, or national, perspective. Part two comprises chapters 4 through 7, and here the differing regional perspectives are discussed, compared and contrasted. Part three, or chapter 8, is a detailed case study of the strike and its aftermath in one small textile town. Part four, which concludes the book, is a reflective exercise looking at the strike from the perspective of nearly seventy years. I hope these divisions make the story easier to follow.

As always, there are many people and institutions responsible for whatever merit this book may possess. My La Trobe University colleagues Bill Breen, Tim Murray, and Alan Frost have read the whole manuscript, as has Bruce Clayton of Allegheny College. Tony Wood and Warren Ellem have read sections of it, and their many suggestions have improved it considerably. Marilyn Lake, Steve Niblo, Giselle Roberts, Rhys Isaac, Jim Patterson, Bill Baker, Tim Minchin, Richard Watson, Erik Olssen, Shane and Graham White, and the late Paul Bourke have all helped me clarify my ideas or shape the narrative. My vice chancellor, Professor Michael Osborne, has consistently supported my work, as has La Trobe's deputy vice chancellor, research, Professor Fred Smith. The research could not even have been attempted without the generous financial support of the Australian Research Council and the La Trobe University Faculty of Humanities and Social Sciences. My gratitude to them all.

So many archivists and librarians have had a hand in the making of this book that it seems invidious to mention but a few of them. Sharon Karasmanis of La Trobe University's interloan department has been tireless in acting on my many requests. John White of the University of North Carolina's Southern Historical Collection has been similarly assiduous during my periods of residence there. The reference team at Allegheny College's Pelletier Library, where I have also often been based, has always been gracious in its assistance to a sometimes demanding visitor. Gregory Murphy, my Washington-based research assistant, did everything I asked of him—and more. Heather Wilkie deserves special mention for the skill and good humor with which she has turned my Luddite scribblings into perfect typescript. She owns a large part of this book, and my abiding gratitude. Thanks go, too, to Beverly Jarrett, director and editor-in-chief at the University of Missouri Press, for her faith in the project, also to my editor there, Sara Davis. They have both helped to make it a better book.

Thanks, too, to the friends and colleagues with whom I have worked and played over the course of what is now becoming a long and happy life. The La Trobe University history department, Judith and Michael Bassett, Johanna and Bill Breen, Bruce and Carrah Clayton, the late Dick and Ruth Watson, Alan Frost, Jan Jackson, Doreen Lowe, Liz Carey, Gillian

Cell, Karin Liedke, all can claim part ownership of this book, for what it is worth.

Finally, most important, I thank my family—my sister Anne Malcolm and her daughters, Robyn, Johanna, Susie, and Jenny; my own children, Kerry, Nikki, Paul, and Mark, and their partners; my grandchildren, Bill, Hilary, Jim, and Tom Washington, Lucy and Bob Henningham, and Alexander Salmond. The book, however, is dedicated to the memory of my beloved youngest granddaughter, Fiona Innes Salmond, whose life touched mine only briefly, but changed it profoundly.

Part I

The Strike

The National Dimension

Thomas W. McMahon, UTW president.
Library of Congress, *New York World Telegram and Sun* Collection.

Chapter 1

The Textile Industry in 1933

"WHEN I REFLECT . . . UPON THE HARD CONDITIONS in many mill communities," Joseph Daniels, the United States' ambassador to Mexico, confided to Franklin D. Roosevelt, his onetime assistant, "the cry Thomas Carlyle heard out of the French Revolution rings in my ears: 'How have you treated us? How have you taught us, fed us and led us, while we toiled for you?'" He was talking about the situation in the cotton mills of his home state, North Carolina, and yet his views had a wider relevance. As Thomas McMahon, president of the United Textile Workers of America, had warned three years earlier, the general situation in the industry was one of complete demoralization, with management unable to see a way "out of the darkness." "The experiences of the past few years in all branches of our industry—the woolen, worsted, cotton silk and rayon [*sic*]," he warned, could not continue. Already they had "reduced the employees, in thousands of cases, to complete destitution."[1]

No American industry entered the year 1933 more severely depressed than textiles. Indeed, McMahon's gloomy summary reflected the state of textiles throughout the 1920s, as the wartime boom quickly collapsed, and the decade became one of steadily declining prices, cost-cutting on the part of management, and reaction to deteriorating working conditions and wage rates by workers, often in the form of strikes, some spontaneous and short, others organized and more prolonged, almost all unsuccessful. By the onset of the depression proper, if workers had identified the hated "stretch-out"—the need to tend more and more looms, to watch more shuttles, spindles, or dyeing vats—as the root cause of their misery, manufacturers blamed overproduction and constantly talked of the need to cut costs by reducing output and cutting back on labor. There was truth in both analyses, though neither group would concede this to the other. Writing in the *American Federationist,* the contemporary labor economist Gladys L. Palmer categorized the 1920s as a decade of "retreat and decline" in the industry, a time of mill closings, wage reductions, short hours, dwindling union strength, and increased employer arbitrariness. She was referring specifically to the situation in the nation's largest and most diverse textile center, Philadelphia, but most of her assertions had national application.[2]

Nowhere was the decline more obvious than in the cotton sector—North and South. By 1933, the great transfer of the industry from its traditional centers in Massachusetts and Rhode Island to the southern Piedmont was complete. The process had been going on since the turn of the century. Manufacturers, attracted by the lower wage scales in the South, by the plentiful supply of labor in what was becoming an increasingly unskilled industry, by the fact that these new workers were of Anglo-Celtic origin—from the failing farms of the Piedmont and the mountains beyond—rather than from central and southern Europe, and with little experience of labor agitation, again unlike some of their northern counterparts, had progressively moved the industry southward. By 1927, as James Hodges has pointed out, the South already produced 82 percent of the coarse yarn and 71 percent of the medium yarn in the United States, with New England maintaining a slight lead only in the fine goods in which the old centers like New Bedford had come to specialize. By 1933 even this slight advantage had gone. New Bedford's dominance in fine goods was over; cotton textiles was now the South's flagship industry. Between 1925 and 1938 the city lost 80 percent of its remaining cotton spindleage. "Heavily dependent on one industry upon which it concentrated most of its energies," wrote Seymour Wolfbein in 1944, "it prospered as textiles prospered and it suffered from the industry's movement to the South." As such, New Bedford's plight mirrored the New England experience as a whole. By 1933, the southern textile manufacturers had triumphed, but in the depths of depression America, was the battle worth the winning?[3]

Like most commentators, Alice Galenson, whose 1985 monograph on the relocation of the industry remains the most detailed study of the process, considers the wage differential between the two regions as critical in explaining the transfer. The decline of southern agriculture had freed a large pool of unskilled laborers and a dearth of alternative opportunity had kept southern wage rates low. True, New England's labor force was also expanding due to immigration, but so was opportunity. Textile wage rates had to reflect this; there was a limit to how low they could go, given workers' increased mobility. While southern productivity was always lower than in the New England mills, it was not sufficiently so to negate the effect of lower wages.[4]

Of course, other factors contributed to the shift. Two had to do with technology—and timing. Cotton mills came much later to the South than to New England. It was not until the 1880s that the drive to transform the Piedmont began. Fortuitously, this coincided with the development of the ring-spindle, a device that greatly simplified the spinning process, making it at once less skilled and less physically demanding, more accessible to unskilled workers, to women, and to children. Southern manufacturers were able to install ring-spindles as they built mills; northern mills had to replace the traditional mule spindles more gradually, often in the face of bitter opposition from the skilled men who had operated them. Similarly, the Draper loom, which was first marketed in 1894, and which simplified, speeded up, and deskilled the weaving process, was adopted much more quickly and generally in the South than in New England's mills, where both artisans and manufacturers were resistant to the change.[5]

Other reasons for the transfer included the relative lack of protective labor legislation in the southern states, which permitted the widespread use of women in the mills, though it should be pointed out that women had also worked in New England's mills from the beginning, and continued to do so despite state legislation, stemming from the Progressive years, which set maximum hours for them. Moreover, child labor, which had been largely eradicated in New England, still existed in southern mills throughout the 1920s. Southern millowners, too, were but lightly troubled by such northern requirements as workmen's compensation or unemployment insurance.[6]

Some historians have pointed to the lack of labor organizations in the cotton-mill South and the ferocious determination of the millmen to prevent their intrusion as important in explaining the shift to the Piedmont. While it is true that southern mills—unlike their northern counterparts— were relatively free from labor strife until the explosive year of 1929, Galenson asserts that for the first decades of the migration, labor unions were also a relatively unimportant presence in New England's cotton mills, only becoming so after the process was well set in train. This point will be discussed in detail elsewhere, what is important here is to reinforce the notion that it was the wage differential, above all, which explains the industry's decisive shift, and that the collapse of New England cotton, so apparent to us now, was not so to companies until the 1920s. Only then, as the trade writer Dane Yorke put it, did "the columns of the textile press reporting the discontinuance and liquidation and abandonment of New England mills read like wartime casualty lists."[7]

But, as Gavin Wright points out, "the Southern mills were stumbling too," though nowhere near as drastically as in New England. Nevertheless, the wartime boom in cotton textiles had well and truly broken by 1920, as the demand for cotton cloth diminished. Changes in women's fashions had an effect as well, the raising of hemlines at once reducing the amount of fabric required for a dress and ending the market for cotton stockings. The Harding administration's protectionist tariff policies wiped out lucrative foreign markets, as did competition from new international players in the industry like India. Wage rates had tripled during the war years but now grew much more slowly, if at all, and though the numbers employed in the industry continued to increase, many people were unable to find full-time work. Moreover, working conditions deteriorated, as southern manufacturers sought ways to reduce costs, aiming to keep up production by cutting back on the welfare services many had provided as a means of enticing labor in the prosperous years, and by requiring more work from their operatives. The dramatic collapse of the New England cotton industry after 1925 thus masked the equally unpalatable fact that southern cotton was also in trouble, and that the conditions McMahon identified in the depths of the depression—overproduction, massive unemployment, worsening working conditions and general demoralization—were all becoming realities even in the South by 1929. True, most mills were still making some money, unlike their New England counterparts, but at greatly reduced rates and usually at the expense of their workers. In 1927 the average southern cotton textile wage remained what it had been in 1894, about 40 percent less than that paid elsewhere, as the millowners, "powerful as any feudal lords," set their faces firmly against change.[8]

Textile managers all over the nation tried to halt the slide in the various sections of their industry in numerous ways. One was to form combinations, local and regional trade associations aimed at regulating production levels and standards, recommending common wage rates, devising common approaches to the demands of labor unions. Cotton textile manufacturers in New England had started meeting in so-called "dinner club associations" from the mid-nineteenth century. Indeed, the New England Cotton Manufacturers Association had organized as early as 1865. Its membership had originally been restricted to mill agents and superintendents, but by 1862 treasurers had been permitted to join, and after 1872, mill officers from outside the region were also accepted, bringing Pennsylvania, New Jersey, and New York mills into its ambit. Though the association grew slowly, not even having its own premises till the 1890s, it did provide a forum for regional millmen to discuss new technologies, to form the personal alliances which often preceded business combinations, and, increasingly, to worry aloud about the challenge from the South.[9]

By the turn of the century, a number of similar associations had emerged. There was, for example, the Arkwright Club of Boston. Formed in 1880, and with membership open only to company directors, its purposes were overtly political, acting as a lobby group for the manufacturers before the various state legislatures and, at times, the United States Congress. Initially open to manufacturers from the several branches of the textile industry, by 1900 it had become exclusively a cotton organization. Southern manufacturers, too, attempted to form regional trade associations, rather less successfully. Not until 1897 was anything permanent achieved, with the launching of the Southern Cotton Spinners Association. Its structure was similar to the Arkwright Club, as were its aims: to try to control through joint action the cost of transporting and marketing its members' goods, and, increasingly urgently, to limit production, to keep supply and demand roughly in balance.[10]

These loose, essentially private, nonbureaucratic associations were insufficient to meet either the economic challenges of the rapidly changing, consolidating business order of the early twentieth century or the political challenge posed by the Progressive movement to business hegemony and private economic power. Cotton manufacturers, therefore, in the words of Louis Galambos, "created a new type of trade group," the "service association." Better organized than the earlier clubs, with a decent income and with full-time staff members, "selected for their administrative, political, or technical skills," groups like the National Association of Cotton Manufacturers, an outgrowth of the New England Cotton Manufacturers Association, or the American Cotton Manufacturers Association—the old Southern Cotton Spinners Association renamed and with some New England members added—tried to bring order to the industry, again on a regional basis. In 1913 officers from these two associations even created an interregional National Council of American Cotton Manufacturers, which would speak for the entire industry, but it was never more than a paper organization. Sectional tensions and distrust overcame the drive to stabilize the industry on a national basis, while the wartime cotton boom helped reduce the economic urgency for doing so.[11]

The boom was over by 1921, replaced by the long slide into depression, punctuated by sharpened labor clashes, particularly in New England in 1922. In this context, the drive to stabilize the industry on a national level was renewed, and this time the initiative came from southern millers. Relative newcomers to the industry, and less bound by its traditions, men like George Harris of Atlanta's Exposition Mills Complex and Stewart Cramer of North Carolina, argued for an industrywide trade association, with a large and expert bureaucracy, its aim to replace competition with cooperation in an endeavor to control production levels, wage rates, and labor relations throughout the land. Despite some opposition from representatives of the declining New England sectors, anxious about turning control over to the South, the southern millers eventually got their way. On October 20, 1926, the Cotton Textile Institute (CTI) was formally organized as a powerful, centrally directed, nationally focused trade association.[12]

The CTI's first president was a New York corporation lawyer, Walker D. Hines, but its driving force was the secretary, George A. Sloan, who succeeded Hines as president in 1929. Sloan, a Vanderbilt University Law School graduate and a man of boundless energy, enthusiasm, and ambition, was determined to replace the wasteful and cutthroat competition that he saw as bedeviling the industry with cooperation, industrywide planning agreements, and cost reductions, all aimed at reducing production. Thus the CTI could be counted on to support such reformist measures as reducing the working hours for women, ending child labor, and restricting night work in the belief that these would serve to scale back production and thus raise prices. Such lobbying activity was usually directed at state legislatures, though Herbert Hoover, with his belief in industrial self-regulation, was also seen as a source of support, the more so when he moved from the Department of Commerce to the White House. The CTI also quickly developed a policy of strong opposition to labor unions, and especially to collective bargaining, a view that needed no reinforcement, particularly in the South. By 1932 it had become the acknowledged spokesman of the cotton textile industry, and its policies were supported by most of the larger and better-established mills. But it had not succeeded in stabilizing the industry. Its influence over the smaller, marginal mills in both New England and the South was limited, while the depression's severity was testing the limits of voluntary regulation among even the more established producers. Sloan and his institute, therefore, were ready to accept a measure of government control, as the New Era gave way to the New Deal.[13]

Manufacturers in other branches of the textile industry had a long history of combining, usually on a regional basis. The Philadelphia Textile Association (PTA) was formed in 1880. Representing local silk, wool, worsted, carpet, and hosiery manufacturers, its initial purpose as a lobby group was to influence Congress on tariff questions. As regional lobbyists, representatives of the PTA often found themselves at odds with the established national associations representing cotton and woolen manufacturers, dominated as these then were by New England interests. Out of this loose Philadelphia group there soon developed the statewide Pennsylvania Manufacturers Association, again representing numerous divisions in the industry. Then there was the Philadelphia Manufacturers Association, made up largely of PTA members wearing different hats, its aim to combat growing labor militancy in the industry's various sections, each of which were represented on the PMA. For example, when rug workers struck in July 1886, the PMA's Rug and Carpet Section representatives investigated the dispute on the association's behalf. Regional manufacturers' groups became common in the Northeast, with its more diversified textile industrial base. The PMA was to be the most powerful force ranged against the state's textile workers in the 1934 strike.[14]

In single-sector towns, combinations of manufacturers also occurred. Paterson, New Jersey—"silk city" as it was often called—was one such. Most of its nearly 300 millowners were members of the Silk Manufacturers Association, a local branch of the National Association of Manufacturers, and their remarkable solidarity during the great strike of 1913, which paralyzed the city for eight months, was cited by friend and foe alike as a prime reason for its failure. They simply would not give an inch. New England woolen goods manufacturers, too, had their regional associations, though the eventual domination of the industry by the American Woolen Company tended in time to render them superfluous. Then, there were the national associations, the Wool Institute and the Silk Association of America. Most manufacturers had a connection with them, and they both had a role to play in the New Deal's transformed industrial structure, without ever approaching the degree of influence achieved by the CTI. Interregional tensions, such as those between the silk manufacturers of New Jersey and those of neighboring Pennsylvania, were always a hindrance to the development of national perspectives in these branches of the industry. The New Jersey mills, with those of Paterson at the center, produced high-quality fabric for the exclusive New York garment market and for export. Their weavers and dyers were highly skilled and fiercely proud of their craft and its traditions. Those in eastern Pennsylvania developed as an annex of the Paterson mills, but improved technology soon enabled manufacturers to dispense with skill. Producing a cheaper fabric for the emerging mass clothing market, they had a ready and docile labor force in the wives and children—especially the daughters—of the Pennsylvania coal miners. Paid less than their New Jersey counterparts, and much less likely to protest, they were a potent factor in the gradual exodus of the industry across the Pennsylvania border.[15]

One thing is certain, as textile manufacturers in all branches of their industry—wool, silk, cotton, even hosiery—thought about their falling profits, their workers' insistence on higher wages, and their need to adapt to technological advance, they were agreed that they had to get more out of their work force. Thus the "stretch-out" was born. It took many forms: the assignment of more looms to weavers or more vats to dyers; stepping up the general pace of the production process, often according to the advice of efficiency experts indoctrinated with the latest management practices—the end purpose being to increase production without a corresponding increase in the cost of labor.[16]

Workers throughout the industry were quick to recognize the stretch-out for what it was, a diminution of their working conditions and an attack on the skills of which they remained fiercely proud. They resisted the changes vehemently, usually by walking off the job. As early as 1904, weavers in Fall River's Bourne Mills, confronted with management's insistence that henceforth they were each to work twenty looms instead of twelve, voted to strike. Soon, weavers in other mills followed, against the advice of conservative union officials. They remained out for sixteen weeks. An underlying cause of the successful strike in the woolen mills of Lawrence, Massachusetts, in 1912, which shot the Industrial Workers of the World (IWW) to national prominence, had been the move from a seven- to a twelve-loom structure. A year later, when the Paterson silk workers struck, the trigger was the walkout of the broadsilk workers protesting the move from a two- to a four-loom system. Again the IWW became involved in what broadened into one of the nation's most bitter, and mythologized, labor disputes. Unlike in the Lawrence strike, however, the workers lost in Paterson.[17]

The stretch-out became part of the southern cotton mill scene following the collapse of the war boom in 1921. It remained so throughout the decade as millmen sought with increasing desperation to reverse the tide of declining profitability. They replaced men with women and then both with machines; they drastically increased the number of looms per operative; they increasingly resorted to piecework; they boosted the number of supervisors and job-watchers; they restricted every break, including toilet visits; in every way they stepped up the pace of mill operation. "Men with more machines to tend now ran where they had once ambled; women found timepieces—'hank-clocks' they called them—installed on each piece of machinery they used; gone was the chance to chat with one's neighbor, let alone to make the occasional trip home to see the children." The workplace was no longer a moderately benign milieu. It had become a place of tension.[18]

Southern textile workers bundled all these new practices together under the hated sobriquet *stretch-out*. They resisted them throughout the decade, and in 1929, their anger too much to contain, they struck in their tens of thousands. Throughout the Carolina Piedmont that year there was industrial tumult. In South Carolina, for example, there were 81 separate strikes, involving more than 80,000 workers. Even more workers struck in the largest textile state, North Carolina. Some of these disputes, especially the bloody confrontations in Gastonia and Marion, North Carolina, and the "precipitating event" in Elizabethton, Tennessee, have passed, like Paterson, New Jersey, in 1913, into the mythology of American labor history, but most were short-term, local affairs, spontaneous and quickly settled. Yet, this "revolt in the Piedmont" as historian Irving Bernstein termed it, continued intermittently throughout 1930, ending with the defeat of the Danville, Virginia, workers after a strike that lasted from September 1930 till January 1931. However large or small, violent or orderly the individual disputes may have been, the stretch-out was the root cause of them all.[19]

In the last two decades a new generation of southern historians has recovered in detail most aspects of the southern textile workers' world. Extending the work of a contemporary group of talented social scientists, and often using the evidence provided by extensive interviewing of workers and their children, scholars such as Allen Tullos, Douglas Flamming, Timothy Minchin, Bryant Simon, Daniel Clark, and, above all, Jacquelyn Hall and her coauthors have provided us with a multidimensional picture of the "cotton mill people," one which modifies the notion that this was a feckless, improvident, essentially passive work force, largely composed of farmers and mountaineers unable to adjust to the circumstances in which they found themselves. Hall and her colleagues instead describe a process of transition, painful to be sure, in which, over two or three generations, these independent rural folk became mill workers, and developed a distinctive culture of their own within the parameters of the workplace and the mill communities in which they lived. As Ella Ford, who was raised in the mountains of western North Carolina but forced in her early twenties to abandon farming for the cotton mills of Gastonia, once told an interviewer, they had "got into the habit" of being mill workers and town dwellers.[20]

Not only people, but also the physical landscape was transformed by this process of industrialization. Soon, mill villages "dotted the Piedmont landscape," management's answer, as James Hodges aptly remarked, to "the practical problem of assembling a workforce in small towns and rural places." By 1905, "one long mill village" ran along the arc of the Piedmont, communities sprang up everywhere, and those already existing grew exponentially once a mill had come to town, their characters changing in the process.[21]

Burlington, in North Carolina's Alamance County, was one such. Originally named Company Shops because the North Carolina Railroad's locomotives were repaired there, it became one of the region's most important textile towns as the industry grew in the post–Civil War years, initially through the activities of the Holt family. Edwin Michael Holt had built, in 1837, Alamance County's first mill on the banks of a tributary stream to the Haw River. After the war, he proceeded to build an "industrial dynasty" there, by 1900 controlling twenty-four of the county's twenty-nine mills, including Burlington's huge Plaid Mill. The town prospered during World War I's textile boom, and its population grew, as it started to shed its turn-of-the-century appearance of a collection of unincorporated mill villages clustered round a small business district. Burlington's roads were paved in 1913, electric street lights came in 1921, and ten thousand people thronged to cheer as the first switch was thrown, and its sidewalk system was completed in 1929. It suffered along with hundreds of similar communities through the postwar stagnation, but textiles had clearly brought progress as well as a change of name to Company Shops.[22]

Spencer Love completed the process. Love was the son of a Harvard mathematics professor whose family had deep roots in Gaston County, and his grandfather had died in 1907, leaving two declining cotton mills there as his estate. Love's career will be discussed in more detail later, but having served in France as a divisional adjutant during World War I, he returned home determined to put the administrative skills his war service had uncovered to work rebuilding the family fortunes. Moving South in 1919, he soon decided that the Gaston County enterprises were past saving, and that the solution was to salvage what equipment he could, sell as much as possible, and move elsewhere. This he did in 1924, choosing Burlington as his new location and eventually placing his faith in a new synthetic yarn, rayon. He was hugely successful. The town became the center of Love's textile empire of hosiery and cotton as well as rayon mills, in time giving its name to Burlington Industries, the largest textile company in the world.[23]

Burlington's mill workers were typical of those making the transition from farm to factory. Ethel Hilliard and her family came there in 1927, after having drifted aimlessly about the Piedmont. She found work in the Burlington Mills spinning room, where she stayed for the rest of her life. "I would not want no better place to work," she claimed. Management had always treated her well, especially allowing her time off to have her children and then taking her back. Charles Murray had farmed as a boy, but ended up as a weaver at the Glencoe Mill, where he stayed for forty years. James Pharis's family were also from the land, but they, too, left the land for Burlington Mills, where they were "pretty satisfied." J. M. Robinette came "from the mountains" in 1917 to find work in the Plaid Mill. He always hoped to go back but could never afford to. Mattie Shoemaker and her sister Mildred Shoemaker Edmonds were also from the mountains. They came to Burlington in 1928 and made it their home thereafter, as did Herman Newton Truitt's grandfather. He was a farmer who could not make a living from his hard mountain soil, but he did so in Burlington, growing produce and selling it to the new mill workers, most former farmers like himself. In time he opened his own store. Other Burlington workers told similar stories of having to leave the land, of learning about mill life and village living, of the cruel pain of separation then eventual adjustment. In this, they were typical of the new cotton mill work force, men and women all over the South who had recently made the transition from farm to factory and who were, in their changing lives, experiencing the region's modernization.[24]

Burlington was an overwhelmingly "native white" town. Less than 1 percent of its population was described in the 1930 census as "foreign born," and only 6.6 percent as "Negroes." In this it was again typical of southern textile communities. What a contrast they presented to those in New England, New Jersey, or Pennsylvania, with their polyglot ethnic work force and communities. Southern boosters were quick to point this out to manufacturers. Burlington's work force, ran a Chamber of Commerce pamphlet, had all "the outstanding characteristics of their loyal, thrifty and efficient ancestors." They were, therefore, "unlikely to fall prey to the radical outside agitator or organizer."[25]

Most of Burlington's mill workers, as elsewhere in the South, lived in villages built for them by Love and his fellow manufacturers. Love's village of Piedmont Heights, like most others, was not a particularly attractive place, but the houses were well constructed, electricity was provided, and rents were low. Unlike many such towns, it had no company store from which workers were forced to get their supplies, but neither was there a school, church, community hall, or welfare clinic, Love having gone into the business relatively late, after the drive to provide such amenities for workers had lost its impetus due to bad economic times. Rather, its residents used downtown Burlington's stores, facilities, and public buildings for their shopping, their general needs, and their entertainment. Young workers, in particular, shared the new world of radio and mingled at the movies, public dances, the bowling alleys, even in the poolrooms and illegal drinking places with the general townsfolk as they, too, embraced the freer, secular, city-derived youth culture of the postwar world, with the automobile, increasingly, at its center. Most southern mill villages were moving in this direction by 1930. In this, at least, young southern textile workers shared a commonality with their northern, ethnically diverse counterparts: the process of modernization.[26]

Of course, Piedmont Heights, like most mill villages, or, indeed, working-class communities, had its rough side. There was plenty of drinking, gambling, fistfighting, and, less typically, cockfighting. Indeed, James Pharis alleged that Alamance County was known throughout the Piedmont for its "rooster fighting," and Burlington was its center. Carroll Lupton, a local physician, agreed that it was "a pretty rough place," especially at night, but that it eventually settled down, especially after Rev. George Washington Swinney built his church there, Glen Hope Baptist. A former mill worker himself, Swinney provided the community with an alternative focus of considerable influence. Conditions in mill villages varied significantly throughout the South. A few were almost model communities, well planned and developed; others, such as that at the Loray Mill in Gastonia, were neglected, unkempt pockets of resentment. Most, like Piedmont Heights, lay somewhere between the poles, far from ideal living places but spaces nonetheless where mill communities could develop, further aiding workers' transition from farm to factory and into the modern world. They were also, of course, white communities, for only a few African Americans worked in the mills, mainly as janitors. They did not live in the villages. Black women in Burlington, as they did elsewhere, often minded mill workers' children so their mothers could go to the mill, but that was as far as it went.[27]

If the southern textile mill workers were overwhelmingly white, native born, and fresh from the farms, those in the New England cotton and woolen mills, or the silk mills of New Jersey and Pennsylvania, were of entirely different stock and of such diverse experiences that to generalize freely about them is impossible. The textile towns themselves were of similar diversity and with individual histories. The first cotton mill workers were, of course, largely native born, but as Herbert J. Lahne wrote in 1944, "Almost from its very beginnings the New England industry augmented the local labor supply with newly arrived immigrants." The English and Scots were the first, but then came the Irish, pushed out by the disastrous potato famine in 1846. After the Civil War it was the turn of the French Canadians. Living close to the mill centers as they did, like the first southern ex-mountaineers, they initially moved between farm and factory, before opting for the permanency of the mills. By 1880 the French Canadians had taken the industry for their own, he asserted, maintaining their advantage despite the waves of new immigrants from southern and eastern Europe—the Italians, the Poles, the Greeks, the Portuguese—who easily found the unskilled jobs now predominating in the mills. So dependent was the New England industry on immigrant labor that the percentage of its native-born workers remained below that of the foreign-born until as late as 1930, the first time for more than a century that the ratios had been reversed.[28]

Lahne's broad generalizations have some value but must be tempered with hundreds of individual exceptions. Massachusetts's first mill workers, at Fall River, were the children of local farmers. Then came the Scots, English, and Irish, all according to Lahne's plan. True, French Canadians arrived in numbers from the 1870s to compete for the less skilled jobs, but so did a new influx of skilled Lancashire workers, especially weavers, actively recruited by millowners dismayed at the declining skill base of their operatives, and especially at the number of women and children in the mills. More Irish followed in the 1870s and 1880s, but they came via Lancashire's textile country, where they had stopped long enough to absorb certain skills, and also something of labor unions and of English class consciousness. By 1875, 13,000 of Fall River's population were from Lancashire, dwarfing the 5,000 French Canadians in the mills, as well as the native-born operatives. At the turn of the century the Portuguese started coming, both from mainland Portugal and the Azores. There were only 700 Portuguese residents in 1885, but in 1909 there were 10,000, almost all unskilled workers, sometimes displacing the French Canadians, but more often moving them up the ladder. Next came the

Poles and Russians, then a few Syrians and Lebanese. The Italians, so prominent in Lynn, in Lawrence, and in the Rhode Island mills, were very few and far between.[29]

The demography of Fall River's sister city, New Bedford, was not dissimilar. Again, the original mill workers had come from the countryside, but after the Civil War they were quickly joined by skilled Englishmen from the Lancashire mills, as well as the French Canadians. Relatively few Irish seem to have made their way there, but after 1900 the Portuguese were a growing presence. Indeed, in 1937 New Bedford had the highest proportion of people of Portuguese descent of any American city, in part a reflection of its earlier history as the center of the whaling industry. A significant number of Portuguese seamen had always called it home.[30]

Broadly, the same demographic pattern held true for the textile industries of New Jersey and Pennsylvania, native-born workers dominated initially, then they were joined by the artisans of western Europe and the British Isles, later by the peasants from Italy and farther east. In some cases, skilled workers came from there as well, of whom the Polish silk workers from Lodz who went to Paterson provide a good example. Prior to 1890, over 80 percent of New Jersey's immigrants had come from western Europe. Indeed, as Rudolph J. Vecoli has written, "the history of the peopling of New Jersey in the nineteenth century is largely that of the coming of the Germans, the Irish, and the British." From then on, the demographic mix changed. The Italians started to come, so did the Slovenians, the Hungarians, the Slavs, the Jews of eastern Europe, to the extent that by 1930 Italians had become the largest foreign group in the state. Indeed one-third of New Jersey's people were of southern or eastern European origin, and the textile industries reflected this change. Passaic's woolen mills for example, initially the province of the Germans and the English, had by 1924 a labor force "almost entirely composed of Poles, Hungarians, Russian Jews, and smaller Slavic groups." Like the mills of the South, the children of these migrant groups were moving into the mills in increasing numbers, and this despite the early passage of a law designed to prevent such practices.[31]

The "silk city" of Paterson is a good example of the changing industrial demography. Paterson, as is well known, was the "first major planned manufacturing city in the United States," the brainchild of Alexander Hamilton, who first saw the industrial potential of the Passaic Falls. By 1840 it had become an important cotton manufacturing center, the year John Ryle, a weaver from the English silk town of Macclesfield, opened its first silk mill. After the Civil War, the silk industry boomed there, largely as the result of the massive migration of English master weavers. Fifteen thousand came from Macclesfield alone, as "the silk industry of England immigrated practically en masse to Paterson"—along with its machinery. After 1900, however, these proud artisans were joined by other ethnic groups: skilled Italian dyers and weavers from Biella and other northern Italian silk towns; Polish Jews from Lodz, skilled males for the most part, many with a highly developed sense of class consciousness, and having already experienced industrial violence. Less skilled workers came too, mainly southern Italians with no previous textile experience, who by 1900 formed the great majority of the dyers' helpers. Paterson's Jewish textile workers were mainly broadsilk weavers, many from Lodz, or Bialystock in Russian Poland. In Paterson, as the latest arrivals, they were often given the poorest-paying work. Some Dutch migrants were also employed as dyers' helpers, but it was the Italians and the Jews who had come to challenge the English dominance of Paterson's silk labor force.[32]

In Pennsylvania, there was a similar demographic pattern. Philadelphia had become by 1890 the most prosperous and diversified textile district in the United States, and the diversity at least was well reflected in its work force. From 1820, Irish immigrants provided the labor in the growing textile district of Kensington, in shops largely owned by British and German migrant masters. Western European migrants and their children continued to dominate the work force through the 1880s, before, as elsewhere, being joined by the new migrants. Like Paterson, there were Polish immigrants from the Lodz textile district, skilled Italians from the North, unskilled from the South, or already lured away from Paterson's vats, skilled carpet weavers from Brussels, Jewish knitters escaping czarist pogroms. Nevertheless, Philadelphia's immigrant textile labor force remained much more western European-oriented than that of neighboring New Jersey, or even those of the outlying centers like Easton, Bridgeport, Reading, or Hazleton. As late as 1906, most of its foreign-born workers were from England, Ireland, and Scotland, and a steady stream of English operatives continued to arrive throughout the postwar years of decline. They were particularly strong in the woolen and worsted branches, where it was argued "the Philadelphia product has no superior," due to the domination of "the expert English workman."[33]

From time to time, Philadelphia manufacturers allegedly attempted to employ African Americans, usually, but not exclusively, as strikebreakers. If it is true, such moves never worked, Philadelphia's textile mills remained as lily-white as those everywhere. In the whole northeastern region only the giant Sayles Finishing Plant in Saylesville, Rhode Island, seems to have hired African Americans for "inside" work. The Scots, Irish, or English would work with them, it was reported. Italians and Portuguese generally would not.[34]

New England manufacturers, like their southern counterparts were to do, initially built mill villages for their workers, usually because of the need to move them near to the source of power—water. When this was no longer the case, and as the communities grew, the need to do so became less obvious, real estate operators found they could make money renting cottages, row houses, and tenements to the operatives. Company-owned housing in Fall River was generally deplorable. Operatives paid seven dollars monthly, according to an 1895 report, for filthy, disease-ridden tenement accommodation, "where a dozen families draw water from a single faucet"—when it was running. Some tenements had even been built in the middle of a swamp; the air all around was truly "pestilential," and no doubt went a long way toward accounting for the town's high death rate. No wonder the workers tried desperately to move to alternative accommodations as soon as they could. On the other hand, Ernest Denomme recalled growing up in the Harris Village Mill, in Rhode Island's Pawtuxet Valley, with fondness. The village was almost 100 percent French, he remembered, which gave it a real sense of community. Other villages nearby were predominantly Irish or Italian. Residents of one town would often play soccer against those of another, and stage other ethnic sports contests. He clearly enjoyed village living. Most likely New England's villages, like their later southern counterparts, ranged from the deplorable to the decently planned. In any case, they were no longer an important aspect of mill town life by the turn of the century. As the towns grew, workers increasingly looked after their own housing needs, independent of their companies.[35]

This had always been the case in Pennsylvania and New Jersey. From the start, Philadelphia's textile workers had found their own accommodation, initially in the Kensington district, but then as the industry spread and diversified, in many other parts of the city, especially Manayunck and Germantown. In all the districts, however, most workers came to own their own homes. "In the Quaker City," wrote the historian Philip Scranton, "far more commonly than in New York or other major urban sites, working people bought their own houses at modest prices," helped by a multiplicity of tiny building and loan associations, and the ground rent system, which enabled buyers to pay only for the structure, while leasing the land on which it stood. By 1900, most workers in Kensington and Manayunck owned or were buying their modest row houses, usually within walking distance of the mills. Not surprisingly, the building and loan associations from which their workers borrowed were often capitalized by mill management in the interests of industrial stability. Even in the "decade of decline" following the world war, home ownership in ethnically defined districts remained the norm for Philadelphia's textile workers, providing a stark contrast to the mill villages of the South, or even New England. [36]

Paterson's silk manufacturers, likewise, had no need to provide housing for their employees. Though a few of the ex-Macclesfield artisans owned their own homes, most families rented houses, often taking in single men as boarders to help pay the rent. Like workers elsewhere, they too lived in ethnically defined districts, of which the Italian was the largest and came to be regarded, with some reason, as "the international center of Italian anarchism." Paterson's Jews formed two quite distinct communities—those from Germany who were often millowners or managers and who lived on the modern East Side, and the more recent arrivals from Poland, who rented crowded accommodations in "Jewtown," in the city's center. Given the city's turbulent industrial history, the fact that millowners had little control over, or involvement with, their workers' living space often worked against them. During the famous strike of 1913, for example, when strikers could not pay their rent, nor boarders their share, few landlords moved to evict. Indeed, the Association of Jewish Landlords "formally voted not to evict silk workers while the strike lasted." In the mill villages of the South, by contrast, eviction was always the owners' prime weapon in times of labor disputes. [37]

Passaic, a few miles south of Paterson, was a woolen and worsted center—and also an immigrant town. There, however, the comparison ended. Passaic's workers were mainly Slavs, Poles, Slovaks, Ukrainians, and Galicians, formerly peasants, and, like their southern counterparts, recent migrants from the countryside, many still hoping that America would provide sufficient to enable them to buy land back home. A large number were single women, who usually lived in boarding houses run by the Roman Catholic Church, rather than the worsted or woolen mills in which they worked. Deeply religious as they were, their several church spires towered over a city of constant turbulence, ethnic tensions with roots deep in the old Austro-Hungarian empire from which they mostly came; religious strife as Russian Orthodox, Polish Catholic, and Latin or Greek Rite devotees battled for hegemony in their new home. There was also an Italian community in Passaic, though nowhere near as large nor as influential as that of neighboring Paterson, as well as a sizeable Magyar population working in the textile mills but living rigidly apart from their Slavic fellow workers. Passaic's Jewish community came from the same parts of Europe as the Slavs and the Magyars, but neither worked with them nor lived close to them. Passaic was the prime example of an immigrant town, dominated by two large woolen companies, in which most of its inhabitants found work, and indeed may have rented houses and tenements originally built by one or other of these firms, but who nonetheless lived in distinct ethnic communities, each with its own religious, cultural, and social institutions, and more often than not bitterly hostile to one another.[38]

Ethnicity also determined the residential patterns in most New England mill towns and villages. In Fall River the Lancashire weavers were quick to reproduce the social life they had left behind, establishing communities built around pubs and lodges, modeled closely on those of England's north. Before too long they even had a cricket club and played regular matches against the clubs of New Bedford and other communities where English operatives had settled. Match reports appeared regularly in Lancashire newspapers, for, as John Cumbler has shrewdly observed, initially "Lancashire workers saw Fall River as another textile town in Lancashire." Even after distance had frayed the tightness of these bonds, the English-style pubs, the lodges—even the cricket—remained. The Irish workers, too, soon formed branches of their own lodges and nationalist societies, and though ordinary relationships with the English were reasonably good, religious and other differences meant that they preferred to live apart.[39]

Both English and Irish workers disliked and distrusted the French Canadians for their cultural distinctiveness, especially their language, and their antiunion attitude, which made them potential strikebreakers. For their part, the Quebecois, determined as always to maintain their language and culture in an English-speaking world, founded their own social institutions and their parochial schools. The English did not have to force residential segregation on them either, it was a development on which the French Canadians insisted. As for the Portuguese, most of whom came initially from the Azores, they too brought with them some traditional beliefs and customs which they found easier to practice in their own communities. Moreover, as neither the English, the Irish, nor the French Canadians had any interest in expanding their circles, these newer arrivals soon found themselves concentrated in their own village in the south of the city. There they founded Portuguese athletic clubs, debating societies, and taverns. Young Portuguese, however, showed from the start a desire to move beyond their world if the other groups would let them. Alone, they looked on marriage outside the ethnic group as not necessarily to be opposed—quite unlike their French Canadian, Irish, or English neighbors. Though rigid social and residential segregation was moderated in the first decades of the twentieth century, it remained an easily observable fact of Fall River life for as long as the mills were there.[40]

The settlement and residential pattern of Lawrence, Massachusetts's most important textile town, showed elements of the Lahne pattern but with its own distinctiveness. Dominated by the giant American Woolen Company, whose Wood worsted mill was the largest in the world, Lawrence was also a significant cotton manufacturing center. The Irish got there first, well before the Civil War. Then, after 1860, came the English, mainly from the Yorkshire woolen city of Bradford, the Scots, the French Canadians, and the Germans. Lawrence's "new" immigrants, those arriving after 1890, came from four distinct regions: France and Belgium; eastern Europe, mainly Poland (both Jews and Catholics) and Russia (mainly Jews, Ukrainians, and Lithuanians); southern Europe (Greeks, Italians, and Portuguese); and the Middle East (Syrians, Turks, and Armenians). Almost all found work in the mills, where there was a distinct ethnic occupational gradation. The English-speakers had the best-paying, least-onerous jobs, then the French Canadians, with "the dirtiest and most dangerous" assigned to the Poles, Lithuanians, and Italians. Lawrence was rigidly segregated residentially, while the level of ethnic conflicts, high even by the standards of such immigrant communities, kept the town fragmented and the tension level high.[41]

It has been stated often, and with considerable truth, that the ethnic diversity of the New England and middle Atlantic textile towns was a boon to manufacturers, in that it prevented working-class solidarity, and, subsequently, challenges to their economic and class power. Certainly, at the individual level, it could make the workplace a cold and lonely place to be. Edith Landes, an English migrant who came to work in Central Falls, Rhode Island, certainly found it so. Her first years were "miserable" and "lonesome," she recalled, because of the way the mills were "all mixed up. You see, not knowing the different nationalities," she explained, made it very hard to get along. "In England they were all English. In this country, in the mills, we worked with a lot of Polish people, Portuguese people, I worked opposite a French girl who didn't speak very good English." Rather, she spoke "Canadian-French" all the time, and they could hardly communicate. It was a "terribly lonely" time for her.[42]

Landes's experience, though not uncommon, could hardly have been typical, nor the result of a plan to stifle the growth of working-class consciousness among the mill girls. In most textile centers, ethnic groups tended to dominate whole sections of the process, the Italian dyers' helpers in Paterson, for example, the ex-Macclesfield or Bradford weavers in Paterson and Lawrence, the Jewish broadsilk weavers, again of Paterson, the Belgian carpet workers of Philadelphia, the Italians in neighboring Norristown's hosiery plants. The occupational differentiation between skilled and unskilled which generally followed ethnic lines was much more important in hindering growth of class solidarity among workers, and this the management certainly encouraged. It is certain, too, that the very diversity of the textile industry in New England and the mid-Atlantic states, with silk, woolen, and cotton mills often present in the same communities, was also a barrier to the emergence of an industrywide class consciousness. This was especially the case in Rhode Island and Massachusetts. From time to time, however, workers did combine across ethnic or sector lines to challenge those who controlled their lives, sometimes under the direction of national labor organizers, sometimes under local nonunion leaders. Lawrence, that most ethnically fragmented of towns, did so successfully in 1912, under the leadership of the Industrial Workers of the World. The IWW was also prominent in the silk workers' strike in Paterson a year later, which paralyzed the industry for eight months, and from which it never really recovered. The strike's failure should not hide the fact that English weavers, Jewish broadsilk men, and Italian dyers, formerly deeply divided, had for the most part stood together throughout its duration. It could be done.[43]

A bewildering complexity of labor organizations tried to weld together these new industrial workers, in both the North and the South. Unions came and went throughout a fifty-year period, some conservative and skill-based, others more overtly revolutionary, appealing to the unskilled and the most desperate. Not all these new American textile workers were entirely ignorant of industrial conditions and the potential for strife that they often engendered. The Polish silk workers who came to Paterson, for example, were often veterans of labor battles at home, as were the weavers and spinners from northern Italy. The English, in particular, had not only experienced such disputes but had a notion that the best way of protecting their positions was through collective action. Thus in Fall River, in New Bedford, in Paterson, British artisans brought with them a predilection for locally based organization by craft and skill. English "craft separatism" became the model for much of the early union activity among skilled operatives, which meant they had little interest initially in reaching out to their newer, non–English-speaking, unskilled workmates. There were some exceptions. In Fall River and New Bedford, the locally based craft union structure did at least absorb some French Canadian workers eventually, but elsewhere the exclusivity remained. In Philadelphia, German skilled operatives even formed their own German-speaking Textile Workers Union.[44]

At the other end of the spectrum were those organizations that claimed either a national or international constituency and a revolutionary agenda. In the nineteenth century the Knights of Labor were extremely active in Philadelphia's textile mills for a time, less so in parts of New England, and even made a brief appearance in the South. The IWW, as has already been noted, had its time of triumph in Lawrence in 1912, before bitter defeat and eventual collapse the following year in Paterson. After the Bolshevik revolution of 1917, its locally based emissaries tried to penetrate the American textile mills, working particularly among the new migrants, the rural refugees, the unskilled and the dispossessed, with whom the craft-based unions had had little contact. Communist Party members, affiliated with the Trade Union Educational League, the party's industrial arm, provided effective leadership in the bitter Passaic strike in 1926, where they worked with the unskilled and unorganized migrants, and again two years later, in New Bedford. There they found ready supporters among the Portuguese workers, whom the craft-based locals had always ignored. In both strikes the Communists were bitterly opposed by both management and representatives of the American Federation of Labor's own textile union, the United Textile Workers, with whom most craft locals had by now affiliated.[45]

The unpalatable experience of New Bedford, where the strike eventually ended on terms acceptable to the UTW, which party members regarded as betrayal of the workers, caused them to abandon the notion of influencing the established textile workers unions. In the wake of the New Bedford strike, the party created its own umbrella labor organization, the Trade Union Unity League, and founded its first affiliate, the National Textile Workers Union (NTWU). The next year the decision was taken to begin organizing the cotton textile South. Hardened veterans were sent to Gastonia, North Carolina, to take control of a strike against the stretch-out at the troubled Loray Mill, the region's largest establishment. The resultant drawn-out stoppage, the violence, including the shooting of the local police chief, Orville Aderholt, and a strike leader, Ella May Wiggins, the highly publicized trial and subsequent flight to the Soviet

Union of those charged with Aderholt's murder have all assured the Loray Mill strike a place in the mythology of American labor struggles. It should be noted, however, that it marked the only time the NTWU attempted to penetrate the South. Retreating to its New England base, it struggled on for a few more years before disbanding in 1934.[46]

Surprisingly, it was the United Textile Workers of America that proved the most durable of all the unions, local, regional, and national, which were competing for the loyalties of America's textile labor force. Founded in 1901 and containing "both craft union locals of skilled workers such as mulespinners or loomfixers, and industrial union locals of weavers, and other semi-skilled and unskilled workers," with conservative leadership, its president an English migrant and supporter of Samuel Gompers, the UTW made little initial progress. It had no impact in the great battles of Lawrence or Paterson, its cautious philosophy and skilled-worker bias holding no attraction for the growing numbers of unskilled workers crowding into the cotton mills of New England and the South and the woolen, worsted, and silk mills of New Jersey, Massachusetts, and Pennsylvania. As late as 1914, it represented only 2 percent of all textile workers.[47]

Nevertheless, the UTW did make some gains during the war, and afterward, it found itself leading strikes in New Hampshire, Rhode Island, and Massachusetts, disputes which forced its leadership, for the first time, to face the need to organize unskilled and non–English-speaking workers. Moreover, in vice president, later president, British-born Thomas McMahon it had a senior officer who was convinced that the union had no future unless it could organize the southern workers. Though its first organizing drive in the Carolina Piedmont, in 1920 and 1921, failed, as did the postwar New England ventures, it had at least established a presence in the South, the first textile union to do so.[48]

Throughout the 1920s, the UTW's strength ebbed and flowed. In 1922, along with the more radical Amalgamated Textile Workers Union, UTW locals led the prolonged and violent New England strike. The battle, which lasted eight months, had no clear victor at the end. However, the UTW leaders stuck it out, and in a dispute in which local leadership was overwhelmingly foreign-born, and where women, especially Portuguese women, were particularly active, the union had finally gained some credence among these groups. The UTW also assisted the Associated Silk Workers in two strikes in Paterson, in 1924 and 1928, and, as has been mentioned, fought the Communists for strike leadership in Passaic and New Bedford.[49]

In 1929 UTW organizers again moved south. Frozen out of Gastonia, they were also often rebuffed as they sought to join local, unorganized protests, while those that they did lead, in Elizabethton, Tennessee, and Marion, North Carolina, in 1929, and in Danville, Virginia, the following year, ended in defeat. Indeed, the UTW's historian describes the union as being at the "nadir of its fortunes" in the early 1930s, with a mere fifteen thousand workers and no money to pay its local organizers. But it hung on, and indeed gained affiliates, if not members, as established unions like the American Federation of Silk Workers, no longer able to exist independently, joined with it in 1932. By 1934 it had added a woolen and worsted and a rayon department, for by this time the world had changed, and the UTW's continued growth seemed assured.[50]

No one could have predicted that in 1931, as America entered its second year of depression. To repeat McMahon's comment, "general demoralization" best described the state of American textiles. As late as 1933, Benjamin Gossett, president of the American Cotton Manufacturers Association, could describe his branch of the industry as "bleeding . . . to death," and few would have disputed this judgment. In New England, it was even worse, as bankruptcy followed bankruptcy. By 1930, New Bedford's fine goods market had collapsed, and former cotton mill workers had pushed the unemployment rate to double that of the rest of the nation. The woolen situation was no better; in Paterson the depression had simply hastened its decline. By the end of the 1920s, "silk city" was "successful neither for people nor for industry." Philadelphia, the nation's most diversified textile center, had long entered what one historian has called the time of "disarray." Production of woven goods, for example, had dropped by more than 50 percent between 1925 and 1933, carpet production had dropped by 65 percent, wool and worsted, by 80 percent. Even fully fashioned hosiery, which had remained strong till 1930, was now on the slide. "The full-fashioned hosiery industry has been carried around in God's pocket for many years," remarked one manufacturer in 1931. Now, the pocket had developed a hole. Hosiery was the South's one bright spot. When physician Carroll Lupton arrived in Burlington in 1933, at a time when the national economy was close to collapse, and having seen nothing but want and misery on his drive up from New Orleans, the obvious prosperity of the young hosiery workers so captured his attention that he decided to set up a medical practice in the town. It was the only place he had seen in a long while where "a fellow could make a living." The town's cotton mill people were not nearly so well-off, as wages declined, jobs were lost, and the stretch-out became more vicious.[51]

Desperate textile workers responded in various ways. A surprising number struck, despite the thousands waiting to take their jobs. There were strikes over pay cuts in Easton, Pennsylvania's silk mills in July 1931, for example, under NTWU leadership, but most, like those in devastated Paterson, in New Bedford, in Philadelphia, and even in Greenville, South Carolina, were locally led. In August, Paterson's weavers were out, supposedly under UTW leaders. The worsted workers struck in Lawrence in October; they stayed out for nearly two months. In March 1932, the silk workers in Paterson and Easton and the cotton mill people in Greenville were out. In South Carolina's Horse Creek Valley there were rolling strikes from March to June, without any union involvement. Throughout 1932, in fact, Easton, Paterson, Allentown, and Hazleton, as well as the Horse Creek Valley were all sites of constant disturbance, but there were scores more sites as textile workers vented their anger at the desperate situation and the inability of their governments, their employers, or their unions to take decisive action.[52]

But a new player had entered the game. In November 1932 Americans had elected as president a man who had promised a New Deal for the American people and had spoken of doing something for the "forgotten man" at the bottom of the economic pyramid. He had also promised to use the full force of the federal government in bold, experimental ways to deal with the scourge of depression. Textile workers and their employers alike waited expectantly as Franklin D. Roosevelt began the realization of his promises.

Chapter 2

The New Deal

THE NATIONAL INDUSTRIAL RECOVERY ACT (NIRA), WHICH established the National Recovery Administration, was the centerpiece of the early New Deal's industrial policy. It was passed late in the frenetic legislative period following FDR's inaugural, known as the "hundred days," and was hastily cobbled together only after Alabama's Senator Hugo Black had introduced legislation barring from interstate commerce goods produced by manufacturers who worked their employees for more than thirty hours weekly. The senator argued that the measure would both create new jobs and attack the continuing problem of "technological unemployment." Support for the Black bill grew, and after AFL president Green threw his weight behind it, promising large-scale industrial action if it were not adopted, the Senate passed the measure. Roosevelt and his brain trusters, who believed the provision of the Black bill to be irresponsible, even unconstitutional, scrambled to find an alternative. They came up with the NIRA.[1]

Signed into law on June 16, after nearly a month of debate and lobbying, the NIRA attempted to satisfy a range of disparate interest groups: social reformers, public works advocates, trustbusters, labor leaders, supporters of trade associations, economic planners—whether for business or government—and advocates of "codes of fair competition." Title 2, which provided for the spending of more than three million dollars on public works, occasioned little controversy. The core of the legislation was to be found in Title 1. Declaring that a national emergency existed, it suspended federal antitrust laws for two years and permitted business leaders to draw up "codes of fair competition" applicable throughout their industry, allowing them to fix prices and to control output. When approved by the president, these codes would have in some areas the power of law, and could be enforced in the courts. The president could alter codes, amend them, amplify them, or even impose them if no agreement was forthcoming. Organized labor's demands were met by section 7, parts a, b, and c, which gave employees the right "to bargain collectively through representatives of their own choosing" and to join unions unhindered and required employers to agree to provisions setting maximum working hours and minimum wage rates. In return for the inclusion of these provisions in each code, business had achieved effective self-rule. Finally, the National Recovery Administration (NRA) was created to administer the act's provisions.[2]

Upon signing the NIRA into law, the president told assembled reporters, "History will probably record the NIRA as the most important and far-reaching legislation ever enacted by the American Congress." It would put millions back to work, he believed, and would stimulate the economy to such an extent that all would soon be back to normal. Some of his advisors were rather less sanguine that such a mishmash of competing and often contradictory economic notions could ever have that effect, and they doubted that handing so much power to the business sector was sensible, especially given its impotence during four years of devastating depression. Business leaders, unsurprisingly, were generally enthusiastic, even regarding the labor provisions of section 7(a), as sufficiently vague as to minimize the prospect of their having to bargain seriously with employees' unions. Rather, their attention was fixed on the suspension of the antitrust laws, agreeing with the NRA administrator, flamboyant General Hugh Johnson, that this would "eliminate eye-gouging, and knee-groining and ear-chewing in business," the ruinous competition that they believed had brought them all so low.[3]

Even organized labor welcomed business self-rule, for their representatives did not see it as such. AFL president William Green called section 7(a) a "Magna Carta" for workers. John L. Lewis, head of the United Mine Workers, compared it to Lincoln's Emancipation Proclamation. As Bryant Simon commented, "Prose could not quite capture textile trade unionist Thornton Oakley's enthusiasm for the law." He wrote a poem about it, eventually published on the front of the *Textile Worker.*

> Now swells the glad voice of the nation,
> Now breaks the bright dawn of a new day
> Black hopelessness yields to elation
> Exultant thy cry, NRA!

Lo, labor again rolls its thunder,
Lifts choral in vast roundelay;
Lo, powers of greed fall asunder,
By blue eagle rent, NRA!

Ride on! Let thy stars throw their pinions,
With light of truth blaze thou the way,
The call reaches all man's dominions,
Proclaim a new age, NRA!

By the time Oakley's verse was published, his new age, if it had ever begun, was already well and truly over, yet that should not diminish the sense of enthusiasm, nor the expectation with which most groups greeted the NRA's creation, with its proud symbol, the "Blue Eagle."[4]

No industry association was more urgent in its support than the Cotton Textile Institute. As the depression deepened, it had urged voluntary cooperation plans on its members, and on President Hoover, with little success. Nevertheless, it had established itself as spokesman for the industry during the Hoover years, had developed its own bureaucracy, and had established close relationships with federal counterparts. Moreover, both Sloan and the increasingly desperate CTI members that he led had become convinced that their salvation, even their survival, could only be achieved through some sort of government-industry partnership; agreements within the industry, but with no government sanction, could never work. The CTI, therefore, was eager to become involved in the NRA experiment.[5]

Sloan and his associates were quick to present their own plans for industrywide self-regulation, backed by federal law, to the NIRA code-drafting committees as soon as they had begun their work. The president, for his part, used the industry as an example, throughout May 1933, of the need for the sort of partnership he was recommending. Cotton textile manufacturers, he told a radio audience on May 7, had tried desperately to reach agreements on production levels and minimum work standards, but these had invariably broken down because of the refusal of a few rogue manufacturers to cooperate. Now, the CTI was leading the way in cotton textile producers' support for the NRA approach.[6]

Indeed it was. Even before the NIRA had cleared Congress, the CTI had formed a Cotton Textile Industry Committee (CTIC), comprising ten southern manufacturers, six from New England and four from the industry's New York marketing side, and charged it with the drafting of a code of competition. Labor representation was not even considered. The CTIC went about its work with a will, and by June 19, only three days after the NIRA had been signed, a draft code was ready, drawn up entirely without labor's input. The code was extraordinarily detailed, but its most important proposals were a minimum weekly wage of ten dollars in the South, and eleven dollars elsewhere, and a workweek shortened to forty hours for production workers, with plants limited to two forty-hour shifts weekly. Section 7(a) however, was explicitly acknowledged, while the insistence that workers join company unions only was discouraged. Employers went along with the labor provisions because, as one of them remarked, if Washington were to set wages and hours thereafter, without collective bargaining, why would workers bother to join unions? There would be nothing left for them to do. The proposed NRA draft code, the very first to be negotiated, was widely publicized, as were the public hearings scheduled for June 27, which were necessary before it could be finalized.[7]

The hearings occasioned wide public interest, were extremely well attended, and were extensively covered in the media. Sloan presented the code and argued vehemently for its immediate adoption, predicting a massive rise in employment, especially in New England where the distress was greatest. Other northern industry leaders were similarly supportive, though some New Englanders quibbled about the continuance of the regional wage differential. Southerners, led by William G. Anderson, president of the Bibb Manufacturing Company, were loud in its defense, arguing, in fact, that it should be even greater, given the mill village system, a positive benefit to workers, yet costly to maintain. They, too, however, were generally supportive of the code. Senator James F. Byrnes, of South Carolina, was not so enthusiastic. He was worried, along with his mill worker constituents, about the possibilities of nullifying any wage gains, or shorter hours, by greatly increasing individual workloads, exploiting the stretch-out even further, in fact. He had no wish to hold up proceedings, but wanted further study of the problem, recommending the establishment of a joint labor-management committee to do so, and to make recommendations which could subsequently be built into the code. To this, General Johnson, concerned that eyes of the nation were upon him, quickly agreed, thus setting the pattern for the NRA Labor Board structure.[8]

Labor's representatives, finally able to have some influence on the code's development, provided the most trenchant criticism. Predictably, both AFL president William Green and McMahon of the UTW attacked the suggested minimum wage rates, which they considered "obscenely low," the regional wage differential, and the forty-hour week. Green still held out for thirty hours; McMahon would settle for thirty-five. During the debate, McMahon—"a plump, jolly elderly man," was how Frances Perkins described him—was anything but cheerful as he denounced labor's exclusion from the CTIC councils, the first of many times he was to do so in the succeeding months. "I had no hand in making up this code," he angrily informed the hearing's chair, and thus had no commitment to it. Neither Green nor McMahon, however, had any comment to offer on the application of section 7(a), of which they approved. Most industry leaders were troubled by it but decided not to force the issue for fear of holding up the whole process. Instead they quickly agreed to raising the minimum wage to twelve and thirteen dollars, respectively; in return the CTIC was granted its bid to become the code authority with the responsibility for its enforcement. The president made a few minor changes, than signed the code on July 16, the first of the NRA codes, and a model for others to follow, especially in the woolen and worsted and silk divisions. In so doing, he remarked, "I know nothing further that could have been done. I can think of no greater achievements of cooperation, mutual understanding, and good will."[9]

The rapid approval of the Cotton Textile Code was clearly a win for the industry, and its representatives greeted it as such. Sloan, for his part, was exultant and quickly moved to cement further both his growing friendship with General Johnson and the goodwill the CTI had earned with the president. William Anderson talked of the dawning of "a new day . . . for all who are in any way concerned with the manufacture and distribution of cotton textiles," while Donald Comer, of Avondale Mills, emphasized that this was the management's code, not labor's. Most historians have echoed this judgment, some asking, like Bernard Bellush, "how was it possible for the New Deal to sanction such extreme concessions to industry?" and finding the answer in the weakness of the UTW, generally, and the incompetence of its leadership, especially McMahon. Certainly it is true that in industries where labor was better organized, the codes reflected this relative strength, but it should also be pointed out that cotton textile workers and their leaders rejoiced along with their employers at the code's approval. Francis Gorman, the UTW's vice president, soon to lead the union in a national strike against the code's provisions, or rather their nonenforcement, nevertheless deemed it in 1933 "the most progressive step in the industry in many years." The *New York Times* reported that throughout the textile South, the workers were as enthusiastic over the code as their employers. In Greenwood, South Carolina, thousands celebrated its approval by dancing in the streets; in Spartanburg and Greenville, textile workers marched and danced as they celebrated their "industrial declaration of independence." They cared little about the CTI or the code authority; they had, they believed, won shorter hours, higher wages, an end to the stretch-out, and the right to organize. They were thus on the way to better lives; for them the promised New Deal had arrived, and as they sang, they gave their thanks to the man who had made it possible: Franklin D. Roosevelt. In New England, in New Jersey, in Philadelphia, no less than the Carolina Piedmont, textile workers—silk, wool, cotton, rayon—all rejoiced as their codes went into operation.[10]

For a few months things went according to aspiration. In large part because the New Deal's weapon for agricultural recovery, the Agricultural Adjustment Act, was also coming into operation, and it included processing taxes on raw cotton, on wool and on silk, buyers were anxious to secure supplies before these went into effect. This was particularly true for cotton, the first code to become operative, and the result was a huge upswing in demand. Production in July 1933 ran at more than 120 percent of average levels between 1922 and 1927. All over the country, but especially in the South, the spindles were whirring again, employers were hiring, not laying off, and new shifts were starting up, as nearly 150,000 new employees began work. In September 1933, employment in cotton mills stood at nearly 466,000, the highest in the nation's history, and cotton was set for easily its best year since 1928, while there were better times, too, in the textile industry's other sectors. McMahon told readers of the *Textile Worker* that the "wheel of progress" was rolling again, that the new "cooperative spirit between employers and workers" which the NIRA had engendered was such that "all will hail and bless the day on which President Roosevelt had the courage, vision and ability to present such a program for the rehabilitation of industry in our nation." Textiles were moving right along.[11]

Optimism, faith in the future, belief in the New Deal, and support for the NRA were all reflected in the mushrooming of union membership figures immediately after the bill's passage. Workers in all industries took section 7(a) very seriously; between 1933 and 1939 more than five million new unionists were signed up. In textiles the UTW was the beneficiary. Accurate membership figures are hard to obtain, partly because growth in 1933 far outstripped the capacity of union officers to tabulate them, partly because a later fire destroyed much of what records had survived. Brooks calculated that from a membership base of a mere 15,000 in February 1933, UTW membership had grown to 40,000 by September, and to 250,000 by June 1934. Other growth estimates were even more dramatic. NRA research staff estimated that as early as August 1933 the UTW already had 340,000 members, of which 185,000 were cotton textile workers. Whatever figures are accepted, the fact of growth is inescapable. Textile workers, told the "President wanted them to join a union," responded with enthusiasm.[12]

Much of this growth occurred in the South, heretofore hostile territory for organizers, certainly a development southern manufacturers "had not anticipated when they accepted the NRA." They had not taken 7(a) seriously, agreeing to it as UTW vice president Gorman later remarked, "with their tongues in cheek." Now, they had to face the unpalatable fact that their workers held a different view, as they flocked to join UTW locals. Indeed, as Janet Irons argues trenchantly, they had been organizing independent locals long before the UTW arrived. In South Carolina alone, the UTW had at least embryonic representation in 75 percent of the state's mills within a month of the cotton code's acceptance. "Textile workers," said H. D. Lisk, a southern organizer, believed the NRA was something "God had sent to them"—God and President Roosevelt. "I sure am proud . . . of our president as it is the first time the laboring class of people has had anyone to help them," declared an Alabama worker, and there were tens of thousands like him who expressed this pride by signing union cards in the summer of 1933.[13]

Workers were especially hopeful that the hated stretch-out would soon be a thing of the past, all the more so as Hugh Johnson quickly appointed the promised committee to study the problem. Its chair, representing the NRA, was Robert Bruere, a New York economist with strong ties to the clothing industry. Benjamin Geer, president both of South Carolina's Furman University and of a small family cotton mill, was the employers' representative, while George L. Berry, president of the AFL's printing pressmen, represented labor. Unlike his two colleagues, he had had no prior experience with any of the textile trades. No problem was more crucial to mill workers, North and South, than the seemingly arbitrary increasing of workloads. It was why Paterson's silk workers had united in 1913, why the Loray Mill had erupted in 1929; throughout the unstable 1920s it had been a constant source of strife, as managers quickened the pace of operation whenever they could in order to seek competitive advantage. The issues were complex, involving as they did questions of the race to adjust to new technology on both sides, workers' determination to maintain existing conditions of employment, management's equal determination to cut costs. There is no doubt that in cotton mills especially working conditions had substantially deteriorated by 1933, and for this the stretch-out was blamed. Bruere's committee glossed right over these complexities, anxious to reassure owners that the code would not be compromised. They visited a few mills, held a few cursory public hearings, and were ready to report by July 21. Predictably, they had little to say, and certainly nothing that would meet the aroused expectations, or assuage the deep resentments, of the workers.[14]

The study committee's report concluded that though the stretch-out system was "sound in principle," it had been abused by some employers, more out of ignorance than design. Moreover, they could find no feasible formula for regulating work practices nationally, recommending instead a series of grievances committees, starting at the factory level, then proceeding through state boards, to a national body working within the code authority, the Cotton Textile National Industrial Relations Board (CTNIRB). Individual differences over workloads would be dealt with by one of these bodies, with the factory-based mill committees, on which workers and management would be equally represented, doing the bulk of the mediation. The CTNIRB would have "power of final determination," however, and would also appoint the state boards. It came as no surprise when Hugh Johnson quickly accepted the study group's recommendations, and reconstituted the group as the CTNIRB, soon to be generally known as the Bruere Board. In so doing he calmed considerably the growing management fears that it would have to settle disputes henceforth through collective bargaining, for the accepted structure would deal with grievances on an individual basis. Moreover, the creation of the Bruere Board meant that the Cotton Textile Code at least fell outside the jurisdiction of the National Labor Board, which the president created on August 5 to settle all labor disputes, for the NLB had authority only over industries whose codes did not provide for individual dispute-settling boards, as did the textile codes. The prospect of the UTW influencing the development of a body of labor law with general application to the industry was thus gravely weakened.[15]

The Bruere Board and its ancillary committees soon had work enough to do, for it was not long before the reports of wholesale code violations and of owners and managers refusing to abide by its basic provisions began to reach Washington. By October 1933 the brief textile boom had subsided. Initially fueled by a desire to beat code-induced cost rises, demand soon dropped off, prices also fell, but the higher production costs, largely due to the code's wages and hours provisions, remained. Cotton textile manufacturers in particular complained that they were worse off than ever; they had to pay their workers more, while they were working less, and costs of production had greatly increased. Moreover, the perennial problem of overproduction had returned. In this situation, as well as using the code structure to reduce hours further, manufacturers sought other ways to deprive their workers of the new day's dawning they had but recently heralded.[16]

Textile workers protested in many ways, and in time their complaints were formalized through the various structures of the Bruere Board. But they also wrote letters describing the harsh conditions of their lives, and their growing anger at the NRA, to the president, whom they continued to revere, to Eleanor Roosevelt, to Frances Perkins, the secretary of labor, to General Johnson, even to Thomas McMahon. Jacquelyn Hall and her colleagues, who made superb use of the thousands that survive in the National Archives and other depositories, described them thus. "Addressing themselves to the president or to Hugh Johnson, men and women with little formal education labored to explain in writing 'facts from my very heart,' scratching their feelings on cheap ruled pads. They had read about the code or heard the news on the radio and felt duty bound to tell the proper authorities how the Blue Eagle was faring in their locale." "It is one o'clock in the morning," ran one such letter. "I could not sleep for thinking of writing to you and explaining how we are treated." Then "came descriptions of complex grievances that arose out of daily practices on the shop floor and accounts of the myriad ways in which owners circumvented 'this wonderful law.'" Most of them, however, came to focus on three particular grievances: the way manufacturers were increasing, not reducing, the pace of work; the way they were systematically abusing the minimum wage provisions; and, increasingly, the way section 7(a) was also being abused. Far from being able to join their UTW locals, workers, mainly in the South, were being victimized, even dismissed, for so doing.[17]

Thus, Fannie Ford, of Burlington, North Carolina, wrote to the president to tell him what had been happening at the Holt Plaid Mill over the past few months. She, her husband, R. L. Ford, and her son, C. E. Ford, had all been "layed off, for no other reason than they got a union hear [*sic*] and My Husband became president of it." She continued, "What make's me so mad about it is that they have black listed us from working at any other mill around hear [*sic*]. They have the Blue Eagle," she said, but it meant nothing to the Holts. "They sure have done lots of dirty work." Ford had voted for FDR, she had the utmost faith in him, and she knew he would "get this straight," now that he had become aware of the situation.[18]

Carl W. Welch, of Gastonia, told the president how the Loray Mill management was simply "not abiding by the code." He had been work-ing "full time three shifts," contrary to the code's prohibition of three-shift days. Moreover, those who had "tried to organize a union" were swiftly punished, either losing their jobs or having their hours reduced. In nearby Bessemer City, the American Mills were "working women 12 hours a day and paying them $12 a week," under the noses of the lo-cal NRA authorities. Welch, too, had great faith in the president, and understood that he clearly had not heard of this defiance, otherwise he would have moved rapidly to rectify matters. "I know," he said, "and all the poor cotton mill people know that you are doing everything in your power to help us." But the owners had not yet got the message. They had to be told. Welch knew that the president had "the worst job in the world with all the chiselers kicking against you." But FDR had to kick back, on behalf of "the poor people" who loved him. It was an urgent situation, and he hoped the president did not mind him saying so.[19]

Though the bulk of these letters of entreaty came from southern cotton mill workers, New Englanders were also victims of code avoidance, and said so. Mary Aezendes of New Bedford, who worked at the Langshaw Cotton Mill, told George Sloan that since the night shift had shut down, in accordance with the code's provisions, workers were forced to eat, even to shave at their posts, so much had the pace of work increased. "I've worked here for twenty-five years and since the NRA it has been worse than ever." At the Neild Mill, alleged M. Moniz, most union mem-bers had been laid off, while the workload of those remaining had been doubled. Mary Heaton Vorse, the radical journalist, knew New Bedford well. She would have agreed with Aezendes and Moniz that manufactur-ers there, no less than those in the Piedmont, had systematically ignored those provisions of the Cotton Textile Code which their workers had hoped would bring improvement to the quality of their lives. It is impor-tant to remember this, given the way historians have insisted on treating the 1934 strike as primarily a southern, and a cotton textile, affair.[20]

Hall and her colleagues have written movingly about the significance of this correspondence "between ordinary people and their government." In it, they say, "workers who lacked access to education and power— and thus the means of affecting public debate—spoke with candor about the most intimate details of their working lives." For southern millhands, who "inhabited a world in which letter writing was a political act of enormous courage," this was particularly true, given the potential cost. The sheer volume of these letters, as well as their nature, is indicative of the difference Roosevelt had made to their lives, the sense of contact people believed they had established with their government, and their conviction that if only he and they could get past the "chiselers," those impeding the good, then all would be well. "If only the Tsar knew," the Russian peasants reputedly sighed as they dealt with their oppression. These letters had a similar ring to them, and they came from all over the country.[21]

There were some mill workers whose growing anger at code avoidance could not be assuaged by the writing of letters or the filing of complaints. Drafting a code for the silk section of the industry proved impossibly difficult. Eventually a temporary code was signed, but the ink had scarcely dried before silk workers in Paterson, New Jersey, Pennsylvania, and Rhode Island rose in revolt. The problem was that no code, temporary or permanent, could inscribe the historic differences within the industry, the higher wages paid to the more skilled workers of Paterson, compared with those in the other silk states, the internal strife within Paterson between the managers of the larger plants and the "cockroach shops," the rickety, one-room family-owned businesses that had sprung up all over the city, during "silk city" 's decline. Already easily undercutting the larger firms, they were now given code exemption. Throughout all the components of the silk industry, however, there was a generalized anger at the stretch-out; this united broadsilk weavers and dyers, Paterson craftsmen, and the daughters of the Pennsylvania anthracite miners who had historically formed much of that state's labor force, and in late August 1933 they struck, the first sustained action against the NRA.[22]

The Paterson broadsilk workers, angered by the real wage reductions the temporary code had imposed on them, led the way, and by September 1 the industry was at a standstill. The Paterson dyers also went out, as did weavers in some Pennsylvania and Rhode Island silk districts. Though regional demands varied somewhat, basically all silk workers voiced dissatisfaction with the temporary code's wages and hours provisions, and its failure to confront the stretch-out. Weavers wanted a two-loom per weaver limit, dyers a restriction on the number of dye boxes each was expected to run. Moreover, as Frank Schweitzer, secretary of the American Federation of Silk Workers, announced, it was "part of the union plan to obtain recognition of a national union, workers will not return to the mills until a general settlement is made." In other words, the vague provisions of section 7(a) had to be made much more specific.[23]

The 1933 silk strike involved, at its height, more than 50,000 workers. The dyers settled first, in late October, when they accepted terms which included wage hikes, agreement that "no man shall run more than one dye box of eight feet or over," and recognition of the UTW as their bargaining agent. The broadsilk workers held out until December before accepting a conference committee recommendation which also included wage hikes, a formula that maintained the Paterson wage differential, a restriction on loom coverage, and, again, recognition of the UTW as the weavers' sole bargaining agent. Moreover, in an effort to reduce the city's permanent state of industrial strife, Paterson's weavers also accepted the creation of a nonpartisan industrial relations board that was to settle future disputes, which placed some restrictions on their right to strike. This would become important as the general textile strike loomed in 1934.[24]

Thomas McMahon claimed publicly that the silk strike had been settled in the union's favor, and he was right. Despite ongoing minor troubles in the wool section, the silk strike experience had convinced him, as he put it in his Christmas message, that the NRA structure, in spite of some deficiencies, was still capable of bringing "peace in industry and at the same time give justice to all concerned."[25]

Cotton mill workers in South Carolina's Horse Creek Valley were much less sanguine. "Situated just across the Savannah River from Augusta, and sandwiched between Edgefield and Barnwell Counties in Aiken County," wrote Bryant Simon, "the valley anchors the South Carolina upcountry." Cotton milling had come there before the Civil War and had taken deep root, as had a tradition of "homegrown" labor militancy. Horse Creek workers had struck in 1929 and in 1932 against the stretch-out; now in October 1933 they struck on behalf of the NRA, hoping to force local manufacturers to live up to the provisions of the code. "We are striking to have Roosevelt and his program incorporated in the operation of the mills," said strike leader Paul Fuller. "The National Government called us out," said another. Soon there was violence, as owners tried to keep their mills open, strikebreakers were attacked, police officers assaulted and arrested picketers, and Governor Ibra C. Blackwood sent special deputies, highway patrolmen, and a machine-gun unit of the South Carolina National Guard to keep the mills running, thus prefiguring his actions of a year later.[26]

The Bruere Board also came to Horse Creek. Workers were at first enthusiastic; after all board members wore the Blue Eagle, surely then they would see the workers' point of view and would ensure that the code provisions, the violation of which had caused the strike, would be upheld. They were wrong. The board's report made little mention of the vital issues of wages, the stretch-out, or union recognition, simply urging strikers to go back to work, pending further negotiations. Yet when they attempted to do so, they found their way barred—by the National Guard. To be fair, the Bruere Board returned to the valley to press for the strikers to be returned. Again, manufacturers ignored the request; instead they began evicting striking workers and their families from their homes, in defiance of the code, but with the full support of Governor Blackwood. "Under the blue eagle banner," commented Bryant Simon, "the owners ran their plants as they saw fit." Neither the UTW, the Bruere Board, nor the national government, in whose name the workers had struck, it seemed, could make millowners accept all the provisions of the Cotton Textile Code. For all McMahon's Christmas season aspirations, the regional differences remained profound.[27]

As the bleak winter of 1933–1934 became spring, the desperate situation in cotton textiles moved center stage. Neither the Bruere Board nor the system of state and mill committees that had been created with it did anything to tackle the widespread violation of code provisions, while as James Hodges has perceptively noted, neither board nor owners "paid any attention to collective bargaining." "Indeed, the board's whole procedure had been designed as if unions did not exist." The workers who had flocked to them in 1933 thought otherwise and demanded action from their leadership. McMahon, still hopeful of cooperating with both the board and the NRA, was nevertheless forced to sharpen his criticisms of both, and especially of the board's failure to deal with the stretch-out. Moreover, the voice of the UTW had become increasingly that of McMahon's vice president, Francis Gorman. Like McMahon, Gorman was of English birth, the son of Bradford wool workers, and had come to America at thirteen, first to work in a Providence woolen mill. He had become a full-time UTW organizer in 1922 and the organization's vice president in 1928. Along the way he had led strikes in Lawrence and Pawtucket, and had also been in Marion, North Carolina, in 1929, site of a bloody battle between strikers and sheriff's deputies. Forty-four years old in 1934, and a polished orator who had never lost his Yorkshire cadences, Gorman cut a much less conciliatory and benign figure than the UTW's elderly president.[28]

McMahon and Gorman increased the tempo and tone of their attacks on the Bruere Board and the code authority in early 1934, without any noticeable effect. On March 1, however, the NRA, as part of Hugh Johnson's recently announced policy of holding "field days," during which the workings of the various codes were reviewed, scheduled one on the various textile codes. Gorman, not McMahon, appeared for the UTW, and he used the opportunity to flay ferociously the cotton textile code, the code authority and the Bruere Board. Labor had had no part in the code's making, he objected, nor in its administration. Labor's suggestions as to modifications had been ignored; only through the newspapers could the UTW get its views known. In a passionate plea for change, he appealed for labor representation on the code authority and for all to recognize the reality of section 7(a). His pleas, predictably, were ignored. Bruere, who also appeared at the meeting, assured all concerned that his board was, in fact, working very well, with workers' grievances being steadily and fairly dealt with. Those who continued to file complaints, to try to use the machinery supposedly created to help them, knew better, as their faith in the NRA, if not in President Roosevelt, dwindled. Indeed Carl Welch spoke for many when he wrote to the president to let him know how things were in Gaston County. As noted earlier, having assured Roosevelt that the mill workers believed he was doing all he possibly could to improve their lives, Welch had to admit that the owners were still firmly in control, and cared nothing for them, the New Deal's promise, or FDR himself. "It doesn't do any good to go to the NRA Board [*sic*] they say they will see about it and that is all there is to it." Early in 1934, tens of thousands of textile workers all over the land had come to believe, with Welch, that their hopes of a better life had been dashed. "It looks like everything is against us," he sadly concluded his letter.[29]

In late May 1934, Hugh Johnson approved the code authority's proposal for a production cut, as he had done the previous November. For between sixty and ninety days, there would be two daily shifts, totaling thirty hours weekly, with no increase in hourly wage rates. The reason, again, was excessive inventories. Demand in 1934 had been weak, the cotton millmen said, their warehouses were full of unsold cloth, as, for that matter, were those of the silk and woolen goods manufacturers. But again, it was the Cotton Code Authority that got in first, and Johnson's announcement was a giant step toward the national textile strike.[30]

Of course the calls for a further cut in cotton production had been heard for weeks, and there was no doubt as to the seriousness of the situation. There was every reason to believe George Sloan's assertion that in April less than half of what had been produced had been sold. Not every NRA economist, however, thought that further production cuts were warranted, but Johnson did, and that was what mattered. As normal, he made no attempt to consult with the UTW before making his decision to accept the authority's recommendation.[31]

McMahon's anger could not be contained. In a bitter letter of protest, he demanded that hourly wages be increased to balance the reduction in hours, that machine workloads be cut, that wage differentials be scrapped, and that a general conference be held between the UTW and the code authority, as the price of peace in the industry. Gorman, for his part, threatened a national strike if the cutbacks went into effect. "There won't be a cotton mill open in the country in two weeks," he stated, "if this order is carried out." Industry leaders and opinion-makers scoffed at the threat and bitterly excoriated these "foreign-born professional agitators" in thinly veiled attacks on their patriotism. So tense was the atmosphere that Hugh Johnson decided that some sort of compromise was necessary. Accordingly, he arranged a meeting with McMahon on June 1 and invited Bruere and Sloan as well. The meeting lasted two days, with Sloan in absolutely no mood to compromise. At the end, it was the UTW who gave most. In return for one more labor representative on the NRA's labor advisory board, the addition of a member representing textile labor on the Bruere Board—balanced, of course, by an extra industry representative—and access to the code authority in an advisory capacity, McMahon and Gorman canceled the planned strike, for which, it has to be said, they were woefully unprepared. They were still searching for a solution to the crisis in their industry within the evolving and confusing federal industrial relations structure, hoping against all the evidence that it might yet work in their favor.[32]

The manufacturers knew that they had beaten the union and loudly said so. William Anderson called it "a great victory," as he congratulated Sloan. Hugh Johnson, too, praised the settlement, and the fine work of the Bruere Board. For this reason, some contemporaries, and later historians, have been harsh on McMahon, arguing that his accommodationist predilections, especially the decision to abort the strike, played into the millowners' hands, convincing them that they had nothing to fear from the UTW, that the Bruere Board was emphatically their ally, and that they could be much more direct in their drive to destroy the southern locals. Janet Irons, in particular, believes that by accepting membership on the Bruere Board, a body which he had previously bitterly attacked as corrupt, McMahon had sold out his southern constituency, indeed that he had allowed the board to co-opt the UTW leadership. Certainly the union had gained little; nevertheless, a general strike in June could hardly have succeeded, given that many of the southern cotton locals existed on paper only, and that the stronger, more experienced, New England silk and cotton work force was not yet ready to go ahead. McMahon, after all, always had more than cotton, or the South, to worry about. The UTW national office was just beginning to develop structures both to meet the challenges of a vastly increased membership in all its divisions and to provide some centralized direction; the silk section was disunited, with New England and Pennsylvania unionists at loggerheads over wage-rate differentials, and with many woolen manufacturers refusing to cooperate with the section's code authority. A general strike in one branch of the industry, and that the most recently and hastily organized, would be unlikely to succeed. In that context, McMahon and Gorman's decision to play for time, to trade industrial action for board representation, makes considerable sense.[33]

Southern workers, however, remained short on patience, the more so as their employers often used the production cuts to close their plants every fourth week, leaving employees completely without income. Even on working weeks, average earnings were only $11.50, below the supposed $12 minimum. Meanwhile, the Bruere Board continued to self-promote its activities, while giving the complaints it received the most cursory of investigations, which in many cases amounted to no more than a letter of inquiry to the mill concerned. Throughout May and June there were minor strike eruptions in southern mills, usually unorganized, but in July things became more urgent. From July 16, Alabama's textile workers started to walk out in a much more organized fashion, to the considerable surprise, and without the sanction, of the national UTW leadership. McMahon had "killed" the projected June strike, said one worker as he left his loom, "we're not going to let him kill this one." The UTW leaders, therefore, were forced to respond.[34]

The Alabama strike had been largely organized by John Dean, an experienced labor leader from New York with considerable prior experience in the South, whom McMahon had sent to Alabama to step up union activity there. Working with state UTW official Albert W. Cox and longtime organizers Mollie Dowd and Alice Berry, Dean based himself in Huntsville, Alabama's most important cotton center, quickly forming locals there, and in other north Alabama mill towns, taking advantage of the rising level of discontent with the NRA. Apparently acting on his own initiative, the Brooklyn-raised Dean, who "with his six feet of Irish stature," said one observer, "his fighting face and soldierly bearing . . . could easily pass as a soldier of fortune if he had a uniform and a belted sword," called a state strike convention at which representatives of 40 of Alabama's 42 locals voted to strike. Huntsville's five thousand workers went out first, and by July 18 the city's mills had all closed. By the end of the week, workers in Florence, Anniston, Gadsden, Cordova, Jasper, Guntersville, Albertville—even Donald Comer's Birmingham branch of the Avondale Mills—were all out. Somewhere between 16,000 and 23,000 of the state's 40,000 textile operatives had struck against McMahon's wishes. Accordingly, he left it to Dean to sort things out, as he pondered the walkout's wider implications. In fact, the 1934 textile strike had begun. [35]

The textile strike in Alabama will be discussed in more detail later. It is sufficient to say now that it stalled after the first week and remained so until merging with the national strike in September. In the absence of any clear national strategy, McMahon and Gorman left Dean alone. He floundered about as the owners won back control. Many of them, in fact, were happy to have their mills closed, so overstocked were their warehouses. The strike was always confined to the northern part of the state, where Dean had made some progress. The unorganized workers in the Chattahoochee Valley, for example, never showed the slightest inclination to follow their unionized fellow operatives from their looms. Rather, they quickly armed themselves to prevent any possible pressure to force them out. [36]

Largely because Alabama's millowners took a very relaxed attitude toward the forced reopening of their mills, the strike proceeded with little disorder. The only serious violence in the first week occurred in Decatur, where three Huntsville unionists were attacked by an angry mob. Monroe Adcock, president of the Huntsville local, was shot in the left leg, and along with two companions, Isaac Bullard and Burnice Rigsby, severely beaten before being run out of town. The only other incident of note occurred two weeks later, when two men abducted Dean at gunpoint from his Huntsville hotel and drove him across the state line to Fayetteville, Tennessee, before releasing him. Two hours later, Dean was back in Huntsville, walking the streets with Mollie Dowd and Alice Berry at his side to the cheers of a large crowd, protected by an armed guard of strikers. Jim Conner, state commander of the American Legion, was later indicted for the botched abduction, but he was never brought to trial. Apart from that, the Alabama strike fizzled throughout August, as Dean, out of his depth, fruitlessly sought federal assistance to settle it. Neither the Roosevelt administration nor the nation's press, preoccupied with much more serious industrial strife in San Francisco, Seattle, and Minneapolis, paid it much attention. [37]

Nevertheless, the demands of the Alabama strikers did at least get to the heart of the problems in cotton textiles. The strikers demanded a minimum wage of twelve dollars for a thirty-hour week, an end to the stretch-out, reinstatement of workers dismissed for union activity or even adherence, and recognition of the UTW. The mill managers, through Scott Roberts, president of the Alabama Cotton Textile Association, denied that a problem even existed. Whatever their supposed grievances, workers' anger should not be directed against millowners, he believed, but against the federal government. "Workers are not striking against a particular mill," he said. "They are striking against the NRA. Every cotton mill in Alabama is operating under the law of the land, which makes the Alabama problem one for the federal government to solve." Textile workers throughout the nation, as well as their employers, would also come to demand national solutions as the situation worsened in the weeks ahead.[38]

The Alabama strike meant that the problems in cotton textiles would dominate the special convention of the UTW, scheduled to meet in New York on August 13. Five hundred delegates attended, including many from southern locals determined to secure support for a general strike in cotton textiles. Monroe Adcock, recovering from his bullet wound and his beating, was there, his head still bandaged. "I have been wounded in the head and shot in the leg," he shouted, as delegates roared in support, "but I am willing to shed my blood again against the capitalists." One after another, southern delegates told their horror stories of beatings and betrayals, as they demanded a strike vote, "the only language the employers will understand." Norman Thomas, the socialist leader, brought the crowd to its feet with his ringing denunciation of General Johnson and the perfidious NRA. Some southern unionists would later discount their influence in moving the connection toward a strike vote. The newspapers had it all wrong, said O. F. Woolf, a delegate from Calhoun County, Alabama. "New Jersey and the East led the way." Obviously strike support was general, but it is hard to refute the notion that the southern delegates were decisive in swaying the convention. Certainly they influenced McMahon. Unsure of his position on day one, by the convention's end he had become swept up in the strike fervor. Gorman never had any doubts. His call for a nationwide strike to secure throughout the land the demands of the Alabama strikers was met "with wild applause." With only ten votes against, the convention authorized a general strike in the cotton textile industry from September 1, unless these demands were met. Strikes in the silk, woolen, and rayon industries were also authorized, the precise dates of which were to be determined by an emergency strike committee. Only Emil Rieve, president of the American Federation of Fully Fashioned Hosiery Workers and a man who, even more than McMahon, understood the realities of current industrial power balances, remained opposed. "We ought to bite off just as much as we can chew," he warned delegates, "and not be swayed by the enthusiasm for a general strike." His words, if heard, went unheeded.[39]

McMahon, however, though no longer willing to deal with the Bruere Board or the NRA, still hoped that "magic intervention from the New Deal" could avert the strike on labor's terms. Publicly, he asked Roosevelt to intervene. "President Roosevelt," he told his delegates, "is the only man on God's green earth who can stop the strike." Gorman was much less sanguine about the effect of presidential involvement. Not even FDR could force management to meet the UTW in face-to-face talks, he said, and that was what was needed if the walkout was to be averted. Certainly neither Sloan nor Peter Van Horn, chair of the Silk Code Authority and president of the National Federation of Textiles, were in any mood to compromise, and Arthur Besse, chair of the Wool and Worsted Authority and president of the National Association of Wool Manufacturers, was content to go along with his more truculent colleagues. Indeed, there was a general view among the authorities, the employers, and even the general public that the strike call was an empty one, that the UTW did not have the support of the mass of workers in either the cotton or silk industries, while the woolen and worsted sector was so depressed that strike action could not even be contemplated. There was, therefore, no need for worry—and certainly not for compromise. The UTW was simply unable to organize a successful strike. The workers would not rise.[40]

As for the White House, despite McMahon's appeal, the president again showed not the slightest desire to intervene personally in an industrial dispute, though there was some attempt by the Department of Labor at conciliation. Frances Perkins, in fact, had specifically warned the president not to get involved, given the complexity of the issues. Instead, she advised him to ask the recently created National Labor Relations Board, chaired by Lloyd Garrison, to settle the dispute. The Bruere Board also offered to arbitrate. Gorman, whom McMahon had designated strike leader, though entirely dubious about their value, did in fact meet for talks with Garrison several times and was also willing to sit down with Sloan and even Van Horn and Besse, under NLRB aegis, in a last-ditch attempt to prevent the strike. Sloan, however, supremely confident, would not contemplate such a meeting, and without his involvement there was little the hardworking Garrison could do. On August 31, Garrison announced that the NLRB had failed to avert the strike and would now rather concentrate on bringing it to a swift conclusion. The differences between the protagonists were "profound and irreconcilable," he advised Roosevelt, suggesting that the president appoint a special board to draw up a plan of settlement as soon as possible.[41]

Gorman, unsurprisingly, had earlier rejected summarily Bruere's offer of arbitration. With Garrison's admission of failure, nothing else was left to do. On August 30, having moved the strike headquarters to Washington, he announced that the strike in cotton textiles would become effective on Saturday, September 1. Silk and woolen workers would also come out at that time. Thus began the largest industrywide conflict in the nation's history.[42]

Chapter 3

The Strike

ON AUGUST 30, "HIS EYES LINED AND BLOODSHOT FROM lack of sleep," Gorman issued the strike orders. His telegram to all local unions stated starkly that as of 11:30 P.M. on Saturday, September 1, a "strike of all cotton textile workers will begin," as "every resource in the direction of a peaceful settlement" had been exhausted. Wool, silk, rayon, and synthetic yarn UTW members were to "stand by for further orders." In the case of the woolen and worsted workers, located principally in New England and Pennsylvania, these were not long in coming. After Arthur Besse, chairman of the Wool Code Authority, refused to convene a joint union-employer conference to negotiate grievances over the code, they, too, were ordered out. The silk workers came out the next day, having already signaled that they were ready to go. The *New York Times* calculated that when the mills reopened on Tuesday, September 4, after the long Labor Day weekend, nearly one million workers could well have heeded the call—600,000 in cotton textiles, 200,000 in the wool and worsted trades, and 150,000 in silk. Its effects would be felt "from Maine to Alabama," said the paper, in what was to become an oft-quoted phrase. It would be "the largest strike ever directed by American labor." Conscious of the need to gain widespread public support, Gorman was at pains to emphasize the conservative nature of the UTW leadership and their determination to avoid violence. "We have instructed our people to be orderly at all times," he told the assembled journalists and "not to associate with Communists and to stamp out communistic uprisings when they occur." This would not be a rerun of Gastonia, 1929.[1]

Gorman had divided the country into several regions, each with its own leader. John Peel, based in Greenville, South Carolina, was to be

Francis J. Gorman, UTW vice president and strike director, at the strike headquarters, Washington, D.C. Library of Congress, *New York World Telegram and Sun* Collection.

in charge of the key region, the South, the base for the cotton textile industry. Horace Riviere, located in Providence, Rhode Island, was to coordinate activities in New England, assisted by Joseph A. Sylvia. Joseph White would look after New York from his base in Cohoes, while William Kelly, of Philadelphia, would control the silk and woolen workers of eastern Pennsylvania and New Jersey. Gorman would stay in Washington, D.C. There he would wage the public campaign: pressure the politicians, plan tactics, and generally, as Hodges pointed out, "provide a continuous sense of a unified national strike" where none actually existed. In order to facilitate this, he decided very early on to borrow a tactic that the UMW had successfully used—the "flying squadron" of mechanized pickets. Fleets of cars and trucks would race from mill to mill, closing them down, urging the workers to join them in the next leg. These "flying squadrons" worked most effectively in the South, especially in the strike's first week, where "the arrival of the cavalcade of cars and flatbed trucks with groups of workers hanging precariously to the staked sides and shouting encouragement to workers inside was a signal in the early September heat for an exodus of even unorganized workers from their machines." Many a Piedmont mill was shut down as a consequence, and the squadrons' use was eventually extended to New England and Pennsylvania. They were the principal reason for the success of the strike's first week, catching both management and state authorities by surprise. Nevertheless, their long-term effect was negative, for they gave southern governors the excuse they needed to bring out the National Guard, both to protect property and those who wanted to go to work. In such an atmosphere, the chance of violence was greatly increased, and for this reason, the squadrons' activities were soon officially terminated—though the directive was often ignored. Moreover, though Gorman may have disavowed any connection with the "disruptive forces" of Communism, the strikers' opponents were quick to raise the Red bogey. Even before the "flying squadrons" so polarized local communities, American Legion commanders clamored for the chance to "keep order" against the expected Red onslaught.[2]

The strike's reach may have extended from Maine to Alabama, but it was in the Carolina Piedmont, the heart of the cotton textile belt, that most commentators expected the decisive battles to be waged. Joseph Shaplen of the *New York Times,* a seasoned observer of southern labor battles, including the Gastonia strike of 1929, predicted that Gaston County would again be a crucial locality, as would Greenville, where Peel had already opened his headquarters. Throughout the Piedmont morale was high as workers awaited the mills' reopening. Workers in Gaston County planned to celebrate Labor Day for the first time in its history. Shaplen reported labor sentiment to have "grown tremendously" there since the violence of 1929. Symbolically, elaborate plans were afoot again to close down the hated Loray Mill. In Charlotte, a mass meeting of union delegates turned into "an old time Southern camp meeting," complete with shouts and prayers. H. D. Lisk, a UTW organizer from Concord, North Carolina, led mill workers in entreating divine intervention to "help us in our battle for human justice." "God is with us," he shouted, his arms outstretched, "and no power on earth can stand up against those who battle for the right." He hoped there would be no violence. In general, his audience concurred, though "a few murmurs of defiance" reportedly came from workers who "vowed they would not remain quiescent if provoked." The mood of the meeting was determined

Mill workers greet a "flying squadron" of strikers in Greensboro,
North Carolina. Library of Congress, LC-USF 33–020926–M3.

and upbeat. "We fight," cried Roy Lawrence, president of the North
Carolina Federation of Labor, "for the Lord and for our families."[3]

Meanwhile, in New England, followers of other ideologies also made
their entreaties. Ann Burlak, secretary of the Communist-controlled National Textile Workers Union, and known as "the 'red flame' of communism," reportedly told the children of New Bedford millhands to join
their parents on the picket line ready to throw tomatoes at "cops and
scabs," causing the local police to warn her that she would be immediately arrested if she gave "the slightest provocation," which drove her into
hiding. In Paterson, site of many a fiercely contested strike since the epic
battle of 1913, 15,000 broadsilk weavers said they were ready to join in.
Pennsylvania's 75,000 silk workers were also on the alert, while in New
England, the UTW had already appointed "captains" in each textile city,
ready to swing picketers into action on September 4. Employers, too,
were taking precautions. Observers reported substantial imports of tear
gas into the textile towns.[4]

Because of Monday's Labor Day holiday, no clear picture of the strike
call's effectiveness could be gained till Tuesday. Gorman, however, did
make a radio address in which he urged state governors to remain calm

and not to respond to the inevitable requests for troops to maintain order. Its message was lost on South Carolina's Ibra Blackwood. He had already announced his plans to maintain good order by deputizing all the state's "mayors, sheriffs, peace officers and every good citizen," if necessary. In Gastonia, both sides prepared for a replay of 1929, while publicly deploring the prospect of such a recurrence. "Those who remember the tragic times we had in 1929 will not want a repetition of those days in Gaston County," warned the *Gastonia Daily Gazette,* conveniently forgetting its own role in the fomentation of violence. "Let us not have anymore such wild disturbances." The local UTW leadership, for its part, predicted that Gaston County's "response to the strike call would be well nigh unanimous." To reinforce the point, Gastonia's first-ever Labor Day march was an impressive affair. Five thousand workers marched through the town's main street as cheering supporters crowded the sidewalks. Meantime, strike leaders planned the next day's activities, when the mills reopened. There was to be large-scale picketing throughout the county, with especially heavy concentration on the Loray Mill. Joseph Shaplen was deeply impressed by the intensity of the workers. This was not 1929, when the mill community itself had been deeply divided over the strike. There was in 1934 one key difference. "The strike now in progress," he reported, "is obviously a mass movement." Once the mills reopened, the first reports from Gaston County seemed to bear this out. Strike leaders were jubilant at their success, claiming after the first day's activity that 20,000 out of Gastonia's 25,000 workers were already out. The sweetest victory of all was at the Loray Mill, which, they claimed, the city's first flying pickets had quickly closed. Not so, said mill management, the decision to close down had been theirs, taken in order to avoid trouble. Whatever the reason, the spindles were quiet there, as they became throughout the county. "Not a wheel moved today" throughout Gaston County, reported Shaplen on September 6. Flying pickets were in complete control of the area.[5]

Reports from throughout the South told of similar situations. In mill after mill, mainly in the Carolinas, wherever the flying squadrons appeared, work promptly ceased. "Well disciplined shock troops," historian Janet Irons has called them; "moving swiftly from mill to mill in caravans of cars" they had closed at least twenty-seven plants in North and South Carolina by the end of Labor Day, and hundreds more on the next. Gorman claimed that 300,000 workers were already out throughout the land; independent surveys put the number at around 200,000, the Cotton Textile Institute at much less. All agreed, however, that the strike call had been most widely heeded in North Carolina, less so in South Carolina and Georgia, while in Alabama, where the unofficial strike had been going on since July, "little effect was noted." Outside the South, compliance was much more spotty. Forty percent of textile workers were reportedly out in New England, rather less than the upward of 50 percent figure most independent observers agreed on for the South. About 40 percent of the Pennsylvania silk workers were also reportedly idle, but the New Jersey plants had been slow to respond. There had been only minor activity, too, in upstate New York.[6]

There was little violence on the strike's first day, though localized clashes gave some ominous indication of the tensions surfacing in scores of communities. Picketers, described by Mary Heaton Vorse as "a gay band of young girls," barricaded 300 workers inside the Pepperell Mill in Fall River, Massachusetts, taunting the police, who eventually "liberated" them after using tear gas on the angry crowd. In Spindale, North Carolina, women picketers stormed four mills, shouting, "They can't do anything to us. Uncle Sam is behind us," compelling management to close them all. Before coming to Spindale, they had closed the Arcadia Mill, near Gear, South Carolina. At Spindale, the strike's first stabbing occurred. Charles Freeman tried to cross the picket line and "had an ice pick thrust in his back" as a result. Supporters and opponents of the strike alike were surprised at the dedication of the picketers, especially the women. In Houston, Texas, scarcely a major textile center, in a violent battle, women picketers "scratched the faces and pulled the hair of non-unionists," before local police separated the combatants. "Women are taking an increasingly active part in the picketing," Shaplen reported, "egging on their men." They would, he believed, "stop at nothing," so profound was their commitment. It was the flying pickets, especially, that caught everyone's attention. They had clearly taken mill management by surprise, the very swiftness of their "descents" making it impossible to predict their arrival or prepare for it adequately. Strike sympathizers found "the growing mass character of the picketing" profoundly impressive. "The appearance of military efficiency and precision is something entirely new in the history of American labor struggles," Shaplen considered.[7]

Management knew this, and knew well how to combat it, given their close links with state power. Southern governors, traditionally responsive to management's point of view, needed little excuse to intervene on their behalf, and the flying squadrons provided just that. The millowners claimed, after all, that the strike was a farce, the vast majority of their workers had in fact been forced out, and that the state should protect their right to work. The editor of the *Textile Bulletin* angrily argued that even a small cadre of fifty union members, by playing on "two human weaknesses" of their fellow workers, "fear of ridicule and fear of bodily harm," could close a large mill. The workers, he insisted, if left to their own devices, would not have struck. Governor Blackwood called out the National Guard as soon as the squadrons got moving, giving orders to "shoot to kill" if necessary to prevent picketers from entering mills. In North Carolina, Governor J. L. B. Ehringhaus was more circumspect, waiting until Wednesday, September 5. By this time well over half the state's mills were closed; in a few counties, such as Gaston, compliance was as high as 90 percent. Justifying his action, Ehringhaus warned of the "increasing number of strike-bent motorcades" on the move in his state and expressed particular concern about reports of "1000 pickets being prepared for descent on Burlington and other mid-State towns where the strike has had little effect." Only in Georgia were the millowners' entreaties resisted. There, Governor Eugene Talmadge, deeply immersed in a primary campaign for which he needed labor's support, insisted that local authorities could easily handle any threats to persons or property.[8]

Mill management lost no time in persuading local authorities to augment their forces through the use of special deputies, often local workers or townspeople opposed to the strike. In some cases they surrounded the mills with their own private guards and proceeded to wait it out. The presence of these deputies or guards, heavily armed and menacing, added to the tension and the ever-present prospect of violence and bloodshed. Right from the start there were reports of minor scrapes and scuffles, and the strike was less than two days old when the first fatalities occurred. In Trion, in North Georgia, a clash between picketers and workers trying to cross the line resulted in two nonstrikers receiving a severe beating. When company guards intervened, the strikers tried to seize their guns. One of the guards then drew his pistol and fired. Soon everyone was shooting; a worker, J. B. Blalock, and a guard, W. M. Hix, were killed— the latter shot through an open window by a thirteen-year-old boy as he lay bleeding on the mill floor from an earlier wound—and twenty others wounded. That same day guards killed two picketers in Augusta. In New England and New Jersey, too, tension increased as more and more workers left their looms and spindles. The Paterson broadsilk weavers finally came out; in Massachusetts all work was stopped in Fall River and New Bedford, while throughout Rhode Island and New Hampshire and even "in conservative Maine" the strike call was increasingly heeded. The flying squadrons made an appearance in Massachusetts, but Governor

Ely had no plans to call out the state police or National Guard as yet. Strike leaders estimated that 140,000 out of a possible 200,000 were on strike in New England by the end of September 5. Though employers insisted on a somewhat lower figure, even they admitted that the strike was "making rapid gains there"—much more so than they had expected. It was in the context of a movement rapidly gaining momentum, and with violence becoming a regular occurrence, that President Roosevelt decided to intervene. On September 5 he appointed a special three-man mediation board—John G. Winant, former Republican governor of New Hampshire, Marion Smith, an Atlanta attorney, and Robert G. Ingersoll, president of the Borough of Brooklyn—to try to settle the strike. Winant was named as chair.[9]

September 6 was the strike's most tragic day. The site was Honea Path, South Carolina, a town of around three thousand people, most of whom were connected in some way with the Chiquola Mill. The community was bitterly divided over the strike; there was taunting on the picket line and tension in the air. A fistfight between two men was the trigger. Soon "shots from pistols, shotguns and rifles blotted out the two-man fight and strikers, officers and workers waged their intense but short-lived battle for the supremacy of the situation." The *Textile Worker* breathlessly reported that "blazing guns dealt death to six picketing strikers and left upward of 15 wounded in a brief but chaotic encounter between workers and members of a flying squadron in this small one-mill community." More than twenty were in fact wounded that day, the majority shot in the back while fleeing the scene. The six slain were all strikers. Who shot first, and at whom, will never be certain, but most observers then believed that management sympathizers had started the gunplay. Certainly the strike leadership had no doubts. Gorman fired off an angry telegram to President Roosevelt, decrying the use of the National Guard as "strike-breakers," which, he believed, helped create the climate of tension that had resulted in the Honea Path killings. He urged FDR, as commander in chief, to "forbid the use of war materials in time of strike." At an emotional funeral for the dead strikers, George Googe of the AFL spoke of the murder of good union men as he waved aloft a bullet-ridden American flag, and the grieving crowd of 10,000 sang "In the Sweet By-and-By." They had died, eulogized Rev. James Myers of the Federated Churches of Christ, "for the rights of the hard-working man, who is close to God. We are all children of God," was his moving conclusion, "and entitled to better things than we have had so far." And these would come. The strike would go on, Googe shouted, till the battle was won. The squadrons would roll again. Governor Blackwood thought otherwise. Declaring on September 9 that a "state of insurrection" existed in South Carolina, he put into effect martial law, or partly so, in that it applied only to mill property. John Peel, southern strike director, had no choice but to call off the squadrons. To do otherwise would have been to risk their annihilation, he declared. That day strikers marched four abreast down Columbia's main street, most waving American flags as symbols of their patriotism.[10]

Despite the violence, the deputies, and the guardsmen, support for the strike continued to grow. A "howling mob of 1000 men and women stormed the gates of the King Phillip Mill" at Warren, Rhode Island, reported the *New York Times,* after a policeman had allegedly struck a union officer on the picket line. In Paterson, the dyers were planning to join the striking weavers and jacquard workers, while independent surveys showed that at least half of Pennsylvania's 70,000 textile workers were idle. Besse, of the Wool Textile Code Authority, pronounced the situation in his industry "beyond control," while even Van Horn, chair of the Silk Textile Code Authority, admitted that the strike was spreading among silk workers. There was more "flying picket" activity in New England, especially in Massachusetts, while in Saylesville, Rhode Island, picketers and police had already fought a pitched battle, and there was more to come. Ann Burlak, the "Red flame," had briefly appeared in New Bedford, only to be told by union officials that the UTW did not want the assistance of her or any other "Reds." Most important of all, the American Federation of Hosiery workers had decided to join the strike—on a partial basis. The 85,000 workers in nonunion mills—mainly in Pennsylvania and North Carolina—were ordered out. Workers already under union contracts were not affected.[11]

Nevertheless, it was in the cotton mills of the Carolina Piedmont that most believed the strike would be won or lost. Certainly, the first week seemed to have belonged to the strikers, the speed and precision of the flying pickets clearly having taken management by surprise. Union figures purported to show that most of the region's mill workers were idle. In the key state of North Carolina, Peel claimed 85,000 out of 110,000 workers were out. Fifty-five thousand out of 70,000 were on strike in South Carolina, and 45,000 out of 58,000 in Georgia. Although accurate figures are impossible to get, these are almost certainly far too high. The Associated Press estimated that 210 mills in North Carolina were closed, with just under 65,000 workers out, while 281, employing 82,000, were open. There were 298 mills closed, and 254 operating, in South Carolina.

The figures are less important than the fact that of those not working, many could more properly be described as "locked-out" than on strike. In mill after mill, owners, having been closed down by the squadrons, and with surplus stock piled up in their warehouses, decided simply to let the strike run its course, content to keep their gates shut, even when there was no longer a need to do so. Gorman knew well what was happening and that, with the deployment of the guard units, his most effective weapon in the South, the flying squadrons, had been nullified. Time was on the owners' side. Accordingly, on the night of Saturday, September 8 he took to the airwaves, suggesting that the Winant Board arbitrate the strike, and that all mills be closed during the process "so that further murders of our fellow workers may be avoided."[12]

Sloan replied the next day on behalf of the increasingly confident industry representatives. It was, he said, impossible to agree to Gorman's conditions that those mills still working be closed or even to the very notion of general arbitration, as the code authority had no right to make decisions on behalf of individual companies. Gorman had expected a negative response, but he hoped that the public would see Sloan and his colleagues as blocking a settlement, and thus gain the strikers some sympathy. Meanwhile, the Winant Committee, denied the chance to arbitrate, began to investigate the UTW's list of grievances, to hear representatives of the code authorities and the unions, and, it was hoped, to arrive at a set of proposals on which agreement could be reached.[13]

As well as interviewing the strike participants, management and union, the Winant Committee members also heard from the nation. The announcement of its appointment prompted a fresh outpouring of correspondence, from strikers, from mill workers opposed to the strike, from mill managers, from local businesspeople, from those sympathetic to the strikers' cause, from those bitterly hostile to it, and from those with particular axes to grind, scores to settle, or panaceas to present. Some went initially to the president, to Frances Perkins, to Garrison—even to Hugh Johnson, until a vicious public attack on McMahon, Gorman, and the UTW revealed once and for all the NRA administrator's partisanship, but the bulk went to Winant himself. Those that went elsewhere were quickly sent to him. They all provide a window through which the strike can be viewed, and it is worth interrupting the strike narrative flow at this point to reflect on their larger meaning.[14]

The strikers, and those close to them, spoke frankly about the condition of their lives, both in the mill and in the larger world. Often they wrote anonymously, citing fear of reprisal as the reason. "Dear President," wrote one woman from the strike center of Greenville, South Carolina, "I don't know what the textile strike is about really," but "I do know all about the life of the cotton mill worker." She had been raised in a mill village, the child of mill workers, and had worked in the same mill since the age of twelve. "The life of the average textile mill worker is a tragic thing," she asserted, and went on to describe it at length.[15]

"I wish you would come down South to Greenville, S.C.," she told Roosevelt, "and just stand at the gates and watch the Hungry [*sic*] depressed desperate faces of the employees. They are hungry, raged [*sic*] and unkempt?" and the main reason was the stretch-out. "I work day after day with my back bowed, the perspiration pouring down my back. We simply have to fly about our work to hold our jobs." If they left their looms, even to go to the bathroom, they had to rush "as if we were putting out a fire or fighting for our life." There was no justice in such a situation, "in this kind of existance [*sic*]," and she wanted her children "to have some kind of chance." She knew well, she asserted, "that every textile worker in the South would walk out of the mill today if they were not afraid of starvation"—or the retribution of their employers.[16]

This unknown and remarkable woman then went on to tell the president all about the long-term effect of the culture in which she had been raised and still lived. "I have," she said, "gone through sleet and snow winter after winter without shoes or half enough clothing to keep me warm." Her children were now "doing the same thing." Her "own pathetic childhood," she poignantly told him, "is being repeated in my own children." As a child, she had dreamed that "I could some day attend school like other children," but it was not to be, nor would the dream be realized for her own family. And yet they, like most mill workers, were not "as dumb and ignorant as might be supposed." They had just never "had a chance," and that, in a larger sense, was what the strike was about, the chance to be more than "human machines," for that was not what God intended. Hard work was one thing, they knew that, they were used to that. She had worked extremely hard during the world war, she recollected, but today much more was required of her, at one-third the pay. There was, she stated, "a limit to everything."[17]

She was not speaking for Gorman "or any other organization," she concluded, as she urged the president to come to Greenville—with a "false mustache as a disguise, if necessary—but from my very heart, . . . for the human lives around me . . . for the free white people all around me."[18]

This powerful plea, from an unknown, unlettered mill worker, got to the heart of the economic and class injustice the strikers believed they suffered under. Though singular in the force of its language, in its message it was typical of most of the letters. Joseph Jura, a Fairhaven, Massachusetts, striker, also complained bitterly about the stretch-out, and the subsequent overproduction he believed was the result. "Our manufacturers," he claimed, "they speed up and drive these workers for all they can and they have to close on account of so much production." "How can the worker pay without wages?" he asked. "So you see," he told Winant, "we have a reason to strike. A starving man or woman is ready for anything you know, and this even more so if he is mistreated, as textile labor is being treated." For Jura, every mill was "nothing but a sweat shop." All the owners were "a bunch of Blood Leaches."[19]

Jura did emphasize one point which concerned New England strikers much more than it did those in the South. His solution to again achieving a living wage was for the mills to run only one shift of forty-eight hours, "as it was in the good old days." This would guarantee workers "at least 10 months of steady work out of 12," thus making strikes unnecessary. Workers in the South, where two or three shifts had long been the norm, depended on the night shift to enable married women to both work and run the household and were unlikely to see the double-shift system as part of their problem. Rather the opposite, they wished for its return in order to reduce the unemployment now besetting the mill villages.[20]

Nevertheless, it was the stretch-out that most strikers, North and South, complained about. "A textile worker in New England" told Winant that the NRA was bound to fail as long as millowners continued to overload their workers. She should know, she asserted, "because I have been doing two men's work for about two years and making less than one man's pay." She was breaking under the strain. "Every woman who works beside me has been doing the same as I, and they are a workworn lot, each one wishing she could find something else to do and so get away from the slavery." Lawrence Robbins, of Green, South Carolina, made the same point to the president. In 1929, when he had started in the mills, most had a loom limit of fifteen to twenty-five per weaver, now they ran fifty to one hundred, and things were steadily getting worse. Since the adoption of the cotton code, he said, "they have stretched out more than ever, an [*sic*] have turned more people out of work all over the South." The strike was their one hope, he told the president. If it was lost, "I wonder what will become of us in the South."[21]

Many letters described in frank detail the violence and intimidation the strikers were experiencing. In Augusta, Georgia, strikers were not allowed to picket, said Carrie Miller. City police had prohibited them even from visiting friends and relatives who lived near the town's mills. "I have a sister that lives clost [*sic*] to the Mill," she said, "I am not aloud [*sic*] to go see her or any of my friends around there." Osie Jones, with better-developed writing skills, elaborated on Miller's complaint. More than half of the town's 4,000 textile workers were on strike, she said, though the mills were still operating barely, and with some "scab" labor from South Carolina, transported to and from work by taxis and with a police escort. Striking workers protesting this invasion were being rounded up and "sent to jail." They were not allowed to picket or "even to sit on our porches" if these were close to the mill, and police had actually forced residents from their homes by teargassing them. There had been much police violence in Augusta; one picketer had been killed, others seriously hurt, shot and beaten. They had, she said, approached Governor Talmadge the previous week seeking his protection, given that he was at that time busily engaged in a reelection campaign claiming to be the working man's friend. He asked them to wait "until after the election," when he promised to do something for them. Instead, he now threatened to send troops "to keep the mills open." They had supported him prior to the election, too late they now recognized his "true colors." Why, she asked, "are we not allowed the lawful right to picket?"[22]

Jones's letter concluded with a common theme: a desperate plea for the president to intervene. "Is it not possible, and in your power to order all mills in the country closed until a settlement or compromise can be agreed upon," asked Dottie Henry, of Greenwood, South Carolina, of the president. She and her husband were both textile workers, and like "the country as a whole," they were "trusting you to lead us out of this." She did not think the union leaders were "asking for too much," she told him. Lawrence Robbins, too, begged him to intervene, not only to prevent immediate bloodshed, but also to help mill workers to a better life. There was no point in depending on anyone else, especially South Carolina's governor, Ibra Blackwood, "the sorriest white man I ever heard of." Alfred M. Kunze, of New Rochelle, New York, similarly believed that only the president had the power to settle the strike in a manner that would do justice to the working man. "Please President Roosevelt don't put any more hardship on your people," was his plea. "Please stop this strike." Textile workers, then, were beginning to recognize the changing power relationships in the United States; they put their hope and trust in Franklin Roosevelt.[23]

Not all textile workers, however, wrote in support of the strikers. "Yesterday I had an excellent factory position for which I was being well paid," asserted a furious Walter Neidel, of Westerly, Rhode Island. There was plenty of work available, and he and his workmates were just getting back on their feet after a long, lean time. "Today that factory is idle," he said, "because neither the State or National government would afford sufficient protection to assure the safety of the workers against wandering bands of lawless marauders." These violent people "from distant towns" had systematically intimidated "law abiding citizens who were trying to pass through the gates of the George C. Moore plant in Westerly." Neidel was outraged. He had voted for Roosevelt; now the president had to reciprocate and make sure that those who wanted to work were free to do so. In Alabama, there were many who felt the same way, at least according to Alice O'Neal of Gadsden. She wanted to know, she told Roosevelt, "What is a free country." She had always believed that the glory of America "was that each individual was to be allowed to think for him or herself," but the local branch of the United Textile Workers clearly believed otherwise. She and hundreds like her had been unable to work for more than two months, not because they supported the strike, but because of systematic union intimidation and abuse. "They call us yellow scabs" she said, just because they wanted to stay at their looms. Lula Luthi of Florence, Alabama, presented a petition from forty workers from the Gardiner-Waring Company, "loyal to ourselves and our employers" and unwilling "to be led by a foreignor [*sic*] such as Francis Gorman is." They, too, wanted "to go back to work"; they had always been "fairly treated" by their employers, and they demanded federal intervention to guarantee their right to work. Take heed, they warned, "there were many thousands of workers who were forced from their jobs when they had no desire to go," and that they would remember this next time they went to the polls.[24]

Correspondents such as these—and there were scores—underlined the unpalatable truth that though Gorman and the other strike leaders could talk about solidarity, class tension, and employer violence, the inescapable fact was that the workers were not united. Thousands were unwilling strikers, forced out by the picketers when they did not want to go and often kept out thereafter by local union pressure, while hundreds of mills did not close at all; workers sometimes, as in Greenville, were kept at their looms by the presence of the National Guard, but more often, because they were simply resistant to the strike call. Most commentators, contemporarily and subsequently, have ignored this reality, most notably the filmmaker George Stoney in *The Uprising of 1934,* yet it remains a potent reason for the uneven progress of the strike, for much of the violence that occurred during it, and for its ultimate failure. Mary Lethert Wingard, in an article that discusses the failure of workers in Erwin Mill 3, in Cooleemee, North Carolina, to strike in 1934, unlike the operatives in other Erwin Company mills, and this despite "pleading, persuasion and even coercion from flying squadrons," talks of the multiplicity of "cultural and social contours that inform social protest," of which union-led strike action was only one. She makes superb use of political scientist James C. Scott's concept "infrapolitics"—"the circumspect struggle waged daily by subordinate groups" in their confrontation with an unequal balance of power. Communities had to be looked at individually, she argues, as each one was "fundamentally shaped by specific contingencies of personality and place." Cultures of resistance did not always manifest themselves in collective action or union activity and certainly they did not surface at the same time. Individuals, too, differed in their responses to unionization, and this the strike of 1934 certainly made clear.[25]

Elizabeth Parr, a weaver at Rose Mills, in Kensington, Philadelphia, perfectly exemplified the antiunion sentiment of so many workers. Rose Mills, she told Winant, which "provided honest employment at a fair rate of wage" in "pleasant surroundings," should be considered "a boon and a benefaction to any community." Yet its continued operation was in danger, due to "the despicable and thoroughly Un-American practice" of forced unionization. Rose Mills, she said, employed nearly five hundred people, of whom only a "mere handful" were union members. Yet this small group was "making a concentrated effort to force unemployment, disgrace, embarrassment and union affiliation upon the rest of the employees." The NRA was a boon for the workers of Rose Mills. They were working shorter hours yet being paid much more. Moreover, employment had increased. Indeed, conditions were now, since the Blue Eagle, "absolutely satisfactory to the employees."[26]

Nevertheless, they had been "constantly besieged, insulted and threatened by union agitators and their hirelings," in order to force them to join the strike, and the plant had eventually closed to avoid further trouble. "Why must an organization composed chiefly of the foreign element," she asked, "the radical, the communist and the treacherous socialist exist in a country that clearly and concisely refers to itself as the United States (land of the free)." The "red flag" was flying too close to "Old Glory" was her view, as she demanded her right to work and for her employers to run their plant, unimpeded by "criminally inclined" union leaders. After all, her "very existence" depended on manufacturers and her ability to continue to work in their plants. She was of "the soil," she said, but she knew she could not return to it. Farming, for poor people like herself, was no longer remotely an option. She and her fellow workers wanted a future, especially for their children, but it was in danger of being denied them by a group of morally bankrupt men, the UTW leaders. She told Winant that "many of our girls actually cried when informed that they would not have any work until further notice," so consuming was their fear of further unemployment, even though they understood the owner's unwillingness to expose further "to danger and violence the safety and lives of his employees. . . . We have our work to go to we want to work and we are eager to resume our duties," Parr concluded her passionate letter, as she called for federal intervention on behalf of the "American people" against "an organization such as the A F of L." Thus, while strikers and their families called for the president to intervene to protect them against the violence and intimidation of their employers, who were backed by state power, thousands of their fellow workers were equally insistent that the government move to protect their right to work and to save them from Gorman and his henchmen. This division, as much as any other factor, fatally hampered the strike's effectiveness from the day it was called. The textile workers were manifestly not united.[27]

Most businessmen who wrote to Winant or the president, predictably, were profoundly antiunion in their views. Jules L. Beuret of New York, a woolen and worsted retailer, urged Winant not to give in to the demands of "groups acting under orders from Union leaders and touring in a wild and unruly manner from city to city for the avowed purpose of promiscuously accomplishing forced closings of textile plants." To do so would be to acquiesce in "revolutionary development," and "we will then no longer be the United States of America, but instead, the Unionized States of America." John Edgerton, president of the Southern States Industrial Council, told Roosevelt that as the strike was more against the government and the NRA than against "the affected employers of Labor," it was up to the president to put down "mob violence," and he said that the employers should not make any concessions. To do otherwise would be to betray "the overwhelming mass of the laboring people who want to work peacefully and who are as much opposed as their employers are to the audacious and lawless action of an organized minority." A few put their own particular spin on the strike. F. L. Hood, who ran a small furniture-manufacturing firm in Greenville, Tennessee, which had had to close because of the strike, believed Gorman was obviously in the pay of the Republican Party and that the strike was part of a plot to discredit the NRA so comprehensively as to get the "party who is now out of power . . . back at any cost." It was "very evident," he thought, that the Republicans—the "money power" he called them—were behind the strike and "paying large sums of money to destroy property, throw people out of work and close down plants . . . over the entire United States."[28]

Those millowners and others who thought beyond mere union bashing or political plots showed a surprising degree of convergence as to their diagnosis on how to revive the ailing textile industry. A large number of Winant's correspondents saw its salvation in the removal of the Agricultural Adjustment Administration's (AAA) processing tax, a key component of the recently implemented farm subsidy program. Its abolition, said J. S. Ownby of Dallas, Texas, "would bring about higher prices for farmer's cotton without advancing prices to the consumer." This, he thought, would greatly aid the consumption of cotton, thus benefiting the whole industry. Ralph C. Perkins, treasurer of the Pilgrim Mills, Fall River, Massachusetts, argued similarly. "Even rich mills cannot afford to stock goods and keep plants moving in dull business periods because of the fact that so much money has to be put out in the form of processing taxes," he asserted bluntly. "We state this not as a opinion," but as a fact. At Pilgrim Mills "the money requirements involved in financing processing taxes" had meant production cutbacks and a consequent decrease in employment. John H. Rodgers, president of the Hart Cotton Mills, Tarboro, North Carolina, believed the same. "It [the processing tax] is really the root of the evil," he contended, and if it were eliminated there would be such an increase in the demand for cotton goods as to quickly alleviate "the deplorable condition in the industry." Similar plans poured in from all over the country, from millowners, from representatives of agricultural interests, and from public officials. Not only would the textile strike be ended through such actions, they contended, it would have much wider implications. "If you can find a practical way to remove or suspend the processing tax," J. E. McDonald, the Texas commissioner of agriculture, telegraphed Winant, "it would furnish a great impetus for nationwide business revival."[29]

From different correspondents came other panaceas. Many, deeply influenced by Roosevelt's declaration of a "bank holiday," in those first desperate New Deal days, with the consequent closing of the nation's banks until reorganization could be effected, proposed similar action for the textile crisis. "This is to urge you to declare a national textile holiday until the present controversy is settled," implored V. R. Threatt, president of UTW Local 1900, of Charlotte, North Carolina, of the president. There had not been any violence in "this immediate section," he warned, "but it is bound to come if there isn't some adjustment made," adding that "this is written for the employers as well as the employees." Many came from striking workers, increasingly desperate as the "county and strike authorities" increased their pressure. It was "almost impossible for us to keep the peace any longer" without such a move, said C. E. Baxter, of Lincoln County, North Carolina. Strikers in Gastonia petitioned the president in their hundreds to grant "a legal holiday until this strike is settled." There was some employer support for such intervention as well, or so Rev. James Myers, industrial secretary of the Federal Council of the Churches of Christ, thought. He was in Greenville, South Carolina, and urged the closing of all mills pending settlement—along the model of the bank holiday. He had been reliably informed that "some prominent cotton employers in the South would welcome this solution," he told Lloyd Garrison, chairman of the National Labor Relations Board. The demand for the compulsory closing of all mills was much stronger in the South, especially in areas with high levels of violence, such as Augusta, Georgia. James Johnson, a UTW organizer, implored Frances Perkins to close all of the city's mills immediately "to prevent our people from being killed." Such sentiment reflected the continuing perception that the federal government had accepted a new role in the settlement of labor disputes, as it had in American life generally, that it had already created models which could be adapted to bring industrial harmony. It took time for workers to realize the bitter truth, that these assumptions were sadly mistaken as far as textiles were concerned.[30]

Of course, hundreds of ordinary citizens wrote to Winant, Perkins, or the president during September. They were not directly involved in the strike but were anxious to give advice nonetheless, again indicating the new immediacy of the federal government. Often they reflected long-held racial or ideological prejudices. Many New Englanders blamed the strike on the ethnic composition of the region's mills. "If you could go to a Union meeting in Manchester, Lowell or Lawrence," wrote "A Mill Worker" of Dover, New Hampshire, "you would hear little English spoken." In Manchester, "it would be mostly French or Polish," in other localities, a general proliferation of tongues. "For weeks I talked with the more intelligent workers, people like myself," he or she went on, "born in this country and educated in the public schools," trying to find out what the strike was about, but to no avail. Whatever the original issues, they had been appropriated by the foreigners who now ran the union and dominated the mills. H. Turner of New York was similarly concerned that the strike was being driven by "Un-American" elements in the New England mills and that things would not improve until such "agitating strikers" were weeded out. M. Weston, of Athol, Massachusetts, was in no doubt what the president should do with such people. The only way to deal with such people as Gorman or AFL president Green was to "stand all strike leaders against the wall and shoot them" before letting the army loose on their followers. "Don't wait . . . do it now," the writer admonished FDR.[31]

In the South, the focus of community anger quickly became the flying squadrons. "Several thousand strikers from Cleveland and other counties invaded Rutherford County today and in a spirit of mob violence

Police arrest textile strikers in Manchester, New Hampshire.
Library of Congress, LC US 262–113630.

took complete charge of twelve mills," the county's angry sheriff, C. C. Moore, informed the president, from Rutherfordton, North Carolina. All the mills had been forced to close, though all of their employees were "anxious to work." He did not have the manpower to deal with this situation, he said, nor did the state of North Carolina. Federal troops should be sent immediately, he believed, "for the protection of employees desiring to work" and, generally, to provide security for the county's "outraged" citizens. Lee B. Weathers of Shelby, North Carolina, was similarly angered by what the squadrons had done to his town. They had "been going out to peaceful textile plants and compelling those who want work from which to feed hungry mouths, to come out of the mills against their wishes." He, too, called on the president to act immediately to stop further "intimidation, threats and violence" and on God to provide FDR with the "strength" to do so. From all over the South, as well as from other parts of the nation, came similar petitions from local officials, businessmen, ordinary citizens, and mill workers themselves, all protesting the refusal of the unionists to respect the right of men and women to work and demanding swift federal action against them. "If your administration fails or refuses to do this," warned W. H. Burruss of Lynchburg, Virginia, "it means chaos and ruination to the entire Country at this time." For H. H. Stein of Philadelphia, "for a group of dissatisfied workers from Brooklyn to force satisfied workers in Yonkers" to down tools went against all that the United States stood for, and the president had to take immediate, and the sternest possible, action against further "flying squad" activity. There was no doubt that, for those opposed to the strike, the squadrons had come to symbolize such lawlessness and violence that an equally forceful response was not only justified, but demanded.[32]

The strike prompted extreme reactions from America's political Left as well. The Relief Workers Union of Staten Island bitterly protested to FDR and Winant at the "terror used against striking textile workers," complaining that his "promise to the Forgotten Man has turned into bullets," and demanding that all "armed forces" be removed from mill plants and towns. The Communist Party organized meetings throughout New England in support of the "heroic textile workers," while from the Ella May Branch of the ILD, in Brooklyn, came a demand that the president afford protection to Rhode Island strikers, in particular, currently "fighting for their existance [*sic*]" against the forces of repression. Hundreds of telegrams came from the South, from strikers and their sympathizers. "We deeply regret the shooting down of armless [*sic*] men in textile strike," protested John H. David, of the New Orleans Central Trades and Labor

Council, in imploring Roosevelt to use his power to find "an amicable settlement in this strike and all other labor disturbances." G. E. Henderson of UTW Local 1882, in Greenville, South Carolina, gave a graphic account of the potential for violence there. "Three mills have called out National Guards. Orders shoot to kill," he asserted. "All thugs possible deputized. Women and girls in mills not allowed to come out by thugs." Lawlessness and violence had taken over Greenville, he continued, and only presidential action could bring relief.[33]

In summary, letters, telegrams, and petitions that ended up in the Winant Committee's files, whether originally directed to the president, the secretary of labor, or Winant himself, had two points in common. Whether supporting the strike or bitterly opposing the strikers, most writers expressed class-based assumptions about what was happening and believed such class antagonisms were endangering the very fabric of the Republic. "Mobs flaunting constituted authority" had taken control of the streets, lamented Alistair Furman Jr. of Greenville, South Carolina, disrupting long-standing practices and habits of deference, falsely claiming legitimacy by waving "the American flag in front of them," and contending they had the president's support. South Carolinians, he said, had always "supported democracy," but democracy had been replaced "by communism or the rule of the mob," and this they would never countenance. A. J. Muste, of the American Workers Party, explained the strike in similarly class-based terms, though from the opposite perspective, as he called on Roosevelt to "round up . . . all manufacturers who have announced they are organized to violate" the NRA's collective bargaining provisions, for only federal power could control such illegal ravages.[34]

The second point of commonality bears on the first, and is indicative of the increased role of the federal government in every aspect of American life that was the New Deal's most important legacy. Opponents and supporters of the strike alike looked to Washington to end it, to bring the justice—or the retribution—they sought. Whether it be the shooting of strikers, the declaration of a "textile holiday," protection from brutal deputies, the rounding-up of recalcitrant manufacturers, the curbing of the flying squadrons, or the restoration of industrial harmony, it was the president to whom people looked, for he alone had the power to act. "Again I appeal to you in the name of mercy to send Fort Oglethorpe troops to Trion [to] restore order and save what appears to be certain additional bloodshed and deaths," implored Benjamin D. Riegel, a Trion, Georgia, millowner. Only the president had the strength to do so. O. J. Havird of Augusta, Georgia, believed Roosevelt was "the only man in the

United States today that can bring to a peaceful solution of the strike that exists in our nation today." H. W. Colton, of Ogunquit, Maine, the first of his family ever to "vote Democratic," warned that he would not do so again unless the president put "some of the Labor Union Heads in Jail," as he alone could do. Latner J. Widenhouse, a striker from Concord, North Carolina, made the point most poignantly, as he detailed the way his employers had repeatedly violated the NRA code, had shown disrespect for essential American verities as "overseers of plant No. 6 of the Cannon Chain with an arrogance almost unaccountable walked through our praying pickets armed with guns, underneath the American Flag, which was held aloft by two of our men without removing their hats, in respect to the Stars and Strips [*sic*] of Old Glory," and had used troops against peaceful picketers. "Is it fair," he asked, "that we should see our children half naked and our hearts torn out by their anguished cries for milk and food." The workers were the descendants of those "who so nobly defended our cause and who whipped Cornwallis at Kings Mountain," he reflected, must they now be forced either to "Fight or Starve?" Only the president could prevent this; only he could "avert this great catastrophe." "It is in desperation that I appeal to you," was his concluding plea, "to stop this whole sale [*sic*] transgression on the rights of labor at the hands of greedy profit snatching exploiters of labor." Prostrike and antistrike workers alike, managers, and ordinary citizens in their correspondence all revealed the shift in the perceived location of power that the New Deal engendered, to Washington, to the federal government, and above all, to the White House.[35]

The second week of the strike opened with violence—this time in New England. On Monday, September 10, said the *New York Times,* "shotgun fire, clubs and tear gas caused about fifty injuries . . . with 5,000 more mill operatives either quitting or being forced out by closing of plants in Massachusetts and Rhode Island." The worst violence occurred in the Rhode Island textile town of Saylesville. A crowd of more than six hundred had gathered at the gates of the huge Saylesville Finishing Company, which had continued operation throughout the strike staffed by nonunion labor. Minor scuffles turned more serious as the workers changed shifts at 3 and 11 P.M. The state police, augmented by special deputies, lost control at the second change, and, as the crowd surged forward to invade the plant, they fired blindly into it. Two strikers were hit with buckshot while a score or more were injured by bricks, rocks, and billy clubs, as the police added "to the uproar the thump of swinging night-sticks and the explosion of teargas bombs." One, Louis Fercki, was critically hurt, his skull fractured by a club during the fracas at the mill gate. Police reportedly fired so much tear gas that people sheltering in the houses nearby were overcome by the fumes, including twin boys, Robert and Richard Blais, just two years old. The strikers prevailed, however, trapping seven hundred workers inside the mill until first light. There was violence, too, in Danielson, Connecticut, as state troopers, trying to rescue a nonstriking worker from rock-throwing picketers, were savagely beaten by a now thoroughly enraged mob before they themselves could be rescued. In response, the lieutenant governor ordered two companies of the National Guard to the district.[36]

Governor Theodore Green ordered out the guard in Rhode Island as well, but he was too late to prevent an escalation of violence in Saylesville. Picketers and police were back the next day, as were the deputies and, eventually, the National Guard. The battle for control of Saylesville Finishing Company lasted all day and into the night, as the crowd, swollen to 4,000, repeatedly charged the small force of less than 100 local and state police, eventually augmented by 260 guardsmen. Observers noted "many women and boys and girls of school age," swelling the angry throng, pelted the guardsmen with "pieces of gravestones, flowerpots and rocks torn from a nearby graveyard." Indeed, the local cemetery had become a battleground. Troops, firing machine guns from the mill roof, eventually drove the crowd away from the gates. Eight strikers were shot, none fatally, due to the determination of the guard commander to use only buckshot and to fire, for the most part, safely over the heads of those in the crowd. More than 100 were injured by clubs or missiles, however, including 18 guardsmen, before the fighting ceased. Governor Green, meantime, had placed the whole Saylesville district under martial law.[37]

Fierce as the fighting in Saylesville had been, what took place next day in nearby Woonsocket was much worse. Strikers and guardsmen fought for control of the Woonsocket Rayon Plant, and a night of violence left nineteen-year-old Jude Courtemanche dead from a shot in the stomach, four others seriously wounded, and scores with bloodied heads and hands. This time, there was no shooting over the heads. Faced by a shouting mob of nearly 10,000, guardsmen shot to wound, if not kill. "The screams of the wounded stopped the strikers," ran one report. They beat a disorderly retreat to the town's business district, where for three hours they laid waste, looting stores, setting fires, and hurling stones and other missiles before the guard was able to restore order. Governor Green, by now thoroughly shaken, closed all Woonsocket's nightclubs, saloons, dance halls, and stores until further notice, and an uneasy calm returned to the city. Blaming the disturbances entirely on Communist influence—Communists had been "imported" into the state "to forment trouble," he claimed, and he had a few suspects rounded up—he then recalled the state legislature for a special session in order to put through legislation permitting the use of federal troops to restore order if the violence continued. There was, however, no need for further action; the presence of the guard and the imposition of curfew restored a measure of calm to Rhode Island. Interestingly, the UTW also blamed "Red agitators and officials" for the Woonsocket carnage and disorder. The leadership vowed to be even more vigilant against "Communistic activities" in the future. There was violence of a lesser order throughout New England in the strike's second week. By its end, guardsmen were on duty throughout the region to prevent "the spread of riots."[38]

There was violence, too, in Pennsylvania, though not of a level requiring the guard to be mobilized. At the Stehli Silk Corporation Mill, in Lancaster, police had to subdue a line of militant women picketers, who, they alleged, were using "old-fashioned hat-pins to attack workers." In Bridgeport, five employees were hurt and a company car burned out as strikers tried to prevent the reopening of the town's largest woolen mill, James Lees and Sons. There was also solidarity, 6,000 Philadelphia hosiery workers went out in sympathy with the textile workers in an unauthorized action, which the union was quick to dub a "holiday," not a strike. In Hazleton, Pennsylvania, a regional silk-milling center, when strikers formed a flying squadron and successfully closed several mills in neighboring towns and counties, only to find themselves under attack by local police and special deputies, they were given impressive support by other unionists. Led by the United Mine Workers' local, thousands of workers took to the streets on September 12 in what was again defined as a "labor holiday." Joining the town's 3,000 striking silk workers in a "labor parade" through the town's business district were members of all twenty-six of Hazleton's unions, including the motion picture operators, the journeymen barbers, and the musicians. Most obvious however, were the mine workers. Fourteen thousand miners were there, representing 34 locals. It was the largest parade in Hazleton's history.[39]

Observers noted the proliferation of American flags in the throng, and also that marchers carried banners and slogans praising FDR, supporting the NRA, especially section 7(a), and excoriating their bosses, who refused to obey the government's directives. It was a good-humored crowd, however, led by high school bands and cheerleaders, singing "Hang the Mayor to a Sour Apple Tree," to the tune of "John Brown's

Body." There was no violence, no unsavory incidents of any kind; the community had a joyous day out. Even associations not normally sympathetic to union activity, such as the local American Legion post, joined in the fun, its drum-and-bugle corps helping to provide a marching beat. The police presence was benign, the municipal authorities having readily granted the appropriate permit to march. Similar events, similar displays of solidarity, took place in other northern textile towns and cities. Two points of contrast with the South are immediately apparent. There, in the isolated textile villages, there were rarely other unionists to provide support. Moreover the local law enforcement officers never adopted a position of even notional neutrality, while the men of the American Legion clamored to become special deputies. The strikers in Piedmont were much more isolated, much more alone.[40]

Joe Shaplen described the situation in the South as the strike entered its second week as resembling "a war of attrition," and in this he was surely right. If, in its first days, the momentum had been with the strikers, as the picketers closed mill after mill, it was now inexorably swinging against them. The presence of troops and deputies had effectively neutralized that one great advantage; now, with no economic urgency to reopen their gates, the millowners could afford to wait the strike out. Moreover, each day brought reports of some mills reopening, usually with a skeleton staff, and usually with guardsmen at the ready. Most, as in Burlington, North Carolina, were hosiery plants, whose workers had been forced out by the picketers. Moreover, the deficiencies in the strike's organization were becoming obvious, the illusion of a nationally directed, well-planned endeavor was fast unravelling. Gorman had promised that the strikers would be fed, but he had no way of keeping his promise, and as the strike entered its second week, there were hunger pangs aplenty. In such a situation, as Shaplen wrote, "the gains [were] on the side of the employers." Increasingly desperate, Gorman urged the president to send federal troops to the South, "to wipe out the National Guard, take care of strike-breaking governors and control the hired thugs of the millowners," whom he blamed both for the high level of violence, and the nonacceptance of his offer of arbitration. The strikers had generally obeyed the law, he complained. Their opponents had not. There was no response from the White House.[41]

Still, there were many areas where the strike was holding firm, and none more so than Gastonia and Gaston County, "the stronghold" of the UTW in the South. There, one hundred plants remained closed, and as J. E. Cuthberton, president of the Gastonia Central Labor Council declared, they would "stay" that way till the strike was won. An ill-judged attempt to force open the Loray Mill was checked by 300 angry picketers, who barred the gates. Police and special deputies rushed to the scene, but sensing the mood of the crowd, decided not to intervene. Governor Ehringhaus, safe in Raleigh, had no such qualms. He dispatched three more guard companies to Gastonia, ostensibly to assist those petitioners who had expressed to him a desire to get back to work. Fifty militia units were now on duty throughout the state. Add to these the more than 10,000 special deputies on duty in North and South Carolina, and the increased potentiality for violence in such a situation of stalemate, with fraying tempers on both sides, was obvious.[42]

There were scores of minor clashes throughout the South as the week wore on. The symbolic Loray Mill was finally reopened. Workers filed in under the watchful eyes of 150 guardsmen aided by "scores of armed deputies," as six hundred picketers hurled abuse from beyond the gates. The situation, said Shaplen, was extremely tense, though no one, thankfully, was hurt. In Alamance County, however, there was disorder and some bloodshed. The county's center, Burlington, had never been known for its union activity. The virulent antiunionism of the town's leading employer, J. Spencer Love, together with a relatively low unemployment situation, even at the bottom of the slump, had assured that. Nevertheless, in 1933 the UTW had come to the mills there, and with Gorman's strike call, so did the flying pickets. By the end of the week they had shut down most of Alamance County's cotton, silk, and rayon mills, to the surprise and chagrin of Love and his followers, who had expected the strike would miss the community altogether. Governor Ehringhaus duly sent two guard companies to the town, which raised the tension level somewhat, still the strike's first week had passed without violence. Not so the second, and as with Saylesville, Rhode Island, trouble centered around a mill that had remained open throughout the strike. There on September 14, a clash between guardsmen and hardened picketers lately arrived from Gastonia broadened into a general battle, during which five strikers, including a young woman, were bayoneted and many more affected by tear gas. That night a bomb exploded in the yard of the Holt Mill, testimony to the tension below the surface of this supposedly tranquil mill community, where only a few months previously the Chamber of Commerce had boosted Burlington as a town free of labor troubles, its workers inured to the blandishments of "the radical, outside agitator or organizer."[43]

Further South, there were numerous reports of increased picketing in Georgia, while even in Alabama where a stalemate had existed since July, there was some signs of renewed local effort. "A mass attack" of picketers, for example, closed the Clark Mill at Austell. As the second week wore on, Georgia became the focus of attention. There, Governor Talmadge, though philosophically opposed to the NRA and sympathetic to the millowners, had not yet involved the Georgia National Guard for fear of losing primary votes. Owners who petitioned him to do so were told to "keep cool," that local authorities, augmented by special deputies, were easily able to contain the situation, even as local violence increased. Safely reelected on September 12 in a landslide, the governor quickly reversed himself and ordered what historian John Allen has described as "the largest peacetime mobilization of troops in the state's history." He mobilized all 4,000 of the state's national guardsmen, having declared martial law "in all sections of the state where rebellion or violence or insurrection is going on that local authorities are unable to handle." Overnight, troops appeared in Columbus, Porterdale, Barnesville, Griffin, Social Circle, Rome, Macon, Aragon and Cartersville, and hundreds of strikers found themselves prisoners of the military.[44]

Certainly the level of violence in some communities was dangerously high. At the Aragon Cotton Mill, in Polk County, Deputy C. D. Stone led a heavily armed band of nonstriking workers against a group of 120 flying pickets camped at the mill's gates. Many of the weapons had been provided by the mill's general manager, J. C. Platt. As they approached, urged on by a "shouting and cheering" crowd of spectators, Deputy Stone reportedly told his men that if the picketers had not left within five minutes of his ordering them to do so, "I'll give the order to fire. If they harm one of our boys we will kill every one of them." Prudently, the picketers had already left the scene. The mob then decided to trap them on the highway, eventually catching up with a laggard truckload. There was gunfire, and Nat Brown, a nonstriker, fell dead. There was violence, too, in Macon as strikers attempted to free Ralph Gay, a UTW organizer jailed for violating the martial law order. Meanwhile, Talmadge put the finishing touches on his plan to end disorder in the state once and for all.[45]

Surveying the scene in the South as the strike's second week drew to a close, Joseph Shaplen wrote of "two armies, one armed to the teeth, the other with folded arms," facing each other "in the Southland today." The counteroffensive was about to begin, he thought. "Two weeks ago,"

the flying pickets had held the cards, "now it is the soldiers' turn"—
the guardsmen and their deputized auxiliaries. The strikers were as determined as ever, but the power arrayed against them might prove too
great. The "hot-spot" was still Gaston County. There the troops were
most obviously on the move. "Truckloads of soldiers were pouring into
the county and setting up their tents in mill yards and alongside military plants on highways between towns and villages," as the strikers, by
now facing real privation, watched "grim-faced." The armed-camp anal-
ogy fitted the New England situation equally well. There, 5,000 troops
stood guard, ready to assist police and deputies, as mills prepared to reopen. Tension was still extremely high, especially in Rhode Island, and in
parts of Massachusetts and Maine, to where the strike had only recently
spread. There, troops had been issued with specially made metal shields
as protection against rocks and other missiles. Woonsocket and Saylesville
were still "under rigid guard," with the curfew strictly enforced, as troops
patrolled the streets with bayonets at the ready.[46]

Rhode Island authorities believed they had identified the brains behind
the Saylesville riot. "The girl in green" they called her. "Clad in a brilliant
green sweater," this striking young woman had purportedly "led a group
of strikers in a brazen charge on the entrenched, bayonet-bearing mili-
tiamen," before moving on to Worcester, Massachusetts, where she had
been briefly arrested for "throwing rocks" at police, then released. When
she was identified subsequently through photographs as the Saylesville
rioter, a frustrated Governor Green called for her rearrest on the federal
charge of "inciting riot resulting in death." She was, he asserted, one of
the "roving bands of Communists, who had caused all the disorder."[47]

Despite the troops, despite the hunger and privations, and despite the
increasingly frequent reports of mill reopenings, Joe Shaplen thought
the strike was holding up reasonably well. The most detailed Associated
Press figures, which the union leadership and the employers rejected for
opposite reasons, showed that 64,685 were still idle in North Carolina
as opposed to 61,735 back at work. The figures for South Carolina—
38,350 idle, 36,350 working—were similar. In the South, Georgia had
the highest proportion of workers still out—44,480—with only 15,520
at work. It was in New England that the disparities were at their greatest,
however. Only 2,000 were reportedly at work in Rhode Island, 43,000
were still idle, while in Massachusetts 32,950 out of a normal work force
of 116,000 were on the job. In Pennsylvania more than half the textile
work force of 80,000 was still out, and in New Jersey the figure was
15,000 out of 43,000, mainly the weavers of Paterson. The strike had

even touched the Midwest. Half of Indiana's 600 textile workers were out; in Iowa only 29 of the state's 920 workers were at their looms or spindles. Across the nation, AP estimates were that 401,132 workers were still out, 334,957 were at work. Of course, these figures are impossible to verify, but the fact that both the employers and the UTW disputed them hotly may, ironically, afford them some validity.[48]

Nevertheless, though the strike was still spreading to some of the more isolated areas—1,500 employees of the Pepperell and York Mills in Biddeford, Maine, voted to join it only on September 16, for example— the fact that mills elsewhere were beginning to reopen was obviously worrying the strike leadership. Moreover it was clear that, after a week of stalemate, the manufacturers had had enough, and with the troops firmly in place, planned to force the issue. Moreover, the union had been utterly unable to make good its promises to feed its striking members. Thousands of them, without pay for two weeks, faced destitution. "Give us some bread and meat," pleaded E. L. Sandefur, treasurer of the strike relief committee in Charlotte, North Carolina, and "we will get out into the country and get some beans." The cry went unanswered. Only a very few strikers were able to get some assistance from the federal government relief schemes, red tape saw to that in New England, while in the South, despite the law, local officials often refused to furnish aid to strikers. By the week's end, even the union admitted "that 'force and hunger' were sending its people back to work." In such a situation, the employers had gained the upper hand.[49]

The strike's third week opened with extraordinary reports from Georgia, where Governor Talmadge, no doubt making up for lost time, went on the offensive. Under the provisions of martial law, he directed the national guard systematically to arrest all strikers and to incarcerate them in a specially constructed internment camp—soon to be renamed "concentration camp" by the press—at Fort McPherson, in Atlanta. The flash point came in the mill town of Newnan. There, Georgia's adjutant general Lindley Camp confronted a flying squadron of pickets with his own "flying squadron"—eight cars full of heavily armed guardsmen. After a struggle, the guardsmen arrested 140 of the picketers, including a number of women and, improbably, 14 African Americans. The blacks were quickly released, the rest were rushed to Fort McPherson. Soon they were imprisoned there—110 men, 16 women, enclosed by a tall barbed-wire fence—Talmadge's "concentration camp." Its establishment, commented Joe Shaplen, "marks a precedent in American labor struggles." The prisoners, apparently "cheerful" and well treated, were "officially" waiting trial by a military court for offenses committed under martial law.[50]

Reporters rushed to Fort McPherson, where they were able to talk to the prisoners through the barbed wire, as their guards looked on. The women were particularly vocal, confirming that they were being well treated, though bitterly resentful of the fact that they were being held "near the spot where Germans were interned during the war." Most of them were young. Viola Horton was only 17; she was there with her three sisters, Bella, Eula and Olivia, and their father. All of them were from Hogansville, near Newnan, from where they had come to help with the picketing. They were rock-hard in their commitment to the union. "We felt more honored to go out with the National Guard than with the scabs," said one of them, Etta Mae Zimmerman. "Don't forget we are still 100 percent union," shouted another. They all agreed that what had happened was quite exciting. "The troops have been mighty nice to us," said Maude Granger. Besides, they "had closed 14 mills already, and not a lick struck on anybody." Not everyone was as sanguine as these victims about the governor's actions. "Hitlerism" had come to America, said Georgia UTW leader A. S. Hollihan. Few accepted Talmadge's explanation that he had declared martial law as a protective measure for strikers and nonstrikers alike, saving them from out-of-state agitators. Those arrested in Newnan scarcely fitted that description.[51]

The signal events in Georgia deflected attention from events in other parts of the country, as the counteroffensive developed and mills began to reopen, usually with massive protection. In Gaston County, where the strike lines still held "without difficulty," violence was never far away. Picketers at the Hatch Hosiery Company, near Belmont, taunted arriving troops with cries of "Boy Scouts" and "Tin Soldiers," refusing all orders to move out of the way. The *Gastonia Daily Gazette* was outraged. "These boys have been made the target of the vilest and filthiest abuse that could be heaped on one human by another," thundered a typical editorial, "and they have been forced to stand up and take it." The next night Gaston County sheriff Clyde Robinson was attacked by a group of Belmont strikers, who stormed his car and tried to pull him out, shouting "We're going to beat you up." The severely shaken sheriff was rescued by guardsmen, and in the ensuing fracas, two strikers, J. T. Brown and Ernest Riley, were severely bayoneted. Riley died the next day, prompting further violence, plus the allegation that the guardsmen responsible had been drinking heavily before the incident. Throughout the Carolinas, it was claimed, vigilante groups were forming, determined to bring matters to a head.[52]

In New England, Maine had become the new center of strike activity. Here, too, there was violence, though nowhere near as serious as in the South. At the Lockwood Manufacturing Plant, in Waterford, two women who tried to breach the picket line were stoned and quite seriously hurt. The crowd then turned on the mill itself, subjecting it to a "rock barrage" until police intervened. In New Bedford, Massachusetts, police broke up a parade of strikers intent on bringing out the garment workers there, while further south, in Passaic, New Jersey, scene of a prolonged and violent textile strike in 1926, police arrested the leaders of a flying squadron of Paterson silk workers, who had gone there to close as many mills as they could. New England organizer Joseph Sylvia proclaimed the union to be clearly "winning" in his region, while Gorman still insisted that the "strike lines were holding firm from Maine to the Gulf." Joseph Shaplen was, in part, inclined to agree with him. Certainly the counteroffensive had, he thought, failed to produce the expected mass desertions from the strike in the South. Not even the menacing presence of "the greatest army ever assembled in an American labor struggle" had been able to achieve these. Moreover, in parts of the Piedmont, notably Gaston County, scarcely a mill had yet reopened, while in Maine and Rhode Island they were still closing. There was plenty of fight left in the strikers, he thought.[53]

Nevertheless, even Shaplen conceded that all over the Piedmont there was a drift, however unwilling, back to work; as hunger hit, people had no choice. Local leaders recognized this fact, even if Gorman did not, for they saw "the crowds of strikers clamoring for food" at every government relief station in the region. Gorman's announcement that strikers were to qualify for emergency relief, something he hailed as "a great victory," was by this time beside the point. The strike was effectively ending, the workers as much beaten by hunger as by the force raised against them. Nevertheless, in Georgia, where the strike crumbled most rapidly, Talmadge's intervention was the main explanatory factor. The complete prohibition of picketing, and the wholesale arrests and incarcerations destroyed whatever infrastructure the strikers had established. It was in this context that the Winant Board, which had been working away since the strike's first week, produced its report.[54]

The lengthy report was divided into several sections. First it listed the UTW grievances that had brought the strike on, and even hinted that some of them were valid, itself a departure from the past. Nevertheless, it did not "suggest any basic changes in code regulations" or wage rates. Rather, it proposed that the president create a Textile Labor Relations Board to replace the Bruere Board, operating under the authority of Public Resolution 44 rather than under the Cotton Textile Code, and with the power to "handle all Section 7(a) collective bargaining cases," together with those "involving other code provisions for workers in the cotton, silk and woolen industries." So as the real economic position of the cotton, silk, and woolen industries could be determined, and in particular their ability to support both higher wages and higher employment levels, the Bureau of Labor Statistics and the Federal Trade Commission should both study them intensively, or so the Winant Board thought.[55]

As far as the strikers' main grievance, the stretch-out, was concerned, all the report suggested was that it, too, become the subject of a special study by the TLRB, and that until this had occurred, there should be no general extending of workloads. Finally, with the strike ending, the board urged that there be no discrimination against those who had struck, though it did not support the other key UTW demand, that it be recognized as the sole bargaining agent for all textile workers. This, said the board, was not "feasible." It would rather have to be done on a plant to plant basis. The president was pleased with the report. It was, he said, "a good example of the practical way in which industrial problems can be calmly discussed and solved under a republican form of government," thus revealing his woeful ignorance of the reality of economic power balances in the industry and in the United States generally.[56]

The next day, the president finally intervened in the strike, urging the strikers to go back to work and the owners to open the mills. "I want," he said, "to express the very sincere hope that all employees now on strike will return to work and that all textile manufacturers will aid the government in carrying out the steps outlined," indicating that he intended the Winant Board's recommendations to be the basis of a final settlement. The next day, the UTW Executive Council ordered its members back to work. "The union ha[d] won an overwhelming victory," the councilors insisted, "one of the greatest in all labor history," and the strike, therefore, was no longer necessary. The Winant report supported the union's "every contention," exulted southern strike director John Peel. Certainly, they had to put the best possible face on the inevitable, yet "victory" it clearly was not. Sloan knew much better where reality lay. All he did was to agree to give the Winant report "serious consideration." He made no comment on the specific proposal that returning strikers should be reemployed—no questions asked.[57]

The *New Republic* was only one of many journals of opinion to point out immediately the shallowness of the UTW's victory claims. The union's main demands at the strike's beginning had been for a thirty-hour week, weekly minimum wages ranging from $13 for unskilled workers to $30 for the highly skilled, elimination of the stretch-out, and union recognition with reinstatement of workers discriminated against because of union recognition. The Winant report had approved none of these, giving strikers only the vaguest promises that working conditions would be improved after further study. The only positive aspect of the settlement, argued the journal, was the recommendation that future labor complaints be taken away from the Cotton Textile National Industrial Relations Board, with its records of consistently supporting the employers and vested with a new labor board, independent of the textile code. For Gorman and his officers to "hail this 'settlement' as an overwhelming victory is, of course incomprehensible,"—nothing more than "face-saving." Certainly the workers, lamented the journal, "as they return, disorganized and disillusioned, to the same conditions that precipitated the strike," would not share their leaders' jubilation.[58]

Thus, the strike ended in complete defeat for those who had fought the hardest and suffered the most, though its full extent was to be masked for a little time yet. Initially most workers believed Gorman's assurances that "your heroic strike ends in complete victory as of tonight," as they prepared to parade back in triumph to the mills. "Our workers will march back in solid phalanxes under their union banner," exulted North Carolina's Roy Lawrence. "They will go back as a victorious army, conscious of their strength, the justice of their cause and the solidarity which has bound them together in this memorable struggle and will continue to bind them in the future. . . . We have compelled recognition of our just grievances." These, he said, would very shortly be rectified.[59]

There were some who doubted this optimism, including those few Communists still working in the South—relics of the Gastonia strike of 1929. For once they were right. They had played no part in the organization of the strike proper, but now they became active, urging strikers not to give in, to recognize that the UTW leadership had "indulged" in "an open betrayal of the workers." They would "now enter the situation with the intention of keeping the struggle going as far as possible." The only people to take the slightest notice were the police. In Concord, North Carolina, two activists were arrested, allegedly for illegally distributing leaflets. One was Caroline Drew, who had done her duty in the Gastonia strike. In a sad postscript to those days, police found in her bag a photograph of those tried for the murder of Chief Aderholt, together with an "identification card" belonging to one of them, Amy Schechter. Paul Crouch, another Gastonia veteran, also briefly made his presence known, as he planned "to capture control of the strike situation." He failed to do so.[60]

The next day, strikers paraded "joyously" in the South. The flying squadrons were on the move again, this time to call the workers back to their jobs. All over the South they marched in "victory parades," with their flags and banners flying, the flying squadrons leading the way. When they reached the mill gates, however, they often found them still closed, for most employers had no intention of simply taking their striking workers back, no questions asked. When 400 strikers tried to return to their jobs in Lyman, South Carolina, they found their way blocked by the bayonets of National Guardsmen, earlier promises of reinstatement forgotten. The plant there had been open for a week, run by old employees who had not joined the strike and workers hired since September 1. In Lyman, there would be no simple "going back." Reports from all over the region indicated owners were disregarding the recommendations of the Winant Report, refusing to rehire striking workers or taking them back only on the condition that they renounce their union membership. Some who were rehired initially were soon dismissed—once the company had worked through the lists. In Gastonia, again reminiscent of 1929, the mills often hired special deputies to keep the mills pure. "We tried to . . . return to our jobs," wrote Ruby Mitchell, a member of the Loray Mills strike committee, to the president, but "we were met and turned back before we got to the Mill by 100 bad men as they are called that was appointed [*sic*] by the Mill officials to keep us out—Those 100 men had knifes—black jakes [*sic*]—clubs and other deadly weapons." The many reports of such incidents, of lockouts, evictions, and blacklistings of strikers, made it obvious that a terrible revenge would soon be exacted, yet the UTW leadership, now totally without resources, had no choice but to formally accept Roosevelt's proposals for ending the strike on October 3. The code authority, savoring its victory, never formally accepted any settlement, merely agreeing to give the Winant Report "serious consideration." Meanwhile, southern millowners behaved as they wished, driving home to workers the obscene hollowness of Gorman's claim to have won an "amazing victory." Throughout the South, thousands of former textile workers would never work in a mill again. The spirit of defiance they had shown in their march back to work was replaced by disillusion and despair. Nothing explains the subsequent failure of CIO textile union organizers to make much headway in the South more than the bitter legacy of the 1934 defeat.[61]

Further north, in the more sophisticated union culture of New England or Pennsylvania, strikers returned to work with little resistance. Again, the Communists urged them to continue the fight, but there was little disposition to heed their call. In New England troops remained on duty for some days after the strike's ending, as tension slowly lessened. Only in Philadelphia was any serious disturbance recorded. There, picketers who disagreed with Gorman's decision tried to prevent the return to work, and eventually clashed with police, who arrested 49 of them, including the wife of the governor, Cornelia Bryce Pinchot. Elsewhere, even in the flash points of Saylesville and Woonsocket, everything was quiet. In Paterson, the silk mills reopened on September 24, with most of the 15,000 broadsilk weavers at their places. The contrast with the South was again stark.[62]

Thus ended the textile strike of 1934, on terms that, despite Gorman's claims that "the abuses against which we struck are going to be eliminated from our great industry," can only be described as defeat. Moreover, again despite his assertion of victory, and despite the illusion of a national structure that his frequent press releases and radio broadcasts emphasized—a national scope also stressed by the public utterances of George Sloan—the strike was never that. Some liberal commentators, most notably Jonathan Mitchell of the *New Republic,* believed the strike, despite its inconclusive ending, had shown Gorman to be "one of the ablest" union organizers in labor history. He had, Mitchell believed, constantly outwitted George Sloan and the Cotton Textile Institute; he had used the press and radio superbly, his so-called sealed and numbered strike orders had kept everybody guessing. His innovative use of the flying squadrons, said Mitchell, was the "first systematic, nationwide use of automobiles to transport pickets from wherever they were to the place you wanted them to be." Throughout the strike's duration, Mitchell thought, "Gorman has demonstrated a brilliance of strike technique, a soundness of judgement, a capacity for hard, continuous work that are possessed by few other leaders of the workers." The passage of time has tempered such roseate contemporary judgments. James Hodges was surely more correct when he wrote that "behind the facade and the rhetorical smoke, the strike was neither national nor as well organized as most historians have assumed. In reality it was a series of spasmodic, uncontrolled local strikes and walkouts, and it should be seen as a series of events rather than as one cohesive event comparable to later strikes by national unions against integrated national companies or industries."

Thousands of southern workers were untouched by the strike, the mills in which they worked so isolated that the pickets were unable to reach them. Thousands more, technically on strike, could more properly be described as "locked-out," either by the picketers or by their management, who hoped to use the strike to reduce their stockpiles and purge their payrolls of workers deemed troublesome. Moreover, the concentration of attention on the South has meant that the strike's regionality has been insufficiently considered. In New England, in New Jersey, in Pennsylvania, textile workers, too, obeyed Gorman's strike call. Often of different ethnic stock than the southern mountaineers they struck with, certainly with a vastly different experience of union involvement and industrial violence, they made little contact with the cotton hands of the Piedmont, and their goals were often different ones. Thus, to understand the real meaning of the textile strike of 1934, we must turn to these regional and local communities.[63]

Part II

The Strike

The Regional Mosaic

Strikers dancing at the entrance to the Clark Thread Mill near Austell, Georgia, September 1934. Walter P. Reuther Library, Wayne State University.

Chapter 4

New England

REFLECTING ON THE 1934 STRIKE FIFTY YEARS LATER, Solomon Barkin, the veteran organizer and labor economist, and himself a participant, believed that it was at its most "disciplined" in New England. The UTW leaders came from there, the union tradition was longest and strongest, and the mill workers were utterly desperate. Even in New England, however, the strike suffered from the overall lack of preparation and organization that characterized it elsewhere, which, in his view, was the reason for its failure. It was "an uprising of the discontented and disillusioned," he argued, for "the NRA had failed the people." Nevertheless, the UTW leadership were also betrayers. They had not planned for the struggle; rather, caught unawares by the depth of their members' anger, they "irresponsibly announced a strike rather than called it." Only in New England was there the disciplined local base that might have been able to sustain the action.[1]

Certainly the strike spread rapidly throughout New England. As early as September 4 the *Christian Science Monitor* reported that half the region's plants had already closed, and that the strike was just gaining ground. Within a week independent figures indicated that 70 percent of Massachusetts' textile workers were out, 90 percent of Rhode Island's and New Hampshire's, and more than half of Connecticut's. Of the 5,000 textile workers in Vermont, 3,500 were on strike. Only Maine's workers had been relatively unaffected by Gorman's call, but even this was soon to change.[2]

The spread of the strike in New England was accompanied by a high level of violence, especially in Rhode Island, where the most savage battles of all occurred. The National Guard had to be called out in Connecticut as well, after rioting in Danielson and Putnam left 35 strikers, workers, and police injured, and, eventually, even in Maine. There was rioting in several Massachusetts textile towns, especially Dighton, Easthampton, and Ludlow. Indeed state troops were quickly sent to Easthampton and also to Ludlow after a scuffle at the entrance to the Ludlow Manufacturing Associates Mill escalated into a pitched battle, but Governor Ely resisted the pressure for a general mobilization. Even in Vermont there was disorder, as 150 townspeople, "led by constables" and "armed with axe handles and other nondescript weapons," confronted 250 outside picketers who had arrived in the town. Though outnumbered, the townsfolk "drove back the squadron in the best tradition of Vermont independence."[3]

The fierce violence in Rhode Island during the strike's second week attracted intense media attention and masked the fact that Connecticut also experienced considerable localized disorder at the same time. Though textiles were nowhere near as dominant as in Rhode Island or Massachusetts, silk, cotton, and woolen mills were nevertheless an important component of the eastern Connecticut economy. From the strike's beginning, picketers and police had clashed in Willimantic, Putnam, and Danielson, as tensions built throughout the eastern mill towns. The Balding-Hemingway-Corticelli Mill in Putnam was a particular flash point, the intensity and frequency of the clashes between picketers and nonstrikers prompting its president quickly to seek state aid.[4]

It was a riot outside the Powdrell and Alexander Mill at Danielson on September 10, however, that forced Connecticut's lieutenant governor, Roy Wilcox, to mobilize two National Guard companies for strike duty. The riot had resulted in injury to 15 people, including 3 state policemen, and was sparked by picketers pelting workers with rocks as they left for home at the end of the afternoon shift. When the crowd isolated one unfortunate worker and started to punch and kick him, three state policemen rushed to his assistance. They were, in turn, assaulted by the crowd, now completely out of control, despite the entreaties of Joseph Davis, president of the Danielson UTW local, for calm. Davis, in fact, stood with the police in an effort to "put a stop to the trouble," but it took both the firing of tear gas shells and the arrival of the guard companies before order could be restored and the injured given first aid.[5]

There was violence, too, in Putnam the next day, and again the guard was dispatched, this time by Governor Wilbur Cross, forced to return prematurely from his summer vacation. Thirty-five were injured after a riot outside the Belding silk mill, as Cross seriously considered declaring martial law. Instead the mill was closed, and the state labor commissioner,

Joseph M. Tone, was sent to the strike zone to try and calm things down. Tone, moving from mill to mill, spoke to the picketers in small groups, convincing them to obey both the law and the National Guard. "Under our government you must conduct yourselves within the law," he reminded a group of Putnam picketers. "When you do picket duty you must keep moving up and down and of course you can't call anyone a 'scab' or a 'skunk' or anything like that." There is no doubt that Tone, whom the workers respected, was able to lower the tension level, and prevent further large-scale violence in the mill district, as both Governor Cross and J. Nicholas Panz, president of the Connecticut Federation of Labor, explicitly acknowledged when the strike had ended. When the Putnam strikers returned to work, the local UTW president, Thomas Redfern, released a statement which not only praised Tone's intervention, but also thanked the National Guardsmen "for their kindness shown to my local, No. 2223, Putnam, Conn., picket line, the men and women, during the strike." It is hard to imagine a similar statement emerging from a North Carolina UTW branch, or, for that matter, from strike leaders in neighboring Rhode Island.[6]

Rhode Island was where most of the generalized violence occurred in New England. Though it was expected daily in Massachusetts, the strike was so complete in that state's most pivotal textile towns, Fall River and New Bedford, as to minimize the prospect of confrontation between picketers and those wishing to cross their lines. In Lawrence, on the other hand, the scene of so much strike action over the years, the mills, surprisingly to some, did not close. Lawrence's 15,000 workers, it seems, were "weary of fighting, weary of violence in the streets," and were determined not to go out again. They rebuffed picketers sent to convince them otherwise and even cooperated with the police in guarding all approaches to the city. In 1931 the NTWU had led a long, violent, and unsuccessful strike there. Memories of that bleak winter were still raw. Lawrence's workers wanted no more of it.[7]

Rhode Island was different, and the course of the strike there will shortly be discussed in some detail, as will the experience of New Bedford, once the leading producer of fine cotton goods in the whole United States, but in 1934 reeling from the industry's collapse. Finally, the course of the strike in Maine, scarcely a major textile state, and one with the most embryonic union structure, will be scrutinized.

Thomas McMahon was the principal speaker at the Providence, Rhode Island, Labor Day parade. In his address he threw down the gauntlet to the employers, warning them not to stand in the way of progress and that the president was with the workers. "I know that President Roosevelt would rather see workers fight for the justice he demands for all workers," he thundered, than accept further exploitation. "I know better than many that we have a friend in the White House." He told a cheering crowd not to "turn the other cheek" in the forthcoming clash. "Hit back if you are hit," was his advice, because the employers would give no quarter.[8]

The parade which preceded this speech was a huge one, taking twenty-five minutes to pass the reviewing stand at city hall, where McMahon was joined by other local dignitaries, including the city's mayor, James E. Dunne, the local congressman, Frances B. Condon, assorted aldermen, church leaders, and AFL office holders. As was proper, the UTW contingent of 500 marchers headed the parade, but they had plenty of support. "Five bands enlivened the marchers with martial music," reported the *Providence Journal,* there was a "good representation of the Journeymen Barbers, all dressed in white coats and carrying black canes," while the Granite Cutters looked powerful in their blue shirts and khaki trousers. Most of Rhode Island's unions were represented among the 4,000 marchers, and together with the thousands more who lined the route, they provided the textile workers with an important gesture of solidarity as they prepared for battle. There was no disorder at the rally, though police did arrest two local youths, Lawrence Spitz and Walter Petraska, who had interrupted "the exercises by throwing showers of Communist handbills over the crowd," attacking McMahon and his counionists, and exalting the claims of the Communist-led National Textile Workers Union to be true guardians of the worker's interests. All in all, however, it was a good day on which to begin a strike.[9]

Textile mills had come earlier to Rhode Island than any other state in the union. Indeed, the first cotton-spinning machine in America was installed there in 1790, built by Samuel Slater, an English migrant and spinner from Derbyshire, who had defied British laws prohibiting skilled mechanics from leaving home. Slater had sailed for America with the knowledge of the most recent British mill technology firmly in his head. Invited by Moses Brown, a local entrepreneur, to Providence, Slater built first a machine, and then a factory. Initially the local folk whom he had hired as weavers resisted coming to Slater's mill to work instead of weaving at home, disliking the factory discipline he imposed. But the future was on the side of the manufacturers. Soon, factories like Slater's were to dot Rhode Island's river valleys, powered by the swiftly running waters of the Blackstone, the Moshassuk, the Woonasquatucket, and the Pawtuxet, spinning and weaving the raw cotton from the expanding South for the domestic market, protected by tariffs from British competition. Textiles, wrote James Findlay, soon became "the economic base supporting much of Rhode Island's working class."[10]

Yet Rhode Island's time as the nation's dominant cotton textile state was brief. By 1815 "John Cabot Lowell [had] developed the integrated system of cotton manufacturing." Soon neighboring Massachusetts had taken over as the leading producer of cotton goods, though Rhode Island remained an important center. Moreover, from the 1820s, the state's wool manufacturing capability, again using the abundance of waterpower available, was steadily on the rise. By 1832 there were twenty-two woolen mills in Rhode Island, mainly producing the rough cloth the southern planters used for dressing their slaves. Moreover, after 1830, when, increasingly, steam power replaced water in the mills, Rhode Island's textile industries went through a second period of expansion, as did New England's mills generally. By the 1840s, as William McLoughlin has pointed out, so efficient had they become that they could compete with British textiles in the home market.[11]

As textiles expanded, so did the demand for labor. Soon it far outran local sources of supply. Increasingly, the mills became the preserve of the foreign-born, at first Irish Catholics, but as the nineteenth century moved on, they were joined by French Canadians, by Portuguese from nearby Massachusetts, and, increasingly, by successive waves of migrants from southern and eastern Europe. By 1910, nearly one-third of Rhode Island's population had been born outside the United States. Italians made up the largest bloc, followed by French Canadians, English, Irish, Portuguese, and Poles in that order. The state's mills reflected this ethnic diversity, as they did in the other great transformation in textile manufacturing, the shift from male to female labor. By 1920 not only did immigrants and their children make up the bulk of the textile mill workers in Rhode Island, it was a work force which was rapidly becoming feminized.[12]

Rhode Island's economy grew rapidly after the Civil War, still substantially based on textiles. By 1890, Providence was the second largest woolen goods manufacturer in the United States, eclipsed only by Philadelphia, while it led the nation in the production of worsteds. It was still among the five top cotton goods producers, its mills producing a bewildering variety of finished and variety products, from fine muslins to corset cloths. Nevertheless, continued prosperity could not mask forever the truth that the cotton textile industry was already steadily declining, in the face of competition from the South, a trend which accelerated in the early twentieth century. By 1928, 80 percent of all "active spindle hours" now occurred in the South, as New England's industry collapsed. The onset of the depression finished the industry off. In Rhode Island, by late 1932, the textile mill work force generally had shrunk more than 30 percent from the levels of the previous decade, in the cotton mills the decline was much more precipitous, "the most dramatic single illustration," writes Findlay, "of the tragic long term decline in the textile industry" generally. The violence in Rhode Island during the 1934 strike needs to be considered in this context of constriction.[13]

Textile unions were a long time coming to Rhode Island. For much of the nineteenth century there had been no effective presence in the mills. The Knights of Labor had had a brief flurry in the 1880s, but left no lasting imprint on the state's workers, while the militant Industrial Workers of the World, active throughout New England in the first decades of the twentieth century, never enjoyed success in Rhode Island, even on the transient scale achieved in Massachusetts or New Jersey. The AFL chartered the United Textile Workers in the state in 1890 but it, too, made slow progress among the operatives; after a decade less than 10 percent had joined.[14]

The industrial scene was to change dramatically after World War I, in the most prolonged industrial unrest in the state's history. As was true also in the South, the war gave a boost to Rhode Island's textiles, temporarily masking the steady decline. War's end brought cutbacks and recession. Manufacturers cut wages by more than 20 percent in 1921 while increasing the workweek. There was much discontent in the villages, but no retaliation, but when similar measures were announced the following year, locals of both unions active in the state, the UTW and the more radical Amalgamated Textile Workers Union, voted to strike. In a preview of what was to happen in 1934, both unions organized "flying squadrons," shock troops of strikers who went from mill to mill, calling out the workers and manning the picket lines. The 1922 strike, which spread throughout New England, was a bitter and prolonged affair, lasting eight months and ending with no clear victor. Probably, it hastened the decline of the industry. Manufacturers looked longingly to the lower wage rates and more tractable workers of the South, as they made plans to relocate. Certainly, the violence of the time left a legacy of bitter class antagonism in the region. However, it also at last established the United Textile Workers as a presence amongst the workers, in a strike in which local leadership was overwhelmingly foreign-born, and in which women, especially Portuguese women, were often in the vanguard of picketing.

Indeed, Louise Lamphere believes the 1922 strike was a "watershed" in Rhode Island's industrial history, given the widespread involvement of women from "the new immigrant groups."[15]

The bewildering complexity of Rhode Island's ethnic mix defies easy analysis. There were some mills, as in Central Falls, which employed mainly Italians, others which were exclusively French Canadian, Polish, or even French. Woonsocket was well known as a "French town," with its French Canadian district labeled "Little Canada," but it had distinctive French and Belgian pockets of settlement as well. Cecile Bibeault, who worked there all her life, said she never spoke anything but French in the mills, and, indeed, her English remained heavily accented when she was interviewed in 1974. The Sayles Finishing plant, on the other hand, rarely hired Italians or Portuguese, preferring workers of English, Irish, or Scottish descent, and, unusually, showed no discrimination against hiring African Americans, which could have accounted for the extreme hostility directed against it by the Central Falls Italians during the strike. Still other mills were "all mixed up," with no particular ethnic group dominant. Edith Landes, who came from England in 1924, recalled her first years in the mills as "miserable" and "lonesome," and blamed the ethnic mix for this. "You see, not knowing the different nationalities," she explained. "In England they were all English. In this country, in the mills, we worked with a lot of Polish people, Portuguese people, I worked opposite a French girl who didn't speak very good English." She spoke mainly "Canadian French," she said, and they could hardly communicate. It was, Edith Landes said, a "terribly lonely" time, as it must have been for thousands like her, from all parts of Europe. It must also have hampered the development of class solidarity, and with it, union consciousness.[16]

Rhode Island's industrial scene remained troubled throughout the 1920s, the more so as the Communist-led National Textile Workers Union established its headquarters there. Indeed, the next major strike, that of the silk workers in 1931, was NTWU-led. Ann Burlak, the NTWU's "Red flame" and a veteran of the Passaic, New Jersey, textile strike of 1926, organized Rhode Island's mainly female silk workers in a bitter though short-lived protest against recently implemented stretch-out procedures in the silk mills of Central Falls and Pawtucket. Rhode Island's women workers, too, acquired a reputation for militant industrial activity that would be tested in 1934.[17]

As a result of her union activities, Ann Burlak also acquired a cult reputation, which has clung to her over the decades. Indeed, members of the University of Rhode Island's Mill Life Oral History Collection staff, who interviewed hundreds of textile workers during the 1970s, found that though many memories had dimmed, those of Burlak remained strong. Supporters and opponents alike recollected her as a striking figure, always dressed in a red coat and hat, and a powerful speaker, her long red hair as well as her words compelling attention. She was, said Harold Fletcher, a true "Red Flame." Elizabeth Nord, a UTW organizer in the 1930s specially chosen to try and counter Burlak's appeal to women, recollected that "people in droves followed her," and that there was little that she or other UTW organizers could do to blunt her appeal, except to attack constantly the Communists in general, and, as 1934 approached, to reject all NTWU calls for cooperation. Rhode Island State Senator Frank Squambuto, a former mill worker and UTW organizer and a bitter opponent of Burlak's, was in no doubt as to her grassroots popularity. "She was a very aggressive woman," he claimed, but also a very able one. She could have been a real asset to the labor movement, he believed, had she not "backed the Communist horse."[18]

Ann Burlak was born in Slatington, Pennsylvania, the oldest of the four children of a Ukrainian-born steelworker—and an avowed Marxist. She herself started work in a silk mill in 1925, as a weaver, but was soon involved in the 1926 Passaic strike, and in Communist Party activity. In 1929, the NTWU hired her as a full-time organizer, and in 1931 she was appointed its general secretary, the only woman to hold the post. The NTWU itself had its headquarters in Providence. It had been formed in 1929 following the New Bedford strike, as the Communist Party's industrial arm. It was the NTWU which sent organizers to Gastonia, North Carolina, in 1929, precipitating the famous strike at the Loray Mill, which resulted in the conviction of several of its members for conspiracy to murder Gastonia's police chief, and the fatal weakening of the organization. Never powerful enough thereafter to wage labor struggles on its own, the NTWU led a struggling half-life, with few resources, aiming to join existing strikes rather than initiate them. What influence it had was largely through charismatic individuals like Burlak, and by 1934 it was confined to New England, and to the grassroots. Thus McMahon, Gorman, and others, in warning local UTW organizers against any cooperation with Burlak and her associates, were not entirely acting as "Red-baiters." There was some substance to their concern.[19]

Nevertheless it was the less radical UTW which gained most from the changing industrial situation, particularly in the months following the passage of the NIRA. Rhode Island's workers, like their southern counterparts, were responsive to the recruiting campaign, the more so because the union's national leadership, McMahon, Gorman, and John Powers, a member of the national executive council, were from the Ocean State. Moreover, as it became clear that the NRA's promises were not being kept, and that conditions were deteriorating, there was an increasing militancy in the mills.[20]

The strike's first day passed quietly in Rhode Island, with most mills reporting normal operation. The situation changed rapidly, however, when the "flying squadrons" began operating in the state. As the well-organized mobile units, mainly from nearby Fall River and New Bedford, and from various Connecticut towns, moved swiftly throughout the villages, one by one the mills closed. Within twenty-four hours half Rhode Island's plants were idle, as strike leaders reinforced the message of the picketers. "Stay away from your looms," local UTW leader Adelard Gingras urged Blackstone Valley operatives. "We can show President Roosevelt we mean what we say." Though the odd local clash between state police and picketers was reported there were no generalized outbreaks of violence in the strike's first days.[21]

This was to change on September 8, as strikers began picketing the state's largest factory, the Sayles Finishing Company's Saylesville plant. The Saylesville plant had a long history. Established by William Sayles in 1847, and planned as a model village community, its grounds had been carefully laid out with the employees' health in mind, while the mill village houses were intended to provide a model for other enlightened manufacturers to follow. Sayles had been deeply impressed with the manufacturing towns built in Germany by the industrial magnate Alfred Krupp, and he had patterned Saylesville on them. The houses were relatively capacious and built in a variety of styles, thus avoiding the drab uniformity of the South's villages. Moreover, Sayles took a deep interest in the cultural life of the village. He organized workers clubs, lyceums, and discussion groups, and various interdepartmental sports leagues, even lunchtime ice polo in the winter. Saylesville had its own dance band, its own music society, even its own Boy Scout troop, all courtesy of management. The mill was huge; at the height of production in the 1920s it employed 3,000 workers spread over 30 acres of floor space, using the most modern of mill technology, at wage rates well among the best in the state. Moreover, even those hostile to the patriarchal style of Sayles's management conceded that Sayles's workers were a group apart, proud of their community, generally contented with their economic lot, and fiercely loyal to their mill. It was scarcely surprising, therefore, that as support for the strike grew in Rhode Island, and as the flying pickets increased the scale of their activities, the Sayles workers showed no disposition to join them.[22]

Love of the company, however, was not the sole reason for the Sayles workers' decision to stay on the job. Management benevolence masked fiercely antiunion labor policies, and the UTW had never been able to penetrate the plant. Robert Dresser, the plant's manager, lost no time in hiring special deputies to protect company property as soon as the strike call was announced and in producing frequent bulletins for workers, assuring them that their right to work would be protected and that "the strikers have no quarrel with this Plant or with its employees." The dispute, in short, had nothing to do with them, and they were thus free to ignore the UTW call. For the Rhode Island strike leadership, on the other hand, the plant was a major challenge. Nothing would signal success in the state as much as its closing, and for that reason, as the strike gained momentum, it became a prime focus for union action. The stage was thus set for violence.[23]

On September 7, 2,000 angry strikers from nearby mills arrived at the plant's gates. There they clashed with police and the newly hired deputies before being chased off. Deputy Sheriff Hermon Paster, who had close ties with Sayles management, then declared an end to all picketing there, at the same time warning union leaders to limit the number of picketers at all Blackstone Valley plants to four. "That's the law," he declared, as the plant continued to operate three shifts a day, around the clock, presenting a challenge the UTW could not ignore. Accordingly, local strike leaders announced on September 9 that they would "lead a new offensive" against the Sayles plant the following day, which would continue until it closed its doors.[24]

Rhode Island's industrial relations history had hardly been a quiescent one, yet what took place at the Sayles plant gates and in the nearby streets over the next two days was unprecedented, as the outmanned and inexperienced local and state police, eventually augmented by the National Guard, fought a series of running battles with crowds of strikers, estimated by press and police at between 3,000 and 5,000. Most were local, though none were Sayles workers. They were of all ages, included "hundreds of women and girls," and they were abusive—"cursing, struggling strikers" the *Boston Herald* called them—and they were violent; their weapons of choice were rocks, bricks, broken pieces of masonry, anything that could be hurled at the police, the deputies, and the National Guardsmen, for as the situation deteriorated, Governor Theodore Green had mobilized Rhode Island's entire force, only 2,000 strong.[25]

A strike sympathizer in the custody of two National Guardsmen
at the Saylesville, Rhode Island, textile strike, September 11, 1934.
Walter P. Reuther Library, Wayne State University.

Fighting began outside the mill at 3 P.M. on September 10. Initially quelled, it recommenced in earnest under the cover of darkness. At 10:30 P.M. "a crowd of 500 stormed a part of the mill with rocks," in a scene, according to one observer, reminiscent of World War I. The police and deputies fought back with buckshot and tear gas shells; the battleground was illuminated by Very lights. When the shooting stopped, two strikers, Lionel Costa of Pawtucket and Armand Gervais of Central Falls, were rushed to the hospital, bleeding profusely from buckshot wounds. They were followed soon after by Louis Fercki, a local lad. His skull had been fractured during a melee at the gates. The acrid smell of tear gas hung over the scene for hours. Indeed so much had been used that women and children crouched fearfully in nearby homes fell unconscious. Most severely affected were little Robert and Richard Blais, two-year-old twins, whose lives, briefly, were in danger. By 3 A.M. the gas had done its work. The streets were cleared, more barricades built at the mill gate, and most ominously, machine guns mounted on the factory roof. Management announced that the mill would continue to operate two shifts. Only 50 workers had failed to report that day, clear evidence of the union's failure "to compel a shut-down by frightening employees with threats."[26]

For Helen Clark Grimes, a respectable member of Providence's middle class, the spectacle of such disorder—"wanton destruction and bloodshed" was how she described it in her diary—struck at the roots of the social order. "The cops carry steel helmets and night sticks," she wrote despairingly, "and a car containing a riot gun and tear gas bombs" had been parked in the Finishing Company's yard all day. Her mind, she said, "was a whirl of strikes, riots, Communists, Federal troops," and not even the impending excitement of the American's Cup yacht races could distract her. "These darn strikes," she complained, had ruined everything.[27]

There was more to come. Next day the battle was rejoined—and it intensified, its location shifting to the nearby Mosassuk Cemetery. Again the rioting started about 3 P.M., the shift change. As the angry crowd of nearly 3,000 surged forward, surrounding the mill gates and, according to some, trying to set the main building on fire, troops and deputies began shooting from the roof, felling five, including a seventy-three-year-old woman, who was hit in both legs with buckshot. Meanwhile guardsmen and strikers clashed at the gate; in the close quarters, they wielded wooden clubs and rubber hoses against sticks, stones, and bricks. Police reinforcements arrived from Central Falls, and the battle continued into the evening, spilling over to the nearby cemetery. Strikers and troops pursued each other, "creeping over the graves and dodging behind tomb stones." Roman candles and rockets had been added to the strikers' arsenal, their appearance again weirdly illuminating the scene as "the cemetery took on the ghastly appearance of a battlefield." At 11:50 P.M., a fresh force of guardsmen arrived. Forming a phalanx, they charged the picketers and were met by a ferocious barrage of bricks, rocks, and masonry, all lit up by the "flaming fires" of the Roman candles. "The sight of blood streaming down pain-contorted features was a commonplace as rocks split skulls, crashed through the windows of homes and through glass of cars while the fighting surged up out of the streets into the Mosassuck cemetery," wrote one eyewitness, "as children hid under beds, babies cried and dogs scurried for cover." Again outnumbered, the guardsmen finally used their rifles on the crowd. Soon four rioters— Charles Gorcynski, William Blackwood, Fernand LaBreche, and Nicolas

Gravelle—and one guardsman, William Castaldi, lay seriously wounded. Gorcynski died the next day. He was only 18. Eight strike sympathizers were shot that night, and 132 injured, including 18 guardsmen, in the bloodiest single encounter of the whole strike. In the end, however, the strikers achieved their purpose. Management reluctantly closed the Sayles plant at Governor Green's insistence to prevent further bloodshed.[28]

In describing the battle at Mosassuck cemetery, journalists and troops alike found a number of common features. First, they remarked on the extreme youth of so many of the strikers. They were a band of "crazy youngsters," stated one reporter, little more than children "foolishly" advancing on the guardsmen's rifles, "screeching curses, they loosed their missiles in a distinctive hail," far too young to know what they were doing, clearly influenced by the Communist radicals on whom Governor Green placed all blame for the violence. The fact that many of them were young women was also noted—and deplored. Somehow, to have "radical females taunting" the guardsmen added an extra dimension of shock to the sorry scene. Especially noted by all were the bearing and activity of their "field commander," sixteen-year-old Rita Brouillette from Central Falls. She was the girl in the "green dress," who could "hurl stones with a vigor that would have done credit to a boy." The "girl in a green dress" was unafraid of the guardsmen, even when they made ready to fire at her. On she advanced, "the mob" behind her, "but somehow all the eye could see was the girl in green." She did not flinch, but neither did the guard's commanding officer. "Aim," he said, but still she came, the "slight figure in the green dress . . . a fury of action," refusing to retreat. Rita was not hit, rather she was arrested and charged with "intimidation and being a disorderly person," along with six older men, but soon she was reportedly sighted throughout New England, always in her green dress, a mysterious figure indeed, the "Saylesville girl in green." The leader of a band of so-called crazy youngsters soon became a figure somewhat larger than life. Fearless and strong, yet also an outlaw, a member of the "roving bands of Communists" allegedly responsible for all the violence, she was a potent symbol of disorder.[29]

Though the worst of the violence was over in Saylesville, even worse was to come in Woonsocket, further to the north. Labor historian Gary Gerstle has written a superb study of long-term labor politics in the town, *Working Class Americanism,* which includes detailed discussion of the textile strike. Among the points he emphasizes concerning the depression's effect on the town was its differential impact, for it stuck hardest at Woonsocket's already struggling cotton, machinery, and rubber in-

Textile picketer dragged out of the Saylesville, Rhode Island,
finishing plant riot by a state trooper, September 10, 1934.
Walter P. Reuther Library, Wayne State University.

dustries, much less so at the skilled woolen and worsted industry, which, unlike cotton, lacked a southern competitor. Second, even in woolen and worsteds, there was considerable underemployment; men and women, still at work, were nevertheless angry at seemingly capricious management decisions, directly affecting the quality of their lives, and increasingly ready to take militant action in opposition to these. Cotton mill workers, on the other hand, by now largely long-term unemployed, had less opportunity to turn to organization as a solution. It was in this context that Woonsocket's Independent Textile Union developed, first among the woolen and worsted workers, heavily French Canadian in ethnic identification, militant in its industrial philosophy. It was the ITU unionists, not those with the UTW, who seized upon section 7(a) as a means of extending labor's power in the town. As Gerstle points out, the ITU had, by the end of 1934, organized seventeen of Woonsocket's mills, and "stood more than 3,000 workers strong," ready to take on the local employers, who, like their southern counterparts, were determined to weaken the NIRA code provisions whenever they could or ignore them completely when they impeded pursuit of their interests.[30]

It took more than a week for Woonsocket's ITU leadership to heed the UTW's strike call. Initially, its leader, Joseph Schmetz, tried to allay worried employers by stressing his union's commitment to maintaining industrial peace. However, he also warned that his union had class obligations to all textile workers. Thus, when the strike call went out on September 1, Woonsocket's workers remained at their looms; one week later they voted to join the national protest, Schmetz insisting that they were not striking against local manufacturers but in solidarity with the textile workers of the nation, North and South, cotton and woolen, rayon and silk. One by one, the town's mills closed their doors.[31]

Gary Gerstle believes that "the strike might have run a peaceful and orderly course in Woonsocket had it not been for the provocative actions of one manufacturer, Woonsocket Rayon." Alone, it had ignored union demands for a phased closedown, management vowing to stay open unless forced to close. Accordingly, on the evening of September 11, a crowd of two thousand gathered at the mill gates and began hurling rocks and masonry at the mill. Both ITU and UTW leaders denied responsibility for the violence, which continued until National Guardsmen arrived from Saylesville and used tear gas to disperse the mob. Profoundly shaken, Schmetz called for such violence to cease immediately.[32]

He was not to be heeded. The next night a larger crowd gathered, as many as ten thousand, restless and angry. The arrival of a taxi at the

mill gates, ostensibly carrying "scab" workers, triggered a night of rioting that spilled from the mill gates into the nearby streets. The National Guardsmen, heavily outnumbered, could not control the crowd
with tear gas or live ammunition. The mob moved into the business district, where its members smashed lights and windows, overturned automobiles, looted stores, and taunted authorities. As at Saylesville, many
of them were young, many were female. Joseph Schmetz "recalled the
bedlam. The streets became pitch dark," Gerstle quotes him as saying;
and "the populace was electrified by the apprehension of some imminent
disaster. Thousands of people were in the danger zone, groups of the
younger element held conversations in the back alleys, stones were flying
and so were tear gas bombs. Any stone that found its target brought an
exclamation of delight from the crowd. Police tried to disperse the mob,
but to no avail." [33]

More troops eventually arrived, and they secured the business district
as dawn broke. By then, one rioter, young Jude Courtemanche, had
been shot dead, eleven more were in hospital, together with four policemen. The retail area, the heart, says Gerstle, of French Canadian working
life in Woonsocket, was destroyed; the damage bill exceeded $100,000.
Woonsocket Rayon had been so badly knocked about that it was forced
to close. The National Guard immediately imposed martial law on the
city, including a 9 P.M. curfew, a prohibition on all liquor sales, and the
cordoning-off of the business area. The rioting was over; the counting of
the cost was not. [34]

Governor Green's responses to the week of violence reflected both his
inability to comprehend the scale of the disorder and his awareness of the
political tightrope he had to walk. He was the scion of one of the wealthi-
est of the state's textile families, traditionally Republican, but he had been
elected governor in 1932 as a Democrat. Moreover, he had just begun
his reelection campaign, running under the banner of Roosevelt's New
Deal and heavily dependent on labor support. To have moved aggressively against the strikers, as his political opponents were urging, would
probably have cost him the governorship, and this explains why, though
mobilizing the state police quite early in the strike, he was most reluctant
similarly to mobilize the National Guard. He did so only when public
order in Saylesville and Woonsocket had collapsed to such a degree that
further delay would have cost more politically than the mobilization.
Even so his public announcement stressed that the guard's use was not
to be seen as strikebreaking. Rather, he had decided on their mobilization "simply to see life and property preserved and order maintained and

the rights of employers, workers and strikers, and especially the general public, respected." While southern governors made no secret of whose interests the guard was there to protect, for a New Deal Democrat like Green, the situation was more complex and the use of the guard much more politically dangerous.[35]

It was similar political reasoning, together with a severe attack of panic, that caused Governor Green to seek federal intervention into Rhode Island's strike disorder, on the face of it an extraordinary decision. On September 13 he called the Rhode Island Assembly into special session and requested an array of emergency powers directed at ending the violence, including the power to close any textile mill threatened by civil strife, the power to augment the state police by recruiting up to a thousand special deputies selected from the American Legion and the Veterans of Foreign Wars, and most important, the power to request that the president send in the United States Army to help keep the peace. Predictably, he got nowhere. Franklin Roosevelt, though in Rhode Island to watch the Americas' Cup, initially showed not the slightest disposition to assist the governor, and then, after talking with him, said that troops would only be sent if the state legislature specifically asked for them. The national officers of the American Legion and the VFW vigorously denounced the potential use of their members as special constables, while the Republican-controlled state senate refused even to consider his proposals. Moreover, his own party also rose against him. On September 13, the Democratic caucus rejected out of hand all his requests, with the most vehement opposition coming from the state's textile centers, especially those in the eye of the storm—Woonsocket, Providence, and Saylesville. Fortunately the worst of the fighting was already over, yet Green's requests indicated his own sense that he had lost control and reflected Rhode Island's changing political balance, which made the prospect of shifting responsibility to Washington and the White House increasingly inviting.[36]

Green was more successful in locating the blame for the state's disorders, not on the strikers, but on a small cadre of "Reds," hard-core Communists and their sympathizers. Indeed, he had requested emergency powers from the state assembly, not to restore order, or even to end the strike, but to quell the "Communist Uprising." State police conducted "Communist-hunts" in the main textile centers at the governor's direction, seizing radical literature, destroying circulars and handbills, and making arrests. Those seized were allegedly "imports" from New York, Boston, even Lawrence, specially schooled in the art of fomenting violence, for "only radicals trained to incite trouble could be behind the methods used in the strike areas," a view shared, incidentally, by the state's UTW leadership, who issued a statement attacking all such agitators, and urging its members to have nothing to do with them. More "Reds" were rounded up over the next few days, even as tensions in the state eased. On the face of it, Green's charges of a Communist conspiracy lacked any foundation. Though the party did have an office in Providence, its local membership was tiny, and if they participated in any strike activity, it was at the periphery, so effectively had the UTW marginalized them. The NTWU, also based in Providence, was little more than the redoubtable Ann Burlak, and her influence throughout the New England area had, seemingly, been countered by UTW attacks on her, by their refusal to give the NTWU any part in the strike, and by their collusion with local police to deny her access to possible strike rally venues. Perhaps, however, the reports of the "Red flame" having burnt "down to a flicker," were exaggerated. She was certainly in Rhode Island for the strike's second week, and there were rumors that she was on the front lines during the Saylesville rioting, her red hair uncharacteristically hidden under a man's cap, moving among the women, especially the Italians and the "Canucks," urging them on, even directing their missiles. Certainly Burlak talked later about her experiences in Rhode Island during the strike, and especially with the women on the picket lines, so as to give credence to these reports. Moreover, even if she had not been physically present, her influence, the fact that many of these women had been radicalized by her example, should not be discounted. Regardless, by September 14 she had resurfaced, calling for a general strike while standing on a ladder on the Boston Common. Five hundred people heard the "magnetic, husky voice of the young woman," according to news reports. " 'Gosh,' said one pert little office worker on the fringe of the crowd, 'she's a lot better looking than I thought she was. Gee, how can she get up there and rave like that.' " Burlak had clearly been temporarily muzzled by the UTW and the police, but she had not been completely silenced.[37]

Nevertheless, Burlak and the Communists were obviously not solely responsible for what had happened in Saylesville and Woonsocket. Yet by placing blame for the disorder and violence on their shoulders, the governor was able to minimize the political damage caused by the use of the National Guard while constraining his Republican opponents and their owner allies. Certainly, his conduct during the strike appears to have cost him little at the polls. On November 6, he was triumphantly reelected

Ann Burlak, the "Red flame," and Gorman's bitter opponent,
refused permission to speak at a strike rally in Fall River, Massachusetts.
Library of Congress, *New York World Telegram and Sun* Collection.

by an even larger margin that in 1932 and with solid union support. Republican control of state politics was over.[38]

After Woonsocket's night of rage, Rhode Island settled down. The city's textile workers buried their dead—thousands marched behind Jude Courtemanche's casket—but when they reflected on the context of violence in which it occurred, many were inclined to blame deep social tensions within the French Canadian community, exacerbated by economic privation, rather than stick with crude class analysis, or even management's undoubtedly repressive policies. Local police officers, for example, described the rioting as the work of "criminally inclined hoodlums, bent on adventure" who had taken advantage of the tense industrial situation but ascribed no deeper class meaning to it than that. In Saylesville, where workers had not wanted to strike anyway, the plant's reopening on September 18 was greeted with jubilation. More than 90 percent of the employees turned up for work; there was no sign of picketers, no hint of violence. By the time the strike was officially ended, many Rhode Island mills had already reopened, even in Woonsocket, as calm prevailed. Though in other parts of the country, and especially the South, many returning strikers found themselves locked out, denied their jobs despite the terms of the settlement, this does not appear to have been the case in Rhode Island. As early as September 26, the *Providence Journal,* which had been strongly supportive of management throughout the strike, declared that "everything was back to normal." Of more significance was the fact that the state's strike leaders did not contest the assertion.[39]

Of course, Rhode Island was not really "back to normal." As Findlay has pointed out, the events of September 1934, and especially the role played by Governor Green, reflected "the coming to power of a new social and political order" in the state, the end of Republican hegemony, the creation of a New Deal coalition that was a microcosm of that shortly to dominate national politics. In the textile centers like Woonsocket, the strike end did not bring about the collapse of union power but rather the formation of a new and aggressive industrial unionism, eventually under the aegis of the CIO, again reflecting national trends. Yet, in the end, neither national politics nor national unions could do much to reverse the decline in what had been the state's "flagship" industry for nearly a century. The long reign of textiles was over, even as so much else was changing. The violence of September 1934, the worst in the state's history, was seen by some observers as almost preordained, the eruption of fifty years of class antagonisms and hatred. If so, it dramatically symbolizes the textile workers' last stand.[40]

New Bedford, Massachusetts, was once the proud center of the United State's whaling industry, as the town's most famous monument, the *Whaleman's Statue,* attests to this day. Herman Melville's Ishmael stayed there one gloomy December day before joining the doomed *Pequod* and its obsessed master. In the America of the 1850s, New Bedford's harbor teemed with real whalers and their crews. By the time of the Civil War, however, cotton manufacturing had begun to replace whaling as the source of the town's livelihood, and this the wartime demand for cloth accentuated. As William Hartford has shown, in the post–Civil War years, as whaling declined, New Bedford's "locally dominated textile industry would experience dramatic growth." By the turn of the twentieth century the city's mills would employ nearly fifteen thousand workers.[41]

New Bedford's development is often compared with that of Massachusetts's most famous cotton town, Fall River, and certainly in climate and in coastal location, they were very much alike. They were similar, too, in their ethnic mix, both being originally settled by English migrants, often veterans of the Lancashire mills, who were soon joined by a massive influx of French Canadians, then, much later, by the Portuguese. Where they differed was in their product. Fall River produced "medium-grade print cloth"; New Bedford was known as the "home of fine spinning." One important consequence of this was that the general decline of New England textiles was somewhat delayed there, as the growing southern competition was in coarse and medium-grade cloths. New Bedford's mills, in fact, showed an impressive profit for much of the 1920s, unlike the New England industry generally. The crunch inevitably came, a result of northern manufacturers, unable to compete with southern medium-grade products, also turning to New Bedford's specialty. The years from 1928 were bleak indeed for the town's workers.[42]

The presence of significant numbers of Lancashire workers gave union development in both Fall River and New Bedford its distinctive cast. They brought with them a highly developed sense of class solidarity and a predilection for locally based organization by craft and skill. "Craft separatism," as Hartford calls it, became the integral part of "the Fall River model of unionism," and prevailed in New Bedford as well. Their British class predilections caused them, at first, to regard the French Canadians with grave suspicion, though the new arrivals were eventually absorbed into the craft-based local unions with surprisingly little trouble, especially after they had made the commitment to settle, which was a contrast to their treatment in most other regional textile centers. Not so the Portuguese, who held the least skilled positions in the mills. The local textile councils in Fall River and New Bedford made no effort to organize them as they had done the French Canadians and displayed little concern for their problems. The Portuguese responded by forming their own associations outside the textile council mainstream, loosely connected as they were to the UTW and the AFL.[43]

That, briefly, was the context for the industrial dispute which rocked New Bedford in 1928, when these distinctions became paramount in shaping the struggle. That year the fine goods market finally collapsed after years of mismanagement by the few families who controlled the city's economic life. Facing huge stockpiles, and a general destruction of their market, on April 9 manufacturers announced a 10 percent wage cut and strict limits on production. The town's textile council, then loosely affiliated with the American Federation of Textile Operatives, representing only eight thousand of New Bedford's thirty thousand textile workers, and still cast in the Lancashire mold, prepared to strike. So did those craft locals, like that of the yarn finishers, who were affiliated with the UTW.[44]

Outside the craft union structure were the Portuguese, doing the dirtiest, worst-paid work, their prospects of advancement limited by craft union control of the best jobs. Yet, unorganized as they were, they too walked out with the unionists to protest the slash in pay. Enter Fred Beal and William Murdoch, two organizers for the labor arm of the Communist Party, then pursuing its dual union policy, who hoped to use the New Bedford strike to further the party's influence in New England, and who saw the Portuguese strikers as potential recruits. The battle, therefore, was fought on two fronts: workers against management, and workers against workers; the older craft-based locals, now affiliated with the UTW, controlled the bulk of the English and French Canadian workers, and Beal's Textile Mills Committee represented the Portuguese.[45]

The strike dragged on till October, with the UTW representatives doing the negotiations, and Beal and the TMC organizing the pickets and demonstrations, which, increasingly, led to violence. It was eventually settled by compromise, the UTW called off the strike in return for a 5 percent, rather than 10 percent, wage cut. Despite the adjurations of Beal and the Communists to stay out, New Bedford's impoverished workers went back to work—even the Portuguese. Although the Communist involvement had not affected the strike's outcome, Fred Beal was probably the big winner in the short term. He had established his reputation as a fearless champion of the disinherited, and he had provided sufficient national publicity for the party to use New Bedford as the base from which to organize its alternative textile union, the National Textile Workers Union. It was Beal who, the next year, was chosen to lead the NTWU in its first southern foray, the Loray Mill, in Gastonia, North Carolina—and to a place in the mythology of American labor struggles.[46]

The depression hit New Bedford with rare ferocity. As early as 1930 its unemployment rate doubled that of the nation as a whole, and it remained at that level throughout the decade. Even in 1939, 30 percent of its inhabitants were unemployed, with a disproportionate number of those women, over twenty-five years of age, Portuguese, and, above all, former textile workers. Those still in work faced steadily shrinking wage rates, and intimidatory labor practices. Nevertheless the UTW maintained a precarious presence in the town, as did the NTWU, ready to compete again for strike leadership.[47]

New Bedford's operatives, like those everywhere, greeted the passage of the NIRA with enthusiasm and relief. In October 1933, thirty thousand people staged a huge parade in its support, snaking down the town's main street, cheering, Blue Eagle banners thrust high. Membership of the UTW rose dramatically in response to section 7(a), effectively silencing any remaining NTWU competition. It was not long, however, before the complaints of systematic code violations arrived, of increasing workloads—the "stretch-out"—of decreasing wages, of the ending of the night shifts and the increasing of daytime production, of intimidation of union activists. As noted earlier, Mary Aezendes, who worked for Langshaw Mills, alleged that since the night shift had been shut down, workers were forced to eat and even shave at their posts, so much had the work pace increased. "I've worked here for twenty-five years and since the NRA it has been worse than ever," she alleged. M. Moniz claimed that the Neild Mill had engaged in widespread laying off of workers, all union members, and then doubling the load of those remaining. Valeda Ferand, a French Canadian, asked that her letter be excused "because i cant righ much," then went on to describe systematic code violations at the New Bedford Mill, including drastic wage reductions: "I hope you gone fix tha," she implored Hugh Johnson, "so we cant work for are liveng. I am all lone i need work to supor my self." Bruere sent her a form letter in reply, suggesting she read it "carefully." Many of the complaints were anonymous, the writers fearing for their jobs or those of their family members if they signed their names; thus, they were never even cursorily investigated. The workers again flocked to the UTW and talked of strike action.[48]

Mary Heaton Vorse, the left-wing journalist, was in New Bedford the day of the strike call, and she described the mood of quiet desperation among its workers. The strike, she wrote, "was fathered by the speed-up and stretch-out, and mothered by evasions of the code, by the disregard of Section 7(a). People can no longer live on what they are getting: they can no longer exist under the conditions under which they work. Too many skilled workers have been discharged and reemployed as 'learners'—one means of avoiding the minimum wage clause. Too many workers have been forced to do three people's work in one day."[49]

The mills were all closed on the strike's first day, Vorse further reported. There was no violence, there were no pickets, for the workers were all solid for the strike. Both the "new" workers, "the big good-natured Portuguese women who look like full-blown peonies," the "black-eyed little French Canadians who in 1928 had fought like wildcats," and "the old-fashioned type of workers," those of British descent, "middle-aged prissy Americans," who normally held "themselves apart from the foreign workers," were in it together this time. Not quite everyone was involved; the local UTW leader, William Batty, had refused unity proposals from the Communist-controlled NTWU, but there was solidarity among the workers nonetheless, or so Vorse believed. Certainly, the press reported that every cotton and silk mill had closed in the city by September 6 and that strikers there were already leaving to help in other, less solid communities. Moreover, though the police presence was obvious in the streets, there had been no beatings, no arrests, and no serious intimidation. The UTW had achieved its first objective.[50]

NTWU officials were not happy at their exclusion from the strike's leadership, and Ann Burlak remained in the town for a few days, hoping to exert some influence. The *Daily Worker* reported that she was cheered wherever she went, which may well have been true, for she had worked hard with the Portuguese community in the dreary years before the strike, especially among the women, and they revered her. Nevertheless, the truth remains that the NTWU had little influence in New Bedford, despite its continued presence there, in helping direct the strike's course. Rather, the *Daily Worker* had to content itself with vicious denunciation of the local UTW leaders, especially Batty, who it described as "strutting in all the glory of his 300 pound, gray-suited, heavy-jowled egotism." Its urgent appeals to its Portuguese base to desert Batty and his leadership went unheeded.[51]

The contest between the NTWU and the UTW, as personified by Burlak and Batty, deserves further discussion, given that it took place along the battle lines that were so clearly marked in 1928, and reflected those same divisions. Ann Burlak's first call for unity went out as soon as the strike began and was accompanied by a *Daily Worker* editorial insisting that "the unbreakable unity of the entire working class, in every section of the country, must now be reared in defense of the general textile strike." The Communist Party, it went on to argue, would "answer on the picket line the slanders of the employers, jinks of the treacherous UTW national leaders, and of the fascist press attacks." The workers must take control of the strike away from Gorman and his henchmen, it concluded. In an open letter to the New Bedford Textile Council, Burlak proposed an immediate merging of the NTWU and UTW locals so there would be no discrimination against her members.[52]

This was the proposal Batty rejected publicly, effectively ending the NTWU's local influence, except on the picket lines. Burlak remained for a while, urging on the picketers, even urging their children to join in and throw tomatoes at "cops and scabs." The Portuguese women cheered, but Batty and the local strike leaders supported the police, who warned her that she would be arrested if she gave "the slightest provocation." Frustrated, she moved on to neighboring North Dighton, where she hired the local baseball stadium for a strike rally. The UTW organizers pursued her, however, encouraging the stadium's owners to call the police, who prevented Burlak from attending her own rally. She then tried to hold an impromptu "sidewalk meeting," but this was broken up by UTW supporters aided by police. Angry and disillusioned, Burlak left town, this time for Providence. Small wonder the *Daily Worker*'s railings against the UTW grew steadily more strident.[53]

For his part, Batty tried hard, and reasonably successfully, to keep the mills closed and the atmosphere as calm as possible; getting Burlak out of the way helped in the latter aim. He used local radio effectively to explain the workers' position, at the same time acknowledging that the local manufacturers were also in a parlous situation, and to emphasize that unless the strike was settled quickly, many of the town's mills would never reopen. This was a point stressed by New Bedford's mayor, Charles S. Ashley, even before the strike was called. "Some of the local mills have been struggling to stay in business for some time," he cabled the president, in urging him to do everything possible to avert the strike. "They have been on the verge of liquidation several times but have postponed such action in the hope that improvement in business generally would react in their favor as well. It is my candid opinion that in the event these mills are closed by a general strike they will never reopen." Batty knew the mayor was right. It was one of the reasons he was so keen to cooperate with the Winant Board in reaching a swift strike settlement, and this

Winant recognized and appreciated. "I wish to express sincere thanks for the valuable assistance rendered by you in connection with the study of the stretch-out problems," he told Batty after his appearance before the board. "We believe something of permanent and constructive value will result from the study you have made."[54]

The detailed story of the strike in New Bedford can be simply told. At the end of the strike's first day, the only mills still working were the town's three tire fabric plants, and they all closed on September 5. Every mill was out, more than 17,500 textile workers were on strike. No textile town in the United States was shut down more tightly than New Bedford, and it remained so for the next three weeks. Moreover, in contrast to 1928, there was little violence in the town. A few instances of window-breaking were reported to police; Josquin Silvia, who worked in one of the fabric mills, was beaten by picketers as he left work on the strike's first day, but in general, strike activity throughout its course was confined to regular rallies in the town's two main parks, Brookhaven and Hazelwood. There large crowds gathered daily—Portuguese at Brookhaven, French Canadians and English at Hazelwood—to hear reports on activity in other New England strike centers, especially Saylesville, Woonsocket, and Lewiston, Maine, where experienced New Bedford picketers had gone to try and shore up local resolve, and to listen to Batty as he outlined the reasons for the strike and stressed the importance of maintaining solidarity.[55]

For Batty, New Bedford's central strike figure, the strike was never about local conditions. Indeed he was willing to concede the contention of local management that to strike against them was unfair, in that they had maintained code provisions scrupulously, were paying code-stipulated wages, and were regularly bargaining with their workers, as the code demanded. All this might be true, Batty told his troops, but this was a strike about national, not local, issues. This was "the first time workers have been asked to come out on a national issue," he said at the strike's beginning. The issue was the New Deal, and the way manufacturers all over the country, and especially in the South, were defying the new administration by evading the textile code. How local employers behaved, in this context, was irrelevant. Regional UTW organizer Ferdinand Sylvia made the same point at a rally on the strike's first day. This was a class battle, a showdown between workers, with President Roosevelt as their leader, and "the big trust companies and others who are trying to break the New Deal," he declared. That was why they must stand firm. The issue was so much greater than New Bedford and the conditions of industrial life there.[56]

Batty and his local leadership team maintained this position throughout the strike. "Our ace in the hole and our best bet is that of the intervention of President Roosevelt," he told a cheering throng after his appearance before the Winant Board. He was certain that the Winant report would favor the strikers' cause, because the president was behind it. His distress at its recommendations, therefore, and the president's easy acceptance of them was palpable. Unlike Gorman, Batty made "no pretence of being satisfied with the settlement proposed," believing that not only had the UTW leadership let its members down, so had the White House. Nevertheless, he put the best possible public face on it, as he recommended a general return to work. The president would be responsible, ultimately, for the settlement's implementation, he told the last rally of the strike, and would use it to bring "substantial improvements" to their conditions.[57]

Thus encouraged, New Bedford's 17,500 striking workers returned to their looms and benches. They were reportedly "gleeful" about going back, and there were no reports of incidents or blacklisting. True, Samuel Samuels, general manager of the New Bedford Manufacturing Company, initially balked at taking back the 100 young women he had employed before the strike, but a brief, noisy protest at the factory gate quickly changed his mind. "Quiet reigns again" in New England, reported the local paper. It certainly did in New Bedford, after three weeks in which the national picture had clearly outweighed local concerns. Nevertheless, the town's decline continued. The depression, wrote Seymour Wolfbein, "completed the disruption of cotton textiles in New Bedford," and there was little Roosevelt, Batty, the UTW, or the NRA code possibly could have done to check the slide.[58]

"The textile workers of Maine have been under the whip of employers so long," wrote Clarence R. Burgess, secretary of the Maine State Federation of Labor, to Gorman early in 1934, "that they are timid." Moreover, the fact that the labor provisions of the textile code were being ignored in the state "has not helped increase their courage." Burgess believed the situation could only be rectified if the UTW's national executive took vigorous action. "I am persuaded your organization should have a man in Maine for a short time at least," he continued, someone who "could go into one of the textile centers, Lewiston, Biddeford or Sanford, dig out a few substantial violations" and then pursue them vigorously through the NRA code machinery. This might show Maine workers that union membership had a point, it might encourage them "to assert themselves in organization activities." But the push would have to come from the center. The state and local labor organizations were simply too weak to accomplish anything on their own. Burgess's appeal went unheeded. Maine was not a significant textile state, and the UTW's national leaders had much more urgent problems to deal with. What happened in September very much reflected both Maine's relative lack of importance as a textile center and the embryonic state of its union structure.[59]

The Maine textile industry, woolen, worsted, and cotton, developed as an offshoot of Massachusetts's growth. The huge firm Boston Associates first extended the industry into the state by establishing mills in Biddeford and Saco during the 1830s. In the 1840s, other small mills were established while a large cotton concentration grew in Lewiston. By 1860, the state had 6,800 of New England's 81,000 cotton mill workers, and 1,027 of the region's woolen mill operatives. Textiles, then, while well established by the outbreak of the Civil War, did not dominate the economy as it did in the states to the south.[60]

Maine textiles shared in the Civil War boom and the rapid industrial growth of the late nineteenth century, though never approaching paper or lumber as the state's leading industries. Indeed, textiles followed the same pattern as elsewhere in New England, impressive growth, reaching a high point in the 1890s, and then slow decline as southern competition destroyed the industry in the twentieth century. Again, this took place on a smaller, less dramatic scale than in states like Massachusetts and Rhode Island.[61]

One distinguishing aspect of Maine's textile industry as it developed after the Civil War was the nature of its work force. From 1860, the scale of French Canadian migration increased rapidly; many people came to find jobs in the cotton mills of Lewiston, Biddeford, and Saco. By 1900 there were 13,000 such migrants in Lewiston, more than 10,000 in Biddeford-Saco, where they made up 62 percent of the population. More significantly, they made up 70 percent of Maine's cotton mill work force, a percentage that remained constant for the first half of the twentieth century. Maine cotton, therefore, was overwhelmingly a French Canadian industry, its centers French Canadian towns.[62]

The effect of this development had considerable implications for the growth of the labor movement, especially among its textile workers. French Canadians have often been described as the least assimilable of all of America's migrant groups, the least willing to adopt even the language of the larger culture, let alone to participate in its institutions. Throughout the century, and especially in Maine, they have remained committed to their own institutions—their churches, their public schools, their fraternal and cultural societies—and to the constant replenishment of their heritage through trips across the border, to their Quebec or New Brunswick families, or through contact with new arrivals. Even today, Lewiston in particular, with its bilingual business signs and its dominant cathedral, has the feel of a French Canadian city. French Canadians went elsewhere in New England, of course, and played an important part in the textile industry, but perhaps only in Woonsocket did they achieve the cultural dominance they enjoyed in Lewiston or Biddeford-Saco.[63]

French Canadian exclusivity made the task of union organizers extremely difficult, all the more so because the focus of community life, the church, was profoundly antilabor and hostile to strike activity. When Mary E. Drier, vice president of the Women's Trade Union League, visited Maine during the 1934 strike, she was completely unprepared for the vehemence with which the clergy opposed her organization. In Lewiston, she reported, all the priests had instructed their parishioners, both privately and from the pulpit, that to strike was to sin. Moreover, she had become convinced that in so doing they were not simply reflecting the wishes of mill management, but rather expressing deeply held convictions which most of their flock shared. Given such pressures and cultural predilections, it was hardly surprising that the bulk of Maine's textile workers remained unorganized in September 1934.[64]

Nevertheless, Maine's workers, like those elsewhere, became profoundly disillusioned with the workings of the cotton textile code and angry with their employers' manipulation of it. And, again like workers elsewhere, they complained to the president, to Hugh Johnson, to anyone they thought might listen. "Please send some one of your representatives in [*sic*] the Pepperell Mills and see all the injustice that is done here," Juliet B. of Biddeford implored Johnson, "and let them talk with the working peoples [*sic*] and see by themself [*sic*] or unless something is done we will all starve here." She and her husband had simply not been paid for work done, she alleged, and no one at the mill could help them. "It is too bad to be poor," she concluded. Marie Talbot of Lewiston alleged that she had received only seven weeks' pay for nine weeks' work, and when she complained she lost her job. "If you do not believe me, I wish you would find out from [*sic*] your selfs [*sic*]," she concluded, enclosing her pay envelopes as proof. Maine's workers may not have been organized, may even have been hostile to unions, but they were bewildered and angry nonetheless at how the code seemed to be used against them. Was it just, asked Aveline Flagg, that employees forced to learn a new task should be denied pay while they were doing so? This was happening in Lewiston.[65]

Nevertheless, the general view was that Maine's textile workers would disregard Gorman's strike call. The mill workers were "not unionized to an appreciable extent," Col. Spaulding Bisbee, a National Guard officer told Governor Louis Brann, and were thus most unlikely to go out. This advice relieved Brann, a Democrat in a Republican state, who was in the last weeks of a vigorous reelection campaign, and he stated publicly that the state's 13,000 cotton textile workers were "unconcerned" about the strike. Mill executives pronounced themselves equally unconcerned as September 4 approached. Some, in fact, predicted that their business would pick up, due to a slowing of activity in Massachusetts and Rhode Island, where the strike was expected to have more effect. Though regional strike director Horace Riviere quickly made his presence felt in Lewiston, announcing plans for an aggressive campaign in the state, and though employees in a few small woolen mills voted to close as a consequence, the cotton centers of Lewiston, Augusta, and Biddeford remained quiet as strike day approached.[66]

The UTW had decided that Lewiston was the key to success in the state, and it was there that organizers concentrated their initial activity. They met stern opposition right from the start. The mayor, Robert J. Wiseman, a self-described bitter opponent of organized labor, quickly refused the local organizer, J. S. Poirier, permission to use city hall for a rally, declaring that the UTW leaders were "only fattening their own purses," and that in "every previous strike the common people have been the ones who suffered." The Rev. M. E. Marchand, pastor of St. Peter and St. Paul's Church, the largest congregation in the state, directed his parishioners to take no part in the impending "labor troubles," for they would surely produce only "misery and suffering." The workers themselves seemed disinclined to heed the strike call, even without such official encouragement, reportedly tearing down union posters as soon as they were nailed up. Though Poirier was able to secure the Lithuanian community center for his rally, it was scarcely a rattling success. Of the approximately 300 people who turned up, a substantial number were described as "curiosity seekers." The textile workers present reportedly showed no interest in striking, rather echoing the views of their employers that "a general strike in other parts of the country would work to their benefit." If Lewiston was to become the hub of Maine's strike effort, there was clearly much organization and education to be done.[67]

Alarmed, Gorman weighed in from the head office, denouncing both Wiseman and Marchand. "I am amazed that any clergyman should denounce efforts of workers to better their conditions," he said in a prepared statement, "especially in Maine where workers have been so long under the domination" of the state's largest textile firm, the Pepperell Mills. "We will take care of Maine all right," he threatened, adding that "by this time next week I think the mayor and the clergyman will be disagreeably surprised." But how could the UTW make good on this threat in Lewiston, given its weakness on the ground there and its lack of worker support? Gorman's answer was to use an immediate and aggressive organizational drive there before calling people out of the mills, and, in a decision which dictated the course of the strike throughout the state, to bring in seasoned unionists from Massachusetts, Rhode Island, and New Hampshire to help spark the local effort. From the beginning, the impending arrival of "outside agitators" determined the reaction of Maine's local authorities to the strike, and in particular, resulted in the widespread use of the National Guard, not, as in other states, to deal with disorder, but to prevent its occurrence.[68]

Strike day passed quietly in Maine, with only one small rayon plant failing to open, and though there was some picketing next day in Waterville, when the Lockwood Manufacturing Company's mill closed, the local police kept things orderly. In Lewiston all the mills were running as normal; nevertheless, the town was decidedly edgy. A local man, Dave Harfein, said to be "of the Communistic party," who had declared his support for the UTW and who had been caught distributing radical literature, was quickly arrested on a charge of assault, convicted on the testimony of police captain Joseph A. Picard, and sent to jail for thirty days. In pronouncing sentence municipal court judge Edward R. Parent warned Harfein that "men from foreign shores who undertake to disturb the peace of orderly society in a city like Lewiston where Communism is not wanted," could hardly expect "sympathy and favor." Lewiston was "no city for Communistic movements," he declared, a warning to those flying squadron units already rumored to be making their way there.[69]

Nevertheless, the strike slowly took effect in Maine, though not, at first, in the cotton textile mills. In Skowhegan, three hundred workers walked out of the Anderson woolen mill, briefly congregating at the mill gates before being dispersed by two state troopers, one with a drawn pistol. In Old Town both the woolen mills had closed. Meanwhile, rumors abounded of the imminent arrival of the feared Massachusetts flying squadrons, and in Biddeford twelve members of the state highway patrol, several deputy sheriffs, and local police took turns guarding the entrances to the giant Pepperell Mills, so convinced were they that the invasion would shortly occur. Indeed, on the evening of Friday September 7, a crowd of 1,000 gathered to watch the expected battle. They were sorely disappointed, the only excitement they witnessed being the arrest of two men, later charged with drunken driving. Of the Massachusetts strikers there was no sign, though some said they had switched their target to Lewiston and were due there the following Monday morning.[70]

Certainly the UTW leadership, if not the feared "squadrons," "invaded" the town over the weekend, as they tried to raise the level of strike support. Speaking in both English and French, Riviere warned that the strike effort in Maine would fail unless Lewiston's workers backed it. "Lewiston is now the obstacle to complete organization of the cotton textile industry," he told those attending, with no little exaggeration. "It is the only weak spot," and the eyes of Maine's workers were on the town. "A strike started in Lewiston would be followed immediately by strikes in Biddeford-Saco, Brunswick, and other reluctant centers"; of that he was certain. The effort, however, would have to come from Lewiston's workers themselves. "The character of the Maine worker is different," he had learned in the last week. "He is cool, inclined to resent outside interference and prefers to start things himself." The flying squadrons would be there to help, he promised, but only if they were invited to do so. They would not start things off.[71]

That was enough for Mayor Wiseman. Citing the "imminent descent upon Lewiston" of outside agitators from the upper Kennebec Valley, Manchester, New Hampshire, New Bedford, and Pawtucket, he requested Governor Brann to send in the National Guard immediately. Lewiston's workers were "terrified" at the prospect of such an invasion, he alleged, and the local police force "exhausted" and no longer able to maintain order. The workers were against the strike but needed the guard's protection if they were to continue at their looms unmolested. Brann, by now safely reelected, was happy to oblige. Within an hour of the request, units of the 103rd Infantry had surrounded the city's mills, thus effectively ending the prospects for strike action in Lewiston. A few would-be picketers did arrive from various points, eager to help out, but after surveying the tightly controlled scene decided they would be better employed elsewhere. Even Riviere decided to cut his losses and move on.[72]

Most went to Augusta, where the UTW did enjoy brief success. There, employees of the Edwards Manufacturing Company struck on September 10, the first of Maine's cotton mill workers to do so. More than half the workers were unionized, management conceded, and the local leader was Rory Claret, a former prize-fighter with considerable reputation in the town. As picket captain, he was quick to surround the mill with strikers, among whom "hundreds of women could be seen." Throughout the day they "circled before the gates," booing and jeering those still at work, though even the local paper, no friend to the strikers, conceded that "no violence was threatened," and that the UTW leadership had warned that none would be tolerated. George Jabar, president of the Maine State Textile Council, addressed a large meeting of strikers in midafternoon; he praised them for their "orderly and effective picketing" but told them not to break the law "in their efforts to prevent scabs from returning to their jobs." He also assured strikers that there were "outside workers" in the town, whose task was simply to instruct and encourage, not to lead, the local effort. What they were doing, he concluded, had the president's implicit blessing. Roosevelt had "given workers in all trades the privilege of organizing." Sadly, their employers refused to recognize that fact.[73]

Mayor Robert Cony, however, was not convinced that the strike leaders were genuine in their insistence on keeping good order. Moreover, once again the rumors of the impending arrival of "flying squadrons" from out of state abounded. Furthermore, though the crowds outside the Andrews Mill had remained orderly throughout the strike's second day, they had certainly swelled in size, causing mill management and local police "a great deal of uneasiness." The mayor, therefore, decided his duty was clear, and like his Lewiston counterpart, he requested the intervention of the Maine National Guard, in order "to preserve the peace of the community." Within an hour, Company F of the 103rd Infantry arrived for duty at the Edwards Mill. Quickly they cleared the area of picketers, moving the largely good-natured crowd to a nearby park. The only resistance came from Lawrence E. Brawn, a local who had recently run for the state legislature on the Socialist ticket. He was quickly arrested for disturbing the peace and, unable to make bail of $1,000, was taken to the Kennebec County Jail. All was now quiet in Augusta, if, indeed, it had ever been otherwise.[74]

The purpose of the National Guard's intervention in Maine's strike centers, reflected Maine's adjutant-general later, was never to combat disorder, but to prevent the possibility of disorder arising, unlike the course of events in Rhode Island or in the states of the southern Piedmont. "Perfect order," he claimed, "was maintained in all strike zones," throughout the state. Moreover, the guard was always careful to consult with local union leaders, to assure them that its function was protective not punitive, and to work out with them mutually acceptable rules of strike behavior. Certainly this was the case in Augusta, where the guard's commander, Col. Frank Sprague, and state UTW leader J. S. Poirier were quick to draw up rules governing future picketing. In so doing, Poirier was doubtless bowing to reality, yet the guard's presence in the strike communities was bitterly resented. Poirier appealed to Governor Brann for the guard's recall even while negotiating details with its commander. Its presence effectively ended the prospect of the strike's spreading in either Lewiston or Augusta.[75]

Augusta was quiet for the rest of the week. The unfortunate Brawn spent most of it in jail, and the rumors that carloads of "agitators were en route . . . from other New England points" continued, despite a complete lack of any substance. Colonel Sprague described the situation as "alarming," and the adjutant-general even requested that local journalists cooperate to prevent the publication of "highly colored stories based on unfounded rumor," given the "hysteria" they evoked. Again frustrated, UTW officials decided that Augusta, too, was a lost cause and they should concentrate their activities on the state's one remaining textile center, the Biddeford-Saco area, especially huge Pepperell Mills, the largest in the state.[76]

Pepperell Mills had kept working throughout the strike's first fortnight, but its employees had become increasingly restive. On September 14 there were reports that yet another flying squadron was coming from New Bedford, prompting the immediate dispatch of guard units as a precautionary measure; they were "to clean up the situation." On the same day, 1,500 cotton textile workers at Biddeford's Pepperell plant and Saco's York Manufacturing Company voted to join the strike the following Monday. Announcing the decision, a jubilant Amede Cyr, secretary of the UTW local, warned that "no outside agitators or pickets were wanted" in either community. "We do not want any outside pickets nor do we want any Reds or other agitators coming here," he emphasized. "We wish to conduct the strike peacefully."[77]

Late as they were in joining the strike, the Biddeford and Saco operatives gave the UTW its most conspicuous success in Maine's cotton mills. Within a day, the mills in both towns had closed, so complete had been the walkout. There was no violence, though the picketers jeered those few workers who turned up for their shifts. The guardsmen's presence, and their efforts to keep strikers and their opponents well away from each other, prevented anything more serious than name-calling, as, indeed, did the persistent, soaking rain. Though Pepperell's management complained of intimidatory tactics, which UTW officials emphatically denied, the extent of strike support had clearly caught them by surprise.[78]

There was, however, some disorder in nearby Waterville, as strikers attempted to close the Lockwood Cotton Mill. There, the National Guard arrived only after local police and strikers had traded blows at the mill's gate, and most of the mill's windows had been broken. The guardsmen were greeted by a hail of stones and other missiles, and one of them, Pvt. Wilbur Hayford of Biddeford, was "struck in the leg by a flying missile" and required medical treatment. Two men were quickly arrested and charged with assault, and the guard soon restored order. Governor Brann was sufficiently discomfited however, to raise the possibility of declaring full martial law, a suggestion strongly supported by the guard commanders. As the adjutant-general emphasized in his report, Waterville had been the only community in Maine where the guard had been dispatched only after disorder had occurred. "In all other places where troops were placed on duty before the situation" got out of hand "we had no trouble whatever and perfect order was maintained." The inference was obvious.[79]

Meanwhile, Lewiston awaited the launching of a full-scale assault. The local press had been predicting for days a last desperate drive on the part of the UTW to force the closure of the town's mills. Tuesday, September 18, was supposedly the key date. By then, it was alleged, more than forty top organizers would have descended on the town, freed from duty elsewhere by the strike's very success in other states. Horace Riviere was reputedly to lead the assault, he had been chosen as "field marshal of this organizing force," said the *Lewiston Evening Journal,* and would be arriving in the state on Sunday. At a mass meeting that day, plans to "clean-up Maine, the last state standing out against the National textile strike," were to be revealed. Lewiston simply had to be brought into line.[80]

There were, of course, no such plans, the UTW leadership having already written Lewiston off as far too tough a nut to crack, all the more so as the strike was faltering nationally. There was no mass meeting. Sylvia failed to show in the town; even Poirier left it on Monday for the slightly more fertile Augusta fields, and the Tuesday deadline passed without incident, prompting a mayoral statement that Lewiston was now "the banner city of the United States." By refusing to strike, he said, the workers had put themselves "in line for new business which will mean much to keep the textile workers employed during the coming winter." He urged them to continue to resist the UTW's blandishments and "to continue to work in cooperation with the mill authorities." They probably needed little urging, in fact. Lewiston's workers had never shown the slightest disposition to heed the union's call—their lack of organization and experience, the powerful hold of the local power structure, the combination of church, mill, and city hall, plus the pervasive presence of the National Guard, had all seen to that. Clarence Burgess was right. The employers' "whip" had proven too powerful.[81]

Nevertheless, Lewiston was to get its invasion, not by hardened out-of-state labor leaders but by enthusiastic strikers from nearby Biddeford and Saco. On September 19, they arrived, this "flying squadron," to "stage their stuff," to be "profane and obscene to a marked degree," and to invite arrest. About fifty came over in all to put some spine into local workers, but they did not make much of a positive impact. The police, assisted by the National Guard, quickly broke up their noisy demonstration and arrested five women and three men, one of whom, Cecile Herbert, described as "a widow and mother of one child," was quickly found guilty of "assault and battery on Bibianne Bourgoin," a twenty-one-year-old mill worker. Herbert was also arraigned on several charges of intimidation and held on one hundred dollars bail. The others, also arraigned, were sent home.[82]

Various Lewiston women, all mill employees, gave evidence against Herbert and those charged with her. They had been thoroughly frightened by their threatening demeanor, they said. They themselves had had no interest in the strike and had simply wanted to go to work. Bibianne Bourgoin testified that Herbert had accosted her in the street, touched her arm and warned her "not to go to work today, because nobody was going in." She told her of the strike in Biddeford and stressed that the Lewiston workers must come out as well, if they were to win the fight. Bourgoin admitted she had not been hurt, and certainly a mere touch on the arm seemed to stretch the definition of "battery" somewhat, but Judge Edward R. Parent was disposed to allow it. The law was so wide, he argued, "as to include the mere touching of a stranger by another." Employers had a right, he believed, "to see to the protection of their employes [sic] and that working girls have the right to walk the streets without interference." Lewiston, he declared, was "no city for outsiders to enter into and engage in an attempt to keep people from their work." If the mills were closed, payrolls would stop, and everyone would suffer. Herbert, therefore, had to be made an example of, as a discouragement to others, hence her conviction.[83]

Herbert's conviction certainly convinced local UTW organizer Poirier that there was no point hanging around in Lewiston, that its mill workers were not going to come out. "I'm getting out of here myself," he told reporters, as he made for less hostile territory in Biddeford. Moreover, as the only organizer in Lewiston, he was angry that no one had warned him that a flying squadron was on its way. Had he known, he would have tried to stop it, he said, and "his plans were upset" as a consequence of its arrival. Meanwhile, the ringleaders of the Waterville disorder were also jailed, as strike activity in Maine sputtered to a close, the National Guard firmly in control, the textile workers, as they always had been, divided and ill-led.[84]

President Roosevelt's appeal to workers to go back to the mills was quickly heeded in Maine, only in Biddeford was there a determination to remain out until a national settlement had been reached. Once the national union had "declared victory," however, Biddeford workers, like those elsewhere in the state, were soon back on the job. Indeed, again like workers everywhere, they believed Gorman, acclaiming the settlement as "labor's greatest victory." In Biddeford, Ferdinand Sylvia, the regional UTW organizer, declared that FDR would henceforth be known "as the emancipator of the textile workers," as he urged workers to go back. He would stay in the state for two weeks, he said, to help workers adjust to the realities of victory.[85]

In Maine, the return to work was free of incident. The guard was soon demobilized; there were no reports of violence or of blacklisting. Indeed the strike quickly dropped from the state's newspapers, as readers turned to the sensational news that Bruno Hauptmann had been arrested for the kidnapping and murder of Charles Lindbergh's infant son. Certainly, the experience had done nothing to strengthen the standing of the UTW among Maine's workers, especially as the hollowness of the settlement was exposed. Burgess continued to seek help from the national union, claiming the local organizers were simply not up to the job, while reports came in from the locals that most were "nearly defunct." There were, however, a few diehards left, wrote B. J. Dorsky of Bangor, still "anxious to organize," but who was there to help them do so? Certainly not the national UTW leaders, themselves defeated and demoralized, while at the state level, funds and expertise were also "sadly lacking."[86]

Still, it has to be said that, despite the lack of any significant labor history in the state, despite the power and position of the owners and their allies, especially the priests, despite a hostile press, despite all the complexities of ethnicity which made Maine a special case, and despite the pervasive presence of the National Guard, 3,470 of the state's 3,519 woolen and worsted workers, in twelve mills, joined the strike at one time or another, as did about half its cotton mill workers. The state department of labor, using different data, calculated that of the state's 22,000 textile workers, 9,518 had been on strike at one time or another. Of these, 6,045 were cotton mill workers, and the remainder came from the silk or woolen plants. About half of Maine's mills were idle at some stage during the three weeks: 17 woolen, 4 cotton, and 1 silk. Not all remained closed for long, the significant fact is, given the pressures against such action, and labor's weakness in the state, that they closed at all.[87]

Nevertheless, the commander of Maine's National Guard had the last word as to the strike's significance. Above all, wrote Adjutant General Hanson to his Washington superior, the events of September had "brought home to our people as never before the value of having a trained disciplined force immediately available to meet emergencies of this kind which are liable to arise at any time." Maine knew that now. Wherever the guard was posted, "perfect order was maintained," and that was an important lesson for the future.[88]

Chapter 5

Mid-Atlantic States

WILLIAM F. KELLY, SECOND VICE PRESIDENT OF THE UTW, and strike director for Delaware, Pennsylvania, and New Jersey, had hoped to use Philadelphia's Labor Day rally to announce detailed instructions for the conduct of the strike there and was thus rather disappointed when the day dawned cold and wet. Still, 2,500 people turned out in McPherson square despite the steady rain, to hear speakers denounce the textile codes, the NRA—"nothing but soothing syrup," said Edward Heany of the UTW district council—and exhort people to support the forthcoming strike. It was, said Heany, "the dream of the textile workers" to display national solidarity for the first time and would surely be the most effective means of bringing the textile workers of the South "up to the standard of the North." If the strike failed, he warned, "Northern workers will be dragged down to the level of the South," and this could not be contemplated.[1]

The crowd responded enthusiastically and then decided on a little "rehearsal" for the days to come. After a rain-shortened parade, they all trooped off to the nearby Concordia Silk Mill, closed for the public holiday. There they symbolically picketed for thirty minutes before calling it a day and getting in out of the rain. Still, it seemed to be an upbeat preview of what was to come in Philadelphia.[2]

From late August labor leaders had been predicting strong support for the upcoming strike, both in Philadelphia, among the city's thousands of silk, hosiery, and cotton workers, and in scores of smaller textile centers scattered throughout the state. Even before the projected Labor Day rally, the *Philadelphia Inquirer* estimated that more than 20,000 of the city's "cotton goods, woolen and worsted and silk workers" were already committed to strike, and there was similar support elsewhere.

121

The prospect of wage reductions down to southern levels was the key energizing factor, the paper believed.[3]

Certainly in the strike's opening salvos, such predictions seemed justified, as mill after mill closed in the city, pickets braving the heavy rain to ensure they remained "closed tight." Moreover, thousands of workers in textile towns like Norristown and Bridgeport reportedly also answered the strike call. Kelly asserted on September 6 that half the state's mill workers were now out, and though representatives of the millowners claimed his count was far too high, they did concede that the strike was affecting production in Philadelphia and in certain Wyoming Valley towns, especially Bridgeport, Norristown, and Lebanon. Both sides agreed that there had been little disorder, though a few picketers had been arrested outside the Rose silk mill in Philadelphia, while pickets had briefly "imprisoned" 150 workers inside the H. C. Jones woolen mill in Conshohocken. The besiegers had been in high good humor, however, and had immediately released their captives when called upon to do so by a UTW official. Moreover, a number of the state's leading citizens had come out in support of the strikers, most notable the wife of the governor, Cornelia Bryce Pinchot, who had sent them a message of encouragement. Only in Bridgeport, across the Schuylkill from Norristown, had things threatened to turn ugly. The council had hired nineteen special deputies to protect the James Lees Woolen Mill, incensing local strikers, who responded by blocking all rail traffic in or out of the mill. They had strung a rope "with American flags attached" across the railway line and then massed behind it, daring management to remove the patriotically festooned barrier. When "Nathan Fair, yardmaster . . . walked up to the rope and tore it down, together with the flags, the crowd, barely in control, surged forward." One of the deputies the company had hired then drew his gun, thus stopping the tide temporarily. Nevertheless, no goods left the yard that day, and the air of menace was sufficient for Bridgeport to be labeled the strike's "hot bed."[4]

In the silk town of Easton the strike started slowly, the mills initially remaining open despite a call from the local AFSW branch for workers to join the battle. Moreover Easton was unusual in that the NTWU, repudiated almost everywhere else, still maintained a presence there, and it quickly called on its members to support the strike. By September 7, the joint pressure was having some effect. Most of the mills were being picketed by members of "flying squadrons" from Manchester, New Hampshire, Paterson, and Allentown, the first appearance of what was to be a feature of the strike in Pennsylvania, the widespread use of what has often been considered a southern tactic. One by one the Easton mills started to close, as management, fearful of the violence associated with the squadrons elsewhere, decided to wait the strike out.[5]

The NTWU's involvement was a further reason for their concern. The branch had sufficient support among the town's unskilled workers to insist on being part of the local strike organization. Indeed, the strike effort in Easton was run by a coalition calling itself the United Front Committee, an uneasy grouping of representatives of the AFSW, the NTWU, and the Amalgamated Clothing Workers. This body, consisting as it did of fundamentally antagonistic members, provided little effective direction, and in the end unraveled amidst fierce recrimination. Nevertheless, the very presence of Communists in its membership was a potent reason for employers to fear the worst.[6]

The flying squadrons certainly increased the potential for violence, in Easton as in other textile centers throughout the state. Lancaster County, for example, had been quiet until a caravan of more than 400, from Reading, Columbia, York, and Marietta, "many of them women," had "dashed through the county," closing silk mill after silk mill and provoking physical clashes in which five workers were reportedly injured. At the Stunzi Silk Mill in Euphrata they had surrounded the plant and showered workers with broken bricks as they arrived to start their shift. The local police were quickly on the scene, but the squadron had moved on even more rapidly, leaving three workers with head injuries in their wake, and the plant closed. In New Holland they stormed the Frank Mill; in Leola they cut all the wiring to the Leola Silk Company plant before driving the workers out. In Bridgeport, too, the tension increased. In Allentown's silk mills more than 3,500 workers had come out, while in Philadelphia the upholsterers, carpet and rug makers, and the plush and pile fabric makers had all decided to join the strike, as had eastern Pennsylvania's 20,000 hosiery workers. The strike had seemingly become a much more serious affair.[7]

On September 11, the *Inquirer* reported that "all of the textile industry is now on strike with the exception of synthetic yarns and hosiery, and workers in the latter have been ordered to strike Wednesday, at midnight." The "southern" tactic of the "flying squadron" was now being widely used throughout the state and had even reached Philadelphia the previous day, when squadron members had forced two silk mills to close. There had been more trouble in Bridgeport; all Allentown's silk mills were shut tight; and Lancaster had again erupted.[8]

Patrick L. Quinlan, the veteran of many a labor battle, including the 1913 Paterson silk strike, had arrived in Lancaster to take command, along with a force of pickets from outside the county. In response, some managers had sent their workers home, but most kept mills operating. One such was the Stehli Silk Mill, and on September 10 there was serious violence there. A crowd of nearly 1,000, mainly from Reading and Lebanon, had gathered to picket. As the workers arrived for the morning shift, the picketers' mood turned ugly. They bombarded the plant with bricks and stones, breaking most of its windows, "keeping up a steady tattoo on the side of the building." More seriously, women employees trying to enter reported being jabbed with "long hat pins," some of which drew blood. Scores were injured by the missiles, and others cut with broken glass before a force of state and city police, reinforced by special deputies, dispersed the crowd. But it took three hours to do so. Seven people were arrested and charged with unlawful assembly and inciting to riot, including Quinlan.[9]

Philadelphia, by contrast, remained relatively quiet, except for the "yelling and jeering" of the picketers as nonstrikers attempted to enter the mills in Kensington and Frankford, the city's main industrial suburbs. There were also rumors and individual acts which attracted attention. The press was particularly taken with the actions of Sophia Mroz, a twenty-one-year-old woolen worker and a striker, described as "dark" and "glamorous," who had been charged with writing "scab" on the sidewalk outside the apartment of Myrtle Kuhn, a workmate who had remained on the job. Management and labor still differed as to the numbers out, with Kelly insisting that the strike was growing daily, a claim management ridiculed. Still, the city was clearly affected; press reports asserted that the strikers were "holding their own," though making much greater gains elsewhere in the state.[10]

It was in these smaller towns that the potentiality for violence was greatest, and none more so than in Bridgeport. There, officials of the James Lees Company had allegedly imported 65 strikebreakers from New York in order to clear a path through the pickets still preventing any movement around the mill. There were frequent clashes between these guards and the picketers, as the tensions steadily escalated. Increasingly concerned, Governor Gifford Pinchot, who, unlike his wife, had studiously refrained from commenting on the strike, now approached union leaders with a plea to help him restore peace and public order, promising also to investigate the allegations that strikebreakers were operating at the mill. Quickly, management withdrew them, as 3,000 angry workers surrounded the Lees plant, savagely beating three of the guards who had unwisely strayed outside its doors. There would be more violence there in the weeks ahead.[11]

In Hazleton, it was announced that there would be a general strike in the town as a means of showing solidarity with striking silk workers there. Christopher M. Sterba has published a fascinating account of this event, and the following paragraphs are drawn from it, expanding on the brief earlier discussion, as an attempt to provide a case study of one small community's reaction to the national challenge.[12]

Hazleton's silk workers, who were mainly women, often the wives and daughters of the district's anthracite miners, had, like those elsewhere, responded enthusiastically to the wages and hour codes of the NRA's section 7(a), for the company which employed most of them, the Duplan Silk Corporation, had historically been viciously antiunion and had successfully fought all attempts by the American Federation of Silk Workers to form locals there. Unlike other members of the town's work force—the miners, the bakers, the brewers, the transport workers, and the shirt factory workers—they had remained unorganized despite this strong union tradition. Consequently, as with the cotton mill operatives of Greenville and Gastonia, they rejoiced as the national government seemingly tipped the balance of power their way. Surely Duplan could not resist the sweep of New Deal reforms. When the silk workers of Pennsylvania, New York, and New Jersey struck in September 1933 over dissatisfaction with aspects of the textile code, Hazleton's largely unorganized workers joined the battle enthusiastically—and were in danger of defeat. Local police power was used against them to stop picketing; the Duplan Silk Corporation's control seemed as secure as ever. Fortunately for the workers, the area's United Mine Workers locals intervened on their behalf, putting pressure on the mayor to lift his antipicketing orders, eventually forcing Duplan to mediation. In October, UTW Local 2033 was formed, and Duplan was organized at last. But the local was a weak one, easily dominated by the company, and tensions in the mill, accordingly, remained high. Hazleton's workers were ready, therefore, to respond to the September strike call.[13]

The town's strikers proved to be resourceful and dedicated squadron members. On September 13, "a group of buses and cars filled with Hazleton silk workers travelled first to Scranton, and then to the Empire Silk Company mill on the outskirts of Wilkes-Barre." There they stormed the mill, hurling rocks and other missiles, forcing frightened female employees to take shelter in offices, bathrooms, anywhere that afforded some protection. Most of their Hazleton assailants were also women, who, according to eyewitnesses, were much more outwardly aggressive in their behavior than their male companions. "They'd do all the hollering and everything" said one. "They were more militant . . . the men would be more reserved." The young women of Hazleton, like their southern counterparts, "modern girls," usually of central European backgrounds, and often from mining families with a strongly developed sense of class, made up the majority of the town's silk workers by the mid-1930s. They were often also the prime bread winners—and the main victims of the stretch-out policies of Duplan and other Hazleton employers. Thus, says Sterba, "a potent combination—youthful rebelliousness, workplace frustration, and a family heritage of strike experience— . . . came together in flying squadron raids."[14]

The silk workers were strongly supported by Hazleton's other workers, both organized and unorganized, and it was largely in response to their demands for more drastic action against Duplan that the Central Labor Union, supported by UMW local president Michael Hartneady, agreed to the notion of a one day "labor holiday," on September 12, accompanied by a great "solidarity" parade, unless Duplan, which alone of the local silk mills had remained open throughout the strike, agreed to shut its doors. There was no response, and so on the appointed day the city closed down. There was no newspaper, the buses did not run, the movie theaters closed as, most important, did the town's factories and coal mines. It was an impressive display of local labor solidarity.[15]

The labor parade was a most colorful affair. "Joining the 3,000 striking silk workers were members from the city's craft and industrial unions"—twenty-six in all, from the brewers to the musicians and motion picture operators. The miners brought up the rear, fourteen thousand of them, "representing thirty-four locals of the UMW." Many marchers carried American flags, others banners and slogans supporting the New Deal and section 7(a). The bakers wore their white workclothes, the painters "the familiar caps of their profession," most, in fact, wore the garments of their trades or their best suits and Sunday dresses. The American Legion provided the music; the local high school football team "paraded in full uniform." The orderly, lighthearted procession stretched for nearly four miles. It was supported by the local municipal authorities, and the police were there to help keep order, but as unobtrusively as possible. It was thus a further impressive demonstration of local civic and economic support for the striking silk workers, something, as Sterba points out, they often lacked in other parts of the country, especially in the South.[16]

Within a fortnight the strike was over, and Hazleton's workers returned to their plants. Duplan, which had tried to stay open, eventually had to shut down. For its workers, emboldened by their action on the picket lines, and buoyed by the local solidarity the parade had so starkly symbolized, ousted local 2033's conservative leadership. The newly formed local immediately forced management to close for the rest of the strike. Thus the textile strike of 1934, though regarded as a failure nationally, had its local successes. One was in Hazleton, Pennsylvania, where workers in the city's largest silk mill finally got a truly independent local union, one that would reflect their aspirations and concerns, not those of their employer.[17]

Meanwhile, the strike grew more "turbulent" in other Pennsylvania centers, nowhere more so than in Bridgeport. There the strikebreakers shipped in from New York were causing disturbances of sufficient seriousness as to prompt Governor Pinchot's investigation. Outside James Lees, thousands of strikers and spectators lined the streets at each change of shift, "forming a gauntlet" that workers going home had to run, as they were pelted with "stones, bricks and sticks." At the same time, Philadelphia-based flying squadrons started moving out of the city, provoking violence in such nearby centers as Chester. And the strike had briefly shut down Philadelphia's hosiery mills. Even those hosiery workers currently working under contracts, and thus specifically exempted from strike action, decided to come out in sympathy anyway. When Emil Rieve, head of the American Federation of Hosiery Workers, angrily ordered them back to work, they at first refused to go. They were, they said, "handling cotton and silk yarns made in plants where strikes were in progress" and were thus "helping the reactionary mill owners of the South to put down the strike." They were simply not prepared to continue to do this, even if it meant defying their national leadership. It took Gorman and Rieve's combined insistence to get them to return, which they did with the greatest reluctance. Again, local determination and indignation had far outrun national policy.[18]

Every day now brought further reports of violence in the state. In Philadelphia itself, women strikers rioted at J. Sullivan and Sons Manufacturing when the company refused to release pay owed to them unless they signed for it. The women, fearful that their signatures would be used against them illegally, refused, and the explosive situation was only defused when a police captain, Norman Renney, persuaded company officials to release the money upon identification only. Governor Pinchot was forced to send a contingent of the state police to Chambersburg to try to control spreading violence there, while on September 17 a flying squadron invaded the Perkasie Silk Mill, forced its way through locked doors, and shut off power to the looms of its 175 employees.[19]

A detachment of state police had remained at Lancaster's Stehli silk plant after the earlier violence there. They had to contain another outbreak a week later when out-of-town picketers clashed with local workers, who were also on the picket line. One of the visitors reportedly dropped "a large bundle of newspapers bearing the emblem of Communism." Police immediately arrested him, and as he was being led away he appealed to his fellow strikers to free him. "Don't let him take me, workers," he cried. "Come to my rescue." The local pickets allegedly "jeered and laughed at his protests," whereupon, in a bizarre twist, members of the visiting flying squadron attacked them. The police joined in, and there was a brief but violent melee before order was restored. One local picketer was hurt, and three squadron members were arrested, in what was surely one of the strike's most unusual confrontations. The strike might have been winding down in the South and New England, but in Pennsylvania it entered its third week still gathering momentum, with the regional UTW leaders vowing to escalate the struggle even further, especially given that they now had the authority to call out the carpet, rug, rayon, knit goods, dyeing, and synthetic yarn workers as well. Rieve, however, kept his hosiery workers well out of it. He had opposed the strike at the August convention, and he remained opposed. He saw it for what it was, an ill-planned enterprise, doomed to fail, and he wanted no part of it. The historian Philip Scranton has described him as the Philadelphia labor leader who best understood the potentialities of the Roosevelt administration's approach to labor-management matters and the futility of such strike action in a depressed economic situation. His was the way of the future, Scranton argues, and without his participation the strike in Pennsylvania was bound to stall.[20]

As the stoppage entered its third week Philadelphia's owners had had enough. They held a series of meetings chaired by Col. Millard Brown, president of the city's Textile Manufacturers Association, in order to try to form a common strike strategy. Deciding to use the courts, they filed requests for a series of injunctions to restrain all strike activity, including picketing. Members of the UTW leadership team were named as defendants, together with the leadership of affiliated locals such as the Woolen, the Worsted, and the Upholsterers and Plush Workers Unions. Incensed by their action, Governor Pinchot's wife, Cornelia, decided to make quite explicit her support for the strikers' cause, addressing a mass meeting in a Kensington lyceum, and then joining a picket line. She withdrew only when told of the Winant recommendations and the president's subsequent appeal for a return to work. "You can count on me in this fight," she shouted, "I am in it to the finish," before lunching at the Bellevue-Stratford Hotel. Meanwhile, her husband tried to mediate a settlement between silk workers and their employers, as reports of escalating violence increased, and as police and strikers battled at the gates of the Runnemede Worsted Mill at Clifton Heights.[21]

Outside Philadelphia, there were similar signs of a determination to bring things to a head. In Easton, upon receipt of a petition from "local plant operators, business and professional men, and bankers," the city council decided to hire more police, while at the same time authorizing the mayor to regulate picketing in the city. He did so immediately, mass picketing was to be prohibited, there could be no more than sixteen on the line at any one time, all of whom had to be employees of the picketed establishment. Out-of-town picketers were specifically warned off. They would be severely dealt with in the future, said Easton's police chief, Frank C. Frederick, now that he had the manpower to do so. By this time Easton's silk workers had lost their enthusiasm for the struggle. The United Front Strike Strategy Board had split asunder, with the UTW and NTWU factions bitterly opposed as to strategy, and, eventually, by whether to abide by the strike settlement. In this context, mill managers judged it safe to reopen, and their employees were happy enough to return—despite the bitter opposition of the NTWU. By September 26, most mills were working to capacity, with no reports of discrimination against strikers. In Lancaster, too, the mills were reopening, some, like the Stunzi, under heavy guard. By September 25, reported the local newspaper, everything was "back to normal."[22]

This was not invariably the case. Many of Pennsylvania's textile workers greeted the news of the strike's ending, and Gorman's subsequent claim of victory, with disappointment, skepticism, and, in some instances, downright anger. Union leaders expressed the view that "victory would have been more complete had the strike continued for another week"; rank-and-file strikers, ready "to fight it out to the bitter end," instead prepared "with dismay" to return to work. Indeed the knit goods workers, who were not affiliated with the UTW, decided to stay out. They had originally struck in support of Gorman; now they decided to continue the struggle on their own.[23]

Throughout the state the mood was ugly, and tensions remained high, as slowly the production lines started to hum. As in the South, management attempted to screen returning workers in order to weed out the most prominent unionists, and there were local clashes as a result and, later, complaints to Washington. In Bridgeport, the violence there was the most serious of the whole strike period, even though the strike was officially over, again illustrating the huge divergence between national strike policies and directives and local realities. Officials at the troubled James Lees plant refused to take all strikers back immediately, claiming there were insufficient orders to employ the full work force. Moreover company officials insisted that no one who had been involved in acts of violence during the strike would ever be rehired. The strikers insisted on full reemployment or none at all and voted to remain on strike. Again there was violence, huge angry crowds at the mill gates daily; those who wanted to work were abused and attacked, the cars and buses transporting them chased and stoned despite police escorts. On October 1 a crowd of 2,000 attacked "an automobile caravan of homegoing workers," injuring three of them, plus two bus line officials who had also been transporting workers. Only the timely arrival of the state police prevented real mayhem. Two days later unionists again attacked the buses and cars carrying afternoon shift workers home. This time the deputies fired bullets and tear gas at the crowd, and when the smoke cleared away one man was dead and more than one hundred people, men and women, hurt. "The ordinarily quiet manufacturing town of Bridgeport . . . erupted yesterday afternoon into a mad carnival of violence and destruction," stated the *Philadelphia Inquirer.*[24]

As the town remained at flash point, the local priest, Rev. Joseph Tomio, appealed to FDR to intervene, and police arrested five specially sworn local deputies and charged them with the murder of twenty-three-year-old Elwood Quirk. Not a striker, he had just finished his shift at a nearby plant and was on his way home when he noticed the huge crowd outside James Lees. Curious, he decided on a closer look, arriving just as the cars tried to run the gauntlet of strikers, who signaled their approach "with an Irish salute, a long, drawn out 'Y-O-O-O H-O-O-O.'" Then the insults as well as bricks started to fly, and soon the bullets and tear gas, as deputies fired indiscriminately from their cars. "Quirk slumped to the side-walk," others were also hit, including a young woman who "hobbled away," assisted by friends, and the mob "took to its heels." A few, a very few, stayed with Quirk, eventually carrying him to hospital, but it was too late.[25]

The next day Hazletine S. Leven, the county sheriff, declared martial law in Bridgeport; the arrested deputies were released on $5,000 bail each and smuggled out of town to avoid a "neck-tie party." The textile strike in Bridgeport was swiftly drawing to a close. In the church basement which had served as strike headquarters, five hundred men and women agreed to a peace plan which would submit all disputes over rehiring to the chairman of the regional labor board, and all strikers charged by their employers with violence would have their cases heard by a joint committee of the UTW and officials of the Lees plant. With that, work recommenced at James Lees. When Elwood Quirk was buried on October 6, the priest of St. Augustine's Catholic Church, Rev. James V. McEnery, described his death as "another tragedy in the cause of justice." The casket was taken to the cemetery by an honor guard of strikers, two thousand strong, men and women with Italian, Polish, or Irish names; very different were these folk from the transplanted Celts of Honea Path, and yet, at the end of it all, both groups stood silently in a graveyard. Later, St. Augustine's dedicated a memorial window in Quirk's honor.[26]

Philip Scranton was inclined to downplay the importance of the textile strike in Pennsylvania, pointing to the continued depressed condition of the industry and the total lack of any improvement as a result. "McMahon's Folly," he called it. In this he is surely right despite the violence and the flying squadrons. Moreover, given the fact that many manufacturers, fearful of conflict and resultant damage, immediately closed their mills and thus added to the number of workers ostensibly out, the UTW's figures of those on strike were surely inflated. Nevertheless, the strike there was important, if only as a way-station in the sorry story of the state's industrial and regional decay. As such, it bears comparison with what eventuated across the state border, and specifically, in what had once been the flagship of the American silk industry—"Silk City," Paterson, New Jersey.[27]

The silk manufacturing city of Paterson has a place in the mythology of American labor battles similar to that of Lawrence, Massachusetts, Gastonia, North Carolina, or even Flint, Michigan. The great struggle of its 25,000 silk workers in 1913, assisted by the colorful IWW trio of Big Bill Haywood, Carlo Tresca, and the frail-looking but fiery Elizabeth Gurley Flynn, was national news for more than six months. At the conflict's height in early June, the city was completely shut down, and more than a thousand strikers and their families took part in a massive pageant at Madison Square Garden organized by the leftist revolutionary journalist John Reed, at which the events of the strike were dramatically reenacted. The spectacle concluded with Haywood delivering an impassioned oration as the "Marseillaise," and the "Internationale" played in

the background. The strike's dramatic impact, as symbolized by this famous event served to mask the fact that it was a failure. Strikers returned
to work in August having gained nothing from their resolution, their rallies and their sustained nonviolence against the combined forces of city
officials, millowners, a hostile press and pulpit and an increasingly violent
police force. In John Updike's fine novel *In the Beauty of the Lilies,* set
partly in Paterson, it is the violence of the owners which causes the Rev.
Clarence Wilmot to lose what was left of his faith, but in reality Paterson's
clergy stood resolutely for the status quo.[28]

Paterson's history as a manufacturing city had been punctuated by industrial violence, which would continue for the next fifteen years even
as its importance as a silk center declined. As has been discussed earlier,
Paterson's silk workers, or substantial sections of them, were out again in
1919, in 1921, 1924, and 1928, with skirmishes and shorter stoppages
in most of the years between. These all occurred against the backdrop of
the steady demise of Paterson as the nation's key silk center. From 1913,
Paterson's larger manufacturers had begun to move their businesses elsewhere or to build up what had formerly been their Pennsylvania sub-
sidiaries, producing lower cost, less exclusive products, requiring a less
skilled work force. Into the vacuum moved former skilled weavers and
dyers, who had dreamed of having their own shops. By 1920 Paterson's
silk industry was increasingly dominated by "cockroach shops," small,
family concerns, usually operated out of the home or rented space in
what had once been larger mills. They were, of course, operating on the
economic margins, and, as family businesses, were totally nonunion.[29]

Throughout the 1920s more mills moved—others closed. The silk market had changed. Paterson's mills continued to produce quality fabrics,
using traditionally skilled weavers demanding high wages. But the market, now a mass one, increasingly wanted inexpensive fabric and this the
mills of Pennsylvania and Rhode Island could supply, using basic looms
operated by women and children—"the wives and daughters of the anthracite miners," as they were commonly categorized. More of Paterson's workers were unemployed and moved into the "cockroach shops."
The bitter strike of 1924, which lasted four months, simply hastened
the process of decline. The Associated Silk Workers still had some apparent strength; the strike ended with workers gaining a pay increase. Yet,
from 1924 the city's production levels declined steadily, and mill closings accelerated, as manufacturers either moved to Pennsylvania or shut
up shop. As Nancy Fogelson has commented, "the victory meant little
to silk workers left in a city with diminishing opportunities for jobs." As

the mills left, she said, so did the young people. "Within a generation," Fogelson concluded, "Paterson became a city of the old, the sick and the poor."[30]

In this context, what happened in September 1934 should be considered merely as another episode in the city's long story of industrial decline, and indeed Paterson's silk workers, together with the UTW, had already made their protest against the NRA and the Silk Code Authority in the prolonged strike of 1933. These events have already been briefly discussed. What should be emphasized is the extraordinary contrast between Silk City and the South. Paterson was a labor town, even in decline, with a long tradition of labor conflict—and collective bargaining. Silk workers, be they dyers, jacquard workers, broadsilk weavers, or hatband workers, had been represented over the years by a bewildering complexity of unions, often short-lived, often local. Some, like the National Textile Workers Union, were frankly militant in their philosophies, others much more accommodationist. What was different in 1933 was that one union now represented all branches of the silk industry, and that was the UTW. The other point worth noting is that in one respect Paterson and Gastonia were the same—Paterson was as much a silk town as Gastonia was a cotton one. Its workers had no interest in the textile industry's other branches; what happened in Easton or Lancaster, Pennsylvania, also silk towns, had some meaning for them, but not events in Hogansville, Georgia.[31]

The 1933 silk strike was, as has been noted, the first directed against the NRA's code provisions—in this case the temporary silk code—which had completely failed to comprehend the historic differences within the industry, especially the wage differential between the skilled weavers of Paterson and those paid in the other silk states, producing lower-quality fabric for the mass market. Add to that the fact that the code seemed to protect the "cockroach shops," together with the generalized, industry-wide anger at the stretch-out, and the long tradition of labor militancy, and the walkout is easily explained. Moreover, sophisticated silk union men saw the potential of section 7(a) in aiding their drive for a closed shop, provided it could be made more precise, and this was a further potent reason for striking.[32]

The 1933 silk strike paralyzed much of the industry from September till early December. The dyers settled in late October, gaining wage rises, recognition of the UTW as their bargaining agent, and, most significant, agreement that no one should have to run more than one eight-foot dye box, their particular stand against the stretch-out. In return, they pledged not to strike during the course of the one-year agreement. The broadsilk workers did not settle until December, also gaining wage rises, a restriction on loom coverage, and recognition of the UTW as their bargaining agent. Moreover, Paterson's weavers had their wage differential maintained; indeed Pennsylvania and Rhode Island silk men would not have settled had they been forced to pay Paterson's wage rates. The city's manufacturers did insist that, in return, the weavers also accept some restriction on their right to strike in the future. They successfully proposed the creation of a nonpartisan industrial relations board to which all future disputes had to be referred and a ban on further strike action by Paterson's weavers unless and until 40 percent of looms elsewhere in the industry were certified as idle. In the euphoria of their December victory, few unionists had thought through the implications of this clause, yet it was to be crucial in determining Silk City's response to the general strike call in September 1934.[33]

There were delegates from Paterson at the UTW's convention in August 1934, but their role was muted despite the support of the American Federation of Silk Workers for a general strike. Indeed the city's manufacturers were quick to point out that even if the rest of the silk workers heeded Gorman's strike call, there would be no strike in Paterson, the contract signed the previous December precluded it. As for neighboring Passaic, it, too, was expected to remain quiet. How could it be otherwise there, with the woolen mills "at their lowest ebb" in many years, with only 2,500 woolen workers employed out of nearly 24,000, with no union presence, and with most of the plants closed for a week, not from fear of industrial violence, but because there was no work to be done.[34]

Yet the strike did come to Silk City and to the desperate Passaic Valley. The NTWU caused a brief flurry of concern when rumors circulated that it was about to merge with its former "arch enemy," the Associated Silk Workers, in order to form a united front to fight the strike. This would have been anathema to the UTW leaders, and Eli Keller, general manager of the ASF, was quick to scotch the notion. Keller was at this time under tremendous pressure from the national strike leadership. Having called out the silk workers, Gorman was desperate for Paterson's weavers to join in, the 1933 agreement notwithstanding. Paterson was still Silk City after all, its past labor battles already part of the UTW mythology, something to be used in the coming struggle. For this reason, therefore, he was happy to certify on September 4 that more than 50 percent of the nation's silk workers had already struck, thus relieving Paterson's weavers of their constraints.[35]

Gorman's figures were so vastly inflated as to be fictitious, something he probably knew full well. Certainly J. J. Kehoe, chair of the city's industrial relations board, did not believe them. In an angry statement he agreed "that when a total of 45,601 silk and rayon looms in the producing areas outside of Passaic and Bergen counties had been stopped due to the general strike, the Paterson union members will be declared free to join the general strike without incurring any liability under the contract dated December 29, 1933." This figure had not been reached, he asserted; the union had not even come close. The Paterson weavers, due to walk out at 10 A.M. on September 5, would therefore be in breach of the agreement they had signed less than a year before.[36]

But they came out anyway, disregarding Kehoe, disregarding Peter Van Horn of the Silk Code Authority, who agreed that manufacturers operating under the code were perfectly prepared to meet the strikers' demands as to the stretch-out, wage rates, and hours of work. They would not concede code recognition of the UTW, however, though individual plants and sections of the industry were perfectly free to do so. In calling out the weavers, Keller insisted that as more than 40 percent of looms outside the city were idle, the 1933 agreement had not been breached. Again Kehoe was vehement in his denial, while Van Horn estimated that less than 15 percent of the nation's silk workers were out. Moreover, he pointed out that due to depressed market conditions, only 4,000 of Paterson's looms had been operating the previous week, less than 10 percent of capacity. Thus, to talk of a mass walkout was scarcely accurate. This mattered little to the 1,500 weavers who crowded into the local union headquarters to hear Frank Schweitzer, general secretary of the American Federation of Silk Workers, declare that "the eyes of the country were on them." Paterson was the "key to the success of the whole silk strike," he shouted over tumultuous applause. As Silk City went, so would the industry.[37]

What of the dyers, the other key to strike success? George Baldanzi, president of the American Federation of Silk and Rayon Dyers and Finishers, very much wanted Paterson's support, something the officials of local 1733 were keen to give. The problem was that the agreement they had signed in October 1933 contained no escape clause, as the weavers' had; it allowed no local strikes during the course of the contract. Could this and should this be broken? Baldanzi and the local thought so; McMahon and Gorman believed otherwise. For the union to abjure such a good agreement at this time would be disastrous public relations, they reasoned. So, off to Washington went Baldanzi and the men of local 1733 to try and win the strike leadership over. Meanwhile the dyer plants kept running, and management took out full-page advertisements reminding their workers what they had won in 1933.

1. Recognition of the affiliated unions of American Federation of Labor.
2. The highest wage paid in the entire textile industry.
3. A five-day, forty-hour week, as provided by the code authority of the NRA.

This agreement, they told workers, was binding until October 24, 1934. Management had "abided by its terms sincerely and honestly." They expected their employees to do no less.[38]

The manufacturers eventually had their way. Tiring of the national strike leadership's indecisiveness on the matter, they eventually sought redress through the New Jersey Court of Chancery, seeking an injunction preventing the UTW "and its agents from striking, picketing or even discussing a walkout in the dyeing industry" during the course of the current agreement. Vice Chancellor Charles Egan proved sympathetic, granting a sweeping order restraining dye house workers from striking and also restraining Gorman from advocating otherwise. Gorman, by this time preoccupied with the unhappy course of the strike elsewhere, and especially the violence in Rhode Island, had already decided that this particular fight was not worth it, and that the UTW decision to call the dyers out should be rescinded. Without them, of course, the strike in Paterson was weak; though the jacquard workers did briefly join the weavers, the dyers, as the largest single industrial group, were essential to its success.[39]

Attention in the strike's second week now turned to Passaic. Despite the extremely depressed conditions in both the woolen and cotton mills there, and the fact that the workers were largely unorganized, the UTW leadership decided that they should try and reestablish a presence in what had once been a center of national industrial attention, hoping to capitalize, in particular, on memories of the battles of 1926. Accordingly, William F. Kelly, UTW national vice president, spoke there on September 3, reminding his audience of their proud record of struggle, and urging them to reenlist in the war. "Your strike in 1926 was a sectional strike," he told them, "but this war embraces the entire country. . . . Strike along with us and we will win a victory for democracy," he concluded, announcing that picketing would begin the next day. Accompanying reporters could not help but notice the general lack of enthusiasm among the 600 who turned out to hear Kelly speak. Their memories of 1926, perhaps, were not positive ones.[40]

Passaic's workers had their collective memory jogged even further the following week with the return to the city of Albert Weisbord and Vera Buch, the charismatic duo who had led the 1926 wool strike. At that time, they had been enthusiastic members of the Communist Party and its labor auxiliaries, which were in the vanguard of the drive to forge a new, socialist America. Since then, their revolutionary careers had taken a dive. Founding members of the NTWU, both had been involved in its disastrous southern adventure in Gastonia in 1929. Subsequently quitting the party one step ahead of the purgers, they formed in 1931 a new leftist organization called the Communist League of Struggle, which attracted neither money nor a following. Living precariously and powerlessly on the fringes of America's splintered Left, they were, not surprisingly, drawn back to the scene of past glory.[41]

Weisbord's reemergence could hardly be called a roaring success. Only about 200 turned up in Pulaski Park, scene of many of his passionate orations in 1926, to hear him speak, and they were notably unenthused at his insistence that "the eyes of the textile world were on Passaic." This was not a local fight; it was a national struggle, he shouted, and President Roosevelt was as much the enemy as the NRA and the manufacturers. This was not what the crowd wanted to hear, given that most of them were likely to be unemployed anyway. They began to heckle their onetime hero. Discomfited, Weisbord called them "slackers" for not joining the cause and angrily left the podium. He did, however, leave word that he would be at "105 Monroe Street to talk to any of those who desired further information." The likelihood that he was mobbed by enthusiastic supporters is small. The industrial world had changed profoundly since 1926. Weisbord, like so many others had found that "you can't go home again."[42]

Passaic's mayor, John R. Johnson, despite strong evidence that most of the town's workers had no interest in joining the strike, had decided that peaceful picketing would be permitted there—under certain conditions, the most important of which was a guarantee of open access to those plants that were operating. Daily Keller brought striking weavers from Paterson, who duly picketed under the watchful eyes of the local police. However, when some workers at the Eureka Print Works decided to join the strike after all, Johnson decided there was a limit to community tolerance. The next day, declaring that as "all employees in the mills want to work" there was thus no need for continued picketing, it was henceforth banned in Passaic. Police then forcibly broke up those picket lines already established.[43]

This was too much for local labor leaders and for the American Civil Liberties Union, who announced that they would be seeking an injunction against the mayor. Keller, for his part, decided to lead a picket line at the Botany Worsted Mills as a symbolic protest. Accordingly, about 900 strikers from Paterson drove past the mill in trucks, alternately taunting the mill workers and inviting them to join them in their protest. They then stopped the trucks and climbed down to march past the Botany plant but were met by Passaic's finest, "grim-faced police with upraised clubs." Their weapons were soon put to use. The crowd was dispersed, and Keller and two supporters were arrested. Meanwhile the Botany Mills workers watched from their windows, showing "but an apathetic interest in the disorder outside the gates." Quickly released, Keller insisted that the picketing would continue, though not necessarily in Passaic, tacitly acknowledging that the strike had little support in that depressed town. Rather, they would let the Court of Chancery settle that particular issue. New York's liberal community was up in arms, however, and threatened a full-scale invasion of the town's textile center. Again, police were at the ready, but only one invader eventually arrived. This was Mrs. Corliss Lamont, wife of the head of the ACLU and a prominent New York socialite. The "slender, stately brunette, attired in a blue tailored suit," posed for photographers in front of the Botany Mill, but, finding no picketers present, quickly returned whence she came. By the time the Court of Chancery was ready to hear the ACLU's request for an injunction, the strike was over and the point moot, as Johnson had withdrawn his no-picketing order. He was, he said, "manifestly pleased" to do so.[44]

Back in Paterson, the strike had stalled. Gorman never called the dyers out; the jacquard workers were always divided and, indeed, Gorman in the end decided that their 1933 contract, too, should be honored and told them to go back to work. Only the weavers stayed out till the national declaration of "victory," and, as Van Horn had pointed out, most of them had not been working anyway at the strike's beginning. The "cockroach shops," of course, totally ununionized, continued to operate throughout September. In his enthusiasm, Schweitzer may have claimed that Paterson was the key to the national strike's success. The reality was that Paterson was to the strike, and the strike leaders, somewhat of a sideshow, as the city had become to the silk industry itself. It was hardly surprising, therefore, that Keller came to spend most of his time in Passaic.[45]

When the national strike was over, and Paterson's weavers prepared to return to work, they found their employers in a defiant mood over whether their December 1933 contract was still valid. The employers had made it clear that once they struck on September 5, that was the end of the matter. They considered that the weavers had unilaterally abrogated the agreement, thus relieving them of any further obligations under it. When the workers returned, it had to be understood that those were the terms. Most workers were forced to return under these conditions, particularly as Keller had recommended they do so, pending further negotiations with the manufacturers. There were some who wished the strike to continue, however, in defiance of the UTW national leadership, and that revealed a serious split within the local branch of the Associated Silk Workers Union. Indeed, a group of dissidents, mainly former members of the NTWU, stormed the strike headquarters, denouncing Keller as a "scab," and Gorman as a "big bum." "Throw out the leaders—they have betrayed you"—one shouted, urging the weavers to continue the struggle. They were not heeded, and by the end of the week most who had left their looms were back at work, many with their wages cut, the 1933 contract effectively dead. Involvement in the national textile strike had scarcely brought them better lives.[46]

What of the dyers, whose situation Gorman had never gotten around to addressing in September? Still angry, they continued preparations to strike once their 1933 agreement had expired. Out they went on October 25, demanding a closed shop, a 30-hour week, and an hourly pay rate of $1 for men, slightly less for women. Reluctantly, Gorman sanctioned their action—he was in no position to do otherwise actually—but he refused to allow the broadsilk workers to join then, despite the policy of wholesale wage cutting in which their employers were by now engaged. The employers, hoping to avert even more strife, offered local 1733 a guaranteed 57.5 cents an hour for a forty-hour week, continuation of the present contract, and enhanced union recognition, but they still would not countenance the closed shop. The strike, affecting 25,000 dyers in New Jersey and New York City, lasted till December. The closed shop was always the major obstacle, the one point the employers refused to concede. Local 1733 was eventually forced to accept that reality. They went back to work on December 4 having won a 36-hour week, a 66-cents-an-hour minimum wage for men, 48 cents for women, and an agreement that employers would henceforth fill future vacancies with union men, but would not dismiss nonunion workers currently on the job. The agreement was to run for two years and also included the establishment of a joint labor board to which all future disputes would first be referred. Local 1733 of the Federation of Silk and Rayon Dyers of America had won a significant victory, for, through attrition, the closed shop would eventually come. No wonder Paterson's streets were crowded on December 3, as 7,000 dyers marched and danced in a massive "victory parade." Lost sight of in the celebration was the important fact that the crucial solution to the closed-shop issue, the clause which brought the two sides together, had been proposed by a federal government conciliator, Nathan W. Shefferman of the National Textile Labor Relations Board. Increasingly, the federal labor bureaucracy would be a key player in the reconciling of labor disputes.[47]

Industrial peace would remain precarious in Paterson. The next year the broadsilk weavers were again out, but the outcome for them was much bleaker than that achieved by the dyers. The issue concerned the "cockroach shops," by now clearly the majority of the city's silk producers and easily able to undercut those few larger firms still in business. A *New York Times* report got to the root of the matter. "These shops," it asserted, "worked for the most part by the town's poorest citizens," had "multiplied rapidly during the past six years." They were easily set up; cheap looms were always available from bankrupt firms, or they could be bought on easy terms. The depression had meant that there was plenty of space available as well. Paterson's manufacturers had always seen unions as their main adversary, especially so after the paralyzing strikes of 1913 and 1919. Indeed, they had contributed to the growth of the "cockroach shops" by trying to buy off striking weavers, suggesting that they set up shop for themselves, sometimes lending them money to do so, certainly promising commissions to get them started. Yet unions had never been the main cause of Silk City's decline, argued the report. Rather, "ruinous competition" had killed off the larger plants, and this the manufacturers had contributed to by their encouragement of these family concerns. Belatedly, they now realized this. Their weavers were out, with UTW sanction, in a protest strike against the family shops, trying to force their owners to meet union conditions for their workers. In this, for once, they had the tacit support of their employers, who had come to see this as their only possibility of survival. But it was far too late. There was no chance of "a general contract," mutually suitable to the large-scale manufacturers, the commission weavers, and the city's 270 family shops, being negotiated. The strike collapsed, and with its failure, so collapsed

Silk City as a union town and as a major textile center. The family shops had won.[48]

Even more than in Pennsylvania, the course of the 1934 strike in Paterson illustrated how different its impact was on various regions of the United States and on the branches of the textile industry. Even the terms of the discourse would have been incomprehensible to the young strikers of Hogansville, Georgia, or even Gastonia, North Carolina, let alone the complexities of the structural issues the silk workers had to negotiate. In Gastonia, in Greenville, and in Huntsville, the strike was a climacteric, a precipitating event, which set the course of industrial relations within southern textiles for decades to come. In Paterson it was merely another episode in a tumultuous history of the labor conflict which accompanied industrial decline. What had already happened the previous year, the 1933 strike and its outcome, was infinitely more important, and, indeed, decisively shaped the nature of the town's 1934 response. The weavers' strike the following year, too, had more significance, in that its failure symbolized Paterson's demise as the nation's most visible silk-producing center. In that context, 1934 was a mere way station of minor significance.

In Paterson, the only issues of concern were the decline of the silk industry, Paterson's position within it, and the operation of the silk code, in particular, its failure to reflect the historic differences in silk's regional organization and wage structure. These were complex matters, their origins rooted in past battles and management decisions, and were far removed from those besetting cotton textiles, for example. Workers understood the NRA codes differently as well. Paterson's weavers and dyers, with their strong traditions of organization, hoped to use section 7(a) to achieve the closed shop, an advance they believed, mistakenly, would halt their decline. Cotton mill workers saw 7(a) differently—and much more simply. For them it was a chance to increase their strength; it provided a hope, at least, of negotiating some genuine redress of their basic grievances.

Nevertheless, there was some commonality to be found between the largely ethnic labor force in Paterson or Passaic, and the Anglo-Celts of the southern textile mills. Both had had enough of the stretch-out, of their employers forcing them to tend more dye boxes or run more spindles, and had welcomed the NRA codes as a means of checking the practice. When it became clear that their employers had no intention of compliance, they prepared to strike. Then, when it was similarly clear that the increased pay the codes seemed to promise would not be forthcoming, this fired their resolve. Most important of all, however, and common across the regions, was the conviction of all textile workers that they were being used, betrayed, denied the better lives that the New Deal had seemingly promised. This was why they walked out, in Paterson no less than in Pawtucket, Rhode Island, or in the Carolina Piedmont, considered the strike's epicenter, to which we now turn.[49]

Chapter 6

The Carolinas

DESPITE THE STRIKE'S IMPORTANCE TO THE WOOLEN and silk workers of New England and the mid-Atlantic states, it was the cotton mill people of the South who had provoked it. Their grievances, their desperate anger, had forced a reluctant UTW leadership into action, and it was in the southern mill counties that the strike would be won or lost. The crucial battleground would be the Carolinas, a fact recognized by all: the UTW leaders, Sloan and his associates, and the increasingly engaged national media. Moreover, within the Piedmont, Gaston County, North Carolina, with its more than 100 mills, far the greatest number of any county in the nation, and its 25,000 workers would be the strike bellwether. If the UTW could win there, it might then be able to control the whole region, or so Joseph Shaplen thought. There were other centers almost as important, however—Spartanburg and Greenville in South Carolina, Durham, Greensboro, and Concord in the Tarheel state. All over the Piedmont, in fact, the cotton mill towns were soon to become the multiple sites of battle.[1]

The strike's first days, as has already been noted, clearly belonged to the UTW, as the "flying squadrons" sped along the highways and back roads, bringing out mill after mill. Gaston County was by no means the only place where most mills were quickly closed. In Spartanburg, Greensboro, Chester, Shelby, and Gaffney, all over the Piedmont and beyond, mill workers, in Bryant Simon's words, "stood firmly behind the union." In Durham, North Carolina, the strikers shut down all the cotton mills in the town, and they remained closed throughout the strike, as the town's workers joined the flying squadrons operating throughout the state, their families sustained by gifts of food and credit from sympathetic local merchants, a good example of Janet Irons's contention that the strike held

Picketers outside a textile mill in Greensboro, North Carolina.
Library of Congress, LC USF 33–020924–M3.

strongest in those communities where past experience and demography had forged strong bonds between millhands and the general population. In Columbia, South Carolina, support for the union was so strong that no picketing was needed to keep the mills tight shut. And yet, even in the strike's first week, with the flying squadrons operating freely, and the manufacturers on the defensive, no more than 70,000 of about 111,000 cotton mill workers were idle in North Carolina. The number was higher across the border, perhaps 40,000 out of 65,000, but the strike in the Piedmont was never total, no matter what the union asserted. Scores of mills continued working throughout September. Again to quote Simon, "flying squadrons could not crack some of the . . . [m]ost hardened antiunion fortresses. Strikers made only shallow inroads into those communities most recently rocked by labor unrest," like the Horse Creek Valley, or "where discrimination, the recruitment of rural laborers, evictions, and blacklistings robbed workers of a core of indigenous activists." Then came the National Guard, the killings at Honea Path, and the strike leadership's consequent decision to abandon their most potent weapon, the flying squadrons. From that time, the strike in the Piedmont was on the defensive. Only a few more mills came out; many more reopened, often with guards and special deputies standing by, bayonets at the ready. Through it all, Gastonia and Gaston County remained firmly fixed in the national focus. For many, what happened there *was* the strike, and for that reason alone, the local course of events merits detailed investigation.[2]

They marched in Gastonia on Labor Day 1934, for the first time in the city's history. The day was crisp and clear, as a "monster parade" made its way down Main Street shortly after noon. The *Gastonia Daily Gazette* estimated that there were about 2,000 in the line, but other observers put the figure much higher, closer to 5,000 in fact. Mill girls dressed in white and proudly waving the Stars and Stripes were in the lead, then line after line of grim-faced workers followed. The marchers proudly carried placards supporting the forthcoming strike, other union banners, Blue Eagle standards, as well as their American flags. They stepped along with spirit,

Labor Day parade in Gastonia, North Carolina, September 4, 1934.
Library of Congress, LC US 262–123745.

Mill girls striking in Gastonia, North Carolina, September 1934.
Library of Congress, LC US 262–123746.

but there was "no disorder," the *Gazette* noted approvingly, while at the same time their very solidarity shocked many Gastonia residents, who feared for the social order. The strike represented "the gravest emergency which has confronted our people since Reconstruction Days," asserted one such. Though the *Gazette,* a tool of the millowners, deplored the general turn of events and the prospect of further "wild disturbances," the editor remained impressed by the Labor Day turnout. It was indeed "a monster parade," he conceded, and, as such, signified that a real problem did exist. After the parade had ended the participants rallied in the town's main park. There, amid cries of solidarity, local UTW leaders outlined their strike plans. There would be extensive picketing of local mills when they opened the next day with the heaviest concentration at the gates of the Loray Mill, the most obvious local symbol of class power.[3]

The *Gazette* was far less sanguine about the parade which took place in the city the following day, when the "flying squadrons" reached town. Twenty-eight cars and two trucks, all packed with strikers, arrived from

Belmont, closing mill after mill and picking up supporters as they journeyed. When they passed through the city's Loray Mill section, "throngs of strikers gathered there cheered uproariously," as film newsreel crews frantically tried to record the parade's progress. These spectators were mainly young, said the paper, "idle women, boys and girls, looking for excitement" but with no orderly leadership. They reached the Ragan Spinning Company at 11 A.M. Its management had been forewarned of the crowd's progress; nevertheless the strikers' behavior on reaching the mill took everyone by surprise. They did not come to the office, complained a furious Caldwell Ragan, the mill's treasurer, as decent folks would have done. Instead, they "broke into" the plant, pulling the switches, stopping all work, "without giving us any chance to close it ourselves." Mill management, he said, "had to go into the mill and call the mob together from among our spindles." Ragan's sense of proper order had been well and truly violated by this action, and he said so with all the anger he could muster. It "was a damnable outrage," the way he and his fellows had been treated. "I addressed the numbers of the mob from a platform," he informed the sympathetic press, "and told them what I thought of their outrageous conduct, in this running through the mill without first coming to the office and making known their demands which we were prepared to grant, if in reason." The strikers were unimpressed. They booed him soundly, but agreed to let him have till 1 P.M. "to clean up our mill," when it would be closed, ready or not. Ragan complied.[4]

"The Loray Mill Division of the Manville Jenckes Co., of Pawtucket, R. Island here is not abiding by the code," wrote Carl W. Welch of Gastonia, North Carolina, to President Roosevelt on December 11, 1933—recall once more his desperate words. He had been working "full time three shifts which should not have been allowed," he went on to say, moreover as soon as "the people here tried to organize a union" they either lost their jobs or had their hours drastically reduced. The Loray Mill, however, was no different from others in Gaston County, he said. In Bessemer City the American Mills, notorious even by Gastonia's standards, were "working their women 12 hours a day and paying $12 a week." Complaint to the local NRA authorities was useless: "they say they will see about it and that is all there is to it." Welch well understood that the president had not heard of conditions in Gaston County, otherwise he would have moved swiftly to rectify them. "I know and all the poor cotton mill people know that you are doing everything in your power to help us." But somehow the millowners had so far not got the message. They were "letting their mills stand because by want to [*sic*] big a profit." He knew, too, that the president had "the worst job in the world with all the chiselers kicking against you," and he assured him that "the poor people are for you 100%." Nevertheless, it was becoming urgent that "you put all these mills back at work," and he hoped the president did not mind him saying so.[5]

Welch's letter was typical of hundreds that the president and General Johnson received from the desperate textile workers of Gaston County, the nation's "combed yarn manufacturing center," which by 1934 would boast more mills that any other county in the nation. They all echoed its twin themes of abuse of the code's provisions and intimidation of those who protested. Above all, they complained of the stretch-out. "Since the NRA came into force," wrote C. H. Lowe, another Loray employee, "they have hired an [*sic*] discharged two thousan [*sic*] people," as those who remained were forced to cover more and more machines. "Winter is just around the corner," she warned, and with so many of Gaston County's workers without jobs, "there is going to be a lot of suffering." John R. Moore, president of UTW Local 1312, told Bruere that both the Flint Mill and the Groves Thread Company had raised mill village rents 40 percent the day the code went into effect and had installed electricity meters on all houses. The stretch-out had been applied so viciously, he continued, "we have to do so much or we can't make nothing." Most Flint and Groves employees were earning no more than $5 weekly, less two dollars deducted for "cold [*sic*] and wood." Disillusioned and angry, Gastonia's workers increasingly looked to the federal government for relief, for as Lucy Mays told "Dear Roosevelt," the millowners were manifestly not "doing us write [*sic*]."[6]

Gastonia, "the city of spindles" and the county seat, had in 1929 been the site of the most sustained of the wave of strikes which rocked the Piedmont's textile mills that year, an event which both bitterly divided the community and which soon passed into the mythology of American labor history. In April young organizers from the National Textile Workers Union, an affiliate of the Trade Union Unity League, the Communist Party's industrial arm, taking advantage of the bitter discontent prevailing among workers at the Loray Mill, the largest in the Piedmont, led a strike, with some brief success. A combination of inept Party leadership, however, and the violent antipathy of the mill management, supported by local and state law enforcement authorities, and a ferocious, mill-directed vigilante group, the Committee of One Hundred, proved too strong, and by mid-May the strike was all but over. Then, the death of Gastonia's police chief, Orville Aderholt, the subsequent arrest and trial of the strike leaders deemed responsible, the climate of violence which this engendered (culminating in the slaying of a local strike leader, Ella May Wiggins), and the insistence of the party leadership on using the trial to further their revolutionary call all served to sweep Gastonia into national, and briefly, international focus. Those eventually convicted of conspiring to murder the police chief were exalted as heroes of the class struggle by some, perpetrators of alien notions and revolutionary violence by others. The citizens of Gastonia found themselves in a riven community; the strike and its aftermath opened wounds which had scarcely healed half a century later.[7]

Never again did the National Textile Workers Union venture southward, its leadership having learned the bitter lesson that the South was indeed foreign territory and that the party, if it had any future there, was more likely to find it among the region's black sharecroppers than the white textile workers with their ferocious and easily exploitable racism. Nevertheless, the conditions that had brought the NTWU initial success in Gastonia had not changed. Wages remained low, the stretch-out was intensified, and men and women continued to lose their jobs and to live in conditions of increasing degradation and poverty as the depression bit ever deeper. In vain did William Green, the conservative president of the AFL, warn manufacturers that such conditions could not continue. Speaking about Gastonia's year of violence to the Senate Committee on Manufactures, he ridiculed the notion that the workers had been duped into following a false ideology. "These southern workers know nothing about the philosophy of Communism; they do not know what it means," he asserted. "It is all Greek to them, but in their hour of distress they accept the support and the help of anyone who extends the friendly hand." Management did not listen as workers in Gastonia and throughout the Piedmont grew "ready to explode."[8]

Initially, Franklin Roosevelt seemed to have extended that hand through the NIRA, and especially through section 7(a). In Greenwood, South Carolina, workers "frolicked" in the streets upon hearing the news of its signing. Soon, they were flocking to join the UTW, secure in the knowledge that the president wanted them to do so. By August 1934, at least 300,000 had paid their dues, of whom 16,000 were in Gaston County.[9]

Joining the UTW meant little, however, unless the manufacturers also wanted them to do so. The writer Hamilton Basso who was in Gastonia just before the strike began, wrote in the *New Republic* of the deep mood of betrayal within the worker community. "It is impossible to emphasize the faith they had in the code," he said, but nothing much had changed. "About the only thing the NRA has brought the Southern textile worker," Basso thought, was the conviction that he had a right to join a union and even this the millowners were determined to deny. Basso called the coming strike "the big showdown," claiming "it is to the textile worker what the San Francisco strike was to the longshoreman." It would define where textile workers stood "with the administration," and vice versa, and whether the code meant anything, or was "just another scrap of paper." Gastonia's workers knew well what the stakes were and stood ready for the battle.[10]

Joseph Shaplen, the seasoned southern correspondent for the *New York Times,* who had covered the events of 1929 for his paper, thought that "labor sentiment had grown tremendously" in Gaston County in the past five years. Though the Communists had gone without trace, belief in unions had not. Symbolically, "elaborate plans" had been made to strike the Loray Mill again, while local UTW officials were confident that the response to the strike call would be well-nigh unanimous. Gastonia's employers conceded that support for the strike was high. H. McKelvie, resident agent for Manville Jenckes, said that the Loray Mill would be closed at the first hint of trouble, so determined was he to avoid the violence of 1929.[11]

The *Gastonia Gazette* was quick to remind the community of what had happened five years before. "Let Us Keep Cool Heads in Gaston County" urged its headlines, as the county had had "more than our share of trouble arising from strikes." So "Let the mills close down and remain closed until the differences have been adjusted. Let us not have any picketing. Trouble and bloodshed always comes when there is picketing because there is no such thing as peaceful picketing." The paper had been assured that none of the county's mills would attempt to run in defiance of the strike call, and though "unjust to those who want to work," it was probably for the best, as "those who remember the tragic times we had in 1929 would not desire a repetition. We are all friends and neighbors," was the paper's plea. "Most of us were raised together here in Gaston County. Most of the cotton mill operatives know their superiors by their first names or a more popular and affectionate nickname. The same is true about the operatives. Both they and their superintendents and many of the executives have played baseball many a day." The lesson of 1929 had been well learned in Gastonia and the surrounding mill communities. As the *Gazette* commented, the county and city had still not lived down the "unfavorable publicity" they had received that summer, nor recovered from the social disorder that had occurred.[12]

If the symbolic beginning of the strike in Gaston County was the Labor Day march, it was the arrival of the flying pickets, seasoned veterans from neighboring Shelby County, which got things going in earnest. Shaplen reported they had taken the town so completely by surprise that they quickly shut down virtually all its forty-five mills before fanning out into the country. The Loray Mill did not even wait for the pickets. A nervous management closed it well before their arrival. By the end of the strike's first day, said Shaplen, the "shut down was nearly complete in the whole of Gaston County" which had already become "the principal stronghold of the UTW." In Spindale, picketers stormed four mills, forcing their closure. Many were women, who shouted, "They can't do anything to us. Uncle Sam is behind us." Shaplen was impressed by several aspects of the first day's strike activity in Gaston County: the speed at which the flying pickets worked, their "surprise descents" making it very difficult to prepare for them, the fact that local strikers were quick to join the picketing activity, giving it "the appearance of military efficiency and precision . . . entirely new in the history of American labor struggles," and, above all, that so many women were clearly involved. "Women are taking an increasingly active part in the picketing," he reported, "egging on their men" but also putting their own bodies on the line with a determination that made violence always a probability. Indeed, the strike's first stabbing had occurred during the "assault" on Spindale. There, Charles Freeman had an ice pick "thrust in his back as he attempted to enter one of the mills to report for work." His assailant, reportedly, was a woman. Though Freeman's injuries were not serious, the incident was nevertheless significant, in that it was the first manifestation of a recurring theme during the strike—violence not between management and workers, often aided by state officers, but between workers themselves, between those who looked to the union for relief and those who preferred to stay with the old ways. By nightfall on September 5 the UTW's control of Gaston County was complete. "Not a wheel moved [there] today," Shaplen reported, as North Carolina's governor, J. L. B. Ehringhaus, contemplated the sending of troops, a move his South Carolina counterpart, Ibra C. Blackwood, had already enthusiastically embraced.[13]

Caldwell Ragan's outraged response to the forced closing of his mill, the sense of disorder it engendered, the jubilant cheering, the obvious disrespect for authority the strikers showed, their insolence and brazen conduct, their very youth, and above all, their refusal to "first come to the office" and make their demands known, instead proceeding directly to the operating rooms and pulling the switches was typical of those of management throughout the South. The *Gastonia Gazette* called the action of the picketers, "mob's law, anarchy,—a group of ignorant boys and girls following in the wake of two or three head-strong, dangerous scattered-brained youths," more concerned with posturing before "the admiring eyes of some of their feminine followers," than in talking responsibly with management. Those thrown out of work were anxious and bitter; the general tension level in the county was rising, and "if the mobs kept roaming around the country seeking trouble they will find it, and there might be bloodshed." Still, it was probably best, the paper thought, to wait it out, despite all the provocation, for a few days more, then "this tension will have eased a bit, and things will be much easier to adjust and pacify." Nevertheless, the guard might yet have to come again to Gastonia.[14]

Certainly there were many, both in Gaston County and throughout the state, who were pressing the governor for action. John W. Haynes of Lexington, the president of Clifford Mills, chided him for failing to maintain the right to work, "at any cost against the anarchist, communist brigands and union leaders now roaming at large over North Carolina, destroying property and intimidating employees who have no grievance and only wish to continue to earn a living for themselves and their families." A petition from the employees of Gastonia's Hanover Mills requested "that troops be sent here immediately" so that they could all go back to work. "If possible get them here tomorrow," the petitioners implored. Meanwhile, strike observers reported "every textile plant in Gastonia is closed" and support for the strike in Gaston County generally to be exceptionally strong. There were daily rallies in the town, wrote Jack P. Lang of the state department of labor, which were enthusiastically attended. Workers carried banners bearing slogans such as "Make the Chiselling Manufacturers Meet Our Terms," he said, while rally speakers emphasized that the president was on their side. "As long as the Stars and Stripes are over the White House we have a friend that will protect us," explained UTW organizer George F. Kendall, "The President has said we could strike." Gaston County, then, like so many other communities, was divided between those who wished to go on working, and those determined to claim the benefits they believed the NRA had given them, and secure in the knowledge that the president backed their cause.[15]

Governor Ehringhaus did start mobilizing the guard on the evening of September 5, using the growing disorder throughout the South, especially the activities of the flying squadrons, as his excuse. The first troops were not sent to Gaston County, however, but to Marion and Concord, where the threat of violence seemed more pressing. Gastonia remained quiet, as, indeed, did the whole county, but with all its 104 mills shut down. *Charlotte Observer* reporter Legette Blythe, who had covered the drama and violence of 1929, was surprised by the relative calm. "Gastonia, center five years ago of one of the greatest industrial upheavals ever to take place in the United States," he wrote, "was quiet yesterday," and with no indication that "disorder might develop." The community, he thought, had learned from those painful months, and the terrible events which had devastated Honea Path the day before would not be repeated there.[16]

Troops would, however, come to Gastonia soon enough. On September 8 a delegation of 14 Gaston County workers went to Raleigh to see the Adjutant General of the North Carolina National Guard, J. Van B. Metts. They wished to return to their jobs, they said, but were prevented by picketers from doing so. They begged him to send troops to protect their right to work. Fifteen Loray Mill workers made a similar trip the very next day, bearing with them a petition for protection signed by a further 802 of their fellows. Though there had still been no violence in the county, the governor had the excuse he wanted. He ordered three guard companies into Gastonia immediately. Though jeering picketers delayed the opening of the Loray Mill overnight, shifts started the next day, returning workers protected by the national guardsmen's bayonets in scenes, thought Legette Blythe, all too reminiscent of 1929. The arrival of the guards had changed the equation in the "textile capital of the world"; management, on the defensive in the strike's first days, was now beginning to regroup. As well as the symbolic Loray Mill, four other Gaston County plants had reopened by September 12, all under National Guard protection, and others planned to do so as soon as more troops arrived. Though John E. Cuthberton, president of the Gastonia Central Labor Council, angrily declared that "the mills in Gastonia are closed and will stay closed," the reality was otherwise, and tension increased throughout the county.[17]

The Gastonia community was clearly divided. On September 10, 1,500 nonunion workers had marched to city hall, demanding protection in order to be able to return to work. Moving on to the courthouse, they filled it to overflowing, cheering one of their number, J. D. McCullough, "a lean, brown, bare-headed figure in shirt-sleeves," as he spoke of his desire to feed his family. Because of the strike he had to "come up town and beg for something to eat," he complained then broke down in tears. Gastonia's mayor, E. B. Denny, said he sympathized with their plight and certainly supported the dispatch of a delegation to Raleigh pleading for more troops, for in the end the community could not "set by and let children starve." It was in this context that some of the city's mills once more started to run.[18]

Nevertheless, most of Gaston County mills stayed closed during the second week of the strike despite the presence of the National Guard and the growing tension between workers themselves. Partly, this was because management did not always share the keenness of some of their workers to return. Since Gaston County's warehouses, like those elsewhere, contained plenty of unsold goods, there was no compelling need to maintain high levels of production. Moreover, the violence of five years ago had had its effect, or so Blythe thought. To force mills to open "might precipitate bloodshed," and that the millowners wanted to avoid. They "would rather stay idle," they had told him, "than embroil the community in violence even resembling that of 1929." It was important symbolically to get the Loray Mill working again, albeit at a very limited capacity, and to get a few more going as well, just to demonstrate who was now regaining control. Still, by the end of the week only five of the county's 104 plants were operating, as much due now to the reluctance of management to force the issue as to the strength and solidarity of the workers. Shaplen thought there was good reason for management's nervousness. The Loray Mill had only opened after 600 picketers had been forcibly held back from the gates by guardsmen aided by "scores of armed deputies"; more guardsmen had been rushed to Gastonia in order to keep it open, and strikers were now openly and angrily taunting the troops. A "showdown" was surely due in Gastonia, he feared.[19]

Despite this, by the end of the strike's second week, support for the UTW remained strong in Gaston County. J. L. Hamme, a Gastonia attorney with strong ties to the UTW, tried to explain why. "In this immediate vicinity the heads of INDUSTRY, are forcing the violence," he told Ehringhaus. There was no doubt, he insisted, "that the strikers of this community are acting in the only possible manner in which the benefits of the NRA may be realized." The aim of the New Deal was to spread employment, he said, and this the workers knew well. For the manufacturers, however, there was no such obligation, hence their increasing of the stretch-out. "Let's put some pressure on industry to respect it's [*sic*] solemn contract," Hamme requested the governor. The state should be supporting the textile workers in their struggle, not impeding their efforts.[20]

Specters from the county's violent recent past now resurfaced in the district. First came Paul Crouch, a Communist Party organizer, who had visited Gastonia from time to time during the 1929 strike. He briefly reappeared in nearby Charlotte, denouncing both Gorman and Governor Ehringhaus in equal measure and urging strikers not to abandon the struggle, but simply to leave the UTW. The strikers were not amused by the suggestion that they return to those who had led them in 1929. They threatened to lynch Crouch, forcing local police to lock him up "for his own protection." A few days later his wife, Sylvia, a local strike leader in 1929, and a NTWU worker, Belle Weaver, were arrested in Gastonia for distributing handbills urging workers to continue the struggle under their leadership. They, too, were menaced by UTW members and held briefly for their own protection. In nearby Concord, another "presence" from 1929, Caroline Drew, was discovered and arrested at the home of a local striker. She had with her a handbag containing, among other items, an identification card belonging to Amy Schechter, former "fiery participant in the Communist disorder" of 1929. The Communist Party had had no influence on the strike's course in Gaston County, as was the case elsewhere. Nevertheless, the arrival of these people in the community, with their connections to 1929, added to the quickening tension and prompted the formation of local vigilante groups.[21]

Shaplen's "showdown," when it came, occurred not in Gastonia but in neighboring Belmont. On the night of September 17, after strikers had subjected guardsmen stationed there to sustained abuse—"the vilest and filthiest . . . that could be heaped on one human by another" was how the *Gastonia Daily Gazette* described it—a fracas occurred. Tension had been high at Belmont since the strike's beginning, and that evening it overflowed. A mob, led by women, one reportedly "carrying a six month old baby in her arms," attacked Belmont sheriff Clyde Robinson outside the gates of the Knit Products Company, dragging him from his car with threats of "we're going to beat you up." Guardsmen quickly surrounded the sheriff, there was a brief, fierce struggle, and when it was over, the sheriff's automobile was revealed to be extensively damaged, and two men lay severely injured by guardsmen's bayonets. One of these, Ernest K. Riley, a Mt. Holly striker and UTW member, died soon afterward. There were allegations, strenuously denied, that the men who stabbed him had been drinking heavily, and a vigilante band formed in the town.

Riley's funeral was an occasion for workers to reinforce their class solidarity. More than 2,000 attended the simple service, including Riley's wife and seven children. She was proud of her dead husband, she said, immensely so, for he had died for a noble cause, "he died for organized labor." Her eighth child, born the day after her husband's funeral, was solemnly dedicated to the cause of the UTW.[22]

Jonathan Daniels, editor of the *Raleigh News and Observer,* the state's most liberal newspaper and the only one to show some balance in its reporting of the strike, used Riley's death to probe the deeper meaning of the tension of the past fortnight. "There will be plenty who will regard the corpse of Ernest H [*sic*] Riley as that of a striker, well damned and well dead," he wrote in a remarkable editorial.

> There would be plenty who would make him the martyr of an economic warfare. But there ought to be some who see in his death the basis for a chilling fear that in the midst of all our shining new machines, all our intricate processes designed to set man free and make him full, man himself remains where he began so very long ago in a cave and there slowly learned to fashion man's first tool, and perhaps his last, out of the flint or the saber tooth of the saber-toothed tiger.

The violence in Gastonia in 1929 had taught the millowners little, he despaired. It had all so easily come back.[23]

There was, of course, a military inquiry into Riley's death. Principal witness was the young commanding officer of Company B, 105th Engineers, whose men had been guarding the Knit Products Mill, Capt. Sam Ervin. The young man spoke in great detail about the night's events and painted a dramatic picture of the confrontation that occurred between the "mobs" of at least 3,000 people and the 60 officers and men under his command. In the course of his description he angrily refuted the allegation that some of his men had been drinking on duty. "The conduct of the soldiers, patrolmen and officers on duty at the mill was excellent throughout they [*sic*] day and night of September 18th [*sic*]," he insisted. The future United States senator, like every other witness, could not identify which soldier had bayoneted Riley. The court of inquiry eventually found the act to be lawful anyway, a sad event which had occurred during the dispersal of an "unlawful assembly," which had become a riot. In such circumstances, Riley's death was "a justifiable and excusable homicide," and there was no useful purpose in trying to identify the individual perpetrator. Riley's family and fellow unionists thought otherwise and made periodic attempts to have Governor Ehringhaus reopen the case, but to no avail. In the circumstances, the governor was pleased that the strike had cost only one North Carolina life, and for this he was willing to accept, modestly, much of the credit, for that had been his only purpose in calling out the guard, "to preserve order and prevent bloodshed."[24]

Meanwhile, the strike was fast collapsing everywhere, as hunger, poor central organization, and state repression eventually had their effect. It would have to be said that Gaston County held out more solidly than most as even more troops moved into the area in the wake of the Belmont stabbing. At the beginning of the strike's third week, 171 mills remained closed in North Carolina. About half of these were in Gaston County. Still, even there, people were drifting back to work. Ten mills had reopened in Gastonia by September 21, two in Dallas and Belmont, and seven in Cherryville. With further openings planned throughout the week, and with the picket lines steadily diminishing at those still closed, it was clear that the strike was running out of steam, even in its fighting heartland. Gaston County's local strike leaders, like those everywhere, greeted its end with relief, knowing they could have sustained the effort little longer. The *Gastonia Gazette* rejoiced that the "whir of the spindles and the music of the looms" could once again be heard in the city, following "three weeks of silence in Gastonia's great industrial plants." There was "a general spirit of optimism and rejoicing on all sides" that all would soon return to normal—as if the strike had never happened.[25]

But what would happen to the strikers? They were not long in finding out. Gastonia's workers, like those throughout the South, marched back to the mill gates in triumph, there to find out how hollow Gorman's "victory" was. In nearby Shelby, they marched in silence, "following a gently flowing large American flag, upheld by three stalwarts," whose grinning features told eloquently of their triumph. As always, the reality was different. True, the tensions eased, and the troops soon went away, but the mills remained closed. Sixty of Gaston County's 104 mills were still shut nearly a week after the strike's end, as owners considered carefully whom they wanted to have working for them in the future, ignoring UTW charges of "blacklisting and discrimination." And "blacklist" and "discriminate" they did. The *Gastonia Gazette* explained why. Some strikers "who indulged in violence and threats against person and property are not being employed and will not be," the paper stated, a position it found perfectly reasonable. No one described the strike's local aftermath better than Ruby Mitchell, a member of the Loray Mill's negotiating committee, whose despairing accounts have already been mentioned. "We tried to return to our jobs," she said, but "we were met and turned back before we got to the Mill by 100 bad Men as they are Called, that was appoineted [*sic*] by the Mill officials to keep us out—Those 100 men had knifes—Black jakes—Clubs, and other deadly weapons." When the committee went to talk to the manager, he made his position quite clear. "Before he would work the union help," he promised, "he would Close the Mill down." The union might run the United States, he said, but "He was going to Run the Loray Mill as he saw fit." Those who had struck at Loray, was Mitchell's poignant conclusion, had been "throwed out in the streets to the mercy of the world." There was little mercy available in Gaston County for those who had battled in the strike of 1934, Gorman's victory declaration notwithstanding.[26]

Martha Gellhorn, who visited many textile towns in both the Carolina Piedmont and New England immediately after the strike's end on behalf of the Federal Emergency Relief Administration, reinforced this dismal view. Her reports to FERA director Hopkins made grim reading as she described the lives of "feverish terror" and extreme privation which was the common lot of textile workers, made even worse by the poststrike climate of repression. Gaston County she found particularly depressing. It was, she wrote, "my idea of a place to go to acquire melancholia." Workers were undernourished, inadequately housed, and worked beyond the bounds of human endurance. Indeed, she said, "the health problem" was so bad she did not "know where to begin." There was not one county clinic or hospital in the whole of Gaston County and only one health officer, a man so incompetent that "he cripples and paralyzes his patients who won't go back." The signs of fatigue were easily discernible in faces of the workers, especially those of the young women—old before their time. Add to these general conditions the threat of management vengeance, and Gellhorn's conclusion that Gaston County presented "a terribly frightening picture" seemed an understatement.[27]

Across the state line, in Spartanburg, South Carolina, D. W. Anderson, treasurer of Pacolet Mills, the town's largest employer, believed that the strike call would have little effect in the town. Most of his employees would not leave their posts, of that he was sure. The UTW had prepared the ground well in the district, however, and Anderson's judgment was soon shown to be wrong. By September 3, 18 mills in Spartanburg County were idle; 9,000 of the county's 14,000 textile workers walked out. Their actions were deliberate; management did not close their mills, the workers did.[28]

As if to reinforce their determination, and under the direction of the resourceful J. O. Blum, secretary of the South Carolina Federation of Textile Workers, the Spartanburg strikers quickly formed themselves into a series of flying squadrons. With the local situation under control, Blum's aim was to use the determination of the strikers as a "flying wedge," assisting other less militant locals throughout the state. This ambitious aim was never remotely realized, Governor Blackwood and the National Guard saw to that. Yet, in the strike's first few days, the "roving strikers from Spartanburg" received considerable regional and national publicity as they sped along the back roads of Spartanburg County and beyond, American flags flying from their car hoods, reinforcing local pickets, even taking control of the local effort where necessary in order to close mills quickly. Along with Gastonia, Spartanburg was considered to be the Piedmont's most severely affected center in the strike's first days, and the flying squadrons its most potent weapon—especially after they had enlarged their reach and moved to do battle in Greenville. For Governor Blackwood, and for local law enforcement officers throughout the state, their activities were to be feared, and state officials moved rapidly to resist their encroachments.[29]

Of course, the rumors attending the Spartanburg squadron far outran the reality of its achievements. It was effective only in the strike's first days, and after the twin disasters of the violence in Greenville and the Honea Path shootings, Blum recalled his shock troops. They were "resting up" he said, and preparing to move again into Greenville County. He was at pains to point out, also, that "not a member of the flying squadron is armed," despite all the assertions to the contrary. "Our sole weapon is moral persuasion," he asserted, "and we are simply asking our brother workers for their cooperation in this effort to get justice and to show them the numerical strength of our union." In reality, the massing of the South Carolina National Guard had ended the Spartanburg squadron's effectiveness. Despite Blum's assertion, it would never ride again; it was just too dangerous. Recognizing this reality, as had Peel, Blum disbanded it on September 10; its brief period in the public eye was over.[30]

With the end of the squadron, the task for Spartanburg's workers was to keep the local mills closed—to hold the line. There was little chance of bringing new strikers out; the National Guard was in town to prevent that, aided by "a large number of special officers," deputized in the strike's first hours by county sheriff Sam Henry. Moreover, R. H. Ashmore, commander of the Spartanburg post of the American Legion, was anxious that his organization be given a significant role in the defense of the local community. "If the situation at any place demands that the legion could help preserve law and order," he insisted, "then I think it is the duty of the legion to answer that call."[31]

In this growing atmosphere of repression, and amid increasing calls for vigilante justice, Spartanburg's strikers, "young men and young women," stood resolute. Most mills remained closed, with well-organized picket lines in place. Only in the strike's third week was there any significant disorder. On September 19 deputies used tear gas and fire hoses to disperse a crowd of several hundred which had gathered outside the Powell Knitting Mill, which had been closed since the strike began. There was stone-throwing, the deputies responded, and twenty-three strikers were arrested and held briefly in the county jail. Given the tension elsewhere in the state, Spartanburg escaped lightly, due in large part to the resolution of the strikers. Faced with such determination, local manufacturers, even in the third week, and with the strike effort flagging, decided not to provoke violence by using the guard to force mills open. It is significant that the incident at the Powell plant occurred only after six female stockroom workers had been smuggled inside. To the strikers this was the thin end of the wedge.[32]

Nevertheless Spartanburg's strikers were relieved when Gorman declared victory. They were hungry and knew they could not hold out much longer. The fact that Roosevelt had reportedly approved the settlement was particularly reassuring to them. "We'll do anything for the president," one picketer remarked on hearing that FDR had asked them to go back to the mills. "And the President is going to play fair with us." Their faith in the New Deal undimmed, Spartanburg's strikers marked the strike's end with a "gay parade" along Main Street. Marching behind a United States flag, "blaring horns," singing, with "happy faces," they stopped all traffic in the town. Then they stopped picketing and presented themselves for work, confident in their victory. Some mills opened promptly and took all their workers back. Indeed, D. W. Anderson of the Pacolet Mill joined the members of UTW local 1994 in celebration. There was a chicken supper and a dance outside the plant, with music provided by the Pacolet Mill Band, followed by a parade of over 1,000 workers down to the center of town. Anderson reportedly marched partway with them. Other employers were not as forgiving. Generally, the mills opened slowly; returning workers were screened against lists of strikers and UTW members, and, as elsewhere, some were never taken back.[33]

If Spartanburg, as historian Bryant Simon has pointed out, was as solidly prounion as any textile center in the state, neighboring Greenville was the opposite. As more than one-third of South Carolina's nonstrikers resided in Greenville County, it is scarcely surprising that the city became the state's prime battleground. Spartanburg's flying squadron achieved its notoriety there as strikers fought management and state power for control of the plants and the streets. "In preparation for the strike," Simon has written, "Greenville managers further strengthened their defenses by arming loyal workers with pistols and picker sticks. When the UTW did finally call out its followers," the governor responded with extra troops. "The combination of private and public might," he argues, "and the specter of eviction of local activists that would inevitably follow a union defeat, . . . allowed the owners to keep their machines running." Despite the support of the Spartanburg squadron, Greenville's repressive atmosphere ensured that the struggle there was lost.[34]

On September 6, 1934, Deputy Sheriff R. L. Putnam shot and killed John Black, an unemployed worker with a reputation as a hothead, close to the Dunean mill in Greenville, South Carolina. Black had been watching a noisy strike demonstration at the mill gates when Putnam ordered him away, angrily "telling him he didn't work there and had no business whatever on mill property." Black left, furiously vowing to return. When he did so, Putnam, claiming he saw the flash of a knife in Black's hand, shot him several times at close range, the first fatality since "the strike turmoil descended on the area," said the *Greenville News*. Probably the reason for the shooting was more personal than political, for it transpired that Black and Putnam had been bitter rivals for the favors of an "unnamed" woman for years. If so, the deputy had used the tension of the strike situation to settle the score.[35]

Certainly Greenville was tense enough that September. Easily the most important textile center in South Carolina's Piedmont region, which was why the UTW had chosen it as the southern strike headquarters, the town had also long been a center of regional unrest. There had been strikes there in 1929, 1932, and again throughout 1934, and fearing the worst, Governor Ibra C. Blackwood had rushed guardsmen to the city as soon as the strike call went out, in accordance with well-laid battle plans. Within days, "Khaki legions of South Carolina's National Guard" roamed the city and ringed the mills with orders to shoot to kill "if rushed by pickets." As has been mentioned, city police and special deputies reinforced them till the "vicinity fairly bristled with guns, bayonets and clubs." Nonstrikers began taking their weapons to work, in contravention of local ordinances but with the quiet connivance of the authorities. In neighboring Easley, townsmen and workers had bought up all the arms and ammunition available in the town's two hardware stores, as the district "prepared for armed conflict."[36]

Greenville's textile workers had welcomed the textile code with jubilation. When its signing was announced on June 16, 1933, they had frolicked and danced in the streets and public places, and a few days later paraded, in more solemn mode, through the town in support of the textile code and in solidarity with the new president. Yet their celebration was short-lived. From the code's adoption, complaints flooded in concerning the way in which the town's many mills had conspired to subvert or ignore its provisions.[37]

As was the case everywhere in the South, the majority alleged that since the code's implementation, stretch-out conditions had become much worse. Dorothy Taylor told the president on February 11, 1934, that the American Spinning Company's weavers had walked out that day, and "stoped [*sic*] all others from their work." This wildcat action was supported by their fellow workers, however, for the weavers were "only asking for the right things"—an end to the stretch-out. The management was "not going by your codes at all," she informed FDR. Rather they had "got the whole mill speeded up until they are working the People to death." There was no time to eat lunch; in the spinning room "the hands are doing as much work in 8 hours as they did in 12 hours." Long-term workers had been laid off, basic safety precautions ignored, and, most galling of all, the mill had been fenced; the gates were now kept locked, "and when you are sick and want out you have got to walk nearly a mile to hunt the gate man." In short, management were now "treating the people worse than convicts."[38]

"The people aint struck for higher wages," Taylor assured the president, "but they want a new supt. and to get rid of the minute man and to be treated like human beings and not like slaves." They wanted the "stretch-out taken off them"; they wanted to be allowed to "speak to each other at work," as had once been the case. In short, they wanted a little dignity in the workplace, a measure of control over their lives. "Mr. Roosevelt ever [*sic*] one knows you have done a great part by the people and we are asking your help," she concluded, "may gods rirches [*sic*] blessing rest on you, and that you may all be happier thru the coming future." Taylor asked that her name not be disclosed, as "they would never work me any more and will make me move" if management learned of her complaints, a request the Cotton Textile National Industrial Relations Board, to which her letter was referred, ignored. What happened to her subsequently cannot be known, yet in her plea to the president, she caught precisely the plight of the textile workers, their fading hopes, their great desperation, and their faith that through President Roosevelt they may yet find a better future.[39]

Mrs. Dill, another employee, also wrote to the president about the February walkout. Like Taylor, she stressed that they were not asking for more money but for the removal of the superintendent, an end to the stretch-out, and decent treatment. "The supt. don't want you to leave your work long enouhgt [*sic*] to get a drink of water," she complained. H. E. Trammell, head of the mill's grievance committee, was equally specific. The weavers had walked out, he asserted, not in search of higher wages, but because of the speeding-up of their looms, which "produced overwork," but also bad work, in which they could no longer take pride. A routine investigation, incidentally, found mill management innocent of the violating of any of the textile code's provisions, but by this time the strikers had returned to work, their grievances unanswered.[40]

Workers at the Conestee Mill walked off the job in late July, after a long series of complaints to the Bruere Board of systematic ignoring of the textile code wage rates, of mass sackings, and of a particularly onerous stretch-out situation, allegations which board investigators, even with their predilection to support the management, found justified in part. Yet nothing changed, the walkout was a final act of desperation, eventually sanctioned by George W. Smith, local UTW organizer. This certainly prompted counteraction of a sort. A posse of specially sworn-in deputies was recruited to guard the mill and disperse pickets, and within a week eviction orders were served on those striking workers who happened to be members of the union. Syble Brown, a sixteen-year-old striker described the scene for Eleanor Roosevelt. Had she been in Conestee that morning, she said, she would have seen "shining guns Looking [*sic*] in the face of poor Gray [*sic*] headed widows," who were simply seeking their "wrights" [*sic*]. In 1928 her mother, a weaver and a widow with five small children to support, had run 22 looms, and made from $19 to $22 weekly. By 1934 she was running 60 looms, at about half her former wage. She simply could not keep up the pace, so "they turned her off" without warning, leaving the family destitute. They had recently organized a union in Conestee, she said, to try and stop such illegalities, and the strike was their last desperate resort. But they had been met with guns, further sackings, and now evictions. "There is [*sic*] many hungry women and little children here this morning," she told the First Lady, imploring her to send help, for "you and Mrs. Perkins is [*sic*] the greatest women in the world." Again, the walkout at Conestee, like those in

Alabama, was an act of desperation, and it prefigured what was soon to happen throughout the Piedmont and beyond.[41]

Throughout Greenville's many mills the pattern was similar, with complaints of rapidly deteriorating work situations and diminished rates of pay since the textile code came into operation. Minnie Stone, of the Dunean Mill, told Hugh Johnson of what was becoming a common practice, and that was the replacement of town-dwelling workers, usually in the mill village, and with some tradition of full-time work, with farming folk who would presumably work for less. Moreover, they were unlikely to be as favorable to the union as those for whom mill work was all they knew. "I never have seen this mill this way before," she explained, "taking Jobs [*sic*] away from the employees on the hill and giving to people living in the country what can make a living." People like her had "nothing to look for to make a living, but mill," she wrote desperately, but management cared nothing for that—"they don't go by law, they go by their own rule." Management were not even "paying the wages they are suppose [*sic*] to pay," Stone alleged, "they have went against the code."[42]

Most of Greenville's mills, in fact, seemed to have "went against the code." At the Easley Cotton Mills, men prominent in the UTW local were all discharged despite section 7(a) and despite proven records of long and good service to the company. Ed B. Smith attempted to use his influence as president of the local branch of the Improved Order of Red Men on behalf of D. C. Bush, a former employee of the Poinsett Mill. Bush had been fired, Smith told South Carolina senator James F. Byrnes, for no reason other than he had testified against the mill at a code authority stretch-out hearing, having been pressured by federal officials to do so. Three of Smith's daughters were dismissed at the same time. Women at the Matthews Mill who complained at being "stretched to the limit," were told by their "boss man" to quit complaining "or go home and nurse [*sic*] our baby." "Mr. Roosevelt your honor," implored one of them, G. C. Hudson, "I do know your hands are full. But please hear me just for pity sakes," and send someone to investigate, and "if it is in your power please give the Matthews Cotton Mill a new set of bosses." Bruere Board investigators did check out her complaint but, as was normally the case, found no evidence of code violation. Bush's complaint was also found to be unsustainable. True, he had testified at a stretch-out hearing, but he had been sacked for inefficiency at the workplace and refusal to obey his supervisor, nothing more. Indeed, said the Poinsett plant's general manager, W. B. Perrin, "he had instructed overseers to lean over backward with reference to any employees who appeared, or were willing to appear" at the hearing. No doubt some employee complaints were spurious or mistaken, arising from personal grievances or a misunderstanding of the code's provisions. Nevertheless, the sheer volume of complaints is what impresses today. Greenville's mills, for whatever reasons, were places of tension, dispute, and desperation. Too many barely literate workers poured out their pleas to those whom they believed might help to be in any doubt of that. Little wonder the UTW leadership chose the town to be its southern strike headquarters.[43]

Millowners in Greenville had prepared for the expected strike more thoroughly than anywhere else in the nation. For months sheriffs' deputies had attended union meetings, had trailed union organizers, and had recruited a small corps of paid informers. The town's Ku Klux Klan chapter, allegedly made up of mill overseers, had been fanning the flames of antiunion sentiment for months, while the mills had systematically purged their work force of the most prominent prounion workers. Management was determined to keep Greenville's mills running, and in the atmosphere of repression which they had created in the preceding months, their chances of success were high. According to Bryant Simon, by the time the strike call sounded, many Greenville workers were quite simply "afraid to strike."[44]

Certainly the strike started slowly. The *Greenville News* reported that only about 11 percent of the county's workers had obeyed the strike call, and though the town was tense, all mills were still running. Indeed, the atmosphere was "as quiet as a Sunday School picnic," with workers in most plants having voted emphatically against supporting the strike. The only exceptions were the Dunean and American Spinning plants. There the afternoon shifts had to be abandoned due to insufficient workers reporting for duty, while picketers declared their intention of keeping both mills from opening the next morning, and this despite the presence of the National Guardsmen. Nevertheless, though the air was tense, management's prestrike strategy seemed to be succeeding.[45]

It was the flying squadrons which changed the situation. The next day the local press reported that a "howling, threatening" mob, about 500 strong, and well armed with clubs and other weapons, was on the move in the Piedmont, closing mills as they went, and heading straight for Greenville, determined to crack the "stronghold of antistrike sentiment." Most of them were from the heavily unionized towns of Spartanburg, Gaffney, and Cowpens, with the Spartanburg squadron particularly prominent, and they meant business. Posing for newsreel cameras, members time and again stressed their determination to close down Greenville's mills. In response, a second guard unit arrived in the city, and Greenville citizens nervously awaited the battle to come. Many, in fact, called on Governor Blackwood to declare martial law. "We believe prompt action on your part imperative," telegrammed F. W. Poe, if the Honea Path shootings were not to be dwarfed by the expected violence in Greenville. The very air was heavy with foreboding.[46]

The battle for Greenville began in earnest around noon on September 5. The Spartanburg squadron had reached the city's outskirts, after having closed down 5 mills in Greer the day before. Arriving in a motorcade of 105 vehicles draped with American flags, which stretched for over half a mile, they proceeded to the town's four largest mills—Dunean, Victor Monaghan, Judson, and Woodside, gathering local support as they went. These they surrounded, shouting to the workers inside to "come on out—we won't hurt you," and there they met the South Carolina National Guard. At the Dunean mill, the guard's captain, Harry Arthur, told his men not to be afraid "to shoot to kill," if necessary. "This is the hard-boiled company of the outfit here," he informed waiting newsmen. "My men have instructions to shoot and shoot to kill if any effort is made to rush them: not to wait for anything else." To reinforce the point, the "troops jabbed menacingly forward with their bayonets whenever union pickets pushed towards the mills but shed no blood."[47]

Fortuitously, no one was shot in Greenville that long afternoon, though disorder reigned in the streets. Both the Dunean and Judson mills closed for brief periods; the other two remained open. The most serious violence occurred at the Judson mill, during the 2:30 P.M. shift change. As the workers filed out they were roundly abused by those picketing, and "several women armed with clubs began bouncing the clubs off the heads of women workers." Several were badly bruised, and one was knocked unconscious, though no one, seemingly, required hospitalization. As he rushed to their rescue, Deputy Sheriff Charles Batson was himself attacked by a group of strikers. He drew his pistol, but before he could fire, guardsmen had forced back his would-be assailants, probably preventing more serious injury. At the Woodside and Victor Monaghan mills, the guardsmen's presence confined the disorder to a few scuffles between strikers and those still at work, always likely in the charged atmosphere of the strike, while at Dunean management decided to send its workers home for the afternoon. For Mason Turner, a local strike leader, this represented victory. "We've got Dunean closed down and were all going to keep it closed down," he asserted.[48]

In fact, the events of the afternoon of September 5 represented a decisive victory for Greenville's mill management, and showed already in which direction the national strike was going. The flying squadron departed the next day, leaving all the mills operating under the guards' protection, as the aroused citizenry continued to clamor for the imposition of martial law. The tension contained, local and school authorities decided, for example, to delay the opening of the school year lest the town's children be menaced by the striking hordes. It was in this context that deputy Putnam shot and killed his rival in love. Moreover, there were a few further instances of disorder. At the Woodside mill on September 7, guardsmen used tear gas to disperse a crowd of several hundred attempting "to rush troops and reach workers who were drawing their weekly pay envelopes at the mill office." The strikers' phalanx was led by women, again draped in American flags, to which they drew attention as they moved toward troops guarding the mill's office. "You ought to respect the flag," these women reportedly shouted as they approached the entrance. "Get of the way. We want to see the management."[49]

The appeal to the flag, so general a feature of the strikers' imagery during 1934, had no effect on the guardsmen. They charged at the women with bayonets fixed, drove them back across the street, and then released their tear gas grenades. Quickly the crowd dispersed. It was the last such confrontation to be seen in Greenville during the course of the strike. By the end of the week, all the town's mills were in full operation, even Dunean. Indeed, workers there were reputedly so grateful for the guards' intervention that they wrote an open letter to Governor Blackwood thanking him for his actions in enabling them to stay at their looms and spindles. The guardsmen remained on duty but in a much more relaxed atmosphere, even allowing themselves to be photographed chatting with female picketers. The picketers themselves swapped their more aggressive actions for square dance sessions on mill property, accompanied by a string band. The "flying squadrons" did not return, recognizing, as did southern strike director Peel, that management had won the battle in Greenville. Nevertheless, those who had taken part in the strike, albeit briefly, found, as did workers throughout the region, that there were no jobs for them anymore, despite the conditions on which the strike was settled. Scores returned to the mills on September 24, only to discover that the new workers who had replaced them during the strike were to stay in their jobs. Around 800 Greenville workers, those who had obeyed the strike call and had stayed out, would not work in the town's textile mills again.[50]

The strikers never had a chance in Greenville. The careful planning by mill management as the strike deadline approached, the early deployment of the troops, their effectiveness in limiting the activities of the Spartanburg "flying squadron" on September 5, and their continued presence in the town all ensured that the mills would remain open, that the brief measure of success enjoyed in Gastonia or Spartanburg would not be repeated. As such "the battle for Greenville" on September 5 was a central event in charting the direction of the strike throughout the Carolina Piedmont. It showed, decisively, which way the wind was blowing.[51]

In Anderson, South Carolina, indeed throughout Anderson County, the mills were largely unorganized, and their employers were confident that, left on their own, Anderson's textile workers would ignore the strike. Indeed, employees at both the Orr and Anderson Mills quickly voted to do just that, support which prompted local business houses to pay for a full-page advertisement in the town newspaper congratulating "the Textile Employees of Anderson For Sticking to their Work." They were all "proud of the high type workers of the community," ran the text, "and we are impressed with their action in considering local problems on their own judgement for the best interest of themselves, their families, their city, their State and their Nation."[52]

But would they be able to maintain this position, the town's leaders wondered, as the flying squadrons came, and as the tensions increased throughout the state? Rumors that Anderson County was next in line after the battle of Greenville was over prompted much concern, despite the moving of additional National Guard units into the area, though not to Anderson itself. Then came the shootings at Honea Path, only a few miles from Anderson. Workers and employers alike were horrified and determined to resist any attempts by "flying squadrons from Spartanburg or Greenville to force them from their frames." Little matter that the battle in Greenville had already been lost, and that the Spartanburg squadron had gone home for good, the transformation of Anderson from dusty mill town to "armed camp" quickly occurred, a potent symbol of the tension the strike had aroused in so many similar communities.[53]

People came to work in Anderson with pistols, rifles, and shotguns. These they "laid on their machines" as they went about their tasks. The town's only recreation space, Cater Park, was taken over by the sheriff's office, headquarters for a force of "six hundred specially deputized mill workers and ex-servicemen," armed to the hilt and ready for battle. Every member of the police force was on duty, quickly trained in the use of "special tear gas apparatus." The "people's army" comprised representatives from every mill in the city, having been specially sworn in at a mass meeting. Anderson County sheriff W. A. Clamp explained that Governor Blackwood had asked him to enlist enough citizens to maintain law and order, and to organize them "along military lines." There was plenty of "arms and ammunition available," he assured anxious citizens; moreover, Clamp and his men had developed a complicated system of signals and alarms, including use of the city's fire alarm bell, which would provide ample warning of any invasion.[54]

The deputies were left in no doubt as to the seriousness of their task. E. E. Epting, president of the local American Legion Post, believed their current call was just as vital to the country's interests as the one they had answered in 1917. R. E. Ligon, general manager of Gluck and Equinox Mills, conflated the two crises even further. "What right have foreigners to come here and tell you what to do?" he asked the assembly. "I want to see our mills run all they can, for Anderson County's welfare depends more upon the mill people than any other group." After the battle of Greenville was over, Sheriff Clamp, now preoccupied as he was with events at Honea Path, conceded that the threat of a general invasion of Anderson had receded somewhat. Consequently, he broke up the 600-strong force into smaller units and sent them to guard individual mills. The company of World War I veterans were kept together, however, under the command of Ben Cleveland, a decorated survivor of the French battlefields. Their intelligence wing, using radio equipment, planned to monitor the strikers' planning sessions, and then, using "pre-arranged signals," would mobilize the whole "protective force within a few minutes," if necessary.[55]

The necessity never arrived. The "invasion" was nothing more than the creation of the community's anxious minds. Most of Anderson's mills remained operational throughout the strike. The guards remained on duty, however, ready for trouble. They were particularly concerned lest strikers "crippled" the power lines, and the veterans in particular were exceedingly watchful against this. Indeed, to accommodate the demand to be part of the town's defense, Sheriff Clamp swore in even more deputies. One thousand were on duty at the end of the strike's second week, as Anderson's residents, having heard of the violence in Rhode Island, in Burlington, North Carolina, and in Polk County, Georgia, were thankful that through their vigilance and resolution, they had saved their town from similar disasters.[56]

By turning itself into an armed camp Anderson avoided any disturbances during the strike of September 1934. Most of its mills continued working; its millhands, their employers, and the general community alike experienced mild paranoia, but that was all. Elsewhere in Anderson County, in Honea Path, people were not so lucky. There the community hysteria which brought out the veterans in Anderson spilled over into the single most savage bloodletting of the whole strike.

Fifteen-year-old Mack Duncan smelled trouble the minute he turned up for the 6 A.M. shift at the Chiquola Mill in Honea Path, South Carolina, on Thursday, September 6. The strike had deeply divided the mill community, and one shift had already stopped running. As he approached the mill, he saw a huge crowd massed at the gate, mainly strike supporters, and he was able to get inside only with the aid of a policeman. Once inside, he was given a picker-stick and told to use it if any strikers tried to disrupt their work. "These were hickory" he recalled, "and they were hard." Some inside the mill carried rifles and trained them on the angry strikers outside. He did not see what happened, Mack Duncan recalled, but "all of a sudden you heard shooting. I don't know whether you've ever been around where there's a lot of fireworks going off, but I'd say for about five minutes it was just a din, bang, and it was bad." When the shooting stopped, six strikers lay dead, another critically wounded (he died later), and upward of a score had been hit. The killings at Honea Path was the strike's bloodiest single incident. As George Stoney and his interview team discovered, the memory of it remained forever seared in the minds of those who were there.[57]

Honea Path was a small mill community of 2,740 people in Anderson County. Its one industry was the Chiquola Mill, which so dominated the town that its superintendent, Dan Beecham, was also the mayor. It was also a thoroughly class-divided community. The "people up town" did not associate with the mill folk, Mack Duncan remembered. "They looked on them, as the colored people say now as white trash" and called them lintheads. Mill children were not even allowed to attend the town grammar school but had to go to one owned by the company. It epitomized the company-controlled Piedmont town.[58]

Isolated as they were, Chiquola Mill workers rejoiced when the Cotton Textile Code briefly promised them a better life, and like workers everywhere wrote their bitter letters of complaint when it did not deliver. Sweepers and cleaners were both doing more work than ever before, asserted T. E. Adams, but were receiving, in effect, $3 a week less due to reclassification. "It takes men to do it [the work] and never get caught up," he said. L. B. Killey apologized for intruding on Hugh Johnson's "valuable time" but wanted him to know that since the adoption of the code his job as a sweeper had been so downgraded that he was now earning little more than the "colored women that use water and chemicals to clean the floor," yet he, and all the sweepers were "white men, a lot of them with families to support." These, and similar complaints, received the usual, noncommittal letters of acknowledgment but no further action.[59]

Partly for this reason, the UTW came to Honea Path. By September about half the Chiquola workers had joined the local, an impressive enough feat, given Honea Path's isolation, the management's ferocious hostility and the relative lack of outside support for local organizers, but one which exacerbated the tensions in the community. Once the strike call had gone out, these boiled over. Not enough went out to close the mill completely, but one shift had to be shut off. Mack Duncan recalled the tension of the time. "After the people struck, they began picketing the mill," he said, "and as we'd go to work they'd try to stop us and talk to us, keep us from going in. . . . If some of the strikers saw you they'd make the scab sign at you, saying you was a scab." The tension increased daily; strikebreakers, many reportedly new workers from nearby farms, needed police escorts to get through the angry picketers at the mill gates. There were constant shouting matches and fistfights between the warring sides, and after three days the community was "near the breaking point."[60]

Then came the rumor that a flying squadron was coming to Anderson County, hoping to force its mills to close completely. This was enough for Sheriff Clamp, who swore in his 600 special deputies to help him repel the threatened invasion. At least 70 of these were from Honea Path, many of them nonstriking mill workers there. These deputies would all be armed, the sheriff warned. Indeed, he "had several machine guns available for use." By dawn on September 6, a number of these men had taken up positions inside the mill, that seems certain. Kathy Lamb, whose grandfather was a night watchman there, told the Stoney team that he had been sent home early, but not before he saw armed men arrive, many of whom he recognized as nonunion workers. Mack Duncan saw them, too, their guns "sticking out the mill windows." Some were very young, "to me they were boys," he claimed. "They weren't men, but some of them were a real good shot with rifles."[61]

Before dawn on September 6, a flying squadron left nearby Belton to join the crowd already at the Chiquola mill gates, many of whom had camped there overnight. Local supporters, singing hymns and some, as usual, waving American flags, were there to meet them. Inside, as Bryan Simon reported, "longtime lawmen, newly deputized officers, and the mayor readied their defenses." Beecham quietly swore in about 100 extra officers, bringing to 126 the total of special policemen on the mill grounds. They were all armed with shotguns and pistols, as the nerves of everyone present stretched to breaking point. There were the usual heated arguments, and here and there a fistfight, as nonstrikers reported for work. Duncan witnessed one of these, between Buck Shaw, a striker, and a nonunion man named Cummings. Shaw hit Cummings on the head with a picker stick, somebody else hit Shaw, and it was on. There is no doubt that the strikers were spoiling for a fight, nor that they had effectively blocked the mill's main entrance. Yet they had clearly not anticipated what happened next, when, in Duncan's words, "all of a sudden you heard shooting." [62]

"Sudden shots from pistols, shotguns and rifles blotted out the two-man fight" was how the *State* reported the brief burst of gunfire that ended the strike at the Chiquola Mill. "One striker after another dropped to the ground, dead or wounded," claimed another eyewitness, to be "carried away as pickets retreated." No one knew who fired the first shot, the reporter went on to say, and that is as true today as it was then. What can be said is that while the strikers and the flying squadron members carried clubs and picker-sticks, those confronting them had guns and had been told to use them if there was any threat to the mill. Management had even secured one of Sheriff Clamp's machine guns firmly in place—only to find that no one knew how to operate it. [63]

That did not matter. The rifles and shotguns did their deadly work well enough. How long the shooting lasted is not known, some witnesses thought two minutes, others five. What is indisputable is that after it stopped the space in front of the mill resembled, according to some there who had seen them, the battlefields of the First World War. Everyone who could had fled, leaving only the dead, the seriously injured, and those who stayed to offer them comfort. Many remembered "the agonized sobs of the women as they rushed to the sides of their dead." Mack Duncan never forgot the scene, "I got sick myself from seeing so much blood," he recalled. R. A. Aitkin also remembered the shooting. He saw several men die, but what stuck with him most was the sight of a town policeman and a mill supervisor finish off two men who had already been knocked down. "Lee Crawford and Ira Davis, they shot them after they knocked them down on the ground," he said. "Kicked 'em over and shot 'em again. And when Yarborough was standing up with both hands up, they shot him in the back with buckshot." Ethel Aitkin, his wife, tried to flee the scene as soon as she saw the guns, but after the shooting had started, she stayed to comfort the dying. She recalled cradling one man's head in her arms and fanning him as best she could with his hat until he died. Both the Aitkins had no doubt where the shots came from. "The non-union was inside the mill shooting 'em outside the window. If there had been guns on both sides there'd have been plenty of killing. It was just like shooting a hog in a pen." Later autopsies confirmed that the dead had all been shot in the back. "Old man" Yarborough had ten separate bullet wounds. Sue Hill's father had five bullet wounds in him, including two in the back. Her uncle, Jess Michael, had been a local UTW organizer, and she remained convinced that her daddy had been deliberately murdered as a consequence. For Sue Hill, for the Aitkins, indeed for all who lived through those few minutes, their lives, and those of everyone in the Honea Path community, had been irretrievably altered. "It was never the same town anymore," Hill asserted. "You were kind of afraid to talk because you didn't know who was for the union and who was against the union." Before long, the town's demography reflected this division. Strikers overwhelmingly lived in one section, nonstrikers in another, and Dan Beecham still controlled both.[64]

As Janet Irons has pointed out, it was not long before a myth grew up around the events of September 6, one indeed encouraged by authorities at the time, and that was that the killings were a tragic accident, the result of fistfights between strikers and nonstrikers outside the mill which had got out of control when someone pulled a gun. There had been no advance planning, no order to shoot, the tragedy was simply a product of the tension of the time. Those who were there knew better. Dan Beecham had killed her father, said Sue Hill. He and his men were inside the mill, and he "told them to kill everybody that was on the mill ground if they could." Kathy Lamb's father, James Hughes, was similarly definite. Though only eight years old at the time, he had seen the whole battle. The "union men" had not gone to the mill that morning "looking for trouble," he told an interviewer. They were unarmed. It was the police who had "done the shooting," and the shots had come from inside the mill, from the second-floor windows, just as Mack Duncan recalled. More than six decades later, there is no reason to doubt such recollections. Indeed, many others, then and later, have confirmed them.[65]

The Chiquola Manufacturing Company refused to permit the mill churches to hold funeral services for the slain strikers. The mourners would not have been able to fit in anyway. Instead, they were held on a grassy bank on the town's outskirts, with some "big trees" for shade. More than 10,000 gathered there on September 8 to lay Ira Davis, Lee

Crawford, Maxie Peterson, R. T. Yarborough, K. M. Knight, and Claude Cannon to rest, as National Guardsmen patrolled the mill property. They watched George L. Googe, southern director of the AFL, dramatically display an American flag, its fabric torn by bullet holes. "See the bullet holes where they shot through the flag on the picket line," he shouted. "This can't go on."[66]

After a chorus of "In the Sweet By-and-By" from representatives of local churches, Rev. James Myers of New York, industrial secretary of the Federal Council of Churches of Christ in America, a man long familiar with mill-management violence, gave the main eulogy. Those who had died, he declared, had done so "for the rights of the hard-working man, who is close to God." They had died fighting for decent working conditions, a cause which dated back "to Jesus' conception that we are all children of God and entitled to better things than we have had so far." Had these principles of democracy been recognized by mill employers, he thundered, "these men need not have died." Trade unions, Myers concluded, helped "lift the lot of everybody." It was "a test of Christian character," therefore to join one, and the slain men should be revered as examples of "Christian unselfishness" for having done so. Those listening frequently interrupted his words with applause and shouts of "Amen." Again, the connection between the cause of labor and the cause of Christ had been well and truly made.[67]

Other speakers emphasized similar points. To tumultuous applause, J. A. Frier, president of the South Carolina Federation of Textile Workers, "dedicated the rest of his life" to leading the textile workers on to victory "even if some of our number should fall by assassin's bullets." John Peel read a message from Gorman, who was unable to attend, which, after condemning "the cruel and senseless death" of the strikers, declared their killing not be utterly in vain if from these sacrifices "we gain a new determination to carry on this greatest of all American strike struggles." Googe, too, took heart from the certainty that as a result of their sacrifice "the New Deal shall come to mean in the fullest what it was intended to mean for labor." The working men and women of America would surely see that Honea Path became "a shrine for the future uplifting of labor in America." As they quietly followed the coffins to the cemetery, most mourners sang the hymn "Thou Art Gone." A few, however, chanted "Remember Honea Path. Remember Honea Path."[68]

All over the county, shocked by the killings, friends of labor called on Roosevelt to act decisively to prevent further outrages. "We deeply regret the shooting down of armless [*sic*] men in textile strike" protested

John H. David of New Orleans, imploring the president to use his powers to find a quick settlement to the strike. The Relief Workers Union of Staten Island remarked bitterly that Roosevelt's "promise to the Forgotten Man had turned into bullets." Hundreds of telegrams and letters reached the Winant Committee offices, expressing similar outrage and calling for urgent federal action both to punish the murders and to prevent further bloodshed. In that sense, Googe's expectation that the Honea Path killings would galvanize the working people of America into action on behalf of the textile workers had some point.[69]

Yet the strike effort in the South certainly suffered as a result. The White House did nothing, while Governor Blackwood, interpreting the shootings as further evidence that South Carolina was in a "state of insurrection," imposed "partial martial law" on September 9. He directed his troops to see that all who wanted to work were able to do so, and it was under military protection that the Chiquola Manufacturing Company reopened on September 9. In response, Peel saw no alternative but to disband his flying squadrons, his most effective strike weapon. To keep them active, he believed, was to risk their being "shot down like dogs," given what had happened at Honea Path. Employers, he protested bitterly, had been given a state license "to arm thug after thug"; if he had advised his squadrons to do likewise, he would have been arrested for insurrection. Besides, he had no stomach for further slaughter. Without the squadrons, the strike effort in the Piedmont was greatly impeded, while the very example of Honea Path showed to southern workers just what they had to overcome. Though the strike front remained intact, the optimism of the first week had ended. For workers at the Chiquola Mill, the struggle was over with the burying of their dead. They were barely aware that their town had gained national attention. Sue Hill believed few had even realized the strike was a general one, so isolated had their lives been. "We thought it just came to our little community," she said. Now that community had to live with its consequences.[70]

There had to be an inquest, of course, into the deaths of the seven men. Ninety-nine people came to Anderson to testify, many relatives, friends, and fellow picketers of those who died. Some bore half-healed bullet wounds sustained during the shootout. Their stories were harrowing and overwhelmingly pointed to a well-planned, coordinated attack, originating from inside the mill. Lily Campbell, for example, said that she saw "Claude Campbell, Tom Stalcup and Charlie Smith shooting from an upstairs window," and that Smith had later shot Lee Crawford "as he lay struggling on the ground," testimony her friends and fellow strikers Angeline Culbertson and Leckey Jones confirmed. Most in fact, identified police officers and special deputies, as well as Dan Beecham, as being responsible, and some even claimed to have heard a mysterious "signal whistle" from the mill just before the shooting began. After two days, the coroner's jury identified three town policemen, including the chief, George Page, and eight special deputies as being responsible for the deaths of three of the men—Lee Crawford, R. T. Yarborough, and K. M. Knight. The other four were deemed to have been shot by "Party or Parties Unknown." The county solicitor thereupon announced that he planned to hand bills of indictment against the eleven so named to a grand jury later in the year, but that was as far as it went. No one was ever found guilty of the shootings.[71]

In Honea Path, people got on with their lives as best they could. Dan Beecham, while taking no responsibility for the killings, did at least offer Sue Hill's mother a job in the mill for life. She had no choice but to accept, despite her hatred of the man she fervently believed responsible for her husband's death. Only after they had replaced the sidewalk on which her husband had died could she "walk in that direction," said Hill. She had a hard life from then on, but then, so did most other folk in the devastated community. It remained a small town, Sue Hill explained, and in such places, "people don't forget very easy." The legacy of the Honea Path shooting still defines the community, as George Stoney and his team were to find. Likewise, in Burlington, North Carolina, the aftermath of the strike polarized the community even more than had the events of September, as a later chapter will attempt to show.[72]

Chapter 7

Georgia and Alabama

ELL BEFORE THE OFFICIAL STRIKE CALL, VIOLENCE and disorder had begun in Georgia. The summer of 1934 had been a bad one in the state's mills. In July, a strike at the Georgia Webbing and Tape Company in Columbus had closed the plant. When management attempted to reopen on August 10, a scuffle between picketers and workers broke out, during which W. R. Sanders, thirty years old, a striker, and a member of UTW Local 1605, was killed. Later in the month UTW picketers at the Atlantic Cotton Mills in Macon attacked a group of black moproom workers as they attempted to enter the plant. One of them, Caesar Cosly, was cut across the back in the scuffle, while a woman had her clothes torn off by the angry crowd before sheriff's deputies gained control of the situation. Macon had been tense all summer, ever since the arrival in the town of a young, activist UTW organizer, Ralph J. Gay, in fact. He had been working there since early June, and his particular targets were the local mills of the giant Bibb Manufacturing Company, whose president, the reactionary W. D. Anderson, was also head of the National Textile Manufacturers Association.[1]

It was at Macon's two Bibb plants, the Payne Mill and Bibb Number 2, that the textile strike officially got under way in Georgia, two days before the official strike call. On August 30, there was violence at the Payne Mill as "a group of from 40 to 50 picketers, many of them women, crowded onto the railroad tracks at the plant and delayed movement of the switch trains for more than an hour." The crowd was eventually dispersed by police, who made free with their blackjacks, allegedly striking one woman on the arm, but not before workers and mill guards had come to blows and angry picketers had briefly held sheriff's deputy Romas Raley captive in his car. There was disorder, too, at the Bibb Number 2 plant, as picketers shouted insults at those entering the mill. "Women mixed their shouts with those of men and pressed towards the fence," a local journalist commented disapprovingly. Concerned at the tension, Gay addressed the picketers, warning them against violence, and urging them not to prevent workers entering Macon's mills. Mill management would surely "plant" agents-provocateur among them, he said, deliberately inciting them to acts of violence, which would then be blamed on the union. "We are going to win this strike" without violence, Gay promised. "If we are going to starve it will be on the picket lines and not in the mills. Don't undertake to mob anybody on the picket line," he implored. "You are winning this strike, but you've got to win it every day. If you get public opinion down on you, you are lost." Police arrested twenty picketers at the Bibb plants that day, and this was before the official strike call. There would be many more arrests to come.[2]

Crucial to the strike effort in Georgia, as throughout the South, was the attitude of the governor, the singular Eugene Talmadge. Normally, Talmadge could have been expected to have supported the state's textile manufacturers, much as Governors Blackwood and Ehringhaus were soon to do. Closely allied with such giants of the industry as Anderson, Talmadge had been busily engaged for months in courting the state's urban business community to add to his rural electoral strength. Moreover, he was becoming openly critical of the New Deal, concerned that the flood of federal money it had generated would undercut his own power base, dependent as it was on the disposition of patronage. In particular, he hated the NRA, both as an unwelcome symbol of the extension of federal power and specifically, through 7(a), its removal of the rights of employers to control workplace conditions in their own plants. Georgia's textile manufacturers, then, confidently expected the governor to support them to the hilt as they prepared to do battle with Gorman and his organizers.[3]

The New Deal was extraordinarily popular with Georgia's voters, however, and Talmadge knew it. In September 1934, he was engaged in a reelection campaign against an opponent, Judge Claude Pittman, who, while a political novice, had enthusiastically wrapped himself in the New Deal mantle and had spoken glowingly of the NRA and its potential benefits for ordinary working people. In response, Talmadge decided to rein in his natural antilabor tendencies and, indeed, to reinvent himself as a friend of the working man. "I am a laborer myself," he told a campaign crowd in the mill town of Dalton, Georgia. "You can look at my hands, and the color of my skin, all tell it." In particular, he emphasized the fact that he had never used soldiers to put down a strike, even when requested to do so. This became a key component of his stump speeches. Talmadge, therefore, was in no position to prime the National Guard as the strike deadline approached. When the mayor of Trion, who was also vice president of Trion Mills, specifically asked him to do so, the governor refused. Local authorities had ample power to deal with any disorder, he averred. Thus the strike started in Georgia with the governor effectively sidelined.[4]

Events in Trion were soon to test Talmadge's reliance on local power. For more than a year employees of the several divisions of the giant Trion Company had deluged Washington with bitter complaints of alleged code violations at their workplace. The company, it was claimed, had only kept to the code for "about three to five weeks," before rearranging its work practices in such a way as to reduce drastically the amount paid to its pieceworkers. Many sent their pay slips as supporting evidence, showing that they had never received the code minimum of $12 for a thirty-hour week. Paul Maxwell told General Johnson that he was only receiving $3 to $5 weekly at the Trion Glove Mill, yet was being charged $6 a week for board. "We Wont [*sic*] you to do same [*sic*] about it," he said. "We can't work for that," thoughtfully enclosing a stamped, addressed envelope to facilitate a speedy reply. B. B. Dimpsey, of Summerville, Georgia, said his wages had been reduced to $9 for a forty-hour week at the cotton mill. He was "loyal to my employers," he said, and "proud" of his job as a "lume" [*sic*] cleaner, "but under changed conditions I can't have a decent living. If I am due to have more under the NRA I would like to have it," Dimpsey concluded. These scores of letters were routinely answered by the sending of mimeographed sheets, complex extracts from the textile code, detailing the correct procedure for filing complaints. "If, after reading the enclosed extracts from the Code," ran the form letter, "you are in doubt as to procedure, the committee would be glad to have you write again." Unsurprisingly, few did. Instead, they listened to the local UTW organizers.[5]

There was also ample evidence that the company dealt harshly with those who made complaints or were engaged in union activity. UTW President McMahon intervened personally on behalf of A. J. Curtis, a UTW member who was summarily evicted from his mill house once his union connection was known, in direct violation of the code. Indeed, so widespread were the complaints against Trion of systematic violation of the code's labor provisions that they were drawn to Bruere's personal attention, though there is no evidence that he took any action on them. The atmosphere in Trion, then, as the strike began, was distinctly ugly.[6]

Trion exploded in violence on September 5, the day after the strike began. Following Talmadge's refusal to send the guard, local authorities swore in forty-six special deputies to protect the plant, especially given the news that a flying squadron from nearby Rome was shortly to arrive to reinforce local strikers. When the Rome contingent appeared, the atmosphere, though undeniably tense, was at first reasonably civil. The strikers first asked the deputies to step aside: "Buddies why don't you give up your guns and join our side?" they shouted. When this request was ignored, the strikers' mood hardened. They moved to disarm the vastly outnumbered deputies, most of whom turned in their arms on request. One, Granville Ball, did not; instead he fired at the crowd then fled into the mill, along with at least two others. Several strikers had been hit, and one, Harvey Burnette, seriously wounded. Incensed, the picketers demanded that Trion's chief of police, Arthur Bloodworth, so far a bystander, enter the mill and arrest Ball. He refused.[7]

Only then did events get out of control. The enraged strikers stormed the mill determined to hunt Ball down. They soon found him, along with Trion's deputy sheriff W. M. Hix, both with guns drawn. A fierce firefight followed. Who shot first can never be known, but when it was over Hix and one of the Rome sympathizers, J. B. Blalock, lay dead, and a least twenty had been wounded. Hix, most observers agreed, had been shot through a window by a youth, "a small boy," who had "levelled an automatic pistol" at him "then shot him again as he slumped on a table." Some said the "boy" was in fact a youth of eighteen, who then fled the scene. He was never identified, nor can the sequence of events preceding the shootings be pieced together. What can be said is that the strike had claimed its first lives.[8]

There was violence and disorder in many Georgia mill centers that day. In Macon, Anderson was as determined to keep the Bibb mills open as Gay was to close them. At a huge Labor Day rally, cheering textile workers, waving banners with "Kill the Stretch-out," "Labor's for the NRA. Where Do the Bosses Stand?" and "Do We Look like Outlaws?" and other such slogans boldly painted on them, heard Gay promise them victory, because they were on the right side of history. "If I had got up before you 10 years ago as I do now and attempted to organize you," he thundered, "mill owners would have taken steps to get rid of me. Now, thank God, we have the support of Franklin D. Roosevelt, who sympathizes with us, and recognizes our right to organize and who, I believe, is the agent of God."[9]

Strikers outside the Trion Cotton Mill in Trion, Georgia, on September 6, 1934. The previous day Deputy Sheriff W. M. Hix and strike sympathizer J. B. Blalock had been killed during fighting. Walter P. Reuther Library, Wayne State University.

The next day the strikers' resolution was put to the test. At the Bibb Mill No. 2 gates, angry picketers attacked T. E. Garrett, chief of city detectives, and overturned a car carrying mill officials to work. Police and sheriff's deputies kept the mill open briefly, but soon only the dye room was working, staffed by African Americans who had been escorted through the picket lines. According to some witnesses, they crossed unwillingly, "Cap, don't do that, I don't want to go in there," one allegedly protested, but his police escort "seized him by the belt" and pulled him into the mill yard, keeping "hold of his belt until he had the Negro inside." Anderson, meanwhile, appealed again to Talmadge for troops, as the pickets remained resolute in defiance of police and mill guards. When the request was refused, he angrily closed the plant's doors, vowing not to reopen until the governor had changed his mind.[10]

In Augusta the strike began reasonably quietly but soon turned violent after a battle between police and picketers at the huge Enterprise Mill. Finding themselves surrounded by a hostile mob, two police officers decided to shoot their way out. They were in "a tough spot," explained the police chief, and had no option but to fight back. Three picketers were seriously injured in the firefight, one of whom, Norman Leon Carroll, later died. He was buried as a working-class hero; 7,000 attended his funeral and heard local UTW official Paul Fuller remind them that Jesus too "was a labor leader, and was crucified by the same reactionary forces that today are fighting the labor movement, a movement which is going through the same persecution as did Jesus, for each tried to free the people." This was the symbolic importance of Carroll's death, a death which fanned class tension in Augusta to flash point levels, where it would remain throughout the strike.[11]

In Newnan, where Talmadge was due to speak, frightened workers urged him to call out the guard, echoing the demands of their employers. They even demonstrated at this rally, carrying banners bearing such slogans as "You used the troops to keep away from a federal court summons, let us have them to return to our jobs." The governor remained adamant, urging them to "keep calm." The primary election, after all, was only five days away.[12]

Elsewhere in Georgia, however, mills closed quietly, sometimes as a result of picketing, sometimes through management action, but largely without violence. Columbus, where there had been violence early in August, reported no incidents at all in September, with all mills closed by management decision. There was some picketing, but the crowds were generally good-natured, though some special deputies were jeered at outside the Bibb Mill. The experience was salutary, most of them reportedly "took off their badges and pistols and resigned their posts" forthwith. Other mills, of course, continued operation, largely unaffected by the strike call. Douglas Flamming has written that for workers at the Crown Mill in Dalton, Georgia, "the 1934 General Strike was largely a picnic." There was no violence in Dalton, and what picketing there was was "symbolic." Flamming goes on to make a crucial point about the strike, not only in Georgia, but throughout the nation. "Every town and mill village had a different experience," he wrote, the national scope of the strike notwithstanding. "In some towns, the strike provided almost no response. In others, a virtual war broke out—sometimes between opposing groups of workers, sometimes between union hands and National Guard troops brought in by management." This intensely localized response, in Georgia and elsewhere, argues Flamming, places limits on how far the strike can be interpreted as a national event. Rather, it represented "a period of transition when the workers' village-level focus, which characterized the paternalistic system, was shifting toward a regional and national perspective." Flamming confined his analysis to the southern industrial milieux, yet its explanatory power holds good for other regions of the nation, in particular the focus on conflict between opposing groups of workers. Southern millhands were not alone in differing, sometimes violently, over unionization. Rhode Island workers did, Maine workers did, even Pennsylvania workers did, and in the tense atmosphere of September 1934, such differences could easily result in violence and battle, a fact many labor historians have found hard to acknowledge.[13]

Local conditions may explain why there was violence in Trion, Augusta, and Macon but good humor in Dalton and why workers in Newnan, who wished to continue working, petitioned the president for protection from those in Hogansville who came to stop them. At times the line between "picnic" and violence was a thin one. Picketers at the Clark Thread Mill in Austell danced to a string band and held a party on mill property. The band had also been playing, however, as these same strikers, many from Atlanta and Douglasville, had blocked all roads leading to the mill, had "shoved back automobiles that tried to enter," had jeered and otherwise abused nonstriking workers, had "sang [*sic*] songs lauding the union and disparaging 'scabs'," had "joined in a square dance in the street while the string band played mountain tunes," and, eventually, had forced management to close the mill. The mill guards, reported the *Atlanta Constitution,* had been powerless against the belligerence of the picketers, "perhaps half of them women."[14]

In other communities, it was the police and special deputies who quickly took control, and nowhere more so than in Augusta. The Winant Committee files leave no doubt of that. In an unsigned letter to Lloyd Garrison, one desperate striker alleged that "we textile workers haven't had the showing of a dog." They were "beaten and shot down on the picket lines," the correspondent said, "and are not even allowed to sit on our front porches in our own home." The police had deputized young boys, had "told them to shoot to kill and to knock them on the heads with picker sticks furnished by the management of the mills." Others were willing to identify themselves as they described similar treatment. As briefly discussed earlier, Carrie Miller confirmed that the Augusta police had prohibited all picketing, had beaten and shot at those continuing to do so, and had even stopped workers gathering on their own front porches. Osie Jones reported likewise, also claiming that Augusta's mill managers were bringing "scab" workers from neighboring South Carolina by the taxi-load in order to break the strike, all under police protection. "One innocent picket" (doubtless Leon Carroll) had already been "slain," she said, and others critically wounded. The police had intimidated women and children simply for gathering near mill property; all requests for protection, to the City Council, to Governor Talmadge, had been ignored. Meanwhile, Augusta continued in the grip of police "terror."[15]

Talmadge, Jones alleged, had in fact promised to "take action" after the election was over. On Wednesday, September 12, he defeated Pittman in a landslide, carrying 155 of Georgia's 159 counties. Immediately he began making up for lost time, and in so doing, turned to the National Guard with a determination and a thoroughness which even outdid that of his colleagues, Blackwood and Ehringhaus. With his reelection, the textile strike in Georgia was effectively broken.[16]

The governor was soon to declare martial law "in all sections of the state where rebellion or violence or insurrection is going on that the local authorities are unable to handle," thus providing the authority for the largest peacetime mobilization of troops in Georgia's history. Soldiers soon occupied the major strike centers, their commanders given authority to arrest strikers and picketers, to try them before military courts, to suspend the functioning of the civil courts and, if they deemed it necessary, the writ of habeas corpus itself. There was no doubt that what the governor had ordered was unconstitutional and would have been found so. It was, however, undeniably effective, finally providing protection for Anderson and his fellow owners as they determined to get their looms and spindles working again.[17]

Indeed, Talmadge had not waited to declare martial law before sending in the troops. As early as September 14, reacting to reports that armed strikers were massing for an attack on the Atco mill in Cartersville, he dispatched two infantry companies there, "with orders to protect textile plants and their workers in the vicinity from molestation or harm at the hands of textile strikers." Under the personal direction of Adj. Gen. Lindley Camp, they lost no time in demonstrating who was now in charge, setting up machine gun emplacements all round the plant, including some on the roof—even though only 100 of Atco's 700 workers had actually walked out and the plant had remained in full operation. "I want the flying squadrons in Georgia to stop," said the governor in announcing his action. "I want all violence and intimidation, carrying arms, big sticks and baseball bats to stop." From now on, he said, he intended to protect all workers who wanted to return to their jobs. At the same time, the state's leading millowners met in Atlanta to draw up a list of plants which would be reopened on Monday, September 17, all under the protection of the National Guard. The governor and mill management, then, were to act together in the planned breaking of the strike.[18]

Talmadge's dramatic intervention encouraged millowners to take strikebreaking action on their own behest. W. D. Anderson did what he had been itching to do all along and brought in "three railroad coaches of strike breakers, imported from New Jersey," to guard the three Bibb plants in Porterdale as they prepared to reopen. This was too much even for Talmadge. Quickly he dispatched four guard companies to Porterdale with orders to protect the Bibb mills and send the New Jersey men home. Both tasks were quickly accomplished.[19]

In Macon, where strike support had remained strong, preparations for the reopening of the Bibb Mills were eased considerably by the arrest of Gay, the dynamic local leader, on a warrant sworn by H. W. Pittman of Bibb Manufacturing. He was charged with "intimidation," in that he allegedly prevented employees, owners, managers, and proprietors of the town's mills from going to work, and held on $75,000 bond. Two strikers who appeared at the Bibb County jail to visit him were also arrested. He was kept there for five days, released only after the strike had been effectively broken. Sheriff's deputies, meanwhile, had rounded up the most prominent of Gay's local leadership cadre in a nighttime raid on a "secret meeting" near Payne City mill village. The strikers were planning a "midnight reign of terror," said Sheriff James R. Hicks Jr. The arrested men said that they had simply come together for a prayer meeting, an explanation the sheriff discounted. Gay was given a thunderous reception at a rally celebrating his release. There they all exulted over their victory, in that brief time of triumph before the reality of its hollowness had overtaken them.[20]

One final killing occurred in Georgia. On September 15, at the Aragon mills, four miles out of Rockmart, "a flying squadron of three automobiles" allegedly "shot Matt Brown, mill guard, to death as they sped past the post where he was on duty." One of the cars was soon captured, and its occupants, Otto DeVaney and Pinky Osborne, both strikers from Rockmart, arrested and held without bail in the Polk County jail. Soon, ten further suspects had been rounded up and also jailed in Cedartown. State troops were quickly sent to Aragon, but not before Rockmart's deputy sheriff, C. D. Stone, had deputized a number of the mill's "loyal workers," armed them with "pistols, rifles, shotguns and automatics," and led them to where the squadron was thought to be camped, having announced that he was tired of waiting for the governor to move and that he "intended to run every striker out of the county." Fortunately, and prudently, the strikers had already left. The governor's determination to break the strike and his use of the National Guard gave brief sanction to further vigilante activity. In vain did O. E. Petry, secretary of Georgia's Federation of Labor, deplore the violence of "the owners and the deputies in recent days," the violation of law and civil liberties which were occurring, the continued refusal of "the textile mill operators to comply with their code and the law." Those back in power were not listening.[21]

On September 17, those mills which management had determined to reopen did so under the terms of martial law and the protection of the National Guard, now deployed throughout the state. Before the day ended, however, both Talmadge and his soldiers had become the focus of national attention, the result of a confrontation in Newnan, a textile village about 100 miles southwest of Atlanta. Its residents had not been strike supporters, indeed they had petitioned Talmadge and Roosevelt repeatedly for protection of their right to work. Flying squadrons, however, had ensured that the town's mills had shut down. A few miles down the road from Newnan was Hogansville, location of the Stark Mill. "People in Hogansville were strong for the union," recalled Opal McMichael of Newnan. The Stark Mill workers, led by charismatic local UTW organizer Homer Welch, had not only obeyed the strike call, but had provided the pickets which had forced Newnan's mills to close. On September 17, as the guard approached, Welch and his supporters determined on one last try.[22]

At 2 A.M. that Monday morning, trucks started rolling from Hogansville, Rockmart, and La Grange, carrying strikers bound for East Newnan and picket duty. It was a trip they had made frequently over the past weeks, recalled Etta Mae Zimmerman of Hogansville, "one of those flying trips," she called it. She quite enjoyed this particular ride, despite the early rise as, to wake themselves up, the picketers sang the latest popular songs. Her sister, Leona Parham, who usually went with her, had missed the truck this particular morning, having gone to get some breakfast, but their father, J. M. Zimmerman, though not a mill worker, climbed aboard at the last minute to be with his daughter. Just before they reached East Newnan, their leader, Homer Welch, stopped their singing to lead them in a brief prayer, reminding them of the seriousness of their purpose. They were on their way "to help the workers close the mill," and because "Roosevelt was wantin' people to organize. Said it over and over." Not only God, then, but the president was on their side.[23]

Eugene Talmadge, however, was not. No sooner had the travelers joined the crowd of picketers, their sympathizers, and curious onlookers outside Newnan Cotton Mills Number 1 plant, than another type of "flying squadron" arrived, eight carloads of specially trained and heavily armed guardsmen with two army "spotter" planes circling overhead. Adjutant General Camp led the command, directing operations from his own car. The soldiers advanced on the strikers, bayonets held high, "tear gas bombs swung at belts" or glowing "red in officers' hands." There was a brief battle before the picketers were subdued and divided into two groups: those who lived in Newnan; and those, like Etta Mae, her father, Viola Horton, Maude Granger, and Homer Welch, who came from somewhere else.[24]

The people from Newnan were told to go home and stay there. So were fourteen African Americans, "accidentally nabbed in the coup by General Camp," who were almost certainly just in the wrong place at the wrong time. Camp did not know what to do with them, eventually they were escorted "to the edge of the mill lot and told to retreat in an orderly, or disorderly fashion, as they liked, but to use a certain alley instead of the street where troops and workers stood." They sped away from the scene, one calling over his shoulder as he ran, "We ain't got no business here, nohow."[25]

As for the "out-of-towners," the squadron members, they were not set free. Rather they were rounded up and forced onto the back of waiting army trucks. Soon the convoy "pulled away from the mill"; as it did so the crowd still massed outside let forth "a mighty cheer." The mill whistle blew; they went inside and work began again at Newnan Cotton Mills Number 2. Those on board the trucks, 112 men and 16 women in all, had no idea where they were headed. In fact, they were on their way to Atlanta, to a hastily constructed detention facility at Fort McPherson, soon to be dubbed a "concentration camp" by the delighted media. The enclosure, encircled by barbed wire, had last been used to intern Germans during World War I. Now, said General Camp, it had been refurbished in order to hold flying squadron members until they could be brought before a military court.[26]

Though most of the prisoners were men, it was the young women who gained national attention, and the press pursued them relentlessly. Most were from Hogansville, often more than one from the same family, and they gave as good as they got. When Viola Horton proudly told reporters she was one of four sisters sent there, someone shouted, "They got your pa, too." "Make it five then," retorted Viola. Her sister Belle said that her biggest problem was "what to wear," as the overalls they had been given were scarcely becoming. The food was good though, according to E. N. Brown of Hogansville—"a little better than I have been getting during the depression." Etta Mae Zimmerman allegedly told reporters that they all "feel more honored to go out with the national guard than with the scabs"—a remark that received national publicity, though after fifty years she said she could not remember making it. Maude Granger, described as "a woman of about 20," said that the troops were "mighty nice" to them, something Etta Mae confirmed in recollection. "They were good to us," she remembered, and there was no "hanky-panky," even when their guards had to follow them to the "little johnny" which had been hastily dug "down in the woods." The whole experience, in fact, was quite exciting. Of course, she said, "I was young enough then that I enjoyed everything."[27]

Minnie Carroll, also from Hogansville, agreed that she had "a grand time" in Fort McPherson and even kept a "camp diary" in which she recorded the adventure. Probably written with the help of a journalist for the *Atlanta Constitution,* which published it, she told of an atmosphere more like that of a holiday camp than a prison. The food was "dandy," lots of "ice-cream and coke," there was plenty of time for checkers, for cards, or just flirting with their guards. When friends and family from Hogansville came to see them, as they were permitted to do, it was just like "being with your friends for an all-day visit" or picnic. They were given clean, new clothing—duck slacks and dresses. "Mine was an embroidered pink dress, very pretty and fit me fine." One evening the soldiers "put up a radio," and they staged an impromptu dance; the next day one of the Horton sisters, Belle, gave the rest of the girls a "finger wave." It was "funny how women feel better when their hair is primped up," Minnie mused. She was sorry when the strike ended, and she was "not anxious" to leave Fort McPherson. Eventually, the guards and their prisoners had to part, with much swapping of addresses, though Minnie doubted "if any real romances" were under way. They left the camp, again on trucks, blowing kisses to their captors and shouting, "Goodbye, general, we had a good time." Even allowing for a large amount of journalistic license, it is clear that these young women had suffered little as a result of their incarceration. As Etta Mae recalled, there were "lots of laughs and jokes." It was good fun.[28]

The media was not similarly interested in the 112 male strikers also sent to Fort McPherson, including Hogansville UTW leader Homer Welch after he had been charged with carrying a concealed weapon. In the absence of reports to the contrary, however, it can be assumed that their treatment was similarly benign. J. M. Zimmerman, Etta Mae's father, however, saw past the good food and the clean clothes. Furious at what he considered the illegality of the governor's actions, he wrote to Talmadge bitterly protesting what he had done. "You had my daughter and myself herded into a barn," he complained, "penned up like cows, not because we had committed any crime or any violence, but because you wish to keep us in slavery." He had always been a Talmadge man, he said, but no longer. The journalists complained the men were generally much less willing to talk to them than were the women. Moreover their numbers were augmented as the guard took control of the strike areas. Six were sent there from Rockmart, two from Porterdale, and those arrested in Macon after the midnight raid were also sent there. Later, two dozen alleged members of a "flying squadron" arrived, having been arrested near Columbus. Their excuse that they were simply on their way to a "weiner roast" was not believed. The fact that all the detainees were relatively well treated could not, in the eyes of the state's UTW leadership, mitigate against the illegal use of state power which had placed them there.[29]

Illegal or not, Talmadge's declaration of martial law, and the consequent deployment of troops throughout the state, effectively ended the textile strike in Georgia. One by one the mills reopened, and striker and nonstriker alike went back to work, some unwillingly, others rejoicing that the union had lost. In Rockmart 1,500 textile workers paraded through the main street flanked by National Guardsmen and carrying banners stating "Open the Gates. We Want to Work," "Meet Me on the Job This Week," or "100 Per Cent Non Union." They were, enthused a watching reporter, "clean bright workers typical of the best of Georgia's citizenry," a far cry from those flying squadron thugs who had so recently breached the state's industrial peace. In both Aragon and Trion, where there had been such violence, the mills were again open. In Georgia, the official ending of the strike, and Gorman's victory declaration, were superfluous.[30]

Nevertheless, the millhands believed Gorman for a while. Augusta's workers staged a huge victory parade. Triumphantly they marched through the town, their banners proclaiming their jubilation. "We Now Have a New Deck for the New Deal," said one. "Leon Carroll did not Die in Vain," read another. "Labor is 100% Behind President Roosevelt," said a third, and, most ironic, "We Have Won—Why Worry." In La Grange, 2,500 picketers folded away their tents before parading through the town, triumphantly shouting, "we are burying the stretch-out." It was not long before they all knew better, as the mill gates remained closed, for many their jobs forever lost. For a brief time, however, they had savored the feel of victory.[31]

The ending of the strike had one final effect. Those held at Fort McPherson or, like Gay, in various county and city jails, were quietly released, most never to answer the charges laid against them. And, as the internees returned to their workplaces, they found the same variation in treatment as elsewhere. Some were rehired without any difficulty—Etta Mae Zimmerman, for example, went back to work as soon as she got home from Fort McPherson. Yet her sister Leona, who had missed the truck to Newnan on September 17, and thus had not been detained, was not taken back. All over the state it was the same, blacklists, refusal to rehire, conditional reemployment, or no problems at all, again testimony to the intensely local nature of this strike, both in the activity of the workers and the responses of management.[32]

Etta Mae Zimmerman made this point with clarity when being interviewed for *The Uprising of 1934*. The interviewer was anxious to probe her recollection of what it meant to have been part of a significant national event, working as part of a regionwide, even a nationwide, movement for industrial change. "No," said Etta Mae, she had never thought of the strike as that, nor of her participation as being part of an "organized hundreds of thousands of people." It wasn't like that for her at all. "It was just this community and Newnan and La Grange." And that was the essence of the textile strike of 1934, in Georgia, in much of the South, and, indeed, the nation.[33]

Alabama was scarcely the epicenter of the South's cotton textile industry; that was firmly in the Carolinas. Nevertheless, the mills provided employment for 40,000 of the state's workers—one in three of all manufacturing jobs, in fact. Most were in north Alabama, with Huntsville sometimes referred to as the second largest cotton mill town in the South—Gastonia was the first. Gadsden, Decatur, Florence, Jasper, Albertville, Anniston, and Gainsville were also significant textile towns. Like cotton mill people everywhere, Alabama's mill workers were angry and disillusioned by June 1934, furious at the way their employers seemed able to evade NRA code provisions with impunity, no longer willing to endure the steadily worsening condition of their lives. Events in Alabama then, provided the "precipitatory moments" for the general textile strike of 1934.[34]

The veteran labor organizer Eula McGill, in 1934 treasurer of her UTW local in Gadsden, Alabama, recalled the enthusiasm with which textile workers in the northern part of the state flocked to the union once the NRA had become law and their increasing anger as their hopes went unrealized. The whole Huntsville area, in particular, she recalled as being "very militant." Women were particularly strong for the union, she said, for they faced one problem male workers were able to avoid— sexual harassment. "Of course we didn't think about it in those terms in those days," she said; nevertheless, the reality of trading jobs for sexual favors was a commonplace in Alabama's mills. Women's jobs were threatened if they did not comply with the foremen's demands, she said. These men were without shame, sometimes "taking" girls on the mill floor itself with no pretence at discretion. The enthusiasm with which rank-and-file workers formed locals far outran the capacity of the regional and national offices to provide trained organizers: "we's [*sic*] all leaders," McGill said. "We didn't have nobody else. We had to lead ourselves. . . . The rank and file people in the textile industry in those days did the organizing and did the running of the union and did the handling of the strike, because, as I say, the union didn't have enough paid representatives to commence to direct." One reason McMahon hastily dispatched veteran organizer John Dean to Alabama was to fill this leadership vacuum and to channel the wealth of local enthusiasm.[35]

As Robin Kelley, among others, has suggested, Alabama had a stronger tradition of militant unionism than other southern states. The coal, iron, and steel industries in particular had been centers of union strength, and in 1934 all were involved in prolonged labor strife. Even in the cotton belt unions had gained a precarious foothold. The Communist-led Sharecroppers Union had twice been involved in violent resistance to employer attempts to smash its fragile base. Nevertheless, Alabama's textile workers joined UTW locals, as McGill pointed out, not so much out of any sense of solidarity with their fellow workers as from the continued degradation of the quality of their lives. Eva Brantley, of the Lincoln Mill in Huntsville, a skein winder, told of the way the stretch-out affected her. Goore, her foreman, simply took two hands off her frame, leaving two women to do the work formerly covered by four. "I'm tired of this damn bunch any way," he responded to their protest, "and when you all think that I'm going to pay you 30 cents an hour you are certainly mistaken for I am not going to do it. If you fool with me I will fire every damn one of you and get a new set of hands." Within half an hour, Goore was back, harassing her, said Brantley. He wanted to know who her mother was, as he had been told "she was in the village talking union." That he would not stand for. "She must cut that damn stuff out," he threatened.

"I won't have you in here and her running round over the village talking Union [*sic*] I mean that." A few days later, Brantley was laid off without explanation. She was scarcely surprised.[36]

M. H. Goodwin, a weaver at the Lincoln Mill, alleged that he was fired summarily, supposedly for bringing dice to work. The real reason, he said, was that the previous day his foreman had discovered that he had joined the UTW local. "It has always been a violation of the rules of Lincoln Mills to shoot craps," Goodwin conceded, but in this case there had been no crap game, and there were plenty of witnesses to confirm this. The reason for Goodwin's dismissal lay elsewhere. At the UTW's special convention in August 1934, speaker after speaker denounced the subversion of the NRA in Alabama. "When we first received word about the Textile Code, the Blue Eagle, and our right to organize and bargain collectively," said J. P. Holland, secretary-treasurer of the Alabama State Textile Council, "it seemed too good to be true. It was a real New Deal for us." But it had not worked out that way. "Thousands of our people earn less today than they did two years ago," Holland alleged. "The minimum was not and is not enforced. I'll send you hundreds of pay envelopes to prove it." John B. Goins, president of the council, told of workers' barracks made of concrete and with tin roofs, which were so hot in the summer months that they were uninhabitable. Even the flies died of heat prostration, he said, and yet workers were now forced to pay rent on these substandard dwellings.[37]

This was the swelling anger and frustration that Dean was sent in June to harness. It was an easy task, for as Janet Irons has written, "the Alabama workers had been suffering for months under the kind of intensified discrimination against union members" that workers in other states "were only beginning to experience." Quickly, the southern-born but Brooklyn-based veteran moved throughout the state, meeting with the locals, finding the prostrike sentiment to be overwhelming. By early July, only two of the state's 42 locals had voted not to strike should a statewide stoppage be called. Some locals, in fact, jumped the gun. On July 12, workers at Gadsden's Dwight Mill walked out. Two days later, the Saratoga Victory Mills in Guntersville was struck. Hastily Dean scrambled to arrange a meeting of all Alabama's locals for July 15. There, after seven hours of debate, delegates agreed on a statewide strike, effective July 17. In so doing, they took a decisive step toward a general textile strike.[38]

The UTW leadership was caught completely unprepared by the Alabama strike, which it had in no way authorized or even anticipated.

After initial gestures of support, therefore, McMahon and Gorman decided to leave Dean on his own and watch events develop. As has been earlier noted, after the first three days, the strike stalled. Always confined to the northern part of the state, especially the Huntsville area, it never involved more than half the state's workers. In the largely unorganized mills of the state's south, work went on unimpeded. Given the lack of any national or even statewide overview, it is hard to describe what happened in Alabama as a strike at all, but rather as a succession of individual walkouts, instigated by local leadership. Eula McGill's recollection was that Alabama's workers had had to lead themselves, they had no larger focus, and the progress of events in July and August amply justified her perspective. In this situation, and despite his abduction and triumphant restoration, Dean steadily lost what influence he had. By mid-August, he had effectively turned over the strike leadership to John Goins, president of the Alabama State Council of Textile Workers. By this time even the leadership had stopped calling it a statewide protest.[39]

Nevertheless, as has been already discussed, the events in Alabama did serve to set the agenda for the UTW's special convention. The Alabama strikers' demands went to the basic problems in cotton textiles, eventually becoming the demands of the workers as a whole. Moreover, the experiences of the Alabama strikers, their accounts of their lives, their suffering and their faith in the union provided the convention's emotional backdrop and were decisive in pushing it toward a strike vote. Back in Alabama, local UTW leaders made preparations to merge their walkout with the national effort, confident that the enlarged focus would bring more workers out. UTW officials predicted that at least 2,000 more would answer the strike call, in what they described as the "test tube of the unions for the general strike."[40]

There were a few optimistic signs in the strike's first days. Throughout August the Gadsden Central Labor Council had been planning a huge Labor Day celebration, and this now took place with the national strike call as a backdrop. On September 3, more than 5,000 men and women marched through the city, with striking employees from the Dwight Mill forming by far the largest single contingent. Led by a float depicting a woman spinning yarn from "an antique spinning wheel," the Dwight marchers stretched for two city blocks, shouting strike slogans as they progressed. Delegations from other striking mills followed, again displaying messages of support for Gorman and the strike effort. In Birmingham, Dean briefly reappeared, telling a cheering Labor Day crowd that "there are no local issues now. It is a national strike and Alabama members of the union will not go back to work until the strike is settled by the national general committee." Indeed, Dean was a busy man that Labor Day, for he also appeared in the Huntsville parade, waving to the crowd from an open car, flanked by officials of the Huntsville Trades and Labor Council. More than 6,000 took part in the parade, including "more than a thousand youngsters, members of the junior union league." They carried banners reading, "We want free school books," and "We refuse prison-made school books." The women's trade union league followed the children, than came "negro members of the federal trade league," carrying a huge banner which read, "Don't be a scab. Join now." The textile strikers held pride of place, however, the parade concluding with a rally in Martin Park, at which Dean, among others, spoke. Elsewhere, a few small mills closed for the first time, and in Anniston 200 employees of the Anniston Yarn Mills, which had been shut for three weeks due to lack of orders, now officially declared themselves to be on strike.[41]

In the end, however, nothing much changed in Alabama following the national strike call. Those mills already closed remained so, but few joined them. Indeed, the main thrust after September 1 was to take every possible action to prevent further closings, and here, as elsewhere, mill management and local law enforcement officers worked in tandem. In Boaz, on September 3, special deputies guarded the Boaz Cotton Mill, where employees had previously refused to strike, and where picketing had recently been authorized. Local residents, specially sworn in for the occasion and armed with shotguns, quickly arrested four bewildered picketers, who were charged with trespassing. Fifty strikers from nearby Albertville arrived, but after observing the display of weaponry, they decided to move on. Meanwhile, many workers kept their weapons within easy reach—"to defend my job," said one.[42]

In the Chattahoochee Valley, rumors that flying squadrons from Georgia were about to arrive to picket five mills there caused employees to arm themselves with clubs and sticks as they stood guard throughout the night. They would not allow any picketing, of that they were certain. The squadrons did not arrive, but the atmosphere remained tense for several days. A group of fifty cars did descend on Opelika from La Grange, Georgia, but after surveying the detachment of "400 citizens and officers," heavily armed with machine guns and gas bombs who stood guard over the mill there, they decided to keep on moving. "Grim faced sentries," had blockaded all roads to the mill, "mute evidence of the community's determination to tolerate no effort on the part of union organizers or others to interfere with operations at the plant." In Sylacauga, where the town's five mills were all working, UTW reports indicated that "nearly every male citizen was armed and outposts were maintained on every highway to prevent outsiders from attempting to force mill workers to join them." In such an atmosphere, there was little Goins and the other state leaders could do to extend the strike. Instead, their efforts became increasingly confined to urging their members to "refrain from all violence, sheath all weapons and stand by in a peaceful and orderly way until this strike is won." So concerned was Goins at the potential for violence in Alabama that he embarked on a hastily arranged statewide tour to reinforce the message and to remove "trouble makers, agitators and foreign influences from our picket lines."[43]

Goins's intervention may well have been timely, given the rising tide of tension in the state. But it did mean, as he himself conceded, that the union was always "on the defensive throughout the strike," unable to take any initiatives or even respond to what national direction there was. Still no one was shot and killed in Alabama. The single most serious act of violence occurred in Russellville. There, Ike Robinton, a voluntary organizer for the UTW, had planned to attend a mass meeting called by Goins as part of his statewide tour. The meeting was broken up by armed men, as local police stood by observing but taking no action. Robinton was told in no uncertain terms to leave town, but as he hastened to comply, his car was shot at. Three bullets penetrated the bodywork, but he was uninjured. The Russellville Mill had been operating under guard since the strike call. Tensions in the town had been high for weeks, and had finally boiled over. Though police eventually arrested six local men for disorderly conduct, they were quickly released, and that was the end of the matter. In fact, said Russellville's chief of police, J. C. Stone, Robinton had probably fabricated the whole story, or perhaps the so-called shots were no more than the sound of a defective car exhaust. He "might have been driving ahead of an old back-firing Ford in which a crowd of boys were riding," he explained, declining to comment on the obvious presence of bullet holes in Robinton's vehicle.[44]

Robinton was in the news again, briefly, in a quite different context. On September 17, Birmingham police confiscated 25,000 circulars allegedly distributed by Alabama's Communist Party, trying to associate itself with the cause of the textile workers—the only known attempt by the party, mainly active among the state's African American workers, to do so. "The Negro masses are also behind this strike," declared the handbill, stating that "thousands of Negro toilers in the Share-Croppers Union of Alabama are themselves striking in the cotton fields for $1 a hundred pounds of picked cotton," and they have raised "the slogan of solidarity" with the textile strikers, "to help close the mills to win the strike." Addie Adkins, an elderly African American woman had been arrested for possessing these circulars, and police were actively seeking her white female accomplice. Ike Robinton was invited to comment on these matters. In no uncertain terms he warned "union men" to keep clear of the Communists and "to turn over to the police" immediately anyone caught distributing Communist propaganda or even "advocating Communist theories." In Alabama, as elsewhere in the South, the Left was unable to exert any influence with the local strike leadership. The legacy of Gastonia was a long one.[45]

The guns continued to bristle in Alabama until Gorman made his notorious declaration of victory and called off the strike. In Opelika "guard shacks" had been constructed in several streets, while deputies mounted a heavy machine gun at the main entrance to the Pepperell Mill. Eufala's citizens, concerned at rumors that Georgia strikers were again about to invade, took to patrolling the highways in anticipation of their arrival. "We are prepared for trouble if and when it comes," said the sheriff, but it never did. Given the tension in the state, the obvious truth that the strike was going nowhere in Alabama and the fact that workers had been on the defensive since mid-July, it is surprising that they did not greet its ending with more enthusiasm. In fact, strikers at Gadsden's Dwight Mill initially decided to defy their national leaders and remain on strike. Only a court injunction against the local leadership forced them to go back. Huntsville's strikers, too, drifted back reluctantly, and in Anniston picketing continued for a few more days. Nevertheless, the strike was over in Alabama and elsewhere. It had accomplished nothing.[46]

In common with their compatriots elsewhere in the South, Alabama's employers ignored those terms of the settlement aimed at protecting strikers' jobs. Union leaders and strikers alike were denied reemployment; those permitted to return found the same intolerable conditions as before—stretch-out, discriminatory rates of pay, and a ferociously enforced ban on union activity. In Gadsden, Dwight management quickly moved to evict all union members from mill housing. The workers had no choice but to comply. Nearly three months of protest had brought them nothing except grief and deprivation. Little wonder that the UTW was broken as a credible force for labor in the state.[47]

Mollie Dowd, the veteran UTW organizer, provided a mournful postscript to the strike's failure in Alabama and the millowners' revenge. She had been visiting Winfield, where the local union president had been kidnapped by armed men, employees of a Birmingham private detective agency, taken to Birmingham, and there arrested on trumped-up robbery charges. She had tried to secure his release to no avail. Throughout the state, she reported, strikers and union members were being denied employment, evicted from their homes, and most desperate of all, being struck off the relief rolls. "Some of these folks are literally starving," she said. The mills were still under guard "with machine guns on every corner" and management determined to root out all vestiges of union power. "Damn Roosevelt," one told her. "I didn't vote for him in the first place and he cannot tell me how to run my business." They positively enjoyed watching their workers starve, Dowd alleged bitterly, "They say, 'Let them starve,' they asked for it." Even speaking to a former striker could be fatal. The strike effort in Pritchard, eight miles from Mobile, had been led by a young woman who took over when "the men were afraid." Now the manager had not only run her out of the village but was also firing anyone "she speaks to or happens to visit." The state relief administrator, Thad Holt, was simply a tool of the owners, she claimed, "he does exactly what they say." He had decent people working for him, but they could do nothing. "The Relief Director at Guntersville cried as she described the desperation of the former strikers, but she said, 'you see how my hands are tied—Here is telegram from Thad Holt who is my boss, saying "cut off all relief, and do it now." ' "[48]

Dowd had no illusions as to who had been the victors in the strike. "You seem to think we won something," she told her friend and fellow UTW organizer, Elizabeth Nord. "I just cannot see it and things here are in a much worse condition than they were three months ago." She was scathing about the UTW's national leadership, especially Gorman and McMahon, who, she believed, "seem to have forgotten Alabama altogether." "You see Alabama has had three months of it while the National had had only three weeks." Dowd was "worried to death about our poor people," but neither Gorman nor McMahon seemed to care. She was proud of what the Alabama UTW representatives—Dean, Cox, she herself, and "the girl with me"—had done. They had been out for three months "and not even a fist fight in the whole time." This had shown some leadership, she thought; at the very least it indicated "that someone has stayed on the job." But in all that time, not once had Gorman or McMahon given them "one word of appreciation or a pat on the back." Rather, Alabama, the local leadership, and those who had followed them had been abandoned to the vengeance of those against whom they had been encouraged to fight. It was a cruel conclusion.[49]

Part III

The Strike

A Local Study

Strikers in Burlington, North Carolina, greet a convoy of "flying pickets."
Library of Congress, LC USF 33–020936–M4.

Chapter 8

The Burlington Bombing—
A Case Study

T HE MILL MANAGERS AND COMMUNITY LEADERS OF
Burlington, North Carolina, expected that the strike would pass
them by altogether. After all, the hand of the depression rested
comparatively lightly on the town, dominated as it already was by the
boosterism of J. Spencer Love and a hosiery industry which had continued to expand throughout the depression years. "Why on earth should
Burlington's workers be dissatisfied," asked "Observer" in the columns
of the local newspaper. "Look at the people who man the looms, they
are the type of our best citizenship—their homes are well furnished,
lawns and gardens well kept; they own their automobile, radio, their
children are bright-eyed, getting their schooling. This is the spirit of
American tradition and the spirit of the 'New Deal'." "Observer" was
wrong. Burlington's workers were soon caught up in the surge of events.
There was violence, the guard came, there were bombings and destruction. Moreover, the retribution exacted by Love and his fellow owners
was of such dimension as to make the town briefly a center of national
attention and to divide it for years to come. As such, it provides a useful
case study of the strike's long-term effect.[1]

There have been textile mills in Alamance County, North Carolina,
since well before the Civil War. Almost certainly the Alamance Mill, built
in 1837 by Edwin Michael Holt on a stream close to the Haw River was
the first. Producing undyed yarn which was sold locally, it was typical of
the small mills that developed in the antebellum Piedmont. Indeed, the
Alamance Mill prospered, for, as Jacquelyn Dowd Hall and her coauthors

noted in *Like a Family,* in 1853 a French dyer showed the Holts how to mix dyes, and soon the mill was producing what became known as Alamance Plaids. This sturdy plaid cloth was sold from covered wagons throughout the Carolinas and even reached eastern Tennessee. It made the Holt family a fortune.[2]

The Holt factory survived the Civil War to become one of those providing "a thread of continuity between textile manufacturing in the old South and the New." After the war, the family proceeded to "build an industrial dynasty," in Alamance County, and by the turn of the century they controlled 24 out of the 29 mills located there. One was the Plaid Mill, it was built in 1883 in the town of Company Shops, so named because the North Carolina Railroads engines were repaired there. Soon Company Shops would be renamed Burlington and become one of the Piedmont's most important textile towns, as the industry provided the economic underpinning for the New South. In time, Burlington would give its name to Burlington Industries, the largest textile company in the world.[3]

All that lay in the future in 1900. Hall and her colleagues, as has been noted, described Burlington as being less of a city than a collection of unincorporated mill villages clustered round a small business district, the typical appearance of southern textile towns as manufacturers determined to retain control of their industry in all of its aspects. Though the town grew rapidly in the next twenty years, though it prospered during the boom of the First World War, and though it, too, acquired the accoutrements of modernization—paved roads, electric street lighting, a sidewalk system completed in 1929—what changed it most profoundly was when Spencer Love moved his operations there and created Burlington Mills. For a time, Spencer Love was Burlington.[4]

Love, the son of a Harvard mathematics professor, was born in 1896 in Cambridge, Massachusetts. His family had deep roots in Gaston County. His great-grandfather had owned slaves there, and his grandfather Grier Love, was "a pioneer of the Carolina textile industry" and the quintessential New South businessman, with an iron determination to develop the cotton industry, both in Gaston County and elsewhere. He succeeded initially but like many of his kind overreached himself. The uncertainties of the industry in the early twentieth century, together with an unwise investment in the building of the huge Loray mill in Gastonia absorbed most of the earlier profit. When he died in 1907, his son, Robert, took over management of the two remaining mills, but he could not halt the decline of the family's fortunes. The wartime boom helped only briefly; the postwar, industrywide depression was devastating.[5]

Upon graduating from Harvard in 1918, Spencer Love went straight into the army. Serving in France as a divisional adjutant in the last days of the war, he saw enough of its horrors to make them a permanent part of his memory, but he also learned that he possessed exceptional administrative skills. He returned home determined to use these in a business career, and soon he moved South to work for his Uncle Robert as the "Old Mill" paymaster—and to learn the textile business. By year's end he was its manager, having bought out his uncle—with his father's money. Spencer Love's career was thus launched—relatively inauspiciously.[6]

Turning the "Old Mill" around in the unsettled conditions of the postwar textile industry would have taxed a much more experienced manager than the young Love. Moreover the plant's machinery and buildings were worn and approaching obsolescence. Though he had, by the end of 1922, slightly improved the mill's performance, the operation remained far from profitable, dependent on its small weaving department to keep afloat. Love resolved, therefore, to put all his resources into weaving, even if this meant moving his business, together with what machinery he could salvage from the "Old Mill," somewhere new, having sold off the rest of the plant. Accordingly, Spencer Love arrived in Burlington in 1924.[7]

Love chose Burlington for a number of reasons: its long history as a textile center; the presence of plenty of skilled weavers ready to work for relatively low wages on account of the area's depressed economy; and the willingness of city leaders to help him get started, the more so because the town's first generation of textile millowners, the Holts, the Williamsons, and the Gants, seemed to have run out of ideas. They had let their plants become run-down, recalled Reid Maynard, a local hosiery manufacturer who became a close friend of Love. "They were at a low ebb, a lot of them closed, some of them bankrupt, the others just took their money out and quit. . . . None of these people died poor," he said, they just got tired of the industry. Love's arrival, therefore, was a crucial shot in the arm for the community. Accordingly, the Burlington Mills Company was formed, using $50,000 worth of the "Old Mill" machinery, $200,000 from the sale of its plant, and $200,000 subscribed locally. The first yarn was spun in October, and by the end of the next year, Burlington Mill's first plant, the Pioneer Plant, employed 200 people working round the clock.[8]

Initially, the Burlington operation was no more successful than the Gastonia one Love had left behind. With increasing desperation he searched for a product that would sell, trying "flag cloths, buntings, cotton, scrims, curtain fabrics, and diaper cloth. He even experimented with the coarse cotton dress cloth in the style of the Alamance Plaid which E. M. Holt had made famous in his antebellum mills." Nothing, however, seemed to work, and the dispirited Love contemplated getting out of textiles altogether. Instead, he decided to run with a new synthetic yarn, rayon, recently introduced into the South from Germany.[9]

Rayon made Love a fortune, because his decision to manufacture it coincided with changes in fashion that caused a huge increase in its demand. One of the reasons for the decline in demand for cotton was the spectacular raising of women's hemlines after World War I. When skirts reached to the floor, cotton stockings would do, but with short skirts, women wanted either sheer silk on their legs—too expensive for most—or "artificial silk" (i.e., rayon). "All Times are Hosiery Times in This Day of Short Skirts," ran a typical advertisement in 1929. "Never before has hosiery played such an important part in adding the final touch to the costume." Rayon saved Love, as it did other Piedmont manufacturers. Moreover, earlier than most, he saw other possibilities for its use besides hosiery. First came bedspreads, and then a wide range of dress goods poured from his rayon mills, most of which he built in Burlington's Piedmont Heights area. By 1934, Burlington Mills had become the largest weaver of rayon in the United States, and Love easily became Alamance County's most important businessman. Having started in milling with no historic attachment to cotton, unlike the Holts he found it much easier to keep up with changing fashions and changing times.[10]

The "boosterism" which Love's success engendered captured the entire community in the late 1920s. Burlington's proud boast that it was "the fastest growing town in North Carolina" was a constant refrain in the local newspaper. New mills and stores were greeted with excitement, improvements in existing plant and machinery likewise, as, of course, was its steady population growth. The Chamber of Commerce proudly announced that nearly 10,000 people lived within the city limits by 1930, with the same number living within a four-mile radius of the town. There were 26 hosiery mills there, 20 "other textile" mills, and 30 mills listed as "miscellaneous." Fifty more textile mills operated in Alamance County, outside the city limits. From 1896, when its first hosiery mill was established, Burlington had now become the sixth largest hosiery center in the whole of the United States. Moreover, there had been similarly rapid development in "dress goods, art silk, tapestries and other cotton, rayon and silk fabrics." If there was the occasional twinge of anxiety that the "moral side of our community" might not be expanding to keep faith with other development, the industrial growth was nonetheless exciting and important. Moreover, if the ravages of the Great Depression hit Burlington with less devastation than most southern textile towns, the fact that Burlington Mills kept expanding between 1929 and 1933 goes a considerable way toward explaining why. "He made a go of this thing. Made the town, no doubt about that," recalled his friend, Reid Maynard. To a considerable degree, he did. Textile workers felt the same way. Love and rayon had made things better in Burlington, even during the depression, recalled Betty Davidson, a Plaid Mill employee between 1932 and 1956.[11]

The men and women who worked in Burlington's mills, and who lived in its villages, were typical of those who, all over the South, had recently made the transition from farm to factory and who were, in their changing lives, experiencing what we now term "modernization." First, the town was overwhelmingly "native white," nearly 93 percent of its white population had been born in the United States. Less than 1 percent were described in the 1930 census as "foreign-born" white, 6.6 percent were "Negroes." For the Chamber of Commerce and the town's associated boosters, this gave it a decided advantage. Burlington workers were the best in the world ran its promotional literature, possessing the outstanding characteristics of their loyal, thrifty, and efficient ancestors. They were quick to learn, and, once having acquired skill in their work, they were slow to lose it. They were not of the type which fell prey to the radical outside agitator or organizer. Labor troubles had been few and far between in Burlington. Of course, efforts had been made, from time to time, by outsiders, to foment strikes but these had been met, in practically every instance, with a "cold shoulder." The strong inference was that unions were unlikely to become part of the Burlington industrial scene.[12]

One clear economic division in Burlington, in some ways more important than those of class or race, was that between folk who were hosiery workers and those who were not. Hosiery mill workers were the elite, said Reid Maynard, earning "a third more, or even double, what you got in cotton mills." Moreover the work was cleaner and physically less demanding than working with cotton. There was no lint in the air to stick to your clothes, to your hair, to your skin. Any job in hosiery was desirable, but "full-fashioned work was the real prize." The technical skill needed to run the machines producing fully fashioned, sheer, seamed stockings was considerable, and the wage rates paid operatives reflected this. The fully fashioned hosiery workers, therefore, made up an economic elite amongst Burlington's textile workers; they were better dressed, better housed, often able to run an automobile, sometimes earning as much in a week as cotton mill hands made in a month. Little wonder that a degree of social prestige soon came to attach itself to hosiery work, which made jobs in the mills all the more eagerly sought. Some young people, or so it was reported, disdained the chance to work in cotton mills, even when good jobs were on offer, preferring to wait until something became available in hosiery. Moreover, hosiery workers tended to socialize together; in Burlington they even had their own "hosiery mill baseball league." Though, as Hall and her fellow authors point out, the highest paid work, as with cotton, was reserved for men, women operatives could also earn very good wages. To be a hosiery worker, therefore, was to be "king bee." It was hardly surprising that most hosiery workers had little use for unions, nor that those who did preferred membership in the Hosiery Workers Union to joining with their cotton worker neighbors in the United Textile Workers. The existence of this economic divide meant that Burlington's mill workers could never challenge management power as a single entity. This would become strikingly obvious in 1934.[13]

This division was at its most stark in the depression years between 1929 and 1933. "To tell you the truth, Burlington did not have a depression," Harry Rogers admitted. "I worked every day. The hosiery people were going full blast." He worked a six-day week through these lean years, he said, "so we really worked when other people were starving." Reid Maynard, from the management perspective, agreed. "Burlington never had a depression, we never had to close things down," he recalled, and that was because the demand for fully fashioned hosiery never slackened. As the cotton mills laid off scores of workers who then faced the most fearful privation, the hosiery mills kept working to capacity, kept paying top rates, even kept hiring. As noted earlier, when Carroll Lupton arrived in Burlington in 1933, at a time when the national economy was close to collapse, having seen nothing but want and misery on his drive up from New Orleans, it was the obvious prosperity of the young hosiery workers which so captured his attention and influenced his decision to set up medical practice in the town. It was the only place he had seen in a long while where "a fellow could make a living" he said. Certainly, if the annual Christmas sales figures were any effective measure, business remained brisk throughout the slump, showing "little or no indication that old Santa Claus recognized anything like a depression." Moreover, official statistics did confirm a pattern of steady industrial growth, even during the worst years of the slump. Fourteen new plants were established in Burlington in 1929, another eight in 1930, a further nine in 1931, and five in 1932, the depression's worst year. Total employment in the town, which was 7,283 in 1929, did slump to 6,600 in 1931 but had risen to 8,501 by the end of 1933. Despite contemporary optimism, however, and the evidence of these statistics, the division between the workers was at its most acute during these years, and the tensions the general strike engendered in 1934 were all the more sharp because of it.[14]

For the depression did come to Burlington, despite the disclaimers of its boosters. As early as 1927, cotton workers, especially men, were finding it hard to obtain steady jobs in the town. By 1932, the unemployment situation was so serious that the county welfare superintendent, P. H. Fleming, reported that his office could no longer meet the demands on its resources. The past two years, he said, had seen such an increase in local unemployment that the county no longer had the provision to make even minimal responses to the wide level of distress. Mattie Shoemaker, recalling the privations of those who were laid off, spoke also of the shame they felt as they lined up at the Flannery Street "breadline," there to receive sparse rations of coffee, sugar, bread, and lard. There was, she explained, "no welfare at that time." Welfare of a sort came with the New Deal, and the eagerness with which Alamance County sought Civil Works Administration assistance, once the New Deal recovery programs had reached into the localities, is further evidence of the depression's local ravages. The CWA quickly put nearly 1,600 men to work in the Burlington area. With unemployment and distress, with the rhetoric of the New Deal, and with the NRA came talk of unions.[15]

Alamance County had never been a center of union activity, not even by southern standards. The National Union of Textile Workers first "brought the ideals of permanent trade unionism" to the Piedmont in the late nineteenth century, and in 1900 it provided what leadership there was to a brief but fierce conflict which originated in one of the Holt Mills at Haw River and quickly spread throughout the county. The strike was soon defeated, and before long the NUTW passed from the Piedmont—and from the labor scene. When union activity returned to the South, and the textile mills, after World War I, it was through the activities of the United Textile Workers. Between 1919 and 1921, the UTW fought to consolidate and extend concessions won during the boom years of the war. In North Carolina, its activities radiated out from Charlotte; there was trouble there in Kannapolis, in Concord, and in

Belmont but not in Alamance County. The union activity, and frequent strike action, that punctuated the immediate postwar years elsewhere largely passed it by, and as Spencer Love's influence became paramount, the likelihood of significant union growth became even more remote. Love was determinedly, even ferociously antiunion, and his prejudices were clearly reflected in his labor policies. Burlington Mills was always antiunion, recalled Harry Rogers, "if you ever talked about a union back in those days, it was as good as losing your job."[16]

Yet unions came to Alamance County in the early 1930s and even to Burlington Mills. By this time, Love was aggressively acquiring mills throughout the Carolinas. Along with high wage rates, he and his managers also put in place various cost-cutting devices based on the new techniques of scientific management which had caused worker discontent since the mid-1920s, including the stretch-out. Burlington's workers, like those elsewhere, were required to run more machines and at a faster pace. The workplace was modernized; work routines were analyzed and changed in the name of greater efficiency; and if some workers found their positions, pay packets, and prestige enhanced, others experienced the opposite. Four years of radical restructuring of mill practice was bound to cause tension, and provoke reaction, especially as workers believed that what little remaining control they had over their work practices was being taken away. Moreover, cotton workers in Burlington were experiencing similar privations to cotton workers everywhere; for them, four years of depression had started to bite deep. Slowly, painfully, and secretly the local UTW built up its membership among the disaffected of the work force, buoyed initially by the passage of the National Industrial Recovery Act, and the hope for a better life its provisions seemed briefly to herald.[17]

Soon, however, the familiar complaints of breaches of the cotton textile code, of NRA wage scales being ignored, of violations of hourly limits, of discrimination against union members, above all, of the stretch-out being applied beyond endurance came from Burlington's workers, too, in late 1933 and throughout 1934, as local employers learned to live with the changed industrial situation. Many concerned practices at the Holt Plaid Mill, where, it was alleged, a systematic campaign of discrimination against union members had long been in effect and had not been modified as a result of section 7(a), company assurances to the contrary. Thus, Fannie Ford wrote to President Roosevelt to tell him that she, her husband, R. L. Ford, and her son, C. E. Ford, had all been "layed off" from the Plaid Mill "for no other reason than they got a union hear [*sic*] and my Husband became president of it." Moreover "what make's me so mad about it," she continued, "is that they have black listed us from working at any other mill around hear [*sic*]. They have the Blue Eagle," she said, "but they sure have done lots of dirty work." She had voted for him, she concluded, and was sure he would "get this straight."[18]

Lee Neal, a Plaid Mill weaver, in a notarized deposition, stated that he, too, had been warned by the Plaid Mill Company's secretary treasurer, Walter Williams, to stop his union work and specifically warned against stating that workers dismissed for union membership would have to be reinstated. He would be "damed [*sic*] if he would ever work these folks anymore," Williams allegedly shouted, as he told Neal "to walk the chalk line and behave myself or I would be fired." C. D. Wilson said he had been sacked from the mill simply for carrying a petition on behalf of the Fords. Pearl Norris, too, alleged that she had been dismissed from the mill because of her membership in local 1777, and had been systematically denied work thereafter.[19]

Such allegations were routinely investigated—and routinely dismissed—usually because the company denied them. The Fords had not been dismissed for their union membership, Williams said, but rather because she "and her family are numbered among the set of employees who were laid off some time ago because the management of this mill moved some looms away from this plant to another of their mills in a different town." Moreover, as Williams and seven other mill officers had all made sworn statements to the effect "that it is not the policy of the mill to discriminate against union labor in anyway," and that all employees were free to join local 1777 if they wished, such charges of discrimination simply could not be sustained. The employees, of course, knew better, but given the partiality of the code authority officials, they could do nothing to change the way things were.[20]

There were other complaints against the Plaid Mill. J. E. Livingston, a machinist, alleged he was being paid the agreed wage rate for thirty hours while being forced to work a forty-four–hour week. Others alleged a range of rate and stretch-out violations, but routine denials by the company were accepted by compliance officials. Though there were complaints of code violations in other Alamance County mills, the preponderance came from Holt employees, most of whom happened also to be members of local 1777. This, then, was the context for what was to take place in September.[21]

The great textile strike of 1934 began quietly in Alamance County. Millowners reported no disturbances on its first day, with "all mills running." Indeed, most believed the strike would miss the community altogether, given the relative lack of privation in the town. "Observer," the *Daily Times News* columnist, was sure the strike would bypass Alamance County, unless, of course, "it should be prolonged and tie up raw materials."[22]

This optimistic view was soon proved wrong, as the flying pickets arrived in town on September 5. "Under cover of darkness and drenching showers," reported the *Raleigh News and Observer,* they had forced five mills to close by 9 A.M. that day, and another eight the next, essentially shutting down "the cotton, silk and rayon industry of Alamance County." Most of the flying pickets were young men, who went about their work with "occasional whoops and hoorays." They were, reported the local paper, lads "in their impulsive, daring age, lacking the background of experience to provide them mature thought. Few of the older men of families were there," and few women workers seemed to be deeply involved. "They trekked out along with the men," but then most of them went home. The strike, to them, was "the affair of the men," concluded the paper, though it was noticed that "some of the ladies, interested in proceedings, dressed and returned to mingle with the crowds about the mill gates, merely to see what was going on. There was little to be seen, merely men, more men, men of industry and men from all ranks of the city out to listen—and do little talking."

There had been no violence in Burlington, however, and it was clear that while many workers supported the strike, others were angry at being forced to quit work. Governor Ehringhaus lost no time in dispatching two companies of the National Guard to the town to protect both mill property and those workers who wished to remain at their posts.[23]

The presence of the flying squadron had a profound effect on the local community, where the general assumption was that if they had not "made a display here," there would have been no walkout, "in a community in the midst of economic conditions as favorable as maybe found in the entire United States." The town's business leaders cried "invasion." Burlington had been "singularly free from labor disturbances during its entire history as a growing industrial center," lamented the *Daily Times-News.* Wages had always been high, living conditions ideal, and the labor force overwhelmingly local, three factors which together made "for a happy and satisfied community of people." But all had changed with the arrival of the "invading forces," men and women in "open rebellion" against the code authority, "the direct representative of the United States government." Public opinion in Burlington, initially at least "halfheartedly" in support of the workers, had changed as a result of the action of these "riotous mobs" and was now ranged firmly against the strikers. Curiously, some of the local strikers seemed to share this view. Sonny Davis, president of the UTW local, disavowed some of the pickets' activities and deplored any tendency toward violence. He also made the point forcefully that they were definitely not local people. Speaking after eleven picketers had been arrested for "forcible trespass" after entering the Whitehead Hosiery Mill and attempting to force members from their jobs, "the mild spoken young leader" pointedly refused to endorse their action, telling a union rally on September 9 that though the strike must continue, it must do so without further violence. By this time some Alamance County mills had already reopened, many with a skeleton work force.[24]

As most Burlington factories remained closed, community attitudes hardened. On September 11, there was a union parade in the business district, this time involving "older people and young women," as well as men. The procession was orderly, led by a striker carrying an American flag, thus "indicating the patriotic spirit of those championing the strike cause." Behind him, strikers held banners attacking the stretch-out, supporting the UTW, and specifically calling for the forcible closing of the Plaid and Mayfair mills, both of which had kept open throughout the strike. That night more pickets arrived in Burlington, "blowing horns and yelling." Ominously, so did more guardsmen, trailing the pickets as tension mounted in the town. Later there was a demonstration at the Standard Hosiery Mill, as the picketers tried to get the workers out, "the smell of violence was in the air," and, according to press reports "many women and children . . . feared for their personal safety."[25]

There was violence aplenty on September 14, as workers attempted to enter the E. M. Holt Plaid Mill to begin the 7 A.M. shift. They were met by a large crowd of strikers, most of them identified as local "peaceful pickets" through the wearing of special ribbons on their coats or dresses, but there were also some hardened unionists from outside the community, fiercely determined to shut the mill down. There was a melee, as National Guardsmen dispersed the angry crowd with tear gas and bayonets. During the struggle, five strikers, including a young woman, suffered bayonet wounds, although none of them was seriously hurt. The girl was Gracie Pickard, sister of local UTW secretary Walter Pickard, one of the most prominent of the strike leaders. The guardsmen might have had it in for Gracie, for she had baited them noisily since their arrival in Burlington. Earlier, they had bundled her into a truck and driven her around the town, a warning to her and other women not to become involved in the strike. They did not frighten her in the least. Rather, her brother Walt said, "my sister stood proud, knowing it was for the union." There was outrage in the town, by no means all of it directed at the guardsmen. Mattie Shoemaker, a mill worker and nonstriker, expressed herself delighted that the "Pickard girl" had met her just deserts, for she had been on the receiving end of Gracie's tongue all week for her refusal to support the strike. Deputy Sheriff Davis was also pleased at Gracie's injuries, all the more so because she had been put in the county jail once her wounds were treated. "You know that thing," he told Mattie, "that's what he called her. 'That thing' he didn't call her a lady. . . . 'You know that thing that talked to you this morning? Well she sure is on the inside looking out. She's down at the County jail.'" For his part, Sonny Davis was again critical of the flying squadrons, some of whom allegedly tore the ribbons from the clothes of the peaceful picketers, and the associated violence. "If we can't win fair and clean," he said, "I don't want to win. I have told our members to refrain from any rough stuff and don't intend to stand for it." Burlington's mayor, E. B. Horner, deemed it time to issue a general call for the upholding of law and order in the community. Attacking the flying squadrons for their "wild riding" and "loud and boisterous conduct," he assured the community that the local union leadership had advised him "that this group is no part of their activities." Accordingly, he urged all citizens not to follow the squadrons about, as some "curiosity seekers" had been doing, but rather "to refrain from congregating or joining in automobile processions on our streets." In that way the squadrons would become isolated, and all could see what they were, invaders from other parts of the South.[26]

The tear gas and the bayonets were bound to provoke a response. That night, a bomb, intended for inside the plant, exploded in the yard of the Holt Mill. First reports were of a "massive blast" which did considerable damage to the mill and its surrounds, but in actuality less than $100 worth occurred, mainly in shattered windowpanes. A second bomb was found, unexploded, the next day under a loom at the Stevens Manufacturing Company. Had the two gone off properly both mills might well have been wrecked. The bombs were thrown from a passing car, which eyewitnesses identified as being occupied by two men.[27]

Burlington's law enforcement officers, urged on by mill management, were determined to apprehend the bombers quickly. Sheriff H. J. Stockard immediately announced an award of $1000 for information leading to their arrest. Personally, he was of the opinion that "it was the work of communists who have been reported in the community" since the strike began. Throughout the next day, National Guardsmen "stopped automobiles throughout the area," searching for those "terrorists" and for more dynamite, several hundred sticks of which had recently been reported stolen from a local warehouse. No more explosives were found, but it was not long before various suspects were held for questioning over the crime.[28]

First to be held was a local striker called Emmett Johnson, detained after a taxi driver, Mack Flores, told police that Johnson had boasted he had thrown the dynamite and had asked Flores to "keep his mouth shut" about it. Johnson denied the allegation and produced several witnesses who placed him in nearby Altamashaw at the time of the bombing, but he was held nonetheless. A few days later three more strikers, Tom Canipe, "Tete" Howard, and J. S. Harraway were charged, not with the bombing as such, but with robbing the Kirk Holt dynamite store the previous evening. The search continued for other suspects, with the local officers soon to be aided by the importation of four private "coal and iron" police from Fayette County, Pennsylvania, employees of the coal magnate and notorious strikebreaker H. C. Frick. These men, all of whom, it later transpired, had lengthy criminal records and long histories of strikebreaking, were brought to Alamance County by a consortium of millowners headed by Spencer Love in order to help restore industrial order. "The socialists and communists, particularly the latter have temporarily taken charge of the situation in Burlington," Love told his sister. The people had to be brought "to their senses" and the strike broken no matter what the cost.[29]

Soon, two more local boys were arrested and charged with the actual bombing, Florence Blalock and Howard Overman. Both had lengthy records of petty criminality and had served time on the state's road gangs. Blalock had already run afoul of Sheriff Stockard earlier in the year, having been held on suspicion of having committed several robberies in Alamance County. He had also been charged by neighboring Orange County officers with carrying a concealed weapon. Then, in October, came the arrest of the "dynamite plot"'s alleged mastermind, local UTW official John "Slim" Anderson, together with H. F. Pruitt and Jerry Furlough, another local, who, it was rumored, was ready to be a witness against his former conspirators. Moreover, Overman had apparently confessed his part in the plot to the Pennsylvania detectives, while Blalock had done the same, while drunk, to an acquaintance. Sheriff Stockard had seemingly done his work well in rounding up so quickly the perpetrators of what he described as a "terrorist attack."[30]

The bombing of the Plaid Mill knocked the stuffing out of the strike effort in Burlington. Local UTW leader Davis once more condemned the violence and talked of resigning his position. He personally had no time for the flying squadrons, he said, nor did he believe that any local striker had thrown the dynamite. "Outsiders coming from other towns had done 'the dirty work,'" was his conclusion. Echoing the views of the business community, Davis agreed that he had led the local walkout out of sympathy for the national cause, not from any dissatisfaction with local work conditions. Though newspapers reported that the rank and file did not share all his conservative views, their resentments were by now more directed at the National Guardsmen than the millowners. "There is plenty of pure American blood in the veins of the Alamance County textile workers," wrote one reporter, "and the same is true of the mill owners."[31]

The bombing had, in an odd way, brought the antagonists together. Not even the Socialist leader Norman Thomas, who made a visit to Alamance to rally the workers to the cause, could do much to halt the drift back to work. Spencer Love thought Thomas had "stirred the people up to rebellion and sedition against the status quo" in an effort "to arouse passion and class sentiment," but later even he admitted that the Socialist leader had not had much success. "The mills in Burlington are open again," Love told his sister on September 18. Sonny Davis confirmed this a few days later. Only a handful of workers were still out in Alamance County, he admitted. The strike there was effectively over. It had been an odd affair from the very beginning. Workers hated the stretch-out, that was certain, yet, according to the *Greensboro Daily News,* they were just as likely to blame their foreman for their discontent as they were the millowners like Love. Furthermore, the local UTW leaders like Davis were not always pleased at the tactics of the flying pickets, nor the atmosphere of violence their activities engendered. Davis insisted that there be no drinking or disorderly behavior on the picket line, threatening to turn over to the local police any striker caught offending, a view not exactly within the spirit of union solidarity, according to a "rough element" among the strikers. What had solidified the strikers, however, had been the arrival of the National Guard and their attacking of picketers with bayonets. Their presence had "crystalized strike sentiment," reported the *Greensboro Daily News,* and had boosted union membership, albeit briefly. Conservative strike leaders and the "rough element" alike condemned the guardmen's presence. They were, said the paper, "about as popular as a grave digger at a wedding party." Had it not been for the bombing, antiguard feeling might have kept strike sentiment alive in Burlington for a few more days—at least until the national leadership had recognized their defeat and declared it victory.[32]

The editor of the Burlington paper reached similar conclusions. Local 1777 of the UTW had reacted to the national strike call, he insisted, not local conditions. Conceding that the union had gained members during the strike because of the presence of the National Guard, he nevertheless considered it a disaster, and for this he blamed the violence of the flying squadrons. "The community" he lamented, "throughout its history a peaceful constructive community made up of purebred American citizenship, had never before faced a strike of any consequence. It was a new experience, one that few thought likely to occur. But it did."

The question now was could Burlington put the tension and violence behind it? The strikers, disregarding the reality that working conditions in the town were "as ideal as may be found in the industry," had acted out of misplaced sympathy with the national cause. They had lost, but so had the town as a whole—the strike had shattered its spirit of unity and trust, its sense of common purpose. Local businessmen made the same point a few days later. In a full-page newspaper advertisement headed "What Has Been Gained," sponsored by the Chamber of Commerce, the local Rotary chapter, the Kiwanis, the Burlington Merchants Association, and the Business and Professional Women's Club, they called on all workers to put "the agitators behind them," and to start rebuilding the "happy and prosperous community" that had existed before the squadrons came. Mill management could then again prove to be much better friends to the workers than the "agitators in the north who have brought on this costly strike," if only mutual trust could be reestablished.[33]

The strike had ended in Alamance County. Now came the aftermath, the revenge. As occurred throughout the South, and in defiance of the nationally negotiated agreement, Burlington's strikers often faced discrimination when they tried to return to work. Harry Rogers said it was widely believed that Burlington Industries maintained a "black list" of people never to be employed there and that everyone involved with the strike was on it, something subsequent research has confirmed. Most dramatically, and symbolically, however, revenge involved the determination to punish those accused of planning and carrying out the bombing of the Plaid Mill, for in the minds of mill management and those who did their bidding, an example had to be made. In the weeks that followed, of the ten men arrested on various charges relating to the bombing, a "core six" emerged who would eventually be convicted and jailed. Four would escape punishment because of the evidence they gave against their fellows. Though the arrests were made by the local sheriff, H. J. Stockard, it became clear through evidence presented at the trial that the strikebreakers hired by mill management had been crucial in building the case against the men.[34]

Of the "core six," John Anderson was the most significant figure. A Republican, and a longtime political opponent of Sheriff Stockard, he was also a striker and active unionist. Indeed, at the time of his arrest he was president of the Piedmont Council of UTW and an activist in the recent strike. J. P. Hoggard, J. S. Harraway, and Tom Canipe were all local men, mill workers, unionists—and strikers. Hoggard, in fact, was one of the local leaders. Howard Overman and the illiterate Florence Blalock had no record of strike activity or even of union membership but had bad reputations within the community. Both had police records, were "known to be heavy drinkers," had lived feckless, dissolute lives, and having had road gang experience, had previously worked with dynamite. The other four, three of whom would eventually provide the bulk of the state's evidence—Avery Kimrey, Jerry Furlough, Charlie McCullom, and H. F. Pruitt—were a varied lot. Kimrey was a striker and a unionist with no police record, but both Furlough and Pruitt had previously been convicted of serious crimes, while Furlough's army career had ended in dishonorable discharge. McCullom's life had been punctuated by periods in jail, mainly for liquor offenses. As early as 1907, however, he had served forty days on a Rockingham County chain gang for assault. He had also been jailed for stealing chickens and, in 1920, for attacking Tessie Wilson, a "Negro woman." One of Burlington's most disreputable citizens, he was a frequent drinking companion of Florence Blalock's. It was on the testimony of these three, Furlough, McCullom, and Pruitt, that the state relied to build its conspiracy case against the others.[35]

The trial of the alleged conspirators began in the Alamance County Superior Court in Graham on November 28, 1934, before Judge E. H. Cranmer and a jury later alleged to have been handpicked by Sheriff Stockard. Local interest was intense, and the courtroom was packed, as it would be throughout the trial. According to the *Daily Times News,* there had never "been a case in Alamance county . . . that attracted more attention than this." The charges were several: conspiracy; breaking and entering with intent to commit a felony; the larceny of dynamite; the receiving of dynamite knowing it to be stolen; the attempted bombing of the Stevens Manufacturing Company; and last, but by no means least, "injuring the property" of the Plaid Mills. The trial lasted only a week, and its course is worth following, if only to witness the determination of the community to punish those who had recently transgressed against the economic order, and the lengths its pillars would go to ensure this.[36]

The prosecution team, county solicitor Leo Carr assisted by Thomas D. Cooper and Maj. L. P. McLendon, presented evidence that, to say the least, was mainly circumstantial. Most of the evidence against Hoggard, Canipe, and Harraway had to do with their being seen near the Kirk Holt Hardware store the night it was broken into and the dynamite stolen. They were identified by a Lee Rumple as being in the area, in a car, along with two women, for they had assisted him as he attempted to push his own car out of a bog, an act of kindness they would soon regret. However, the only one of the three Rumple had known before that evening was Hoggard, who had subsequently come to beg him to forget there were women in their company "as they were all married men, and it might go home and cause trouble." The accused men admitted being in the general vicinity of the hardware store and agreed that they had stopped to help Rumple and his companions. They emphatically denied, however, having anything to do with the theft of the dynamite. Rather, they were on their way back from "Mack and Mack's," a Belmont store where they had gone to buy moonshine and had found the stuck car while taking a shortcut by Pine Top School. They were, they admitted, union men but had nothing to do with any of the violence associated with the strike. Numerous defense witnesses, including Canipe's wife, were able to back up the essentials of their story. Hoggard complained bitterly about the way the "Frick Men" had treated him upon his arrest. First, they had put him in a cell, he claimed, and "lit some stuff which perfumed the room" and made him dizzy, and then bluffed him into admitting his part in the conspiracy by saying that all the others had confessed. At no time did they identify themselves as private detectives, but rather as "federal officers." They had, they claimed falsely, already recovered unused dynamite from his "cow-feed box." All the three accused men had wanted that night, he plaintively stated, was "corn liquor." They had no need of "chemical liquor." The fact that they had been on the road and in the vicinity of the dynamite store was enough for the jury. Moreover, they were all union men, and Hoggard was a strike leader. They were duly convicted and sentenced; Hoggard received four to six years, Canipe and Harraway, two each. Yet even the prosecuting attorney had conceded that there was no real evidence against the three of them. They were punished for disturbing the socioeconomic order, not for criminal action.[37]

The evidence against Overman and Blalock, who supposedly manu-factured and threw the bombs, came from confessions allegedly made either to the Frick detectives or to Charlie McCullom. Though the night watchmen at both the Holt and Stevens Mills saw objects being thrown from a passing car, they were unable to identify the perpetrators, though one of them, A. E. Goodman, agreed, when pressed by the defense, that he *didn't* see "Slim" Anderson. S. E. Howard of Uniontown, Pennsyl-vania, deputy sheriff for A. C. Frick Coke Company, provided the bulk of the evidence against Overman. He had come to Alamance County on September 17, in the wake of the bombing, at the behest of "a group of private citizens and mill owners, through the direction of the Sheriff," to help in the investigation. On October 12, at a cabin in the Correct Time Inn, a local hotel of most unsavory reputation, in his presence and that of officers Jones, Steward, and Delph who had come South with him, Howard Overman allegedly signed, of his own free will, a full confes-sion to the crime, after saying that he would not take the rap alone, and they should "find Blalock" as well. No threats had been made, Howard insisted, and no reward or inducements offered, save permitting "the boy" to have a slug of whiskey once it was all over; they had thoughtfully purchased a bottle on their way to the inn.[38]

Defense lawyer Henderson saw things rather differently, alleging that Overman must have been so drunk after the deputies had finished with him he could not possibly have known what he was signing. "Don't you know that as a matter of fact when the boy came out of there you fellows had him staggering drunk?" he accused. There was plenty of evidence to back up this contention, as well as sufficient to show that the Frick men were not exactly saints either, that they had been regular patrons of a lo-cal bootlegger, and that Burlington's "whores" had paid them frequent visits at the Correct Time Inn—all charged to expenses. D. P. Steward, Howard's partner, argued that giving Overman a drink was no more than a sociable act, but under cross-examination conceded that by the time they had brought him home in a taxi, he was so drunk that he couldn't even find his way to the front door—a fact the taxi-driver corroborated. Steward also conceded that in his effort to get Overman to confess, he had told him that as all his coconspirators were "talking," he might as well do so, rather than take all the blame for the conspiracy. Overman himself denied all the charges against him. His account of what happened at the Correct Time Inn, predictably, emphasized the drinking. He drank so much, he said, that he had vomited, whereupon "a nigger" had brought him some soup. Eventually he had signed a blank piece of paper and been taken home, only to be rearrested later in the night. His wife confirmed his state of insobriety. He had just talked "blabber mouth," she said. "He could hardly talk he was so drunk." Overman denied taking any part in the bombing or ever working at the Plaid or Stevens Mills. At the time the bomb was thrown, he alleged, he had been drinking at Odell's Cafe, where he had got into a fight, something on which a number of witnesses agreed. He confirmed a long history of arrests for liquor offenses, however, and had twice served time on the roads.[39]

Clearly Howard Overman was not Burlington's most upright citizen. Yet the only evidence linking him with the bombing was the confession extracted by the Frick detectives, and even they admitted to giving him a drink or two. L. F. Going, the jailer who received him later in the evening, was more explicit. Overman was so drunk when he arrived, he said, that he was experiencing "running fits." Throughout the night he "jumps up and hollers," he went on, completely out of control. Clearly, a confession given while in such a state should have been regarded with deep suspicion, leaving aside the nature of its obtaining. It was not.[40]

Blalock, charged as Overman's partner in crime, also allegedly confessed to the bombing, not to the Pennsylvania detectives, but to Charlie McCullom, the town drunk. "I am the man that throwed the dynamite in the Plaid mill," he supposedly told McCullom during a marathon drinking session, adding that it was Overman who had driven the car that night. He also admitted to having robbed the dynamite store. Blalock allegedly implicated the other defendants as well, in particular Anderson, whom he claimed to have hidden the dynamite once it had been delivered to him. The defense lawyers had a high old time of it with McCullom, drawing attention to the amount of time he had spent since his arrest with the Pennsylvania detectives, who were currently paying for his hotel room, his food, and even keeping him well supplied with drink. McCullom agreed that this was so but said it had not influenced his testimony at all and denied that he had been coached in any way. Agreeing with enthusiasm that he was a heavy drinker, with a long string of liquor offenses, he nevertheless vehemently denied the defense charge that he had "been drunk or half drunk ever since the strike" was settled and that liquor had affected his recollection in any way.[41]

Blalock, like Overman, denied all the charges against him. He had also been drunk the night of the bombing, he said, having done the rounds of the illegal drinking establishments with Overman. Contrary to what most thought, he said he had borne his share of picketing during the strike, even though he was not a mill worker, but that was all. Furthermore, he had certainly not spoken to Charlie McCullom about the bombing. Under cross-examination he agreed that he had a long police record, mainly for liquor offenses, and that he had served time on road gangs, where he had learned how to use dynamite. This did not, however, make him a bomber. His mother, who took the stand on her son's behalf, testified that he had been home in bed when the bombing occurred, insensible from drink.[42]

It was Anderson, however, who was marked as the leader of the conspiracy. The evidence against him came from the confessions of three of those accused with him, Furlough, Pruitt, and McCullom. All of them identified the union leader as the "master-mind" of the whole conspiracy. Together they told a complicated tale of intrigue and intent to destroy property, if not to kill. It was Anderson who had planned the theft of the dynamite, which he had then hidden on his mother-in-law's property, so that, in the event of a sudden search of his own home, he would be in the clear. Furlough testified that Anderson had originally wanted him to do the bombing and that the plan had been for him to blow up Duke Power's transformer in Glen Raven. He, Furlough, and Pruitt had moved the dynamite under Anderson's direction, but Furlough said that he had been too frightened to damage the transformer. Anderson had then shifted the point of attack to the mills and had replaced Furlough with Blalock and Overman. "Slim" Anderson, then, had planned both the theft and the bombing, he said, as part of the union's strike campaign, it was as simple as that.[43]

The defense team, Maj. John J. Henderson, former lieutenant governor Elmer Long, and Clarence Ross, aimed at discrediting the three "confessors" as witnesses by pointing to their dubious characters and the fact that they were currently being "kept" by the Pennsylvania detectives, who rarely let them out of their sight. As well as drawing frequent attention to McCullom's drunkenness, they showed that Pruitt also had a long police record, both for drunkenness and carrying a concealed weapon, while even Furlough's own relatives were forced to admit that he was a notoriously mean-spirited man, who failed to provide for his wife and family, who habitually told lies, and who had a particularly violent temper. He was also a union member and part of the local strike organization. As such, he had fallen afoul of Anderson just the previous week—over union violence. A number of witnesses agreed that since the strike began, Furlough had been loudly advocating extreme action, including the dynamiting of mill property, and that he and Anderson had had a very public disagreement as a result. Anderson had "cussed Furlough out" for this, claiming his tactics "were too radical and too rough," and had eventually had him thrown out of the union hall. Furlough, for his part, had vowed vengeance.[44]

When Anderson took the stand, it was to deny having had anything to do with the theft of the dynamite or the subsequent bombing. Agreeing that Furlough had come to talk to him about such activity, he had, he claimed, told him to "get the hell out of here." The night the dynamite was stolen, he said, he and his wife were visiting friends, Mr. and Mrs. Paul Kimmons, a claim both the Kimmonses corroborated, while he was in bed asleep at the time the bomb went off, having spent the evening with his mother-in-law. A parade of witnesses testified as to his good character and that his prime concern during the recent strike had been to quiet the angry voices of those unionists, like Furlough, who were advocating violence. He had, said one, "pleaded with tears in his eyes for no violence." Anderson himself stressed that he had opposed the use of the flying squadrons, and that "we didn't want any rough stuff or any violence or any drinking" on the picket line. He had, he stated repeatedly, nothing to do with the bombing at the Plaid Mill.[45]

The defense rested in a reasonably confident frame of mind. The lawyers had worked hard and successfully to discredit the credibility of the three main witnesses against Anderson; they had at least implanted an alternative explanation of the bombing—that Furlough might have done it in anger after Anderson had expelled him from the union hall—in the jurors' minds; and they had shown that Overman's alleged confession had been made under the most dubious of circumstances. Furthermore, they had also shown that there was nothing to connect Hoggard, Harraway, and Canipe with the theft of the dynamite except their being in the general vicinity of the store on the night in question. In short, Henderson and his team believed they had done sufficient to disprove any notion of a conspiracy existing, while at the same time demolishing the flimsy and manufactured case against their clients.

They had not, however, convinced the jury, carefully selected as it allegedly had been by Sheriff Stockard and kept to its task by intimidation, the odd hint of bribery, and the partiality of the judge's charge. Judge Cranmer, who had described the alleged plot as "striking at the very roots of civilization," repeatedly made it quite clear where his sympathies lay. Describing the UTW leadership as "men living in luxury in fine hotels from the earnings of hard working people," he had nothing but contempt for local folk like the defendants, willing to do the bidding of parasites such as they. Six of the defendants were found guilty and given savagely punitive sentences: Anderson, the man most feared by the local power structure, was ordered imprisoned for eight to ten years; Blalock and Overman for five to seven; and, as noted earlier, Hoggard from four to six, and Canipe and Harraway two years apiece. A seventh defendant, Avery Kimrey, who played no part in the trial, and who may or may not have been in the car with the others the night the dynamite was stolen—it was never clearly established one way or the other—received a two-year suspended sentence. Furlough, the state's chief witness received a brief suspended sentence on one count only, the others all being nol-prossed. All three witnesses—Pruitt, McCullom, and Furlough—were promptly given jobs at the Plaid Mill. Spencer Love and his companions had had their revenge.[46]

The verdict was popular with Burlington's business community. The *Daily Times News* called it a "triumph for justice and law and order in Alamance County and a warning to agitators everywhere that disorders of this nature will not be tolerated." Community feeling had never approved of "any incidents which occurred during the recent strike," the editorial insisted. "A small minority raised all the fuss, while a great majority condemned their actions." It was to be hoped that everyone now knew that "nothing is ever gained by violence" the main lesson of the verdict, and Burlington would once more be a true community, without the class tensions the strike had stimulated.[47]

A curious incident which occurred at the conclusion of the trial, as the convicted men were being hurried to jail pending the posting of appeal bonds, indicated, however, that such tensions had not yet departed. A large crowd had gathered to watch them leave. Blalock, handcuffed to Overman, appeared first. Suddenly, he struck out at Deputy Sheriff Alec Davis, who was closest to him. Deputy Lee Davis, also nearby, thereupon swung at Blalock with his "blackjack" but missed, hitting Alec Davis on the nose instead and "inflicting a painful but not serious injury." The crowd cheered lustily. A few minutes later, D. P. Steward, one of the Frick deputies, appeared. He immediately found himself surrounded by an obviously hostile crowd who jeered him, called him names, and cried "get him, get him." Steward, "used to meeting toughs at their own game in the Pennsylvania mining areas," drew both his own blackjack and his pistol and, thus armed, forced his way through the mob to a waiting automobile. The crowd action, their support for the condemned bombers, and their clear hostility to the "Pennsylvania detectives," was indication that the class tensions that Burlington's better citizens hoped were gone were in fact still very much present.[48]

Few people outside Alamance County had shown much interest in the trial of the Burlington bombers, but this was to change once the savagery of their sentences became known. At the nearby University of North Carolina, in Chapel Hill, where much of the state's liberal community lived and worked, there was outrage and a call for action, while in New York the International Labor Defense, the legal arm of the Communist Party, announced that it intended to coordinate the appeals of all the convicted men. The ILD had cut its teeth in the South in 1929, when it took over the defense of those accused of conspiring to murder Gastonia's police chief, Orville Aderholt, during the violent strike of that year. More recently, it had become deeply involved in the famous trial of the Scottsboro boys. The defense of the Burlington bombers presented an opportunity to broaden the party's support base in the South, something the Gastonia enterprise had singularly failed to achieve. Scarcely had the sentences been handed down, therefore, than a Workers Defense Committee was organized under ILD auspices, with instructions to make contact with sympathetic members of the Chapel Hill academic community. Don West, one of the founders of the Highlander Folk School and now a party member, was sent to Burlington to coordinate activities. There, he worked under the alias Jim Weaver, partly because he was wanted in Atlanta on charges of inciting insurrection. Quickly he assumed the chair of the defense committee. West remained in Burlington for several months before his real identity was exposed—ironically, not by a company spy or informant, but by Leonard Green, a New England socialist hired by the UTW's state president to conduct a confidential inquiry into the guilt or innocence of the accused men. Fearing extradition, West went underground and left the state; subsequently, Green made public his belief that the Burlington bombers were probably guilty as charged, for which he was duly censured by Norman Thomas.[49]

Those members of the Chapel Hill community who became activists on behalf of the convicted men included J. O. Bailey, and his wife, Loretta, of the university's English department, the young historian C. Vann Woodward, Olive Matthews Stone, then a graduate student, William T. Couch, director of the university's press, the socialist and English teacher E. E. Ericson, and, most important of all, the Pulitzer Prize–winning poet and dramatist Paul Eliot Green. West recalled making contact with Green immediately he arrived in the area and said that the playwright "was very active" in the Workers Defense Committee "after we got him convinced that it was really a frame-up." Green's recollection was that working with the ILD was a disaster; the Communists were less interested in helping the convicted men than in promoting their own ideological agenda, exactly the same experience as those who tried to cooperate with them in Gastonia or Scottsboro had had or were to have. Nevertheless the liberals and the ILD people did work together for a while on the Workers Defense Committee, albeit increasingly unhappily.[50]

Paul Green had taken no particular interest in the original trial of the men, but his sympathies were aroused when Don West brought Hoggard, out of jail on bond, to visit him, just prior to the latter's imprisonment. Shortly afterward, Blalock's mother also visited him. She was very much afraid that her son would attempt suicide while in prison and begged Green to use his influence on Florence's behalf. She was a mill worker, he said, and "a very illiterate woman, but tears are never illiterate, they all speak the same language, and motherhood does also." Deeply moved, he visited Blalock in jail, was profoundly shocked at what he saw, and convinced as he listened to the stories and read the trial transcript that there had been a dreadful miscarriage of justice. He worked determinedly, therefore, to secure the release on bail of all the prisoners, pending their appeal to the state supreme court.[51]

Throughout January and February, Green, Couch, and Ericson worked with the Workers Defense Committee in publicizing the case at a series of meetings in both Chapel Hill and Burlington, and at establishing a bail fund. "It's going splendidly here," West/Weaver wrote Anderson on January 10.

> Last night the WORKERS DEFENSE COMMITTEE met in its regular meeting. Paul Green, W. T. Couch. . . . E. E. Ericson, two ministers and some five or so students and others were here from Chapel Hill. There were about fifty or so persons there last night, among them many new workers who are becoming interested. We laid plans for immediate bail (Blalock had been abused, tear gassed, etc. in the Hillsboro Jail). . . . We raised part of bail among farmers and workers. Last night Paul Green definitely promised to go part of bail also. We will fix that up today. . . . The two lawyers from New York representing the ILD have certainly shown these people what an organization of workers expects of lawyers . . . Only by our united, collective efforts can we workers ever hope to effectively fight our oppressors, the mill owners.

The class battle was thus well and truly joined.[52]

As well as attending meetings of the Defense Committee in Burlington, Green, Couch, and their supporters sponsored their own branch of it, on the Chapel Hill campus. The *Daily Tar Heel* carried reports of several meetings held in January and February 1935, including one addressed by Anderson and Hoggard, both out on bail by this time. The students had become intensely interested in the case and had formed their own "Committee for the Defense of the Burlington Prisoners." Hoggard and Anderson, for their part, proclaimed their innocence and described in detail the realities of life in the North Carolina jails of the time. They were kept in the dark most of the time, Hoggard said, and at no time were they even given a change of bedding. Blalock, in particular, was badly treated, because of his hot temper. In one incident he was temporarily blinded by tear gas, shot at him from point-blank range in an attempt to quiet him down. They made it clear how glad they were to be out and how much they appreciated the efforts of those working on their behalf. Acknowledging their deepening commitment to the cause, Green and his supporters formed the League for Southern Labor, its purpose to secure pardons for all the defendants. Soon to change its name to the Southern Committee for People's Rights, its charter members included Green, Couch, Bailey, Phillips Russell, and Woodward.[53]

Of course, the Burlington power structure quickly became aware of the growing support for the convicted men and deplored it. "Have you ever heard of Paul Green at Chapel Hill been rated as a communist?" Spencer Love angrily asked his sister Cornelia. "I have it on definite authority that he has attended several communist meetings in Burlington recently and has participated actively in the ring that is trying to get off the communistic group that set off the dynamite during the strike in Burlington." She did not believe he was, was Cornelia's reply. Rather he was "merely trying to help out a case of injustice," however mistaken he may have been. Spencer Love remained unconvinced. "The men who were convicted in Graham were guilty beyond any shadow of a doubt," he insisted. "If Paul Green is not a communist he is certainly beyond the slightest question associating and affiliating with them in this matter." The evidence in the case, to his mind, was totally convincing, much more so than in that of Bruno Hauptmann, the alleged killer of Charles Lindbergh's young son. Love had become obsessed with the Lindbergh case, currently dominating the nation's news media, and was quick to see parallels in his own circumstances. "It is altogether possible that you may at some later date see the communists come out and defend Hauptmann," was his dark conclusion.[54]

Nothing illustrates more dramatically the heightened class tensions in Burlington and the paranoia of its elite laid bare by the strike than Love's reaction in April 1935 to a fearful personal tragedy. In February 1935 Blalock, who had not yet received bail, escaped from custody and remained free for several months. Taking advantage of the loose security provisions of the Alamance County jail, he and two fellow prisoners had lowered themselves from a second-story window by means of a blanket ladder, after "prizing open" the iron cage in which they had been locked for the night. A month later, Overman, while out on bail and with "some other fellows," robbed a warehouse at Stonefall, North Carolina, near the Virginia state line. While Anderson, Green, and those others who supported the prisoners' cause deplored these events, they were able to keep them in perspective. Anderson even wrote Paul Green and asked him to use his contacts in the mill community to have Overman returned to jail. "I feel sorry for him," he conceded, "as his weakness is whiskey. I understand he was on a drunk. His father has asked me to write to you and request you to turn him over to the law and let him remain in jail. I am of the opinion that that will be the best as he is of a criminal type." Anderson remained convinced, however, that neither Overman nor Blalock were guilty of a bombing, hence his compassion. He knew they were not guilty of any wider conspiracy, "for I did not know him (Overman) until after the arrest." Overman and Blalock, he insisted, were simply victims of circumstance dragged into the case because of their criminal records, unstable personalities, and generally bad reputations in order to make the convictions of the unionists more certain.[55]

Not so Spencer Love—he was appalled at Blalock's escape and convinced that he would attempt to wreak terrible revenge on those who had seen him convicted. Then, in early April, the Love family suffered a fearful blow. Spencer's fourteen-month-old son, Phillip, was found dead in his cot, never having awakened from his afternoon nap. Though there was no evidence of it, Love was insistent that the tragedy was not accidental and that Blalock was somehow involved. Again citing the Lindbergh infant's death, he demanded that a full autopsy be performed on the child's body. The Duke Hospital staff scheduled to carry it out were warned that the death might well have resulted from "foul play due to some labor disturbance at his [Love's] mill." Love told his sister that he believed Blalock may have poisoned his son, and only reluctantly accepted the medical opinion that "death in this case was the result of an overwhelming bacterial infection." He continued to flirt with the notion that Green and his supporters at the university had somehow engineered Blalock's jailbreak.

Blalock incidentally, was recaptured in Marion, North Carolina, in May. He had been there for some weeks, and could have had nothing to do with the Love family's tragedy. Spencer Love's reaction, the connection he made immediately between his son's death and the unrest in Burlington, is dramatic indication of the effect the recent events had had on him. He could not put them behind him. For the next two years, until discovered, he engaged in large-scale industrial espionage, spying on his workers, alert for any signs of recurring union activity.[56]

Meanwhile, Paul Green, Bill Couch, and the North Carolina liberals did their best to raise money to finance the bombers' appeal. Green was clearly the focal point. Twenty years later he recalled that he had not initially wanted to become involved, "having a play in mind I wanted to write for Broadway." But, as he read the accounts of the trial, and as he "listened to the pitiful story of the defendants," he became increasingly drawn in, financially and emotionally. The account book of the Chapel Hill Defense Committee for the Burlington Workers shows just how much money he personally contributed, while his general files indicate how much of his time was spent addressing meetings, writing letters, trying to bring their case to a wider audience. Lucy Randolph Mason of the National Consumers League was surely correct when she wrote to him appreciatively that "you were a great sport to put your whole living behind these men." For much of 1935, his plans for a new play postponed, Green effectively worked full time on the Burlington bomb case.[57]

It was not a lone effort, of course. Bill Couch did more than his share of speaking, writing, and fund-raising, while E. E. Ericson's forte was writing long letters to newspapers, outlining the events of 1934 and explaining why the appeal was so urgent. Typical was one published in the *Winston-Salem Journal* in May. Describing the trial, he insisted that it was held in an atmosphere tense with the bitter feeling engendered by the strike; in a courtroom where the prosecutor passed lightly over the evidence and spent his time appealing to the prejudices of the jury, where somebody found money to have as a "Special Prosecutor" one of the most prominent lawyers of the state, where the textile union was referred to as "a den of gangsters," and John Anderson, local union man, Republican (so far from being a "dangerous Red") and respected president of the Piedmont Council of the United Textile Workers, was referred to as "the Al Capone of Alamance County."

The prosecution's case, based as it was on confessions from "company stools," or allegedly made to so-called detectives from Frick Coal and

Iron was dubious in the extreme. The defense legal team, "Major J. J. Henderson, ex Lieutenant-Governor Long and Mr. Clarence Ross, had all firmly believed their clients to be innocent," and so did the members of the defense committee, hence the urgency of their appeal. Certainly, letters such as these did secure the case some regional publicity—and the unabated animus of mill management. Love's continued vehemence even created a breach with his sister Cornelia, a librarian at the University of North Carolina. She worked with Green and Couch; she knew they were not Communists "but had got mixed up in it because the dynamiters made [them] think they were persecuted and unjustly sentenced." Perhaps, indeed, they had been, despite her brother's insistence to the contrary.[58]

Of course, working on behalf of the bombers did lead the North Carolina liberals into the company of, and eventually into conflict with, folks who really were Communists or closely allied with party organizations. When Anna Damon, acting national secretary of the ILD, announced on February 1 that the organization would be involved in the appeals procedure, the potential for conflict was always going to be there. Initially, given that there was a Chapel Hill as well as a Burlington branch of the Workers Defense Committee, things went smoothly enough. The ILD people concentrated on working with the Burlington group, especially through Walt Pickard, Gracie's father, now president of the UTW local, following Davis's resignation. He was ostensibly the author of a widely distributed booklet, the *Burlington Dynamite Plot,* published by the ILD, which analyzed the recent events in class terms and linked them into a general class-struggle context. "Not the scabs, not the sheriff and his tear-gas," ran the argument, "not the National Guard with their bayonets, could break that strike. So the mill-owners thought up another way. They'd break our strike, they'd smash our union, with just the kind of frame-up the bosses used in San Francisco to put Tom Mooney away, because he organized the working people. And that was how the Burlington dynamite frame-up began."

The pamphlet attacked the class-divided town of Burlington—"almost all our folks are rayon and cotton mill hands, and just about all of us are poor. . . . While the rich folks in town—the Holts and Loves and Smiths—never put in an hour's work in those mills in their lives"—the empty promises and duplicity of the NRA and the New Deal, and the travesty of the alleged bombers' trial. Concluding with a call for support in defending their brothers, Pickard praised the ILD for "getting all its members and branches and friends behind us in our fight." It would be a hard struggle. "But it's going to take united labor all over the country to get our men free," the pamphlet ended. "The mill-owners think they've broken our union, but we are building it again, step by step. They think they've put our men in jail for years, but we are going to get them out and we are going to show up this whole rotten frame-up for what it is." The name on the title page might have been Pickard's, but the words were Don West's. They echoed a left-wing political perspective considerably removed from that of the majority of Chapel Hill branch members, motivated as they were much more from traditional liberal notions of fairness and justice than from any ideological considerations. The sentiment was now also removed from the position of the UTW's national leadership.[59]

The alleged frame-up was featured prominently in the ILD's newspaper, *Labor Defender,* during 1935. A number of articles, most written by Pickard or Don West, though Ericson also made a contribution, went over the facts of the case, described the various components of the frame-up, emphasized the need for solidarity in opposing it, and praised the "courage and dispatch" with which the ILD had "come to the rescue" of the convicted men. Most repeated the argument laid out in the Pickard pamphlet. One, by Anderson, however, added a new dimension to the story. In it, he vehemently attacked Sonny Davis, local UTW president at the time of the textile strike, first for threatening to call off all local activity because of the explosion, and then for trying to dissolve the UTW local once the strike was over. Davis, he said, had "turned against us . . . and sided with the textile bosses," as indeed, had UTW president McMahon, who had not lifted a finger to help the accused men. They had been abandoned, "just when we need the union most." However, "even if the top officials of the UTW have joined the bosses and turned against us" he stated, "our fight to build our union, and our fight to free our six men sentenced to the pen, is going right on. The Workers Defense Committee, helped by the ILD is fighting tooth and nail against the frame-up." There was in none of these articles, not even the one by Ericson, any mention of the activities of Paul Green and his Chapel Hill group, who had, in fact, raised the bulk of the bail money and would provide for most of the other legal costs associated with the appeal. As had been the case in Gastonia, the ILD hated sharing the spotlight with anyone—especially liberals.[60]

Nevertheless, as the appeal hearing date approached, the liberals and the ILD continued to work together in public, though increasingly unhappily. They appeared on the same platform at rallies, especially those at which the defendants appeared and told their stories. Hoggard, in particular, was most effective. Older than the others, with a good grasp of the language, and a history of union activity, his devastating attacks on Furlough, emphasizing his long-term predilection for violence, were compelling. So, too, was his account of his treatment at the hands of the Frick detectives—"they smoked me and tried to dope me with stuff they burn [*sic*] in the room"—and the miseries of imprisonment. In the Hillsboro jail, to which the prisoners had been originally transferred, he said, he and Canipe were placed in a cell only three feet wide and five feet long. Moreover, "they had a colored boy up stairs [*sic*] over us who was up for murder and confessed and he'd get worried and turn the spigot and run water on our floor." Their cell was thus constantly flooded, he said, but no one paid attention to their complaints. Blalock, he confirmed, had been particularly badly treated, being teargassed on more than one occasion. At rallies and public meetings then, with the defendants present, those who believed in their cause, or were merely using their circumstances, could at least appear united.[61]

Once the ILD lawyers had arrived, and the appeal began in earnest, the divisions between the two groups simply could not be contained. The North Carolina Supreme Court heard the appeal in the last week of August 1935. Col. John Henderson, Elmer Long, and Clarence Ross, all local lawyers, continued to appear for the defendants, but they were joined by David Levinson of New York, retained by the ILD for the occasion. Opening, Henderson argued at length that the state had erred in 1934 by bringing the defendants to trial jointly on the several indictments, that no evidence of conspiracy had been brought out at the original trial, that the jury had been improperly selected, that Overman's alleged confession had been improperly admitted as evidence, and that the charge of Judge Cranmer had been "unfair and prejudicial to the rights of the defendants." Henderson's arguments were thoughtful and exceedingly well presented; however, it was Levinson who made the headlines. Rather than concentrate on the legal points at issue, he vigorously attacked North Carolina justice in general, charging that its courts denied the "laboring and lower classes equal justice" and that "economic justice" therefore, demanded a new trial. Though his diatribe was angrily cut short by Chief Justice Walter P. Stacey, Paul Green thought the damage had been well and truly done. He had earlier predicted to Couch that "these guys are going to ruin the whole thing if we let them get up and plead," and that was precisely what had happened. "These ILD guys got up in the middle of things and started preaching and cussing out North Carolina for the injustice here, the blindness of the people," he recalled and "they took it away from local control." No amount of legal argument could have retrieved the situation after Levinson's outbursts, he bitterly reflected.[62]

And that was how it worked out. Stacey announced the court's decision in November. Confining itself to the narrow issue of whether a crime had been committed, and ignoring the issues of social and economic justice which Levinson had raised, the state supreme court confirmed the sentences on six of the original seven defendants. It found no merit in the defense argument that Judge Cranmer should have originally granted each defendant a separate trial, nor, indeed, in any of its subsequent arguments, believing the evidence sufficient for the jury to have found the men guilty on all counts. The "economic justice" argument had no relevance, Stacey said, for the case had involved "no rights arising out of the relationship between employer and employee." Rather it was "a plain case of violence and wilful injury to property as a result of unlawful conspiracy." That was all there was to it. Howard Overman, however, was to get a new trial. His initial sentence was quashed on the grounds that his confession had been illegally obtained, not, as the defense contended because the Frick detectives had gotten him drunk, but rather because one of them, Steward, had falsely stated that the other defendants had also confessed. "A confession wrung from the mind by the flattery of hope or by the torture of fear, comes in such questionable shape as to merit no consideration," the court determined. Overman's confession clearly fell into that category. Otherwise, nothing had changed. The *Raleigh News and Observer* believed the court's action afforded "little comfort," especially "in the light of the villainy of the detectives who, though paid by private interests, had been sworn as deputy sheriffs of the county of Alamance," but most other press comment was supportive of the court, tending rather to attack "all the ineffectuals in North Carolina," in particular, Paul Green. The *Daily Times News,* for example, deplored "the attempt of a few highly educated and intelligent men at Chapel Hill, associated in various capacities with the University of North Carolina, to make a second Mooney case out of the 'Burlington Dynamiters' trial." All they were doing, said the editor, returning to his well-worn theme, was "widening the gap of class hatred and extending the millenium [*sic*] of caste-eradication ever more distant." It was time for Green and his supporters to let well alone, for their continued efforts were "serving only to stoke new fires of lawless strife between the forces of employer and employe [*sic*]." The millowners, of course, felt entirely vindicated. They had known all along, said Love, that the men were guilty; now there would be an end to the fuss and bother.[63]

Undaunted, the liberal community pledged to fight on—all the way to the United States Supreme Court, if necessary. So did the ILD, as it vowed "to force a new trial for these innocent men." "The future of every trade unionist in America is tied up with the fate of the Burlington prisoners," proclaimed the *Labor Defender.* It never happened. William Couch continued to write angry articles arguing for their innocence, the Southern Committee for People's Rights named them "political prisoners," even as, one by one, the men surrendered themselves to the Alamance County Superior Court and began serving their sentences. The ILD shortly found greater causes to turn to; "nationwide" interest was short-lived, if indeed, it ever had existed, and the Burlington bombers were forgotten—except by Paul Green. There was unfinished business to be done, not the financing of an appeal to the Supreme Court, that was unrealistic. Rather, he continued to do what he could to help the families of the men whose lives had unexpectedly intersected with his. When Canipe's wife wrote seeking a loan in order to save her furniture, she called him her "Dear Friend." She realized, she said "what a friend you have been to Tom and the other boys in the dynamite mess. You will never know how much I appreciate what you have done." Green did not think he deserved such praise. He had not, after all, even been able to keep them out of jail. Still, they were not there for long. Canipe and Harraway were paroled within a year; the others followed soon after, "free men again." "Good times came," he recalled, "and we all moved on to other matters of daily concern, making a living and carrying on our jobs." Paul Green should not have been so deprecatory. He had devoted, for a while, his money and his time to securing justice for the "Burlington bombers," and he had done it, unlike those of the ILD, not for the party, not from ideological imperatives, but for reasons of simple humanity. Thus finally ended the 1934 textile strike for the citizens of Burlington, North Carolina.[64]

Part IV

The Strike

Reflections

Greensboro, North Carolina, police chief reading a striker's picket.
Library of Congress, LC USF 33–020926–M4.

Reflections

"WE DIDN'T HAVE NO BACKING.... WE SHOULDN'T have done it. The South hadn't even begun to organize well by then," remembered Kasper Smith, former textile worker and striker. "What happened in 1934 has a whole lot to do with people not being so union now." The veteran organizer, Solomon Barkin, made much the same point at a 1984 symposium commemorating the strike's outbreak. The strike's leaders had had little "experience with leading large strikes," he asserted; there was no money to sustain the effort; "organizational preparation was practically nil"; there was little support from other unions, the federal bureaucracy or the president, "preoccupied" as he then was "with recovery rather than labor relations." Moreover, the AFL generally had failed its local union base, especially those "which had been spontaneously formed" in the wake of the NIRA's passage. They were essentially left to their own resources during the strike, despite all Gorman's posturing, his so-called sealed orders supposedly sent to the local unions, binding them into a coordinated national effort, his use of the NBC national radio network, again to promote the strike's national dimension. This was a sham, said Barkin. There were no "sealed orders," no national direction, no widespread public or union support. This was not a national strike at all, but rather the sum of thousands of essentially local efforts, often with differing impulses and aims, and this was especially true of the cotton textile South, the strike's supposed epicenter, where the workers' sacrifices were the greatest, the repression the most severe, and the consequences of failure the most long-lasting.[1]

Janet Irons has pointed out that those few historians who have written about the 1934 strike at all have concentrated on its failure, essentially echoing Barkin's judgment. Focusing particularly on the South, they have argued that the strike could not possibly have succeeded there, given the region's lack of "a strong and deep basis for unions," the paucity of experienced UTW leadership; the enthusiasm of the workers for 7(a) was not a substitute for preparation and policy. Southern "homegrown unions" could not possibly have sustained the effort required to maintain a successful strike, especially given the regional forces arrayed against them. Irons herself is inclined to dispute this view, claiming with some justice that southern strikers held up their end of the struggle as well as they could, given the strength of their adversaries—the mill owners and the states. Rather, she argues it was the failure of national leadership, the persistent myopia of Gorman and McMahon in believing a negotiated settlement favorable to the workers could be found, their ambivalence at the increasing militance of southern strikers, over whom they could exert little control, and the disastrous nature of the strike settlement itself, which ensured that workers were left again at the mercy of their employers. These, rather than a lack of union tradition or resolve, were the real explanations of failure in the South.[2]

James Hodges would certainly disagree with Irons over the strength of the South's "homegrown unions." "The union had been badly beaten," he wrote, "and the UTW officials had little choice in their heartbreaking surrender." Workers had, in fact, been drifting back "sheepishly" to southern mills since the end of the strike's second week, and despite the solidarity displayed in a few regions like Gaston County, sheer hunger was accelerating this movement. Elsewhere mills were also reopening, though many manufacturers preferred to remain shut, pending a general settlement, rather than risk damage to their plants. But the South was crucial to the strike's success, and once it was lost, it seemed good strategy to Gorman "to call it off and salvage the wreckage," all the more so since the UTW's coffers were completely bare. "We went as far as we could," he claimed, "short of starting a revolution." Moreover, Gorman believed that even if the strike had failed, and this he, personally, was never willing to concede, it had at least shown textile workers that "the old style of union organizing was dead." Workers had to build for the future, "a permanent union with organization protected through written contracts," and this had to be done on a national level, in keeping with the changing times. The experience of the 1934 strike had convinced a new generation of organizers of this necessity; it was their "baptism of fire." There was a linkage, therefore, between the experience of 1934 and the foundation in 1939 of the Textile Workers Union of America.[3]

Solomon Barkin agreed that though initially the collapse of the 1934 strike did "create a sense of failure and disillusionment," in the long term it prepared the way for the CIO drive to organize textile workers through its Textile Workers Organizing Committee and for the eventual founding of the TWUA. "The TWOC rekindled the independence fire," he asserted, and in the North, at least, people responded. "In New England and the Middle Atlantic states, many employers in 1937 accepted the unions without a fight in part because they knew that the organizational power was alive." Robert Zieger, though more cautious in his judgments, made essentially the same point. When the TWOC drive got under way, the reality was that the "nonsouthern and noncotton sectors in the industry—woolens, silk, hosiery, synthetic fabrics and dyeing—presented far more plausible initial targets for successful organizing and collective bargaining than did cotton textiles." Indeed, Sidney Hillman, TWOC chairman, decided to place most of his organizers outside the South, where the labor climate was much more friendly, arguing that success there would "provide the financial and experiential momentum" for subsequent work in Dixie. When the TWUA was eventually formed, more than 90 percent of its members were from northern or mid-Atlantic mills.[4]

In this connection, the work of historian Lizabeth Cohen is of signal importance in explaining this. In her superb *Making a New Deal: Industrial Workers in Chicago, 1919–1939,* she shows how the depression had destroyed the institutions America's ethnic communities had worked so hard to create as a means of dealing with life in their new world, but which had often served to keep them apart. The depression had not only destroyed their banks, their stores, their self-help societies—even their churches—it had also hastened the arrival of what David Kennedy has categorized as a "sense of common economic grievance that transcended the particular loyalties of the nation's diverse immigrant groups." Barriers which had kept workers apart had buckled under the strain, replaced by an embryonic American working class. The events of September 1934 are indicative of this. The Portuguese and French Canadian workers who joined together to close New Bedford's mills had in earlier struggles found themselves on opposite sides of the barricades. The Hazleton flying pickets were of diverse ethnic origin. Even in the unorganized textile towns of Maine, where the largely French Canadian work force had historically opposed all union activity; they finally defied their priests to join the picket lines and to battle the National Guard. When the strike was over, and they had lost, they did not, as we have noted, desert the union. Rather, they joined the TWUA, took part in its union drives, and also became charter members of the labor wing of the

Democratic Party. Outside the South, then, the strike of 1934 marked an important way station in the developing class consciousness of America's textile workers.[5]

Certainly, the southern aftermath was different, and yet, as Bryant Simon has shown, for a brief time, in South Carolina at least, the politics of race gave way to class-based division, and the strike of 1934 was a catalyst for this. In the wake of their defeat, mill workers swept Olin Johnson, one of their own, into the governor's mansion, and, a few years later, into the United States Senate. For a while they made up the most liberal element in South Carolina politics, and like their northern counterparts, they were Franklin Roosevelt's most fervent supporters. Their liberalism, of course, did not last. As African Americans, willing no longer to accept their segregated lives, pushed against the barriers that constrained them, Johnson drifted away from New Deal liberalism back to the politics of reactionary racism, and he took his textile worker constituency with him. But for a time, as Simon shows so poignantly, it was class, not race which had energized their political responses.[6]

The 1934 textile strike was an exceedingly violent one, as the merging of the northern and southern stories amply illustrates. Clearly this arose in part from the sheer desperation of the strikers, men and women for so long strugglers in a declining industry, their situation, their want, dramatically worsened by depression, briefly provided a glimpse of a better future by the new president, only to have these hopes dashed. Indeed, as their employers used the NRA codes to make their working conditions even less tolerable—the stretch-out was common to all branches of the textile industry in every part of the country—it is scarcely surprising that when they struck they did so with an intensity that could easily become confrontational. Given the mind-set of those who opposed them, their own sense of being caught up, swept along by forces beyond their control, their need to strike back, the extent of the disorder is less singular. The year 1934, after all, was one of industrial tumult. There was violence in Toledo, Ohio, in May as workers battled the National Guard in the city streets. Stoop-laborers fought hired toughs in California's Imperial Valley in June; San Francisco's longshoremen clashed with police in July in the course of a two-month strike there. In Minneapolis–St. Paul, the Teamster Local 574 fought police and vigilantes for months. On July 20, the police opened fire at a picket line. When it was over, sixty-seven workers had been wounded, and two lay dead. The textile strike occurred within a context of industrial disorder, as the newly forming working class began to seek its due.[7]

Still, the heart of the American textile industry remained unorganized. Moreover, those TWOC organizers assigned to the South confirmed what the few local UTW leaders still working there had long known: the failure of the 1934 strike and its bitter aftermath had left textile workers desperate and disillusioned, some actively hostile to further organization, most unwilling to take the risk again. "The smashing of the young UTW locals in the South sent a message throughout the Southern crescent," wrote Hodges, "and the unions retreated." It was Gorman's insistence that a major victory had been won, when in reality the workers were sent back to face their employers unprotected, that had so embittered them. In a series of reports to Gorman in 1936 and 1937 about the current situation in North Carolina, Paul Christopher constantly referred to this sense of betrayal as the main reason for the collapse of most UTW locals. It was "still a thorn in our side," he claimed, exacerbated by the general air of repression. There were only fifteen members left in Burlington's local 1777, he said, and they were forced to meet entirely in secret. "Most of them are literally scared to death." It was the same throughout the South, disillusion and fear followed the failure of 1934. As Franz Daniel, a veteran organizer, remarked in 1960, the memory of the UTW's "deception" was still raw in southern textile towns. George Stoney discovered the same thing thirty years later.[8]

If the influence of the UTW amongst textile workers was seriously weakened by the strike's failure, that of the NTWU was obliterated. The half-life it had lived since 1929 was over. Communist attempts to join in the strike were firmly rebuffed throughout the nation, with the exception of Easton, Pennsylvania, and even there the brief coalition collapsed in acrimonious disagreement. UTW officials cooperated with local police in New England to keep Ann Burlak away from public podiums, at the same time castigating "Communist agitators," for much of the violence that did occur. Throughout the land those opposed to the strike justified repressive action with the need to check such subversion. Rhode Island's liberal Governor Green made common cause with Eugene Talmadge in this regard. Of course, the Communist threat was nonexistent in both Rhode Island and Georgia, but this mattered not a whit. Throughout 1934 Communists were systematically scapegoated, North and South. At the end of it, the NTWU disbanded, its organizers ordered back into the industrial mainstream. Ironically some became tough local workers for the new CIO.[9]

As the strike developed, commonalities occurred in the way it was presented. One such was the emphasis on the involvement of women, especially activist young women, on the picket lines and in the union halls, supporting their men, indeed often outstripping them in the vehemence of their protests. The newsreels, the newspaper reports, the press pictures, the magazine articles focused on women's active involvement, right from the strike's first day. In the regional and local press, from Maine to Alabama, as well as the national dailies, the similarity of emphasis is quite remarkable. For example, Mary Heaton Vorse, the radical journalist, in the first of her many dispatches, wrote excitedly from New Bedford, about those "big good-natured Portuguese women who look like full-blown peonies," and the "black eyed little French-Canadians who . . . [f]ought like wild cats," who had come together to close the city's mills. The sober southern correspondent for the *New York Times,* Joseph Shaplen, a long-time observer of the southern industrial scene, as already noted, likewise devoted much of his first accounts of the strike to emphasizing the involvement of women, women walking the picket lines or as part of the teams of motorized "flying pickets," speeding along the South's highways, invading isolated mills and forcing their closure. He told of the angry phalanx of women in Spindale, North Carolina, who stormed four mills, shouting, "They can't do anything to us, Uncle Sam is behind us," eventually compelling management to close them all. "Women are taking an increasingly active part in the picketing," wrote Shaplen "egging on their men." They would, he believed, "stop at nothing," so profound was their commitment.[10]

As the strike intensified, so did the stories of the girl strikers. There was Rita Brouillette, the Saylesville "girl in green," facing down the commander of a Rhode Island guard detachment; there were the young women of Hazleton, Pennsylvania, ferocious on the picket line; the stalwart "hat pin girls" of Lancaster; Etta Mae Zimmerman and her friends of Hogansville, Georgia, defiant to the last, and eventually confined behind the wire in Governor Talmadge's "concentration camp." Why was so much attention paid to Etta Mae and her friends, indeed to all the women, young and not so young, who were active in the 1934 strike? Perhaps it was to sell newspapers and magazines. George Stoney and his interview team discovered plenty of evidence that both film cameramen and news photographers were instructed to shoot violent scenes whenever they could. Their employers actively sought images of disorder, especially scenes in which women were involved. The respected Charlotte journalist Legette Blythe was only one of the many who recalled this. It may be that they were also instructed to focus on women's general strike involvement, not only to emphasize their disorderly activity, but also to add a note of glamour, of sexual titillation, to their reportage. Certainly when they wrote about the activities of Ann Burlak, secretary of the National Textile Workers Union, the Communist Party's rival to the UTW, which attempted to capitalize on the strike call, they focused as much on her appearance and apparel—her long, bright red hair, her red dress and matching shoes—as on her message. Indeed, she soon became generally known as "the Red Flame." And remember "the girl in the green dress," and how exotic she was made to seem.[11]

Nevertheless, though the media may have sensationalized their activities, women took part in the strike because the issues were just as important to them as to their men—in many instances even more so. Most of these southern mill workers were "modern women," in the terms of Hall's and her colleagues' analysis. Unlike their mothers, who may also have worked in the textile industry, they saw the mills as their permanent workplace, their ticket to the smart life that the radio, the magazines, and the movies told them about, and they were increasingly sensitive to any changes in their work conditions, especially their wages and hours, as a result. Often they were married, with children; some like Ella May, the Gastonia martyr in 1929, were trying to raise them on their own. The sixteen women taken to the Fort McPherson camp, for example, all fit this description. But then, so did the young women in the Hazleton "flying squad." Usually of central European backgrounds, often the daughters of anthracite miners with a strongly developed sense of class, they made up the majority of the town's silk workers by the mid-1930s. They were also often the town's main breadwinners, due to the collapse of the mines, and the main victims of their employers' stretch-out and wage-cutting policies. Thus, wrote historian Christopher Sterba, "a potent combination—youthful rebelliousness, workplace frustration, and a family heritage of strike experience . . . came together in the flying squadron raids." And what of Rita Brouillette, the "girl in green?" Her name suggests she was French Canadian, the people at the bottom of the mill socioeconomic scale, the most depressed of Rhode Island's ethnic communities. Was she merely the leader of a group of young dispossessed, using the strike's general atmosphere of disorder to act out their anger through unfocused violence? Who can say? What can be said is that women mill workers throughout the land were in desperate economic trouble: their wages falling, as were their men's, their hopes of the better life the NRA seemed to promise dashed. There were some factors, indeed, that penalized women particularly, for example in the way employers evaded code wage rates by reclassifying jobs downward;

women workers were disproportionately affected by this. Then, in the cotton mills, the code agreement to move to a two-shift day cut out the third shift, the night shift, usually staffed by married women. For these and other reasons, including widespread sexual harassment, their active involvement in the strike is scarcely surprising.[12]

Hall and her colleagues were the first historians to use systematically the tens of thousands of letters from southern mill workers to the president, his wife, Hugh Johnson, George Sloan—indeed, to anyone who would listen—as they described the desperation of their lives, the misery of the mills, the arrogance of their employers, the way section 7(a) was ignored or evaded, how their working conditions had in fact worsened over the past twelve months, despite all the president's efforts on their behalf. They point out that while political letter writing had always been "a male, and mostly urban, upper-class affair," the preponderance of the letters they analyzed were from women, poor women from the South's textile communities. People from outside the South wrote as well, and while the letters are not as numerous, their general profile is the same. The majority are from women mill workers, describing the deteriorating conditions of their existence, and asking, at the very least, that the laws meant to check this be fairly administered. Listen again to Mary Aezendes of New Bedford—the name is Portuguese—a millhand at the Langshaw Cotton Mill, as she told Sloan that since the night shift had shut down, in accordance with Code provisions, workers were forced to eat, even to shave at their posts, so much had the pace of work increased. "I've worked here for twenty-five years," she said, "and since the NRA it has been worse than ever." North and South, these letters told a similar story. They also represent a decisive step in the politicization of America's female textile mill workers.[13]

When the 1934 strike was over, most employers outside the South honored, albeit grudgingly, the undertaking that striking workers be reemployed without penalty. Those that did not, like Samuel Samuels of the New Bedford Manufacturing Company, were quickly forced to change their minds. In this case, Samuels's one hundred female employees simply started work anyway. But they did not forget the lesson of the strike. Union membership grew throughout the textile industries, the more so when the lusty CIO took over from the UTW. Women, no less than men, joined the TWOC, the new TWUA, and the labor wing of the Democratic Party with which it was increasingly identified. They had become truly politicized.[14] In the South it was different; there manufacturers ignored the settlement provisions. Strikers, especially if they had held local union responsibility, were rarely taken back. The UTW locals withered and died. Southern textile workers had learned their lesson. Never again would they march en masse to labor's call. They still do not. This does not mean, however, that they were not politicized. In November 1934, Martha Gellhorn, writing to Harry Hopkins from Gastonia, North Carolina, in the strike's grim aftermath, painted a devastating picture of deprivation and hopelessness, of promises not kept, of union men broken by defeat, and of the millowners' revenge. The women were less despairing, buoyed by their continued faith in FDR—though no longer believing in his omnipotence. Gellhorn told of one woman she had recently visited, a former mill worker and striker, who had not been taken back. She had five children and was existing on a weekly relief allowance of $3.40. "Her picture of the President (on the wall) was a small one," she said,

> And she told me her oldest daughter had been married some months before and had cried for the big, colored picture as a wedding present. The children have no shoes and the woman is terrified of the coming cold as if it were a definite physical entity. There is practically no furniture left in the home, and you can imagine what and how they eat. But she said, suddenly brightening, "I'd give my heart to see the President I know he means to do everything he can for us; but they make it hard for him; they won't let him."

That is a statement of faith and of hope. But it is also a political statement—about the limits of political possibility.[15]

The anonymous woman in Gellhorn's letter, with her continuing devotion to Franklin Roosevelt, clearly had lost neither her faith in the president nor in the reform agenda he exemplified. For her, the strike had not been against the New Deal but against those who would subvert its intentions, those who "make it hard for him" to do good. For General Johnson, on the other hand, the issue was clear. In calling the workers out, McMahon and Gorman had connived with the NRA's radical opponents to subvert the president's plan for economic recovery. There were no reasons to strike; the codes were working well, including their several grievance procedures. At various times, Sloan, Besse, and Van Horn all expressed the same view, the UTW had struck against "the solemn arrangements" of the NRA and, by extension, against the New Deal itself.[16]

The strikers themselves had no doubt who their enemies were; they did not include federal government, and, especially not President Roosevelt.

They carried high the Blue Eagle in their various parades; above all, they marched out of the mills with the Stars and Stripes unfurled, as a symbol of their support for the New Deal, the NRA, and the better life it had briefly heralded. The flag was with them throughout September, often attached to the "flying squadron" cars that sped along southern highways or the back roads of eastern Pennsylvania; when they returned to work in brief triumph after Gorman's declaration of victory, it was frequently following the same flag. It was even there, bloodied and torn, at the funerals of those who died at Honea Path. The New Deal was never the enemy; rather it was those they saw as subverting it, their employers, those in power who had twisted and manipulated the NRA's provisions so as to deny to them what Roosevelt had made rightfully theirs. How could it have been otherwise? Yes, the NRA was indeed a failure; it could never have promoted recovery nor bought them a better life and was, fortunately, soon to be terminated by the Supreme Court. The strikers could not then have known this, though historians and economists in later years would generally accept it as true. Nevertheless, they were right to distrust their employers and those who worked the codes for their benefit, who ignored the minimum-wage provisions, who refused to acknowledge the intentions of section 7(a). In the end, their anger, their sense of betrayal could no longer be contained, and they forced the strike on the unprepared, inexperienced UTW leadership. It was, said Solomon Barkin, "an uprising of the discontented and disillusioned," not against the president, not against the New Deal—they remained its staunchest supporters—but against those whom they perceived, correctly, as wishing to bring them both down.[17]

Textile workers followed their leaders' call in September 1934 for many different reasons. For the Paterson silk workers it was just another skirmish in their long struggle against industrial decline. Workers in New Bedford were as much concerned with the strike's national implications as they were for their own conditions. Furthermore, "the national scope of the strike notwithstanding," let us recall Douglas Flamming's words. Not every experience was the same, he wrote, "In some towns, the strike provoked almost no response." In others there was compliance; in still others bitter conflict, violence, and bloodshed "between opposing groups of workers" or between strikers and the forces of the state—the National Guard, the special deputies, and state police. A point worth noting in this connection is that the northern states often had relatively sophisticated labor bureaucracies and dispute resolution procedures, and these sometimes worked to defuse potential flash points. There is no doubt that

Connecticut's state labor commissioner, Joseph Tone, played a key role in calming things down in the strike areas and that his success was partly due to the importance of his office. Similarly, in Bridgeport, Pennsylvania, it was the regional labor board which, in the end, found a solution to the Lees plant dispute. Even in Paterson, the local labor bureaucracy eventually exerted its influence. In the South, in contrast, there were no sophisticated state labor bureaucracies; governors sought no advice from state AFL officials, rather they simply told them to get the mills open. There were no independent attempts at conciliation, not even to prevent violence.[18]

Yet, overall, this local perspective was changing to a national one; this was the New Deal's abiding legacy, in labor relations no less than in all other aspects of American life. The 1934 strike needs to be located within this period of transition, a shift shortly to be symbolized with the passage of the National Labor Relations Act. Finally, it needs also to be considered as part of the struggle for economic and social justice which gave the twentieth century its configuration—and which continues still.

Notes

Preface

1. Robin R. Brooks, "The United Textile Workers of America," 349–51, 355, 379. The actual numbers of strikers will never be known. Union figures were always well above the industry count, for obvious reasons, while independent press estimates differed widely. Moreover, thousands of workers, not necessarily UTW members, or even sympathetic to the strikers, were idle because of mill closings, either by management determined to avoid trouble or by "flying squadrons." Whether they should be included in the count is problematic, yet the union invariably did so, hence the claim that at the strike's peak, around one million were idle, making it easily the largest walkout in U.S. history.

Chapter 1   *The Textile Industry in 1933*

1. Josephus Daniels to Franklin Delano Roosevelt (henceforth FDR), Sept. 17, 1934, in Papers of Franklin Delano Roosevelt, Private Personal File 86 (henceforth Roosevelt Papers, PPF), Franklin Delano Roosevelt Library, Hyde Park, New York. *Textile Worker* 19, 1 (Apr. 1931): 6–7.
2. Gladys L. Palmer, "History of the Philadelphia Textile Council," 1137–38.
3. James A. Hodges, *New Deal Labor Policy and the Southern Cotton Textile Industry 1933–1941,* 9–13; Gavin Wright, *Old South, New South: Revolutions in the Southern Economy since the Civil War,* 147–54; Seymour Wolfbein, *The Decline of a Cotton Textile City: A Study of New Bedford,* 33–37.
4. Alice Galenson, *The Migration of the Cotton Textile Industry from New England to the South 1880–1930,* 184–88.
5. Ibid., 39–45.
6. Hodges, *Labor Policy,* 12–13.
7. Ibid., 14; Galenson, *Migration,* 192–94; Yorke, quoted in Wright, *Old South,* 147.
8. Wright, *Old South,* 147–50; Douglas Flamming, *Creating the Modern South: Millhands and Managers in Dalton, Georgia, 1884–1984,* 112. See also my own *Gastonia, 1929: The Story of the Loray Mill Strike,* 6–8; and Hodges, *Labor Policy,* 13–14. Josephus Daniels to FDR, Sept. 17, 1934, Roosevelt Papers, PPF 86.
9. Louis Galambos, *Competition and Cooperation: The Emergence of a National Trade Association,* 20–23.
10. Ibid., 23–36.
11. Ibid., 55–66.

12. Ibid., 92–106; Hodges, *Labor Policy*, 18; Herbert J. Lahne, *The Cotton Mill Worker*, 21–22.

13. Jacquelyn Dowd Hall, James Leloudis, Robert Korstad, Mary Murphy, Lu Ann Jones, and Christopher B. Daly, *Like a Family: The Making of a Southern Cotton Mill World*, 235, 289–90; Galambos, *Competition and Cooperation*, 109–10, 157–69; Janet Irons, "Testing the New Deal: The General Textile Strike of 1934," 161–64.

14. Philip Scranton, *Figured Tapestry, Production, Markets and Power in Philadelphia Textiles, 1885–1941*, 28–29, 46–54.

15. Scranton, *Figured Tapestry*, 180–86; Steven Golin, *The Fragile Bridge: Paterson Silk Strike, 1913*, 21, 59–60, 76–82; Anne Huber Tripp, *The IWW and the Paterson Silk Strike of 1913*, 62, 170.

16. Wright, *Old South*, 154.

17. John T. Cumbler, *Working-Class Community in Industrial America: Work, Leisure, and Struggle in Two Industrial Cities, 1880–1930*, 202–5; Tripp, *Paterson Silk Strike*, 20–21, 61–64.

18. Wright, *Old South*, 152–55; Salmond, *Gastonia, 1929*, 8–9; Hodges, *Labor Policy*, 35–37; Janet Irons, *Testing the New Deal: The General Textile Strike of 1934 in the American South*, 22–25. (Henceforth Irons's dissertation will be identified as Irons, "Testing the New Deal," her monograph as Irons, *Testing*.)

19. Salmond, *Gastonia, 1929*, 9–10; Hodges, *Labor Policy*, 35; Irons, *Testing*, 29–33; Irving Bernstein, *The Lean Years: A History of the American Worker, 1920–1933*, 40–41.

20. Ella Ford, "We Are Mill People," 3–5; Flamming, *Creating the Modern South*; Hall et al., *Like a Family*; Allen Tullos, *Habits of Industry: White Culture and the Transformation of the Carolina Piedmont*; Daniel Clark, *Like Night and Day: Unionization in a Southern Mill Town*; Bryant Simon, *A Fabric of Defeat: The Politics of South Carolina Millhands, 1910–1948*; Timothy J. Minchin, *What Do We Need a Union For? The TWUA in the South, 1945–1955*. For the social scientists, see Lois McDonald, *Southern Mill Hills: A Study of Social and Economic Forces in Certain Textile Mill Villages*; Marjorie A. Potwin, *Cotton Mill People of the Piedmont: A Study in Social Change*; or Dorothy Myra Page, *Southern Cotton Mills and Labor*.

21. Hodges, *Labor Policy*, 26–27; Jacquelyn Hall, Robert Korstad and James Lehoudis, "Cotton Mill People: Work, Community and Protest in the Textile South, 1880–1940," 246 ff.

22. *Burlington Daily Times News*, May 21, 1929, July 1, 1937; Hall et al., *Like a Family*, 25–26, 116, 153; Bess Beatty, "The Edwin Holt Family; Nineteenth Century Capitalists in North Carolina," 511–35; Annette C. Wright, "The Aftermath of the General Textile Strike: Managers and Workplace at Burlington Mills," 84; John A. Salmond, " 'The Burlington Dynamite Plot': The 1934 Textile Strike and Its Aftermath in Burlington, North Carolina," 399–400.

23. Hall et al., *Like a Family*, 240–48; Tullos, *Habits of Industry*, 107–18; *Burlington Daily Times News*, Nov. 15, 18, 1927, Nov. 21, 1929.

24. Ethel Hilliard, interviews with Allen Tullos, Mar. 29, Apr. 3, July 21, Aug. 10, 1979; Charles Murray, interview with Brent Glass, Mar. 4, 1976; James Pharis, interview with Cliff Kuhn, July 24, 1977; J. M. Robinette, interview with Cliff Kuhn, July 1977; Mattie Shoemaker and Mildred Shoemaker Edmonds, interview with Mary Murphy, Mar. 23, 1979; Herman Newton Truitt, interview with Allen Tullos, Dec. 5, 1978, Jan. 19, 30, 1979 (henceforth Hilliard interview etc.), all in

Southern Oral History Collection (hereinafter cited as SOHC), Southern Historical Collection, Wilson Library, University of North Carolina at Chapel Hill.

25. Burlington Chamber of Commerce, "Why Burlington," 1934, 9 (pamphlet found in North Carolina Collection, Wilson Library, University of North Carolina at Chapel Hill).

26. Hall et al., *Like a Family*, 247–50.

27. Pharis interview; Hilliard interview; Shoemaker and Edmonds interview; Carroll Lupton, interview with Mary Murphy, May 18, 1979; Mary Ethel Shockley, interview with Cliff Kuhn, July 24, 1977; Ethel Faucette, interviews with Cliff Kuhn, Nov. 16, 1978, Jan. 4, 1979, all in SOHC. *Burlington Daily Times News,* Feb. 7, June 20, 1927, Oct. 18, 1929, Dec. 22, 1931; Hall, *Like a Family,* 250; Salmond, *Gastonia, 1929,* xii, 3–5.

28. Lahne, *Cotton Mill Worker,* 71–73.

29. Cumbler, *Working-Class Community,* 101–9, 127–33, 219; William G. McLoughlin, *Rhode Island: A History,* 120; Paul Buhle, "Italian-American Radicals and the Labor Movement, 1905–1930," 121–51.

30. Wolfbein, *Decline of a Cotton Textile City,* 7–11, 34–44, 80; William F. Hartford, *Where Is Our Responsibility? Unions and Economic Change in the New England Textile Industry, 1870–1960,* 9–13, 37–39, 74–75.

31. Rudolph J. Vecoli, *The People of New Jersey,* 69–73, 173–85.

32. Nancy Fogelson, "They Paved the Streets with Silk: Paterson, New Jersey, Silk Workers, 1913–1924," 134–35; Vecoli, *People,* 73–75; Richard D. Margrave, "Technology Diffusion and the Transfer of Skills: Nineteenth-Century English Silk Migration to Paterson" in *Silk City: Studies on the Paterson Silk Industry, 1860–1940,* ed. Philip B. Scranton, 9–27; Golin, *Fragile Bridge,* 2–3, 24–31.

33. Scranton, *Figured Tapestry,* 20–21, 103, 215, 221–23, 233, 242–44.

34. Ibid., 269. Interview with Elliot Broadbent, by Harvey Kantar and Tracy Miller (M46), Sept. 14, 1973, in Mill Life Oral History Collection (henceforth MLOC) Special Collections, University of Rhode Island, Kingston, Rhode Island.

35. Lahne, *Cotton Mill Worker,* 26–27. Cumbler, *Working-Class Community,* 115–19. Interview with Ernest Denomme, by Francoise S. Puniello, Feb. 17, 1971 (MLOC).

36. Scranton, *Figured Tapestry,* 27–28, 443.

37. Golin, *Fragile Bridge,* 25–26, 30–31, 49, 133; Margrave, "Technology Diffusion," 14–15, 24–27; David J. Goldberg, *A Tale of Three Cities: Labor Organization and Protest in Paterson, Passaic and Lawrence, 1916–1921,* 19–29.

38. Goldberg, *Tale of Three Cities,* 46–55.

39. Cumbler, *Working-Class Community,* 151–55.

40. Ibid., 158–61.

41. Goldberg, *Tale of Three Cities,* 83–91.

42. Edith Landes, interview with Christine Brown and Priscilla Golding (M93), July 5, 1974 (MLOC).

43. See Goldberg, *Tale of Three Cities;* Golin, *Fragile Bridge;* Tripp, *IWW and the Paterson Silk Strike,* passim; Scranton, *Figured Tapestry,* 42, 123–24, 221–23.

44. Hartford, *Where Is Our Responsibility?* 9–13, 37–39; Scranton, *Figured Tapestry,* 37; Cumbler, *Working-Class Community,* 166–77.

45. Scranton, *Figured Tapestry,* 47–53; McLoughlin, *Rhode Island,* 119–23; Golin, *Fragile Bridge;* Tripp, *The IWW and the Paterson Silk Strike,* passim; Ellen Grigsby, "The Politics of Protest: Theoretical, Historical and Literary Perspectives

on Labor Conflict in Gaston County, North Carolina," 150–55. For Passaic, see Vera Buch Weisbord, *A Radical Life*, 100–136; and Edward P. Johanningsmeier, "The Trade Union Unity League: Communists and the Transition to Industrial Unionism, 1928–1934," 167–68. On New Bedford, see Michael W. Santos, "Community and Communism: The 1928 New Bedford Textile Strike," 233–37.

46. For Gastonia and the NTWU, see Salmond, *Gastonia, 1929,* passim.

47. Brooks, "United Textile Workers," 223–37; Joseph A. McCartin, *Labor's Great War: The Struggle for Industrial Democracy and the Origins of Modern American Labor Relations, 1912–1921,* 166–67.

48. McCartin, *Labor's Great War,* 167–71, 182–83; Irons, "Testing the New Deal," 41–51; Hall et al., *Like a Family,* 187–95.

49. McLoughlin, *Rhode Island,* 190–91; Susan E. Jaffee, "Ethnic Working-Class Protest: The Textile Strike of 1922 in Rhode Island"; Louise Lamphere, *From Working Daughters to Working Mothers: Immigrant Women in a New England Industrial Community,* 183–89.

50. Brooks, "United Textile Workers," 312–50, 355–62.

51. Hodges, *Labor Policy,* 8, 17–20; Wolfbein, *Decline of a Cotton Textile City,* 38–41; Fogelson, "They Paved the Streets with Silk," 147–48; Scranton, *Figured Tapestry,* 410–11; Lupton interview, SOHC.

52. See the *Textile Worker* vol. 19, no. 3 (June 1931): 102, 112–14, 117–19; no. 4 (July 1931): 141, 161–62; no. 5 (Aug. 1931): 235; no. 6 (Sept. 1931): 254; no. 7 (Oct. 1931): 300–308; no. 8 (Nov. 1931): 341–45; no. 9 (Dec. 1931): 396–98, 412; vol. 20, no. 3 (Mar. 1932): 540–42; no. 4 (Apr. 1932): 6, 14; no. 5 (May 1932): 58, 63; no. 6 (June 1932): 85, 94, 103; no. 8 (Aug. 1932): 158–60; no. 9 (Sept. 1932): 189, 196–97; no. 12 (Dec. 1932): 282–84. The best discussion of the locally led southern strikes is in Irons, *Testing,* 29–37.

Chapter 2   *The New Deal*

1. William E. Leuchtenburg, *Franklin D. Roosevelt and the New Deal, 1932–1940,* 55–56; Christopher L. Tomlins, *The State and the Unions: Labor Relations, Law and the Organized Labor Movement in America, 1880–1960,* 104–6; Bernard Bellush, *The Failure of the NRA,* 6–11.

2. Bellush, *Failure of NRA,* 25–27; Hodges, *Labor Policy,* 45–46.

3. Bellush, *Failure of NRA,* 1, 28–29; Tomlins, *The State and the Unions,* 108; Colin Gordon, *New Deals: Business, Labor and Politics in America, 1920–1935,* 172–73.

4. Simon, *Fabric of Defeat,* 84–85; *Textile Worker* 22, 4 (Apr. 1934): 1.

5. Galambos, *Competition and Cooperation,* 165–68, 175–84.

6. Hodges, *Labor Policy,* 48–49.

7. Ibid., 49–50; *New York Times,* June 20, 1933.

8. Galambos, *Competition and Cooperation,* 216–26; Hodges, *Labor Policy,* 50–51; *New York Times,* June 28, 29, 30, 1933.

9. Hodges, *Labor Policy,* 51–55; Irons, *Testing,* 59–60; Galambos, *Competition and Cooperation,* 216–26; *New York Times,* June 27–30, July 1, 11, 16, 17, 1933; Bellush, *Failure of NRA,* 42–45; Ellis W. Hawley, *The New Deal and the Problem of Monopoly,* 221–22. For the Woolen Code, and the Rayon Code, see *Textile Worker*

21, 8 (Aug. 1933): 236–46. For the Silk Code, see *Textile Worker* 21, 9 (Sept. 1933): 264–74.

10. Galambos, *Competition and Cooperation,* 226; Hall et al., *Like a Family,* 290; Irons, "Testing the New Deal," 174–76; Bellush, *Failure of NRA,* 45; Hodges, *Labor Policy,* 55; Simon, *Fabric of Defeat,* 87–89.

11. Hodges, *Labor Policy,* 55–57; *Textile Worker* 21, 7 (July 1933): 197–98; Irons, "Testing the New Deal," 183.

12. Hodges, *Labor Policy,* 60–61; Brooks, "United Textile Workers," 349–51. United Textile Worker Papers (henceforth UTW Papers) in Textile Workers Union of America Collection, State Historical Society of Wisconsin, Box 674, Locals-Status 1934–1936.

13. Irons, "Testing the New Deal," 101; Irons, *Testing,* 69–70; Hodges, *Labor Policy,* 61–62.

14. Hodges, *Labor Policy,* 64–67; Irons, "Testing the New Deal," 176–78; Galambos, *Competition and Cooperation,* 230–31.

15. Hodges, *Labor Policy,* 68–70; Hall et al., *Like a Family,* 307–8; John W. Kennedy, "The General Strike in the Textile Industry, September 1934," 10–11.

16. Hodges, *Labor Policy,* 56–57; Hall et al., *Like a Family,* 293, 299–302.

17. Hall et al., *Like a Family,* 293–95.

18. Mrs. Fannie Ford to President Roosevelt, Mar. 13, 1934, Records of the National Recovery Administration, Record Group 9, National Archives, Washington, D.C. (henceforth NRA Records) Records Relating to Employee Complaints in the Textile Industry, File 398 (henceforth, 398, Employee Complaints).

19. Carl Welch to President Roosevelt, Dec. 11, 1933, NRA Records, 398, Employee Complaints.

20. Mary Aezendes to George Sloan, May 9, 1934; M. Moniz to "Friend" (President Roosevelt), May 8, 1934, NRA Records, 398, Employee Complaints. An exception to the tendency to treat the 1934 strike as essentially a regional one is David Kennedy in his volume in the Oxford History of the United States: *Freedom from Fear: The American People in Depression and War, 1929–1945,* 295–96.

21. Hall et al., *Like a Family,* 293–94, 309–10.

22. *New York Times,* July 19, 23, Aug. 27, 1933.

23. Ibid., Aug. 27, Sept. 1, 1933.

24. *Paterson Morning Call,* Oct. 21, 24, 25, 26, 1933; *New York Times,* Oct. 25, Nov. 29, 30, Dec. 3, 6, 1933; *Textile Worker* vol. 21, no. 9 (Sept. 1933): 259–60; no. 11 (Nov. 1933): 324–25.

25. *New York Times,* Sept. 8, 1933; *Textile Worker* 21, 12 (Dec. 1933): 339.

26. *Textile Worker* 21, 11 (Nov. 1933): 336; Simon, *Fabric of Defeat,* 97–99.

27. Simon, *Fabric of Defeat,* 96–101.

28. *Washington Post,* Sept. 1, 1934; Hodges, *Labor Policy,* 73–74; Irons, "Testing the New Deal," 302–4.

29. Carl W. Welch, Gastonia, North Carolina, to FDR, Dec. 11, 1933, NRA Records, 398, Employee Complaints; Hodges, *Labor Policy,* 76–78; Irons, "Testing the New Deal," 305–7.

30. Hodges, *Labor Policy,* 58, 86–87.

31. Ibid., 86–87.

32. Ibid., 88–89.

33. Ibid., 89; Irons, *Testing,* 86–88; Irons, "Testing the New Deal," 336–42; *Textile Worker* 22, 4 (Apr. 1934): 136–44.

34. Hodges, *Labor Policy,* 90–92, 96–97; Irons, *Testing,* 110–13; James L. Hoffman, "A Study of the United Textile Workers of America in a Cotton Mill in a Medium-sized Southern City: Labor Revolt in Alabama, 1934," 190–97; *Birmingham Age-Herald,* July 17, 18, 19, 1934; *Birmingham News,* July 18, 20, 1934.

35. *Birmingham Age-Herald,* July 19, 25, 1934; *Textile Worker* 22, 11 (Nov. 1934): 482–85. See also memorandum for Frances Perkins, Secretary of Labor, July 18, 1934, in Records of the Secretary of Labor, File 174, General Files of the Secretary of Labor, 1933–1941, National Archives, Washington, D.C.; Irons, *Testing,* 100.

36. Hodges, *Labor Policy,* 90–97; *Birmingham News,* Sept. 5, 1934.

37. *Birmingham News,* July 19, 1934; *Birmingham Age-Herald,* Aug. 6, 7, 1934; Hodges, *Labor Policy,* 97–98.

38. *Birmingham News,* July 18, 1934; *Birmingham Age-Herald,* July 17, 18, 1934.

39. *Paterson Morning Call,* Aug. 25, 27, 1934; *Birmingham Age-Herald,* Aug. 18, 1934; *Birmingham News,* Aug. 18, 31, 1934; Hodges, *Labor Policy,* 94–100.

40. *New York Times,* Dec. 8, 1933, Aug. 18, 1934; *Philadelphia Evening Bulletin,* Aug. 17, 27, 1934; *Birmingham News,* Aug. 18, 1934; *Paterson Evening News,* Sept. 1, 1934; Hodges, *Labor Policy,* 99–100.

41. *Philadelphia Evening Bulletin,* Aug. 28, 30, 31, 1934; *New York Times,* Aug. 28, 29, 30, 31, Sept. 1, 1934; *Birmingham News,* Aug. 30, 1934; Hodges, *Labor Policy,* 102–3.

42. Hodges, *Labor Policy,* 102–4; *New York Times,* Aug. 31, Sept. 1, 1934.

Chapter 3   *The Strike*

1. Hodges, *Labor Policy,* 104–5; *New York Times,* Sept. 1, 2, 1934; "A Chronological Record of the General Textile Strike," *Textile Bulletin* 47, 8 (Oct. 25, 1934): 9–34, 51–57; *Washington Post,* Aug. 31, 1934.

2. Hodges, *Labor Policy,* 105–6; Irons, *Testing,* 128–31; "Chronological Record," 11–13; *New York Times,* Sept. 1, 1934; *Washington Post,* Sept. 2, 3, 1934.

3. Hodges, *Labor Policy,* 104; *New York Times,* Sept. 2, 3, 1934.

4. *New York Times,* Sept. 2, 3, 1934; Mary Heaton Vorse, "Textile Trouble: New England on Strike," 147–48. It was the NTWU that organized the famous Loray Mill strike of 1929.

5. Hodges, *Labor Policy,* 107; "Chronological Record," 22; *New York Times,* Sept. 4, 5, 6, 1934; *Gastonia Daily Gazette,* Sept. 4, 5, 6, 1934.

6. Irons, "Testing the New Deal," 427; *New York Times,* Sept. 5, 1934.

7. *New York Times,* Sept. 5, 1934; *Washington Post,* Sept. 5, 1934; Vorse, "Textile Troubles," 148.

8. Irons, "Testing the New Deal," 438; Hodges, *Labor Policy,* 108–9; *New York Times,* Sept. 6, 1934; *Washington Post,* Sept. 6, 1934.

9. Hodges, *Labor Policy,* 110–13; *New York Times,* Sept. 6, 1934.

10. Hodges, *Labor Policy,* 107–8; *New York Times,* Sept. 7, 8, 9, 10, 1934; "Chronological Record," 25–26; *Washington Post,* Sept. 8, 9, 1934.

11. *New York Times,* Sept. 7, 8, 9, 10, 1934.

12. *New York Times,* Sept. 10, 1934; *Washington Post,* Sept. 9, 1934; Hodges, *Labor Policy,* 108; "The Week," *New Republic* 80, 1033 (Sept. 19, 1934): 141–42.

13. Hodges, *Labor Policy*, 113–14; *New York Times*, Sept. 9, 10, 1934.

14. *New York Times*, Sept. 15, 1934.

15. Unless otherwise stated, the material in the following pages comes from the Records of the National Recovery Administration (National Archives, Washington, D.C.) Records of the Board of Inquiry for the Cotton Textile Industry, Group 401, General Correspondence, Aug.–Sept. 1934. "Just a Laborer" Greenville, South Carolina, to FDR, Sept. 10, 1934.

16. Ibid.

17. Ibid.

18. Ibid.

19. Joseph Jura, Fairhaven, Massachusetts, to Winant, Sept. 7, 1934, ibid.

20. Ibid.

21. "A Textile Worker in New England" to Winant, Sept. 7, 1934; Lawrence H. Robbins, Green, South Carolina, to President Roosevelt, Sept. 8, 1934, ibid.

22. Mrs. Carrie Miller, Augusta, Georgia, to Mr Loyd [*sic*] Garrison, Sept. 12, 1934; Mrs. Osie Jones to Garrison, Sept. 15, 1934, ibid. See also John E. Allen, "Eugene Talmadge and the Great Textile Strike in Georgia, Sept. 1934," in *Essays in Southern Labor History*, ed. Gary Fink and Merle E. Reed, 229–333.

23. Mrs. Dottie Henry, Greenwood, South Carolina, to Roosevelt, Sept. 6, 1934; Robbins to Roosevelt, Sept. 8, 1934; Alfred M. Kunze, New Rochelle, New York, to Roosevelt, Aug. 31, 1934, Board of Inquiry Records, Group 401.

24. Walter Neidel, Westerly, Rhode Island, to Roosevelt, Sept. 7, 1934; Alice O'Neal to Roosevelt, Sept. 12, 1934; Lula Luthi to the President's Mediation Board, Sept. 15, 1934, ibid.

25. Mary Lethert Wingard, "Rethinking Paternalism: Power and Parochialism in a Southern Mill Village," 873–902.

26. Miss Elizabeth Parr to Winant, Sept. 11, 1934, Board of Inquiry Records, Box 401.

27. Ibid.

28. Jules L. Beuret to Winant, Sept. 8, 1934; John E. Edgerton to Roosevelt, Sept. 6, 1934; F. L. Hood, Greenville, Tennessee, to Frances Perkins, Sept. 13, 1934, ibid.

29. J. S. Ownby to Winant, Sept. 12, 1934; Ralph C. Perkins to Harris at Vose, New York, Sept. 13, 1934; John H. Rodgers, Tarboro, North Carolina, to Winant, Sept. 12, 1934; J. E. McDonald, Austin, Texas, to Winant, Sept. 12, 1934, ibid. For a succinct discussion of the effect of the AAA on the growing of cotton, see Wright, *Old South, New South*, 227–36.

30. V. R. Threatt to Roosevelt, Sept. 13, 1934; C. E. Baxter, Lincolntown, North Carolina, to Winant, Sept. 13, 1934; Mrs. Ruth Bayard, Gastonia, North Carolina, to Roosevelt, Sept. 13, 1934; Rev James Myers to Garrison, Sept. 9, 1934; L. James Johnson to Perkins, Sept. 12, 1934, Board of Inquiry Records, Box 401.

31. A mill worker, Dover, New Hampshire, to Winant, Sept. 9, 1934; H. Turner to Winant, Sept. 13, 1934; M. Weston to Roosevelt, Sept. 15, 1934, ibid.

32. C. C. Moore to Roosevelt, Sept. 4, 1934; Lee B. Weathers to FDR, Sept. 5, 1934; W. H. Burruss to Roosevelt, Aug. 30, 1934; H. H. Stein to Roosevelt, Sept. 7, 1934, ibid.

33. Relief Workers Union, Staten Island, to Roosevelt, Sept. 6, 1934; Chairman Roberts, New Bedford, Massachusetts, to Roosevelt, Sept. 7, 1934; Ella May Branch, ILD, Brooklyn, New York, to Roosevelt, Sept. 14, 1934; John H. David, Secretary

New Orleans Central Trades and Labor Council, to Roosevelt, Sept. 17, 1934; G. E. Henderson to Roosevelt, Sept. 10, 1934, ibid.

34. Alistair G. Furman Jr., Greenville, South Carolina, to Roosevelt, Sept. 5, 1934; A. J. Muste, New York, to Roosevelt Sept. 14, 1934, ibid.

35. Benjamin D. Riegel to Roosevelt, Sept. 7, 1934; O. J. Havird, Augusta, Georgia, to Roosevelt, Sept. 10, 1934; H. W. Colton, Ogunquit, Maine, Sept. 3, 1934; Latner J. Widenhouse to Roosevelt, Sept. 13, 1934, ibid.

36. *New York Times,* Sept. 11, 1934; James Findlay, "The Great Textile Strike of 1934: Illuminating Rhode Island History in the Thirties," 21; *Washington Post,* Sept. 11, 1934.

37. *New York Times,* Sept. 12, 1934; *Washington Post,* Sept. 13, 1934; Findlay, "The Great Textile Strike," 21.

38. *New York Times,* Sept. 12, 13, 14, 15, 16, 1934; Findlay, "The Great Textile Strike," 21–23; *Washington Post,* Sept. 14, 1934.

39. *New York Times,* Sept. 12, 14, 1934; Christopher M. Sterba, "Family, Work and Nation: Hazleton, Pennsylvania, and the 1934 General Strike in Textiles," 24–31.

40. Sterba, "Family, Work and Nation," 31–34.

41. *New York Times,* Sept. 11, 1934; *Washington Post,* Sept. 14, 1934.

42. *New York Times,* Sept. 11, 12, 13, 1934.

43. *New York Times,* Sept. 13, 1934; *Burlington Daily Times News,* Sept. 14, 1934; *Raleigh News and Observer,* Sept. 15, 1934; *Greensboro Daily News,* Sept. 15, 16, 1934; "Why Burlington," 9, 32.

44. *New York Times,* Sept. 12, 15, 1934; Allen, "Eugene Talmadge and the Great Textile Strike in Georgia," 236–37.

45. *New York Times,* Sept. 15, 16, 17, 1934; Allen, "Eugene Talmadge and the Great Textile Strike in Georgia," 238.

46. *New York Times,* Sept. 16, 17, 1934.

47. *Washington Post,* Sept. 16, 1934.

48. *New York Times,* Sept. 15, 1934.

49. Hodges, *Labor Policy,* 111–12; *New York Times,* Sept. 17, 1934.

50. *New York Times,* Sept. 18, 19, 1934; Allen, "Eugene Talmadge and the Great Textile Strike in Georgia," 237–38.

51. Ibid.

52. *New York Times,* Sept. 18, 19, 20, 1934; *Gastonia Daily Gazette,* Sept. 18, 19, 20, 1934.

53. *New York Times,* Sept. 18, 19, 20, 21, 23, 1934.

54. Ibid., Sept. 18, 20, 1934.

55. Hodges, *Labor Policy,* 114–15.

56. Ibid., 115; Irons, *Testing,* 152–53; *New York Times,* Sept. 21, 1934. For the president's statement, see also Roosevelt Papers, Official File 407b, Textile Strike.

57. Hodges, *Labor Policy,* 115–16; *New York Times,* Sept. 22, 23, 1934; *Washington Post,* Sept. 22, 1934.

58. "The Textile Workers Lose," *New Republic* 80, 1035 (Oct. 3, 1934): 200.

59. *New York Times,* Sept. 23, 1934.

60. Ibid., Sept. 22, 23, 1934.

61. Ibid., Sept. 25, 26, 1934; Hodges, *Labor Policy,* 115–17; Hall et al., *Like a Family,* 350–53; Irons, *Testing,* 154–63.

62. *New York Times,* Sept. 25, 1934; *Washington Post,* Sept. 23, 1934; Findlay, "The Great Textile Strike," 28–29.

63. Hodges, *Labor Policy,* 106; Jonathan Mitchell, "Here Comes Gorman," 203–5.

Chapter 4 *New England*

1. Solomon Barkin, "Notes Respecting Presentations and Discussions at the Rieve-Pollock Foundations Commemoration of the 1934 General Textile Strike and the 1939 Founding of TWUA," Nov. 12, 1984, Solomon Barkin Papers, Special Collections and Archives, W. E. B. Du Bois Library, University of Massachusetts, Amherst (henceforth Barkin Papers), Box 23.

2. *Christian Science Monitor,* Sept. 4, 7, 14, 1934.

3. Ibid., Sept. 6, 11, 22, 1934; *Boston Globe,* Sept. 20, 22, 1934; *Hartford Courant,* Sept. 11, 12, 13, 1934.

4. *Hartford Courant,* Sept. 6, 7, 8, 1934.

5. Ibid., Sept. 11, 1934.

6. Ibid., Sept. 13, 15, 20, 22, 23, 26, 1934.

7. *Christian Science Monitor,* Sept. 7, 1934.

8. *Providence Journal,* Sept. 4, 1934.

9. Ibid.

10. McLoughlin, *Rhode Island,* 114–17; James Findlay, "The Great Textile Strike of 1934," in *A History of Rhode Island Working People,* ed. Paul Buhle, Scott Molloy, Gail Sansbury, 50–53.

11. McLoughlin, *Rhode Island,* 119–23.

12. McLoughlin, *Rhode Island,* 120. See also Jaffee, "Ethnic Working-Class Protest," passim; Editha Hadcock, "Labor Problems in Rhode Island Cotton Mills, 1790–1940"; Lamphere, *From Working Daughters to Working Mothers,* 171–89; Buhle, "Italian-American Radicals and the Labor Movement," 121–51; Adena Meyers, "Rhode Island Women Activists in the 1934 General Textile Strike," 11–13; Interview with Mrs. Olive Drake by F. Simister, Mar. 1, 1972, Rhode Island Mill Life Project, Rhode Island Historical Society.

13. McLoughlin, *Rhode Island,* 165, 188; Wolfbein, *Decline of a Cotton Textile City,* 26; Jaffee, "Ethnic Working-Class Protest," 14; Hadcock, "Labor Problems," 201; Findlay, "The Great Textile Strike of 1934," 16–29.

14. McLoughlin, *Rhode Island,* 188–89; Hadcock, "Labor Problems," 345–51.

15. McLoughlin, *Rhode Island,* 190–91; Jaffee, "Ethnic Working-Class Protest," 21, 37; Lamphere, *Working Daughters,* 183–89.

16. Interview with Albert Bell, by Paula Kennedy (M94), July 7, 1974, with Cecile Bibeault, by Mark Brown (M119), Nov. 15, 1974, with Elliot Broadbent, by Harvey Kantar and Tracy Miller (M46), Sept. 14, 1973, with Edith Landes, by Christine Brown and Priscilla Golding (M93), July 5, 1974, all in MLOC.

17. Meyers, "Rhode Island Women," 43–47; Lamphere, *Working Daughters,* 190–92.

18. Interview with Emily Desmarais, by Christine and Mark L. Brown (M159), Oct. 4, 1975; with Harold Fletcher, by Pamela Kennedy (M103), Aug. 2, 1974; with Andrew Morotiero by Mark L. Brown (M130), May 14, 1975; with Elizabeth

Nord by James Findlay (M161), Nov. 12, 1975; with Senator Frank Squambuto by Earleen McCarthy (M22), Oct. 22, 1971, all in MLOC.

19. Mari Jo Buhle, Paul Buhle, and Dan Georgakas, eds., *Encyclopedia of the American Left*, 595, 773–75; Bernard K. Johnpoll and Harvey Klehr, eds., *Biographical Dictionary of the American Left*, 54–55. For the Gastonia strike and its aftermath, see Salmond, *Gastonia, 1929*.

20. Meyers, "Rhode Island Women," 51; Findlay, "Illuminating Rhode Island History," 17–19.

21. *Providence Journal*, Sept. 5, 6, 7, 1934.

22. Kate Dunnigan and Richard Quinney, "Work and Community in Saylesville," 173–80; *Working Water: A Guide to the Historic Landscape of the Blackstone River Valley*, 40–41.

23. *Providence Journal*, Sept. 8, 1934; Findlay, "Illuminating Rhode Island History," 22–23; Textile Strike Notice No. 3, Sept. 11, 1934, in Sayles Finishing Plant Records, Ephemera, Manuscripts Department, Rhode Island Historical Society, Providence, Rhode Island (henceforth, Sayles ephemera).

24. *Providence Journal*, Sept. 8, 10, 1934; Findlay, "Illuminating Rhode Island History," 22–23.

25. *Providence Journal*, Sept. 11, 12, 1934; *Boston Herald*, Sept. 13, 1934.

26. *Providence Journal*, Sept. 11, 1934; *New York Times*, Sept. 11, 1934; Textile Strike Notice No. 3, Sayles ephemera.

27. Diary of Helen Clarke Grimes, Sept. 11, 13, 14, 1934, Manuscripts Department, Rhode Island Historical Society.

28. *Providence News Tribune*, Sept. 12, 1934; *Providence Journal*, Sept. 12, 13, 14, 1934; *New York Times*, Sept. 12, 1934; Textile Strike Notice No. 4, Sayles ephemera.

29. *Providence Journal*, Sept. 12, 14, 1934; *Boston Herald*, Sept. 13, 1934; *Washington Post*, Sept. 16, 1934; Meyers, "Rhode Island Women," 62–63.

30. Gary Gerstle, *Working-Class Americanism: The Politics of Labor in a Textile City, 1914–1960*, 97–98, 103–5.

31. Gerstle, *Working-Class Americanism*, 129–30.

32. Gerstle, *Working-Class Americanism*, 130–31; *New York Times*, Sept. 11, 12, 1934; *Providence Journal*, Sept. 11, 12, 1934.

33. Gerstle, *Working-Class Americanism*, 132–33; *Providence Journal*, Sept. 13, 1934.

34. Gerstle, *Working-Class Americanism*, 132–33; Findlay, "Illuminating Rhode Island History," 21–22; *Providence Journal*, Sept. 13, 1934.

35. *Providence Journal*, Sept. 12, 1934; *Christian Science Monitor*, Sept. 13, 1934; Findlay, "Illuminating Rhode Island History," 26; Erwin L. Levine, *Theodore Francis Green: The Rhode Island Years, 1906–1936*, 169–71; Bernstein, *Turbulent Years*, 312–13.

36. Findlay, "Illuminating Rhode Island History," 26–27; *Providence Journal*, Sept. 13, 14, 16, 1934; Bernstein, *Turbulent Years*, 312–13; J. Edgar Hoover to Attorney General, Sept. 15, 1934, Roosevelt Papers, Official File 4076.

37. *Boston Traveller*, Sept. 7, 1934; *Boston Herald*, Sept. 14, 1934; Desmarais interview, Fletcher interview, MLOC; Myers, "Rhode Island Women," 50.

38. *Providence Journal*, Sept. 13, 14, 15, 17; Findlay, "Illuminating Rhode Island History," 26–28; Levine, *Rhode Island Years*, 172–76; Paul M. Buhle, ed., *Working Lives: An Oral History of Rhode Island Labor*, 32.

39. Gerstle, *Working-Class Americanism,* 133–37; *Providence Journal,* Sept. 18, 19, 20, 21, 23, 24, 25, 26, 1934; *Christian Science Monitor,* Sept. 14, 1934.

40. Gerstle, *Working-Class Americanism,* passim, esp. part 3; Findlay, "Illuminating Rhode Island History," 28–29; McLoughlin, *Rhode Island,* 199–200.

41. Wolfbein, *The Decline of a Cotton Textile City,* 7–10; Hartford, *Where Is Our Responsibility?* 74.

42. Hartford, *Where Is Our Responsibility?* 9–13, 37–39, 74–75; Wolfbein, *Decline of a Cotton Textile City,* 10–11.

43. Hartford, *Where Is Our Responsibility?* 9–13, 37–39; Brooks, "United Textile Workers," 223, 265–67.

44. Santos, "Community and Communism," 233–37. Within a month the Textile Council unions had cut their ties with the AFTO and joined the UTW.

45. Santos, "Community and Communism," 238–40; Brooks, "United Textile Workers," 265–66.

46. Santos, "Community and Communism," 241–43, 246–47; Hartford, *Where Is Our Responsibility?* 75; Brooks, "United Textile Workers," 269–70; Salmond, *Gastonia, 1929,* passim.

47. Wolfbein, *Decline of a Cotton Textile City,* 38–41; Hartford, *Where Is Our Responsibility?* 76.

48. Mary Aezendes to George Sloan, May 9, 1934; M. Moniz to "Friend," May 8, 1934; Langshaw Workers to Roosevelt, Feb. 12, 1934; Valeda Ferand to General Jhonsou [*sic*], Dec. 20, 1934; "A Very Bitter Ex-employee" to NRA Commission, Boston, Massachusetts, Aug. 23, 1934, all in NRA Records, 398, Employee Complaints; Wolfbein, *Decline of a Cotton Textile City,* passim.

49. Mary Heaton Vorse, "New England on Strike," 147–48.

50. Ibid. See also *Boston Herald,* Sept. 6, 1934; *New Bedford Standard Times,* Sept. 4, 1934.

51. *Daily Worker,* Sept. 1, 4, 6, 10, 1934; Meyers, "Rhode Island Women," 48.

52. *Daily Worker,* Aug. 31, Sept. 1, 4, 1934.

53. *New York Times,* Sept. 5, 1934; *Providence Journal,* Sept. 7, 1934; *Daily Worker,* Sept. 10, 1934.

54. Charles S. Ashley to Roosevelt, Aug. 27, 1934, Roosevelt Papers, PPF 2070; John G. Winant to William Batty, Sept. 21, 1934, in NRA Records, 401, Board of Inquiry Records; Papers of John G. Winant (henceforth Winant Papers) Franklin Delano Roosevelt Library, Hyde Park, New York, File 137 (clippings).

55. *New Bedford Standard Times,* Sept. 4, 5, 10, 16, 1934.

56. Ibid., Sept. 4, 6, 1934.

57. Ibid., Sept. 16, 21, 1934.

58. Ibid., Sept. 25, 1934; Wolfbein, *Decline of a Textile Town,* 103.

59. Clarence R. Burgess, Secretary, Maine Federation of Labor, to James A. Poole, Central Labor Union, Woodland, Maine, Jan. 18, 1934; Burgess to Gorman, Mar. 17, 1934, both in Maine State Federation of Labor Collection (henceforth MSFC), Special Collections, Folger Library, University of Maine, Box 203, Folder 3–3, Outgoing Letters, 1934.

60. Charles E. Clark, *Maine: A Bicentennial History,* 135–36.

61. Ibid., 140–42.

62. Ibid., 140–43.

63. Ibid., 143–45.

64. Report of Mary E. Drier to National Women's Trade Union League, visit to Augusta, Lewiston, and Waterville, Maine, Sept. 18, 19, 1934, Records of the National Recovery Administration; Records of the Cotton Textile National Industrial Relations Board, RG397, General Records, July 1933–Sept. 1934 (National Archives).

65. Juliet B. to Hugh Johnson, July 30, 1934; Marie Talbot to NRA, Feb. 6, 1934; Aveline Flagg to Gordon James, Augusta, Maine, Apr. 2, 1934, all in NRA Records, 398, Employee Complaints.

66. Col. Spaulding Bisbee to Governor Louis Brann, Sept. 25, 1934, Records of the Adjutant-General (henceforth Adjutant-General's Records) Maine State Archives, Augusta, Maine, Box 227, Folder 61; *Lewiston Daily Sun,* Sept. 3, 4, 1934, *Portland Press Herald,* Sept. 1, 4, 1934.

67. *Lewiston Evening Journal,* Aug. 29, Sept. 1, 1934.

68. Ibid., Aug. 29, Sept. 4, 1934, *Daily Kennebec Journal,* Sept. 3, 1934; Report to Department of War on Activity in Connection with the Strike, June 30, 1935, Adjutant-General's Records, Box 227, Folder S (Strike Correspondence).

69. *Lewiston Evening Journal,* Sept. 6, 1934.

70. *Portland Press Herald,* Sept. 7, 8, 1934.

71. *Lewiston Daily Sun,* Sept. 10, 1934.

72. Report to the Department of War, June 30, 1935; Wiseman to Adjutant-General, Sept. 28, 1934, both in Adjutant-General's Records, Box 227, Folder S; *Lewiston Evening Journal,* Sept. 12, 1934.

73. *Daily Kennebec Journal,* Sept. 11, 1934.

74. Ibid., Sept. 12, 13, 1934.

75. J. W. Hanson to Maj. Gen. George E. Leach, Chief National Guard Bureau, Washington, D.C., Sept. 23, Oct. 1, 1934. Adjutant-General's Records, Box 227, Folder S; *Daily Kennebec Journal,* Sept. 12, 13, 1934.

76. *Daily Kennebec Journal,* Sept. 15, 17, 1934; Charles W. Savage to newspaper editors, Sept. 17, 1934; Adjutant-General's Records, Box 227, Folder S.

77. *Daily Kennebec Journal,* Sept. 15, 17, 1934.

78. *Lewiston Evening Journal,* Sept. 18, 1934. *Daily Kennebec Journal,* Sept. 17, 18, 1934.

79. *Portland Press Herald,* Sept. 19, 20, 1934; *Daily Kennebec Journal,* Sept. 20, 1934; Hanson to Leach, Oct. 1, 1934, Adjutant-General's Records, Box 227, Folder 1.

80. *Lewiston Evening Journal,* Sept. 14, 1934.

81. *Lewiston Evening Journal,* Sept. 15, 17, 18, 1934.

82. *Lewiston Evening Journal,* Sept. 19, 1934; *Lewiston Daily Sun,* Sept. 20, 1934.

83. *Lewiston Evening Journal,* Sept. 19, 1934.

84. Ibid., Sept. 19, 20, 1934.

85. *Lewiston Evening Journal,* Sept. 22, 1934; *Portland Press Herald,* Sept. 24, 1934; *Daily Kennebec Journal,* Sept. 24, 1934.

86. *Portland Press Herald,* Sept. 20, 1934; *Lewiston Daily Sun,* Sept. 25, 1934; J. M. Plunkett to Burgess, Apr. 27, 1935; B. J. Dorsky to Jean D'Avignon, President, Maine State Federation of Labor, Aug. 5, 1935, Burgess to D'Avignon, Dec. 9, 1935, MSFC, Box 203, Folder 3–4, Outgoing Letters, 1935.

87. *Daily Kennebec Journal,* Sept. 24, 1934; *Lewiston Evening Journal,* Sept. 22, 1934; *Lewiston Daily Sun,* Sept. 22, 1934.

88. Hanson to Leach, Oct. 1, 1934, Adjutant-General's Records, Box 227, Folder S.

Chapter 5 *Mid-Atlantic States*

1. *Philadelphia Inquirer,* Sept. 3, 4, 1934.
2. Ibid.
3. Ibid., Aug. 31, Sept. 2, 3, 4, 1934.
4. Ibid., Sept. 6, 7, 1934; *Philadelphia Evening Bulletin,* Sept. 5, 1934.
5. *Easton Express,* Sept. 4, 7, 8, 1934.
6. Ibid., Sept. 13, 17, 1934.
7. *Philadelphia Inquirer,* Sept. 8, 9, 1934; *Lancaster New Era,* Sept. 7, 1934.
8. *Philadelphia Inquirer,* Sept. 11, 12, 1934.
9. *Lancaster New Era,* Sept. 11, 1934; *Philadelphia Evening Bulletin,* Sept. 11, 1934.
10. *Philadelphia Inquirer,* Sept. 11, 12, 1934; *Philadelphia Evening Bulletin,* Sept. 7, 8, 13, 1934.
11. *Philadelphia Evening Bulletin,* Sept. 12, 13, 14, 1934.
12. *Philadelphia Inquirer,* Sept. 12, 1934; Sterba, "Family, Work and Nation," 3–35.
13. Sterba, "Family, Work and Nation," 11–12, 17–20, 22–24.
14. Ibid., 25–27.
15. Ibid., 29–30.
16. Ibid., 31–33.
17. Ibid., 33–35; *Philadelphia Inquirer,* Sept. 13, 1934.
18; *Philadelphia Inquirer,* Sept. 13, 14, 1934; *Philadelphia Evening Bulletin,* Sept. 13, 1934. The Lees guards were soon dismissed, and sent back to New York under police escort.
19. Ibid., Sept. 15, 17, 18, 19, 1934.
20. *Lancaster New Era,* Sept. 18, 1934; Scranton, *Figured Tapestry,* 481–86.
21. *Philadelphia Inquirer,* Sept. 19, 20, 22, 1934; *Philadelphia Evening Bulletin,* Sept. 21, 1934.
22. *Easton Express,* Sept. 21, 22, 26, 1934; *Lancaster New Era,* Sept. 20, 25, 1934.
23. *Philadelphia Inquirer,* Sept. 23, 1934.
24. *Philadelphia Inquirer,* Sept. 25, 29, Oct. 2, 4, 1934; *Philadelphia Evening Bulletin,* Sept. 28, Oct. 4, 1934; Thomas Secreist to John A. Chumbley, Textile Relations Board, Oct. 24, 1934, NRA Records, 397, TNIRB Records.
25. *Philadelphia Inquirer,* Oct. 4, 1934; *Philadelphia Evening Bulletin,* Oct. 4, 1934.
26. *Philadelphia Inquirer,* Oct. 5, 6, 7, 9, 1934; *Philadelphia Evening Bulletin,* Oct. 5, 6, 1934.
27. Scranton, *Figured Tapestry,* 454–55, 483–86.
28. Fogelson, "They Paved the Streets with Silk," 133–48; John Updike, *In the Beauty of the Lilies,* 83–86; Golin, *Fragile Bridge,* 157–77.
29. Goldberg, *A Tale of Three Cities,* 186–203; Fogelson, "They Paved the Streets with Silk," 140–48; McCartin, *Labor's Great War,* 182–83. See also the discussion on the silk industry in Chapter 1.
30. Fogelson, "They Paved the Streets with Silk," 142–46.
31. See Chapter 2.
32. *New York Times,* July 19, 23, Aug. 27, 1933.
33. *Paterson Morning Call,* Oct. 21, 24, 25, 26, 27, 1933, Sept. 5, 1934; *New York Times,* Oct. 25, Nov. 29, 30, Dec. 3, 6, 1933.

34. *Paterson Morning Call,* Aug. 25, 31, Sept. 1, 3, 4, 1934; *Paterson Evening News,* Sept. 1, 5, 1934.

35. *Paterson Evening News,* Sept. 1, 1934; *Paterson Morning Call,* Sept. 5, 1934.

36. *Paterson Morning Call,* Sept. 5, 1934.

37. *Paterson Morning Call,* Sept. 5, 7, 1934; *Paterson Evening News,* Sept. 5, 1934.

38. *Paterson Morning Call,* Sept. 7, 1934.

39. *Paterson Morning Call,* Sept. 14, 15, 1934; *Paterson Evening News,* Sept. 14, 1934.

40. *Paterson Morning Call,* Sept. 4, 1934.

41. Weisbord, *A Radical Life,* passim. For Gastonia, the Weisbords and the NTWU, see Salmond, *Gastonia, 1929.*

42. *Paterson Morning Call,* Sept. 10, 1934.

43. *Paterson Morning Call,* Sept. 11, 12, 1934.

44. *Paterson Morning Call,* Sept. 14, 19, 20, 22, 24, 1934.

45. *Paterson Morning Call,* Sept. 10, 11, 1934.

46. *Paterson Morning Call,* Sept. 25, 26, 27, 1934.

47. *New York Times,* Oct. 14, 21, 25, Dec. 1, 2, 4, 1934.

48. Philip J. McLewin, "Labor Conflict and Technological Change: The Family Shop in Paterson," in Scranton, ed., *Silk City,* 145–56; *New York Times,* Nov. 1, 12, 17, 24, 1935.

49. See NRA Records, 398, Employee Complaints, Paterson, New Jersey, for a record of complaints against firms requiring agreement to wage cuts as a condition of future employment.

Chapter 6   *The Carolinas*

1. *New York Times,* Aug. 31, Sept. 1, 2, 3, 1934.

2. *Washington Post,* Sept. 8, 1934; Simon, *Fabric of Defeat,* 114–15; Dolores Janiewski, *Sisterhood Denied. Race, Gender and Class in a New South Community,* 159–61; Janet Irons, "The Challenge to National Coordination: Southern Textile Workers and the General Strike of 1934," in Staughton Lynd, ed., *"We Are All Leaders": The Alternative Unionism of the Early 1930s,* 87–89. See also Irons, *Testing,* 125–27.

3. *Charlotte Observer,* Sept. 4, 1934; *New York Times,* Sept. 4, 1934; *Gastonia Daily Gazette,* Aug. 31, Sept. 3, 1934; Hall et.al., *Like a Family,* 332; Salmond, *Gastonia, 1929,* 183.

4. *Gastonia Daily Gazette,* Sept. 5, 1934.

5. Carl W. Welch to President Roosevelt Dec. 11, 1933, NRA Records, 398, Employee Complaints. See Chapter 2.

6. Lucy Mays to President Roosevelt, Aug. 23, 1933; C. H. Lowe to General Johnson, Oct. 20, 1933; John R. Moore to Robert Bruere, Jan. 3, 1934, NRA Records, 398, Employee Complaints. For Gastonia's development as a textile center, see Tullos, *Habits of Industry,* 86–87, 105–10; and Salmond, *Gastonia, 1929,* 10–14.

7. Salmond, *Gastonia, 1929,* is the most recent survey of the strike, but see also Liston Pope's classic study, *Millhands and Preachers: A Study of Gastonia.*

8. Salmond, *Gastonia, 1929,* 181–82.

9. Ibid. See also Bryant Simon, "Prelude to the New Deal: The Political Response of South Carolina Textile Workers to the Great Depression, 1929–1933," in Gary M. Fink and Merl E. Reed eds., *Race, Class and Community in Southern Labor History*, 41.

10. Mary Heaton Vorse and Hamilton Basso, "Textile Trouble," 147–50.

11. *New York Times*, Sept. 1, 2, 1934.

12. *Gastonia Daily Gazette*, Aug. 31, Sept. 1, 1934.

13. *New York Times*, Sept. 5, 6, 1934; *Charlotte Observer*, Sept. 5, 1934.

14. *Gastonia Daily Gazette*, Sept. 10, 1934.

15. John W. Haynes to Governor Ehringhaus, Sept. 6, 1934; J. G. Stephenson to Ehringhaus, Sept. 10, 1934; Jack Lang to Major A. L. Fletcher, Sept. 7, 1934; William F. Gaffney to Fletcher, Sept. 6, 1934, all in Papers of Governor J. C. B. Ehringhaus, North Carolina State Department of Archives and History (henceforth Ehringhaus Papers) Box 103, Strike Correspondence.

16. *New York Times*, Sept. 6, 1934; *Charlotte Observer*, Sept. 6, 7, 1934; Ehringhaus, memorandum for files, Sept. 6, 1934, Ehringhaus Papers, Box 103.

17. *New York Times*, Sept. 11, 12, 1934; *Charlotte News*, Sept. 11, 1934, *Gastonia Daily Gazette*, Sept. 10, 1934.

18. *Gastonia Daily Gazette*, Sept. 10, 1934.

19. *Charlotte Observer*, Sept. 12, 13, 17, 1934; *Gastonia Daily Gazette*, Sept. 12, 1929; *New York Times*, Sept. 13, 16, 1929.

20. J. L. Hamme to Ehringhaus, Sept. 5, 1934, Ehringhaus Papers, Box 103.

21. *Charlotte Observer*, Sept. 17, 18, 23, 27, 28, 1929; *Gastonia Daily Gazette*, Sept. 20, 26, 1929; *Raleigh News and Observer*, Sept. 22, 1929.

22. *Gastonia Daily Gazette*, Sept. 19, 20, 1934; *New York Times*, Sept. 19, 20, 1934; *Charlotte Observer*, Sept. 20, 21, 23, 1934.

23. *Raleigh News and Observer*, Sept. 20, 1934.

24. W. W. Bigham to Ehringhaus, undated; R. R. Lawrence to Ehringhaus, Nov. 14, 1934. Ehringhaus Papers, Box 103; Carey Dowd to Ehringhaus, Sept. 14, 1934, Ehringhaus Papers, Box 104 (Strike Commendations). Transcript, Court of Inquiry into Death of Ernest K. Riley, Sept. 21, 1934, Ehringhaus Papers, Box 139 (Adjutant-General).

25. *Charlotte Observer*, Sept. 20, 21, 23, 1934; *New York Times*. Sept. 20, 21, 22, 1934.

26. *New York Times*, Sept. 23, 24, 26, 1934; *Raleigh News and Observer*, Sept. 23, 1934; *Charlotte Observer*. Sept. 25, 1934; Hall et al., *Like a Family*, 351–52.

27. Bernstein, *The Turbulent Years*, 299–300; Martha Gellhorn to Harry Hopkins, Nov. 11, 1934, Papers of Harry L. Hopkins, Franklin D. Roosevelt Library, Hyde Park, New York (henceforth Hopkins Papers) File 66.

28. *Spartanburg Journal*, Sept. 1, 3, 1934. For a much fuller account of the strike and its aftermath in Spartanburg County, see G. C. Waldrep III, *Southern Workers and the Search for Community: Spartanburg County, South Carolina*.

29. *Spartanburg Journal*, Sept. 5, 6, 1934; *Anderson Independent*, Sept. 4, 6, 1934; Simon, *Fabric of Defeat*, 113–14.

30. *Spartanburg Journal*, Sept. 7, 8, 11, 1934.

31. Ibid., Sept. 3, 4, 6, 7, 1934.

32. Ibid., Sept. 6, 19, 1934.

33. Ibid., Sept. 21, 23, 27, 28, 1934.

34. Simon, *Fabric of Defeat*, 114–15.

35. *Greenville News,* Sept. 7, 1934; *Gastonia Daily Gazette,* Sept. 6, 1934.

36. *Gastonia Daily Gazette,* Sept. 7, 1934, *Greenville News,* Sept. 7, 1934; Simon, *Fabric of Defeat,* 114–15.

37. Bryant Simon, "Prelude to the New Deal," 41.

38. Miss Dorothy Taylor to FDR, Feb. 14, 1934, NRA Records, 398, Employee Complaints.

39. Dorothy Taylor to FDR, Feb. 14, 1934, H. H. Willis, Chairman, Cotton Textile Industrial Relations Board for South Carolina to L. R. Gilbert, Secretary, Cotton Tex. Natt. Ind. Rel. Board, Apr. 2, 1934, ibid.

40. Mrs. Dill to FDR, Feb. 15, 1934, clipping in NRA records, Investigation by R. F. Howell of complaints against American Spinning Company, Mar. 29, 1934, ibid.

41. L. R. Gilbert to Cotton Textile National Industrial Relations Board, Aug. 18, 1933, Feb. 10, 1934; Syble Brown to Mrs. Roosevelt, Aug. 2, 1934, ibid. *Greenville Daily News Record,* Aug. 2, 11, 1934.

42. Dunean Mills File, Greenville, South Carolina. Mrs. Minnie Stone to General Hugh Johnson, undated, but received Feb. 1, 1934, NRA Records, 398, Employee Complaints.

43. Easley Cotton Mills File, Greenville County, South Carolina, Ed Smith to Senator James F. Byrnes, Aug. 1, 1933; L. R. Gilbert to Mrs. Hudson, Nov. 1, 1933; Sydney F. Munroe, Assistant to the President, Cotton-Textile Institute to Leon Wolman, Labor Advisory Board, NRA, Aug. 18, 1933, ibid.

44. Simon, *Fabric of Defeat,* 114–15.

45. *Greenville News,* Sept. 4, 1934; *The State,* Columbia, South Carolina, Sept. 4, 1934.

46. *Greenville News,* Sept. 5, 1934; F. W. Poe to Blackwood, Sept. 6, 1934, Papers of Governor Ibra C. Blackwood, South Carolina Department of Archives and History, Columbia, South Carolina (henceforth Blackwood Papers). General Subjects File: Board of Conciliation and Arbitration File.

47. *Greenville News,* Sept. 6, 1934; *The State,* Sept. 6, 1934.

48. Ibid.

49. *Greenville News,* Sept. 7, 8, 1934; T. M. Marchant to Blackwood, Sept. 7, 1934, Blackwood Papers, Board of Conciliation and Arbitration File.

50. *Greenville News,* Sept. 8, 9, 11, 24, 25, 1934.

51. *Greenville News,* Sept. 24, 1934.

52. *Anderson Independent,* Sept. 2, 1934.

53. Ibid., Sept. 5, 6, 1934.

54. Ibid., Sept. 6, 1934.

55. Ibid., Sept. 6, 7, 1934.

56. Ibid., Sept. 14, 1934.

57. Mack Fretwell Duncan, interview by Allen Tullos June 7, Aug. 30, 1979, SOHC. Transcripts of interviews made for the documentary film, "The Uprising of 1934" (henceforth Film transcripts) Box 23, Honea Path, South Carolina, Southern Labor Archive, Georgia State University, Atlanta, Georgia.

58. Duncan interview; Jim DuPlessis, "Massacre in Honea Path," 60–63.

59. T. E. Adams to Hugh Johnson, Feb. 14, 1934; L. B. Killey to Johnson, Apr. 19, 1934, NRA Records, 398, Employee Complaints.

60. Duncan interview; Simon, *Fabric of Defeat,* 115–16; Irons, "Testing the New Deal," 454–56; *Anderson Independent,* Sept. 5, 1934.

61. *The State,* Columbia, South Carolina, Sept. 6, 1934; Film transcripts, Box 23, Honea Path; Duncan interview; *Anderson Independent,* Sept. 6, 1934.

62. *Anderson Independent,* Sept. 7, 1934; *The State,* Sept. 7, 1934; Duncan interview; Simon, *Fabric of Defeat,* 116.

63. *The State,* Sept. 7, 1934; *Anderson Independent,* Sept. 7, 1934; Film transcripts, Box 23, Honea Path.

64. *Anderson Independent,* Sept. 7, 1934; *The State,* Sept. 7, 25, 1934; Duncan interview; Film transcripts, Box 23, Honea Path; DuPlessis, "Massacre," 60–63.

65. *Anderson Independent,* Sept. 7, 1934; Irons, *Testing,* 147–50; Irons, "Testing the New Deal," 459–60; Duncan interview; Film transcripts Box 23, Honea Path.

66. Charles L. Rucker was to die of his wounds later. *Anderson Independent,* Sept. 9, 10, 1934; Simon, *Fabric of Defeat,* 117; *The State,* Sept. 9, 1934; *New York Times,* Sept. 9, 1934.

67. Ibid. Myers had been present at the Gastonia and Marion strikes of 1929.

68. Ibid.

69. Simon, *Fabric of Defeat,* 119; Relief Workers Union, Staten Island to Roosevelt, Sept. 6, 1934; John H. David to Roosevelt, Sept. 17, 1934. NRA Records, 401, General Correspondence, Aug.-Sept. 1934.

70. Simon, *Fabric of Defeat,* 119; *The State,* Sept. 10, 11, 1934; Film transcripts, Box 23, Honea Path.

71. *The State,* Sept. 25, 26, 1934; *Anderson Independent,* Sept. 25, 26, 1934; DuPlessis, "Massacre," 60–63.

72. Film Transcripts, Box 23, Honea Path.

Chapter 7   *Georgia and Alabama*

1. *Macon Evening News,* Aug. 27, 1934; Allen, "Eugene Talmadge and the Great Textile Strike in Georgia," 233–34; Irons, *Testing,* 115–18.

2. *Macon Evening News,* Aug. 31, 1934; *Atlanta Constitution,* Sept. 1, 1934.

3. Allen, "Eugene Talmadge and the Great Textile Strike in Georgia," 230–32.

4. *Atlanta Constitution,* Sept. 4, 5, 1934; Allen, "Eugene Talmadge and the Great Textile Strike in Georgia," 232–33.

5. Report by E. O. Fitzsimons, Trion Cotton Mills, Trion, Georgia, Feb. 20, 1934; Lucille Powell to General Johnson, Sept. 2, 1933; Paul Maxwell to Hugh Johnson, Aug. 18, 1933, B. B. Dimpsey to William Farnsworth, Assistant Counsel, NRA, Oct. 30, 1933, all in NRA Records, 398, Employee Complaints.

6. Thomas McMahon to L. R. Gilbert, Secretary, Cotton Textile National Industrial Relations Board, Jan. 23, 1934; W. L. Mitchell to Bruere, May 25, 1934, ibid.

7. *Atlanta Constitution,* Sept. 6, 1934.

8. Ibid., see also *New York Times,* Sept. 6, 1934.

9. *Macon Evening News,* Sept. 3, 1934.

10. Ibid. Sept. 4, 5, 6, 1934.

11. *Augusta Chronicle,* Sept. 6, 10, 1934.

12. *Atlanta Constitution,* Sept. 6, 7, 1934.

13. *Columbus Enquirer,* Sept. 4, 1934; Flamming, *Creating the Modern South,* 200–202.

14. *Atlanta Constitution,* Sept. 11, 1934; A. E. Fleming, Newnan, Georgia, to Roosevelt, Sept. 5, 1934, NRA Records, 401, Board of Inquiry-General Correspondence, Aug.-Sept. 1934.

15. One of the Augusta Employees to Lloyd Garrison, Sept. 11, 1934; Mrs. Carrie Miller to Garrison, Sept. 12, 1934; Mrs. Osie Jones to Garrison, Sept. 15, 1934, ibid. See Chapter 3.

16. Mrs. Jones to Garrison, Sept. 15, 1934, ibid. *Atlanta Constitution,* Sept. 13, 1934.

17. *Atlanta Constitution,* Sept. 18, 1934; Allen, "Eugene Talmadge and the Great Textile Strike in Georgia," 237.

18. *Atlanta Constitution,* Sept. 15, 16, 1934.

19. *Atlanta Constitution,* Sept. 17, 19, 1934.

20. *Macon Evening News,* Sept. 17, 20, 22, 23, 1934.

21. *Atlanta Constitution,* Sept. 15, 16, 17, 1934.

22 Film Transcripts, Box 9, East Newnan, Georgia; *Newnan Herald,* Sept. 21, 1934.

23. *Atlanta Constitution,* Sept. 18, 1934; Film transcripts, Box 7, East Newnan, Georgia.

24. Ibid. See also *Newnan Herald,* Sept. 21, 1934.

25. *Atlanta Constitution,* Sept. 18, 1934.

26. Allen, "Eugene Talmadge and the Great Textile Strike in Georgia," 237; *Atlanta Constitution,* Sept. 17, 1934; *Newnan Herald,* Sept. 21, 1934; Film transcripts, Box 7, East Newnan.

27. *Atlanta Constitution,* Sept. 18, 1934; *Macon Evening News,* Sept. 19, 1934; Film transcripts, Box 7, East Newnan.

28. Film transcripts, Box 7, East Newnan; *Atlanta Constitution,* Sept. 23, 1934.

29. Film transcripts, Box 7, East Newnan, *Atlanta Constitution,* Sept. 17, 21, 1934; *Columbus Enquirer,* Sept. 21, 1934.

30. *Atlanta Constitution,* Sept. 18, 1934.

31. *Augusta Chronicle,* Sept. 26, 1934; *Macon Evening News,* Sept. 24, 1934.

32. *Atlanta Constitution,* Sept. 22, 1934; Film transcripts, Boxes 7 and 9, East Newnan.

33. Film transcripts, Box 7, East Newnan.

34. Hoffman, "Labor Revolt in Alabama," 206–9; *Birmingham Age-Herald,* July 16, 17, 18, 1934; H. Wayne Flynt, *Poor but Proud: Alabama's Poor Whites,* 92–94; Irons, *Testing,* 123–24.

35. Hoffman, "Labor Revolt in Alabama," 192–93; Film Transcripts, Box 1, Eula McGill.

36. Robin G. Kelley, *Hammer and Hoe: Alabama Communists During the Great Depression,* 43–53, 65–70; Eva Brantley to Mr P. O. Davis, Chairman, State Textile Compliance Board, Nov. 4, 16, 1933, NRA Records, 398, Employee Complaints, Huntsville, Alabama.

37. M. H. Goodwin to Senator Robert Wagner, Nov. 4, 1933, ibid; Oliver Carlson, "Why Textiles Vote to Strike," 95–96.

38. Irons, "Testing the New Deal," 359–62; Hoffman, "Labor Revolt in Alabama," 195–97.

39. Film Transcripts, Box 1, Eula McGill; *Birmingham Age-Herald,* July 17, 18, 19, 1934; *Huntsville Times,* July 19, 31, Aug. 1, 7, 1934; Irons, "Testing the New Deal," 362–63; Hoffman, "Labor Revolt in Alabama," 208–9.

40. *Birmingham Age-Herald,* Aug. 19, Sept. 1, 1934; Hoffman, "Labor Revolt in Alabama," 231–32, 259; *Birmingham News,* Aug. 31, 1934.

41. Hoffman, "Labor Revolt in Alabama," 255–57; *Birmingham Age-Herald,* Sept. 4, 5, 6, 1934; *Huntsville Times,* Sept. 4, 1934.

42. *Birmingham Age-Herald,* Sept. 4, 1934; Hoffman, "Labor Revolt in Alabama," 258.

43. *Birmingham News,* Sept. 5, 7, 10, 1934; *Birmingham Age-Herald,* Sept. 6, 7, 8, 1934; *Huntsville Times,* Sept. 7, 8, 1934.

44. *Birmingham News,* Sept. 10, 17, 21, 1934; *Birmingham Age-Herald,* Sept. 17, 1934.

45. *Birmingham News,* Sept. 18, 1934; *Huntsville Times,* Sept. 18, 1934; Kelley, *Hammer and Hoe,* 22, 73.

46. *Birmingham News,* Sept. 13, 18, 1934; *Birmingham Age-Herald,* Sept. 25, 27, 1934; *Huntsville Times,* Sept. 26, 27, 1934; Hoffman, "Labor Revolt in Alabama," 340–41.

47. Hoffman, "Labor Revolt in Alabama," 341–46; *Birmingham News,* Sept. 24, 25, 1934.

48. Mollie Dowd to Elizabeth Nord, Oct. 10, 12, 1934, NRA Records, 397, TNIRB Records.

49. Dowd to Nord, Oct. 8, 1934, ibid.

Chapter 8   *The Burlington Bombing—A Case Study*

1. *Burlington Daily Times News,* Sept. 3, 1934. For Love see Tullos, *Habits of Industry,* 107–18.

2. Hall et al., *Like a Family,* 25–26; Beatty, "The Edwin Holt Family," 511–35.

3. Ibid. See also Wright, "The Aftermath of the General Textile Strike," 84.

4. Hall et al., *Like a Family,* 116, 253; *Burlington Daily Times News,* May 21, 1929, July 1, 1937.

5. Hall et al., *Like a Family,* 239–40; Tullos, *Habits of Industry,* 107–12.

6. Hall et al., *Like a Family,* 241–42; Tullos, *Habits of Industry,* 112–13.

7. Hall et al., *Like a Family,* 241–42; Tullos, *Habits of Industry,* 112–15.

8. Hall et al., *Like a Family,* 246; Tullos, *Habits of Industry,* 112–16.

9. Tullos, *Habits of Industry,* 114–15, Hall et al., *Like a Family,* 246.

10. Tullos, *Habits of Industry,* 115–18; Hall et al., *Like a Family,* 241–48; *Burlington Daily Times News,* Feb. 18, 1927.

11. Hall et al., *Like a Family,* 241–46; Tullos, *Habits of Industry,* 118, *Burlington Daily Times News,* Nov. 15, 18, 1927, Nov. 21, 1929; "Why Burlington," 9; Allen Tullos, interview with Betty Parker Davidson and Lloyd Davidson, Feb. 2, 15, 1979, SOHC.

12. "Why Burlington," 9, 32.

13. Allen Tullos, interview with Reid Maynard, Feb. 6, 13, Apr. 3, 1979; Mary Murphy, interview with Stella Carden, Apr. 25, 1979; with Ernest Chapman, June 4, 1979; Allen Tullos interview with Frank Webster, Jan. 30, 1979, with Harry Rogers, Feb. 2, 1979; Cliff Kuhn, interview with Harry Lee Rogers, July 21, 1977, all in SOHC; Hall et al., *Like a Family,* 255–57.

14. Maynard interview; Rogers, Tullos interview; Lupton interview, SOHC; *Burlington Daily Times News,* Dec. 24, 1931, July 1, 1937; "Why Burlington," 25.

15. *Burlington Daily Times News,* Nov. 17, 1927, Sept. 24, 1932, Jan. 4, 1934; Shoemaker-Edmonds interview, SOHC.

16. Rogers, Tullos interview, SOHC; Wright, "The Aftermath," 93; Hall et al., *Like a Family,* 101–5, 186–94; Irons, *Testing,* 21–22.

17. Wright, "The Aftermath," 96–98; Hall et al., *Like a Family,* 271–72.

18. "Mrs. Fannie Ford to President Roosevelt," Mar. 13, 1934, in NRA Records, 398, Employee Complaints.

19. Statement of Lee Neal, Feb. 6, 1934, of C. D. Wilson, Oct. 10, 1933, of Pearl Norris, Nov. 10, 1933, ibid.

20. L. R. Gilbert to Mrs. R. L. Ford, Apr. 9, 1934; Frederick W. Darnell to Mrs. Pearl Norris, Dec. 7, 1933, ibid.

21. J. E. Livingston to Hugh Johnson, Oct. 23, 1933, ibid.

22. *Burlington Daily Times News,* Sept. 3, 1934.

23. *Raleigh News and Observer,* Sept. 4, 6, 7, 1935; *Greensboro Daily News,* Sept. 6, 7, 8, 1935; *Burlington Daily Times News,* Sept. 5, 1934.

24. *Burlington Daily Times News,* Sept. 6, 7, 10, 1934.

25. *Burlington Daily Times News,* Sept. 12, 1934; *Raleigh News and Observer,* Sept. 11, 13, 14, 1934; *Greensboro Daily News,* Sept. 11, 1934.

26. *Burlington Daily Times News,* Sept. 14, 1934; *Raleigh News and Observer,* Sept. 15, 1934; *Greensboro Daily News,* Sept. 15, 16, 1934; Shoemaker-Edmonds, interview SOHC. Hall et al., *Like a Family,* 342.

27. *Raleigh News and Observer,* Sept. 16, 1934, Jan. 19, 1936, *Greensboro Daily News,* Sept. 16, 1934; *Burlington Daily Times News,* Sept. 15, 1934.

28. *Raleigh News and Observer,* Sept. 16, 1934; *Greensboro Daily News,* Sept. 16, 18, 1934.

29. *Burlington Daily Times News,* Sept. 21, 25, 1934; W. T. Couch, "Pennsylvania 'Detectives' in North Carolina," 21–25; Spencer Love to Cornelia S. Love, Sept. 16, 1934; James Spencer Love Papers (henceforth Love Papers) Box 2, Southern Historical Collection, Wilson Library, University of North Carolina at Chapel Hill.

30. *Burlington Daily Times News,* Jan. 3, Oct. 22, 23, 1934.

31. *Burlington Daily Times News,* Sept. 15, 1934; *Greensboro Daily News,* Sept. 16, 1934.

32. *Greensboro Daily News,* Sept. 16, 21, 1934; Spencer Love to Cornelia S. Love, Sept. 18, 1934, Love Papers, Box 2; Harry Lee Rogers, interview, SOHC; Wright, "The Aftermath," 100–101.

33. *Burlington Daily Times News,* Sept. 17, Oct. 3, 1934.

34. Rogers, interview, SOHC. *Greensboro Daily News,* Sept. 26, 1934; W. T. Couch "Dynamite in Burlington," 18–21; Couch, "Pennsylvania Detectives," 21–24; Jim Weaver, "Six Personalities in Dynamite Case, Burlington, North Carolina," undated, in Papers of Don West (henceforth West Papers) Southern Historical Collection, Wilson Library, University of North Carolina at Chapel Hill. The charge against Emmett Johnson, the first man arrested, was subsequently quietly dropped.

35. Ibid.

36. See "John L. Anderson et al." Trial transcript in John L. Anderson Papers, Southern Historical Collection, Wilson Library, University of North Carolina at Chapel Hill. *Burlington Daily Times News,* Dec. 4, 1934.

37. Trial Transcript, vol. 1, 76–86. 3: 427–66, 486–99, 523–24; Couch and Bailey, "Dynamite in Burlington," 18–20; W. T. Couch, "For the Defense," *Raleigh News and Observer,* Jan. 26, 1936.

38. *Greensboro Daily News,* Nov. 30, 1934.

39. Trial Transcript, 1: 117, 156–63, 219–20. 4: 666–731.

40. Ibid., 4: 731.

41. Ibid., 1: 242–78.

42. Ibid., 4: 557–603.

43. Ibid., 1: 287–375.

44. Ibid., 2: 1–45. 4: 806–39.

45. Ibid., 2: 116–83, 189–204.

46. Couch and Bailey, "Dynamite in Burlington," 18–19; *Raleigh News and Observer,* Aug. 29, 1935; *Burlington Daily Times News,* Dec. 5, 1934.

47. *Burlington Daily Times News,* Dec. 5, 1934.

48. Ibid.

49. Jacquelyn Dowd Hall, interview with Paul Green, May 30, 1975 (henceforth Green interview); Jacquelyn Dowd Hall, interview with Don West, Jan. 22, 1975 (henceforth West interview) both in SOHC; Broadsheet from Workers Defense Committee, Dec. 28, 1934, in West Papers; ILD Press Release, Feb. 1, 1935, Paul Eliot Green Papers (henceforth Green Papers) Box 125, Southern Historical Collection, Wilson Library, University of North Carolina at Chapel Hill. For Gastonia, see Salmond, *Gastonia, 1929.* For Scottsboro see Dan Carter, *Scottsboro: A Tragedy of the American South.* For Don West see Anthony P. Dunbar, *Against the Grain: Southern Radicals and Prophets, 1929–1959,* 138–42; and Kelley, *Hammer and Hoe,* 63, 126.

50. Green interview; West interview. In 1936, after Ericson had gone to dinner with the Communist Party's vice presidential candidate that election year, J. W. Ford, an African American, UNC president Frank Porter Graham came under great pressure to dismiss the young man. He refused. See memo in Papers of Olive Matthews Stone (henceforth Stone Papers) Folder 27, Southern Historical Collection, Wilson Library, University of North Carolina at Chapel Hill.

51. Green interview.

52. Weaver to John Anderson, Jan. 10, 1934, West Papers.

53. *Daily Tar Heel,* Jan. 16, Feb. 20, 21, 1935; Sherna Gluck, interview with Olive Matthews Stone, 1975, SOHC. Eventually all the convicted men were bailed, except for Blalock.

54. Spencer Love to Cornelia Love, Jan. 21, 25, 1935, Cornelia Love to Spencer Love, Jan. 22, 1935, Love Papers, Folder 102.

55. Anderson to Green, Mar. 19, 23, 1935, Green Papers, Series 1, Box 5; *Burlington Daily Times News,* Feb. 13, 1935.

56. Spencer Love to Cornelia Love, Apr. 23, 1935; Cornelia Love to Spencer Love, Apr. 22, May 28, 1935; Wiley D. Forbes, Department of Pathology, Duke University to Spencer Love, Apr. 30, 1935; Autopsy report on Phillip Hanes Love, all in Love Papers, Folder 103. See also Wright, "The Aftermath," 99–100; *Burlington Daily Times News,* May 16, 1935.

57. Lucy Randolph Mason to Green, May 6, 1935; Roger Baldwin, American Fund for Public Service to Green, Aug. 26, 1935, Account Book of Chapel Hill Defense Committee for Burlington Workers; Paul Green, Statement to FBI, May 18, 1954, all in Green Papers, Box 125.

58. E. Ericson to Editor, *Winston-Salem Journal,* May 15, 1935, in Green Papers, Box 125; Cornelia Love to Spencer Love, May 28, Sept. 6, 1935, Love Papers, Folder 103.

59. Walt Pickard, *Burlington Dynamite Plot,* copy found in the North Carolina Collection, Wilson Library, University of North Carolina at Chapel Hill; West interview, SOHC; Dunbar *Against the Grain,* 140.

60. E. E. Ericson, "Burlington Dynamite Plot," *Labor Defender,* Mar. 1935, 8–9, 22; Walt Pickard, "Headed for the Next Milestone—in the Burlington Dynamite Plot," *Labor Defender,* Apr. 1935, 11; Elizabeth Lawson, "Who Is Behind the Burlington Dynamite Plot," *Labor Defender,* May 1935, 9, 23; John L. Anderson, "Union Misleaders Turn Against the Burlington Six," *Labor Defender,* June 1935, 12; Don West, "Dirty Work in Burlington," *Labor Defender,* Oct. 1935, 14, 19.

61. Meeting transcripts, Green Papers, Box 125.

62. Paul Green interview, SOHC; *Raleigh News and Observer,* Aug. 27, 28, 29, 1935; *Burlington Daily Times News,* Aug. 24, 1935.

63. *Burlington Daily Times News,* Dec. 30, 1935; *Raleigh News and Observer,* Nov. 21, 1935, *Greensboro Daily News,* Aug. 28, Dec. 3, 1935; Love to Cornelia Love, Jan. 28, 1936, Love Papers, Folder 109.

64. *Greensboro Daily News,* Dec. 3, 1935, Jan. 4, 1936; *Raleigh News and Observer,* Nov. 23, 1935, Nov. 20, 1936; *Burlington Daily Times News,* Jan. 3, 1936, Couch, "Pennsylvania, Detectives." "For the Defense," *Raleigh News and Observer,* Jan. 26, 1936; "Five New Victims," *Labor Defender,* Feb. 1936, 3; Mrs. T. J. Canipe to Green, Aug. 26, 1935, Green Papers, Box 5; Green statement to FBI, May 18, 1954, Green Papers, Box 125; Olive M. Stone, "Civil Rights in the South," Apr. 1936, pamphlet in Stone Papers, Folder 27.

Reflections

1. Hodges, *Labor Policy,* 104–6, 117; "Notes," Barkin Papers, Box 23.

2. Irons, "The Challenge of National Coordination," 72–73, 88–89.

3. Hodges, *Labor Policy,* 116–17, 176–77. Gorman was not present at the TWUA's creation. Defecting from its leadership and that of the new CIO he remained with the dwindling UTW, reaffiliated with the AFL, a "pathetic little 'Napoleon' without an army," as he was once derisively called.

4. "Notes," Barkin Papers, Box 23; Robert H. Zieger, *The CIO: 1935–1955,* 75–78.

5. Kennedy, *Freedom from Fear,* 306; Lizabeth Cohen, *Making a New Deal: Industrial Workers in Chicago, 1919–1939,* passim.

6. Simon, *Politics of Defeat;* Irons, *Testing,* 167–69.

7. Kennedy, *Freedom from Fear,* 293–95.

8. Zieger, *The CIO,* 76–77; Hodges, *Labor Policy,* 116–18; Paul Christopher to Gorman, Mar. 3, Dec. 31, 1936, Feb. 22, 1937, Box 1867, UTW Records, AFL-CIO Region 8 Records, 1933–1969, Southern Labor Archives, Georgia State University, Atlanta; Stoney, "The Uprising of 1934."

9. Salmond, *Gastonia, 1929,* 180; Zieger, *The CIO,* passim.

10. Vorse, "New England on Strike," 147–48; *New York Times,* Sept. 5, 1934. See Chapter 3.

11. *New York Times,* Sept. 3, 1934; *Providence Journal,* Sept. 7, 12, 14, 15, 1934; *Boston Herald,* Sept. 13, 1934; *Philadelphia Evening Bulletin,* Sept. 11, 1934; *Lancaster New Era,* Sept. 11, 1934; *Atlanta Constitution,* Sept. 17, 18, 1934. Film transcripts, Boxes 4, 7, 18; Sterba, "Family, Work and Nation," 3–35.

12. Sterba, "Family, Work and Nation," passim; Salmond, *Gastonia, 1929,* passim; Hall et al., *Like a Family,* passim.

13. Hall et al., *Like a Family,* 309–16; Mary Aezendes to George Sloan, May 9, 1934, NRA Records, 398, Employee Complaints.

14. *New Bedford Standard Times,* Sept. 25, 1934; Zieger, *The CIO,* 76–77; Hartford, *Where Is Our Responsibility?* passim.

15. Martha Gellhorn to Harry Hopkins, Nov. 11, 1934, Hopkins Papers, File 66.

16. *New York Times,* Sept. 15, 1934.

17. "Notes," Barkin Papers, Box 23.

18. Flamming, *Creating the Modern South,* 200–201.

Bibliography

MANUSCRIPTS

WASHINGTON, D.C.
National Archives
Records of the National Recovery Administration
Records of the Secretary of Labor

HYDE PARK, NEW YORK
Franklin Delano Roosevelt Library
Harry L. Hopkins Papers
Franklin Delano Roosevelt Papers
John G. Winant Papers

AUGUSTA, MAINE
Maine State Archives
Records of the Adjutant-General

ORONO, MAINE
Special Collections, Folger Library, University of Maine
Maine State Federation of Labor Collection

AMHERST, MASSACHUSETTS
Special Collections and Archives, W. E. B. Du Bois Library, University of
    Massachusetts
Solomon Barkin Papers

PROVIDENCE, RHODE ISLAND
Rhode Island Historical Society
Diary of Helen Clark Grimes
Sayles Finishing Plant Records

CHAPEL HILL, NORTH CAROLINA
Southern Historical Collection, Wilson Library, University of North Carolina at Chapel Hill
John L. Anderson Papers
Paul Eliot Green Papers
James Spencer Love Papers
Olive Matthews Stone Papers
Don West Papers
North Carolina Collection, Wilson Library, University of North Carolina at Chapel Hill
Burlington, North Carolina, Chamber of Commerce, "Why Burlington," pamphlet, 1934
Pickard, Walt, *Burlington Dynamite Plot* (ILD, New York, 1935)

RALEIGH, NORTH CAROLINA
North Carolina State Department of Archives and History
Papers of Governor J. C. B. Ehringhaus

COLUMBIA, SOUTH CAROLINA
South Carolina Department of Archives and History
Papers of Governor Ibra C. Blackwood

ATLANTA, GEORGIA
Southern Labor Archive, Georgia State University
AFL-CIO Region 8 Records, 1933–1969
Transcripts of Interviews Made for the Documentary Film, "The Uprising of 1934"

MADISON, WISCONSIN
State Historical Society of Wisconsin
Textile Workers Union of America Collection

NEWSPAPERS

NATIONAL
Daily Worker
New York Times
Washington Post

MAINE
Daily Kennebec Journal
Lewiston Daily Sun
Lewiston Evening Journal
Portland Press Herald

RHODE ISLAND
Providence Journal
Providence News Tribune
Woonsocket Call

MASSACHUSETTS
Boston Globe
Boston Herald
Boston Traveller
Christian Science Monitor
New Bedford Standard Times

CONNECTICUT
Hartford Courant

PENNSYLVANIA
Easton Express
Lancaster New Era
Philadelphia Evening Bulletin
Philadelphia Inquirer

NEW JERSEY
Paterson Evening News
Paterson Morning Call

NORTH CAROLINA
Burlington Daily Times News
Charlotte News
Charlotte Observer
Daily Tar Heel
Gastonia Daily Gazette
Raleigh News and Observer
Winston-Salem Journal

SOUTH CAROLINA
Anderson Independent
Greenville News
Spartanburg Journal
The State, Columbia

GEORGIA
Atlanta Constitution
Augusta Chronicle
Columbus Enquirer
Macon Evening News
Newnan Herald

ALABAMA
Birmingham Age-Herald
Birmingham News
Huntsville Times

MAGAZINES

Labor Defender
Nation
New Republic
Newsweek
Textile Bulletin
Textile Worker
Time

INTERVIEWS

KINGSTON, RHODE ISLAND
Mill Life Oral History Collection, Special Collections, University of
    Rhode Island, Kingston, Rhode Island
Bell, Albert, with Pamela Kennedy, July 7, 1974.
Bibault, Cecile, with Mark Brown, Nov. 15, 1974.
Broadbend, Elliot, with Harvey Kantor and Tracy Miller, Sept. 14, 1973.
Denomme, Ernest, with Franciose S. Puniello, Feb. 17, 1971.

Desmarais, Emily, with Christine Brown and Mark L. Brown, Oct. 4, 1973.
Fletcher, Harold, with Pamela Kennedy, Aug. 2, 1974.
Landes, Edith, with Christine Brown and Priscilla Golding, July 5, 1974.
Morotiero, Andrew, with Mark Brown, May 14, 1975.
Nord, Elizabeth, with James Findlay, Nov. 12, 1975.
Squambuto, Senator Frank, with Earleen McCarthy, Oct. 22, 1971.

PROVIDENCE, RHODE ISLAND
Rhode Island Mill Life Project, Rhode Island Historical Society
Drake, Olive, with F. Simister, Mar. 1, 1972.

CHAPEL HILL, NORTH CAROLINA
Southern Oral History Collection, Wilson Library, University of North Carolina at Chapel Hill
Carden, Stella, with Mary Murphy, Apr. 25, 1979.
Chapman, Ernest, with Mary Murphy, July 4, 1979.
Davidson, Betty Parker, and Lloyd Davidson, with Allen Tullos, Feb. 2, 15, 1979.
Duncan, Mack, with Allen Tullos, June 7, Aug. 30, 1979.
Faucette, Ethel, with Cliff Kuhn, Nov. 16, 1978, Jan. 4, 1979.
Green, Paul, with Jacquelyn Dowd Hall, May 30, 1975.
Hilliard, Ethel, with Allen Tullos, Mar. 29, Apr. 3, July 25, Aug. 10, 1979.
Lupton, Carroll, with Mary Murphy, May 18, 1979.
Maynard, Reid, with Allen Tullos, Feb. 6, 13, 1976.
Murray, Charles, with Brent Glass, Mar. 4, 1976.
Pharis, James, with Cliff Kuhn, July 24, 1977.
Robinette, J. M., with Cliff Kuhn, July 1977.
Rogers, Harry, with Allen Tullos, Feb. 2, 1977.
Rogers, Harry Lee, with Cliff Kuhn, July 20, 1977.
Shoemaker, Mattie, and Mildred Shoemaker Edmonds, with Mary Murphy, Mar. 23, 1979.
Shockley, Mary Ethel, with Cliff Kuhn, July 27, 1977.
Stone, Olive Matthews, with Sherna Gluck, 1975.
Truitt, Herman Newton, with Allen Tullos, Dec. 5, 1978, Jan. 19, 30, 1979.
Webster, Frank, with Allen Tullos, Jan. 30, 1979.
West, Don, with Jacquelyn Dowd Hall, Jan. 22, 1975.

BOOKS

Bellush, Bernard. *The Failure of the NRA*. New York: Norton, 1975.

Bernstein, Irving. *The Lean Years: A History of the American Worker, 1920–1933*. Boston: Houghton Mifflin, 1960.

Buhle, Mari Jo, Paul Buhle, and Dan Georgakas, eds. *Encyclopedia of the American Left*. Westport, Conn.: Greenwood Press, 1986.

Buhle, Paul, ed. *Working Lives: An Oral History of Rhode Island Labor*. Providence: Rhode Island Historical Society, 1987.

Buhle, Paul, Scott Malloy, and Gail Sansbury, eds. *A History of Rhode Island Working People*. Providence: Regine Printing Company, 1983.

Carter, Dan. *Scottsboro: A Tragedy of the American South*. Baton Rouge: Louisiana State University Press, 1968.

Clark, Charles E. *Maine: A Bicentennial History*. New York: Norton, 1977.

Clark, Daniel. *Like Night and Day: Unionization in a Southern Mill Town*. Chapel Hill: University of North Carolina Press, 1997.

Cohen, Lizabeth. *Making a New Deal: Industrial Workers in Chicago, 1919–1939*. New York: Cambridge University Press, 1990.

Cumbler, John T. *Working-Class Community in Industrial America: Work, Leisure and Struggle in Two Industrial Cities, 1880–1930*. Westport, Conn.: Greenwood Press, 1979.

Dunbar, Anthony P. *Against the Grain: Southern Radicals and Prophets, 1929–1959*. Charlottesville: University Press of Virginia, 1981.

Fink, Gary, and Merl Reed, eds. *Essay in Southern Labor History*. Westport, Conn.: Greenwood Press, 1977.

———. *Race, Class and Community in Southern Labor History*. Tuscaloosa: University of Alabama Press, 1994.

Flamming, Douglas. *Creating the Modern South: Millhands and Managers in Dalton, Georgia, 1884–1984*. Chapel Hill: University of North Carolina Press, 1992.

Flynt, H. Wayne. *Poor but Proud: Alabama's Poor Whites*. Tuscaloosa: University of Alabama Press, 1989.

Galambos, Louis. *Competition and Cooperation: The Emergence of a National Trade Association*. Baltimore: Johns Hopkins Press, 1966.

Galenson, Alice. *The Migration of the Cotton Textile Industry from New England to the South, 1880–1930*. New York: Garland, 1985.

Gerstle, Gary. *Working Class Americanism: The Politics of Labor in a Textile City*. New York: Cambridge University Press, 1989.

Goldberg, David J. *A Tale of Three Cities: Labor Organization and Protest in Paterson, Passaic and Lawrence, 1916–1921*. New Brunswick: Rutgers University Press, 1989.

Golin, Steve. *The Fragile Bridge: Paterson Silk Strike, 1913*. Philadelphia: Temple University Press, 1988.

Gordon, Colin. *New Deals: Business, Labor and Politics in America, 1920–1935*. New York: Cambridge University Press, 1994.

Hall, Jacquelyn Dowd, James Leloudis, Robert Korstad, Mary Murphy, Lu Ann Jones, and Christopher Daly. *Like a Family: The Making of a Southern Cotton Mill World*. Chapel Hill: University of North Carolina Press, 1987.

Hartford, William F. *Where Is Our Responsibility? Unions and Economic Change in the New England Textile Industry, 1870–1960*. Amherst: University of Massachusetts Press, 1996.

Hawley, Ellis. *The New Deal and the Problem of Monopoly*. Princeton, N.J.: Princeton University Press, 1996.

Hodges, James A. *New Deal Labor Policy and the Southern Cotton Textile Industry, 1933–1941*. Knoxville: University of Tennessee Press, 1986.

Irons, Janet. *Testing the New Deal: The General Textile Strike of 1934 in the American South*. Urbana: University of Illinois Press, 2000.

Janiewski, Dolores. *Sisterhood Denied: Race, Gender and Class in a New South Community*. Philadelphia: Temple University Press, 1985.

Johnpoll, Bernard K., and Harvey Klehr, eds. *Biographical Dictionary of the American Left*. Westport, Conn.: Greenwood Press, 1986.

Kelley, Robin G. *Hammer and Hoe: Alabama Communists during the Great Depression*. Chapel Hill: University of North Carolina Press, 1990.

Kennedy, David. *Freedom from Fear. The American People in Depression and War, 1929–1945*. New York: Oxford University Press, 1999.

Lahne, Herbert J. *The Cotton Mill Worker*. New York: Farrar & Rinehart, 1944.

Lamphere, Louise. *From Working Daughters to Working Mothers: Immigrant Women in a New England Industrial Community*. Ithaca: Cornell University Press, 1987.

Leuchtenburg, William E. *Franklin D. Roosevelt and the New Deal, 1932–1940*. New York: Harper & Row, 1963.

Levine, Erwin. *Theodore Francis Green: The Rhode Island Years, 1906–1936*. Providence: Brown University Press, 1963.

Lynd, Staughton, ed. *"We Are All Leaders": The Alternative Unions in the Early 1930s*. Urbana: University of Illinois Press, 1996.

McCartin, Joseph A. *Labor's Great War: The Struggle for Industrial Democracy and the Origins of Modern American Labor Relations, 1912–1921*. Chapel Hill: University of North Carolina Press, 1997.

McDonald, Lois. *Southern Mill Hills: A Study of Social and Economic Forces in Certain Textile Mill Villages*. New York: Alexander Hillman, 1928.

McLaughlin, William. *Rhode Island: A History*. New York: Norton, 1986.

Minchin, Timothy J. *What Do We Need a Union For? The TWUA in the South, 1945–1955*. Chapel Hill: University of North Carolina Press, 1997.

Page, Dorothy Myra. *Southern Cotton Mills and Labor*. New York: Workers Library, 1929.

Pope, Liston. *Millhands and Preachers: A Study of Gastonia*. New Haven: Yale University Press, 1942.

Potwin, Marjorie A. *Cotton Mill People of the Piedmont: A Study in Social Change*. New York: Columbia University Press, 1927.

Salmond, John. *Gastonia, 1929: The Story of the Loray Mill Strike*. Chapel Hill: University of North Carolina Press, 1995.

Scranton, Philip. *Figured Tapestry: Production, Markets and Power in Philadelphia Textiles, 1885–1941*. New York: Cambridge University Press, 1989.

Scranton, Philip, ed. *Silk City: Studies on the Paterson Silk Industry, 1860–1940*. Trenton: New Jersey Historical Society, 1985.

Simon, Bryant. *A Fabric of Defeat: The Politics of South Carolina Millhands, 1910–1948*. Chapel Hill: University of North Carolina Press, 1998.

Tomlins, Christopher L. *The State and the Unions: Labor Relations, Law and the Organized Labor Movement in America, 1880–1960*. New York: Cambridge University Press, 1985.

Tripp, Anne Huber. *The IWW and the Paterson Silk Strike of 1913*. Urbana: University of Illinois Press, 1987.

Tullos, Allen. *Habits of Industry: White Culture and the Transformation of the Carolina Piedmont*. Chapel Hill: University of North Carolina Press, 1989.

Updike, John. *In the Beauty of the Lilies*. New York: Knopf, 1996.

Vecoli, Rudolph. *The People of New Jersey*. Princeton: Van Nostrand, 1965.

Waldrep, G. C. III. *Southern Workers and the Search for Community: Spartanburg County, South Carolina*. Urbana: University of Illinois Press, 2000.

Weisbord, Vera Buch. *A Radical Life*. Bloomington: Indiana University Press, 1977.

Wolfbein, Seymour. *The Decline of a Cotton Textile City: A Study of New Bedford*. New York: Columbia University Press, 1944.

Working Water: A Guide to the Historic Landscapes of the Blackstone River Valley. Providence: Rhode Island Parks Association, 1987.

Wright, Gavin. *Old South, New South: Revolutions in the Southern Economy since the Civil War*. New York: Basic Books, 1986.

Zieger, Robert H. *The CIO, 1935–1955*. Chapel Hill: University of North Carolina Press, 1995.

ARTICLES AND BOOK CHAPTERS

Allen, John E. "Eugene Talmadge and the Great Textile Strike in Georgia, September, 1934." In *Essays in Southern Labor History*, edited by Gary Fink and Merl Reed.

Beatty, Bess. "The Edwin Holt Family: Nineteenth Century Capitalists in North Carolina." *North Carolina Historical Review* 63, 4 (Oct. 1986).

Buhle, Paul. "Italian American Radicals and the Labor Movement, 1905–1930." *Radical History Review* 17 (spring 1978).

Carlson, Oliver. "Why Textiles Vote to Strike." *New Republic* 80, 1031 (Sept. 5, 1934).

Couch, William T. "Dynamite in Burlington." *Carolina Magazine* 64, 6 (Apr. 1935).

———. "Pennsylvania Detectives in North Carolina." *Carolina Magazine* 65, 3 (Dec. 1935).

Dunnigan, Kate, and Richard Quinney. "Work and Community in Saylesville." *Radical History Review* 17 (spring 1978).

Du Plessis, Jim. "Massacre in Honea Path." *Southern Exposure* 17 (fall 1989).

Findlay, James. "The Great Textile Strike of 1934: Illuminating Rhode Island History in the Thirties." *Rhode Island History* 42 (Feb. 1983).

Fogelson, Nancy. "They Paved the Streets with Silk: Paterson, New Jersey, Silk Workers, 1913–1924." *New Jersey History* 97 (Aug. 1979).

Ford, Ella. "We Are Mill People." *New Masses* 5 (Aug. 30, 1929).

Hall, Jacquelyn, Robert Korstad, and James Leloudis, "Cotton Mill People: Work, Community and Protest in the Textile South, 1880–1940." *American Historical Review* 91, 2 (Apr. 1986).

Irons, Janet. "The Challenge of National Coordination: Southern Textile Workers and the General Textile Strike of 1934." In *"We Are All Leaders": The Alternative Unions in the Early 1930s,* edited by Staughton Lynd.

Johanningsmeier, Edward P. "The Trade Union Unity League: Communists and the Transition to Industrial Unionism, 1928–1934." *Labor History* 42, 2 (May 2001).

Margrave, Richard D. "Technology Diffusion and the Transfer of Skills: Nineteenth-Century English Silk Migration to Paterson." In *Silk City: Studies on the Paterson Silk Industry, 1860–1940,* edited by Philip Scranton.

McLewin, Philip J. "Labor Conflict and Technological Change: The Family Shop in Paterson." In *Silk City: Studies on the Paterson Silk Industry, 1860–1940,* edited by Philip Scranton.

Mitchell, Jonathan. "Here Comes Gorman." *New Republic* 80, 1035 (Oct. 3, 1934).

Palmer, Gladys. "History of the Philadelphia Textile Council." *American Federationist* 39, 10 (Oct. 1932).

Salmond, John. "'The Burlington Dynamite Plot': The 1934 Textile Strike and Its Aftermath in Burlington, North Carolina." *North Carolina Historical Review* 75, 4 (Oct. 1998).

Santos, Michael W. "Community and Communism: The 1928 New Bedford Textile Strike." *Labor History* 26, 2 (spring 1985).

Sterba, Christopher M. "Family, Work and Nation: Hazleton, Pennsylvania, and the 1934 General Strike in Textiles." *Pennsylvania Magazine of History and Biography* 120, 1/2 (Jan./Apr. 1996).

Vorse, Mary Heaton, and Hamilton Basso. "Textile Trouble: New England on Strike." *New Republic* 80, 1033 (Sept. 19, 1934).

Wingard, Mary Lethert. "Rethinking Paternalism: Power and Parochialism in a Southern Mill Village." *Journal of American History* 83, 3 (Dec. 1996).

Wright, Annette C. "The Aftermath of the General Textile Strike: Managers and Workplace at Burlington Mills." *Journal of Southern History* 60, 1 (Feb. 1994).

THESES AND DISSERTATIONS

Brooks, Robin R. "The United Textile Workers of America." Ph.D. diss., Yale University, 1935.

Grigsby, Ellen. "The Politics of Protest: Theoretical, Historical and Literary Perspectives on Labor Conflict in Gaston County, North Carolina." Ph.D. diss., University of North Carolina at Chapel Hill, 1986.

Hadcock, Editha. "Labor Problems in Rhode Island Cotton Mills, 1790–1940." Ph.D. diss., Brown University, 1940.

Hoffman, James L. "A Study of the United Textile Workers of America in a Cotton Mill in a Medium-sized Southern City: Labor Revolt in Alabama, 1934." Ed.D. diss., University of Alabama, 1986.

Irons, Janet. " 'Testing the New Deal': The General Textile Strike of 1934." Ph.D. diss., Duke University, 1988.

Jaffee, Susan. "Ethnic Working Class Protest: The Textile Strike of 1922 in Rhode Island." Honors thesis, Brown University, 1974.

Kennedy, John W. "The General Strike in the Textile Industry, Sept. 1934." Master's thesis, Duke University, 1947.

Meyers, Adena. "Rhode Island Women Activists in the 1934 General Textile Strike." Honors thesis, Brown University, 1990.

Index

Pages references to photographs appear in italics.

Widenhouse, Latner J., 66
Wiggins, Ella May, 21, 149, 241
Wilcox, Roy, 84
Williams, Walter, 209
Williamson family, 203
Wilmot, Clarence, 132
Wilson, C. D., 209
Wilson, Tessie, 216
Winant, John G., 52; appeals to, 54, 56, 59, 60, 61, 64, 108
Winant Committee, 54, 65, 107, 175, 183; report of, 75–76, 109, 129
Wingard, Mary Lethert, 59
Winston-Salem Journal, 227
Wiseman, Robert J., 112, 114
Wolfbein, Seymour, 2, 109
Women: importance in strike, 88–90, 92, 95, 98, 100, 106, 115, 123, 124, 125, 126, 127–28, 145, *146,* 239–42, 145–46, 151; importance in work force, 8, 87, 191
Women's Trade Union League, 111
Woodside Mill, 166, 167

Woodward, C. Vann, 223, 225
Woolen Code Authority, x. *See also* Textile codes
Woolf, O. F., 42
Wool Institute, 7
Woonsocket, R.I.: violence in, 67–68, 95, 97–98, 102
Woonsocket Rayon, 67, 97, 98
Workers Defense Committee, 223–24, 225, 228, 229
Working Class Americanism (Gerstle), 95, 97–98
Wright, Gavin, 4

Yarborough, R. T., 172, 173, 174, 176
Yorke, Dane, 4
York Manufacturing Company, 73, 116

Zieger, Robert, x, 237
Zimmerman, Etta Mae, 74, 186, 187, 188, 190, 240
Zimmerman, J. M., 186, 189